CONSTRUCTION COST ESTIMATING Process and Practices

LEN HOLM

JOHN E. SCHAUFELBERGER

DENNIS GRIFFIN

THOMAS COLE

University of Washington

Upper Saddle River, New Jersey
Columbus, Ohio

Library of Congress Cataloging in Publication Data
Construction cost estimating: process and practices / Len Holm . . . [et al.].
    p. cm.
  Includes bibliographical references and index.
  ISBN 0-13-049665-0
    1. Building—Estimates. I. Holm, Len
TH435.C7269 2005
692'.5—dc22

2003070741

Editor in Chief: Stephen Helba
Executive Editor: Ed Francis
Editorial Assistant: Jennifer Day
Production Editor: Holly Shufeldt
Production Coordination: Carlisle Publishers Services
Design Coordinator: Diane Ernsberger
Cover Designer: Thomas Borah
Production Manager: Matt Ottenweller
Marketing Manager: Mark Marsden

This book was set in Times by Carlisle Communications, Ltd. It was printed and bound by R.R. Donnelley & Sons Company. The cover was printed by Phoenix Color Corp.

Pearson Education Ltd.
Pearson Education Singapore Pte. Ltd.
Pearson Education Canada, Ltd.
Pearson Education—Japan

Pearson Education Australia Pty. Limited
Pearson Education North Asia Ltd.
Pearson Educación de Mexico, S.A. de C.V.
Pearson Education Malaysia Pte. Ltd.

10 9 8 7 6 5 4 3 2 1
ISBN: 0-13-049665-0

PREFACE

The ability to predict the cost of constructing a project is an essential construction management skill. This book examines several types of construction cost estimates and the processes used in developing each type. Cost estimating is not an exact science. It requires an understanding of construction materials, construction methods and techniques, construction equipment, and construction labor. To be a good estimator, one also needs practical construction experience.

This book was developed for use as a text for undergraduate courses in construction cost estimating and as a reference for construction professionals. The authors assume that readers have a basic understanding of the construction process and types of construction contracts, as well as the materials and methods used in the industry. While the specific procedures for cost estimating may vary from one company to another, and for different types of construction, there are fundamental principles and processes that are used. It is these principles and processes that are addressed in this book. There are many cost estimating books on the market that address the quantity take-off process, others that provide estimating databases, and still others that discuss development of a lump-sum estimate. We know of none, however, that provide the coverage in this book. It illustrates the process for developing three separate types of estimates: a budget estimate during design development, a guaranteed maximum price estimate for a cost-plus contract, and a bid for a lump-sum contract. The book also discusses analyzing subcontractor quotations as well as estimating jobsite general conditions and company overhead costs.

This book is organized into five sections. The first section provides an overview of cost estimating and introduces a construction project that is used as a case study throughout the book to illustrate concepts and processes and to provide a context for student exercises.

Although the name of the construction company used in this text is fictitious, the project was actually constructed in Kent, Washington. The second section discusses the process for developing budget estimates during feasibility studies and design development, and estimates for preconstruction services. The third section discusses the process for developing a cost estimate for a bid contract, which generally is awarded on a lump-sum, unit-price, or combination lump-sum and unit-price basis. Included are techniques for estimating contractor-performed work, subcontractor-performed work, and contractor project management costs. The section concludes with a description of the process for finalizing a bid on bid day. The fourth section discusses cost estimating for a negotiated contract, which typically is awarded on a cost-plus basis. Both fee determination and guaranteed maximum price estimating are addressed. The final section contains some advanced estimating topics, including automated cost estimating, other types of estimates, and project management issues.

Each chapter has a similar organization. First concepts are discussed and then illustrated using the case study project. Review questions are provided to emphasize the main points covered in the chapter, and an instructor's manual containing the answers to the review questions is available. Exercises also are provided to allow students to apply the principles learned. A listing of all abbreviations used in the text is in Appendix A, and a glossary of cost estimating terms is in Appendix B. Appendix C provides some useful estimating resources, Appendix D contains a Request for Proposal for the case study project, Appendix E contains an Invitation for Bid for the project, and Appendix F contains many of the estimating forms used in the text. These forms were created in Microsoft Excel and can be customized to meet the needs of the user. Italics are used in the text to indicate information that was added to these forms. Appendices G and H contain selected specifications and drawings for the case study project.

ACKNOWLEDGMENTS

This book could not have been written without the help of many people. We wish to acknowledge the following: the Carpenters-Employers Apprenticeship and Training Trust Fund of Western Washington for allowing us to use their building as a case study; Lance Mueller and Associates of Seattle, Washington, for allowing us to use their drawings; Philip Larson for his help with the WinEstimator® information; Mark Lowe for preparing answers to the review questions; and most of all, the many University of Washington students who have used draft versions of this book and provided many valuable suggestions for improvement. We also want to thank the following reviewers of the manuscript for their many helpful comments: William W. Campbell, Montgomery College; Jay Christofferson, Brigham Young University; John Messner, Pennsylvania State University; and James J. Stein, Eastern Michigan University.

Len Holm
John E. Schaufelberger
Dennis Griffin
Tom Cole

CONTENTS

CHAPTER 7   QUANTITY TAKE-OFF   92

CHAPTER 8   PRICING SELF-PERFORMED WORK   120

CHAPTER 9   ESTIMATING SUBCONTRACTOR WORK   142

I

OVERVIEW

CHAPTER 1
INTRODUCTION

CHAPTER 2
CASE STUDY: TRAINING CENTER

1 INTRODUCTION

1.1 COST ESTIMATING PROCESS

Cost estimating is the process of analyzing a specific scope of work and predicting the cost of performing the work. The accuracy of the estimate is a function of how well the specific scope of work is defined and the time available to the estimator. The basic challenges the construction contractor faces are to estimate the costs of constructing a project, schedule the specific construction activities, and then build the project within the estimated cost and schedule. Therefore, cost estimating and cost control skills are essential if the construction contractor is to build a project profitably.

Cost estimating involves collecting, analyzing, and summarizing all available data pertaining to a project. The data may consist of a rough concept of the gross area or volume of a project, or it may be a set of detailed plans and specifications. Using whatever data is available, the *estimator* first divides the project into components or elements of work and then estimates the cost for each of these. The estimate may be based on an estimated gross cost per component or element of work, or it may be based on individual labor, material, equipment, or subcontractor estimated costs for each. The estimated cost for the project is then determined by adding the estimated costs for all of the components or elements of work.

In this chapter, we will examine the design process, the different types and uses of cost estimates in construction, the types of contracts used in the industry, the bid and negotiated procurement processes, and risk analysis. This overview provides a background for the detailed discussion contained in the following chapters.

1.2   DESIGN PROCESS

The first phase of the design process is known as the *programming* phase. This is when the basic project goals are identified, the functions to be performed in the completed project are defined, and general scope and budget decisions are made. If the owner approves the project program at the end of the programming phase, the designer initiates the next phase—*schematic design.* During this phase the designer develops sketches and drawings based on the owner's program. The overall design is approximately 30% complete at the end of the schematic design phase. If the owner approves the schematic design, the designer initiates the next phase—*design development.* During this phase, the designer finalizes dimensions, selects materials, prepares section and elevation drawings, and prepares color boards to show finish materials. The overall design is approximately 90% complete at the end of design development. Last is the *construction document* phase when the designer incorporates owner comments on the design development drawings, prepares door and finish schedules, and completes the technical specifications, thereby finalizing a set of documents for construction.

1.3   USES OF COST ESTIMATES

Cost estimates are developed and updated throughout the design and construction phases of a project, as illustrated in Figure 1-1. The project owner needs to have an understanding of the anticipated project cost before determining project feasibility and financing requirements.

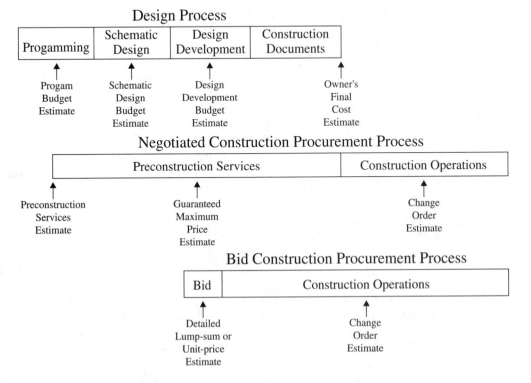

FIGURE 1–1   Cost estimates developed during project design and construction.

The project designer needs to have updated cost estimates throughout the design process to ensure that the project is being designed in such a manner that it can be constructed within the owner's budget. The construction contractor must be able to forecast the construction cost to prepare a bid or negotiate a contract price to win the project and to estimate the cost impacts of change orders during the execution of the project.

Some of the primary uses of cost estimates in construction are as follows:

- Developing an initial project budget for an owner. An initial budget estimate is usually prepared during the programming phase. It may be prepared by the design firm, a consultant, or the construction contractor to estimate project funding requirements. This budget may be used by the owner to obtain financing for the project.
- Determining project feasibility. A cost estimate may be prepared for a project owner to determine whether or not the project is affordable or whether or not anticipated revenues would justify the investment in constructing the project.
- Designing the project within the owner's budget. Cost estimates may be prepared at various milestones during the design process to ensure that the estimated cost of construction is within the budget established by the owner.
- Evaluating alternative design concepts and project components. The design team may be considering alternative building systems or components. Cost estimates for each system or component under consideration usually are prepared to assess the cost impacts of the alternatives being considered.
- Preparing bids. Cost estimates are prepared by construction contractors to determine their bid amounts for a bid procurement process.
- Preparing cost proposals. Cost estimates are prepared by construction contractors to justify their cost proposals in a negotiated procurement process.
- Establishing project budgets. Construction contractors often use their updated cost estimates to establish their project budgets once they are awarded a construction contract.
- Determining cost impacts of *change orders (CO)*. Contract change orders modify the scope of work. The construction contractor prepares a cost estimate to predict the cost impacts of the scope modifications. These estimates are used by the contractor to negotiate an adjustment to the contract value as compensation for the additional work.
- Substantiating claims and resolving disputes. Construction contractors may perceive that they incurred additional work because of a differing site condition or some problem with the design documents. Consequently they may wish to submit *claims* for additional compensation for the cost of the additional work. Cost estimates would be prepared to support the contractors' claims. These estimates also may be used by *mediators* or *arbitrators* in resolving disputes that may result from unresolved claims.
- Preparing a schedule of values used to justify progress payment requests. A schedule of values is a breakdown of the contract value that shows the estimated cost of the major project components. It is prepared from the contractor's cost estimate for the project. The schedule of values is used to justify the progress payment requests on lump-sum contracts.
- Creating historical cost databases. Actual cost data may be collected to create an as-built estimate used to update a cost estimating database that can be used in estimating future projects.

The accuracy of the cost estimate will depend on the completeness of the design documents, as we will see in the next section of this chapter.

1.4   TYPES OF COST ESTIMATES

There are three major types of cost estimates. *Conceptual cost estimates* are developed using incomplete project documentation; for example, during programming and schematic design. *Semi-detailed cost estimates* are prepared when parts of the project have been completely designed, while other aspects have not; for example, during design development. *Detailed cost estimates* are prepared based on fully developed construction drawings and specifications. There is no single estimate for any project.

There are good estimates, and there are bad estimates. Cost estimating is as much a learned skill as it is a science. Estimating material costs generally is not difficult, as it involves measuring the scope of work from the contract drawings. Estimating labor and equipment costs, however, requires knowledge of construction techniques and experienced judgment. The greatest uncertainty is in predicting the productivity of the crews and equipment that will be used on the project. This will vary based on job conditions, crew size, crew experience, and equipment selected. The accuracy of the estimate will depend upon the completeness of the contract documents and the experience of the estimator. The typical accuracy of the various types of cost estimates is shown in Figure 1-2.

Conceptual Cost Estimates

A conceptual cost estimate is a quick method for determining an approximate cost of a project without benefit of a detailed definition of the exact scope of work. Three types of conceptual cost estimates are used in the construction industry. They are rough-order-of-magnitude cost estimates, assemblies cost estimates, and cost indices.

Rough-order-of-magnitude (ROM) cost estimates often are called square-foot cost estimates. Estimating tables similar to the one illustrated in Figure 1-3 are used to predict the anticipated construction cost based on the estimated gross square feet of the project. Some construction firms have developed their own databases for square-foot cost estimating. Others use square-foot estimating tables that are published in cost reference books. One of

Type of Estimate	Construction Document Development	Expected Percent Error*
Conceptual	Schematic Design 0–30% Construction Documents	±10–20%
Semi-Detailed	Design Development 30–90% Construction Documents	±5–10%
Detailed	90–100% Plans and Specifications	±2–4%

*Percent error means the expected variation between the cost estimate and the actual cost.

FIGURE 1–2   Accuracy of different types of cost estimates.

Estimated Building Costs			
Building Type	**Average Cost per Square Foot**	**Building Type**	**Average Cost per Square Foot**
Apartment, 1–3 story	$106	Medical Office, 1–2 story	$125
Apartment, 4–8 story	$108	Motel, 2–3 story	$113
Branch Bank	$160	Office Building, 2–5 story	$107
Classroom Building	$110	Post Office	$88
Fire Station	$108	Restaurant	$130
Hospital, 2–3 story	$155	School	$94
Hospital, 4–8 story	$125	Store	$80
Hotel, 3–6 story	$102	Warehouse	$60

FIGURE 1–3   Square-foot cost estimating database.

the most commonly used reference books is *Square Foot Costs,* which is published annually by R. S. Means.

Let's look at an example.

EXAMPLE 1-1

Determine a rough-order-of-magnitude cost estimate for the construction of a 3-story hospital with approximately 20,000 square feet per floor.

The total estimated floor area for the hospital is

$$(3 \text{ floors})(20{,}000 \text{ square feet per floor}) = 60{,}000 \text{ square feet}$$

The estimated cost per square foot shown in Figure 1-3 for a 2–3 story hospital is $155 per square foot. The total estimated construction cost is

$$(60{,}000 \text{ square feet})(\$155 \text{ per square foot}) = \textbf{\textit{\$9.3 million}}$$

Assemblies cost estimates are developed by using databases to estimate the cost of individual building components, such as the foundation, roof, exterior enclosure, interior, mechanical, plumbing, and electrical. Usually some basic material selections must be made by the designer before the cost of the individual project assemblies can be estimated. The overall project cost estimate is then developed by summing the cost estimates for all the individual assemblies. An example of an assemblies cost estimate is shown in Figure 1-4. A commonly used reference for developing assemblies cost estimates is *Assemblies Cost Data,* which is published annually by R. S. Means.

Cost indices are used to predict the cost of a project based on the cost of a similar project at another location and/or constructed in a different timeframe. An example table of cost indices is shown in Figure 1-5. The cost index numbers are developed by determining

Cost Estimate

Project: Main Street Motel
Estimator: Henry Williams
Date: March 15, 2003

Foundations

Description	Quantity	Unit	Unit Price	Total	Cost/sf
Conventional spread footings	30,000	sf	$1.80	$54,000	
Subtotal				$54,000	$1.80

Substructure

Description	Quantity	Unit	Unit Price	Total	Cost/sf
Reinforced slab-on-grade (4 inch)	30,000	sf	$3.50	$105,000	
Subtotal				$105,000	$3.50

Superstructure

Description	Quantity	Unit	Unit Price	Total	Cost/sf
Concrete support walls (1,000 ft × 30 ft × 17 ft)	35,000	sf	$5.40	$189,000	
Roof structure	30,000	sf	$4.00	$120,000	
Subtotal				$309,000	$10.30

Exterior Closure

Description	Quantity	Unit	Unit Price	Total	Cost/sf
Exterior walls—brick (70%)	24,500	sf	$8.50	$208,250	
Exterior doors & windows (30%)	10,500	sf	$2.00	$ 21,000	
Subtotal				$229,250	$7.64

Roofing

Description	Quantity	Unit	Unit Price	Total	Cost/sf
Roofing	30,000	sf	$4.00	$120,000	
Subtotal				$120,000	$4.00

Interior Construction

Description	Quantity	Unit	Unit Price	Total	Cost/sf
Finishes	30,000	sf	$12.50	$375,000	
Subtotal				$375,000	$12.50

FIGURE 1–4 Example assemblies cost estimate.

Mechanical					
Description	**Quantity**	**Unit**	**Unit Price**	**Total**	**Cost/sf**
Mechanical	30,000	sf	$14.50	$435,000	
Fire Protection	30,000	sf	$2.00	$ 60,000	
Subtotal				$495,000	$16.50

Electrical					
Description	**Quantity**	**Unit**	**Unit Price**	**Total**	**Cost/sf**
Electrical	30,000	sf	$9.50	$285,000	
Subtotal				$285,000	$9.50

Sitework					
Description	**Quantity**	**Unit**	**Unit Price**	**Total**	**Cost/sf**
Sitework	95,000	sf	$3.50	$332,500	
Subtotal				$332,500	$11.08

Total					
Description	**Quantity**	**Unit**		**Total**	**Cost/sf**
Total Estimated Cost	30,000	sf		$2,304,750	$76.83

FIGURE 1–4 Continued.

Construction Cost Index Numbers				
Year	**Chicago**	**Dallas**	**New York**	**Seattle**
2003	49	37	57	45
2002	47	36	56	44
2001	45	35	55	43
2000	44	34	53	42
1999	43	33	52	41
1998	42	33	51	40
1997	40	32	50	39
1996	39	31	49	38
1995	38	30	47	38

FIGURE 1–5 Historical cost indices.

the relative cost of constructing similar projects at various locations in different years. The most commonly used cost indices in the construction industry are those published by *Engineering-News Record* and by R. S. Means. Conceptual cost estimating using cost indices is performed by the following equation:

$$\text{Estimated Cost} = \frac{(\text{Known Cost})(\text{Cost Index for Estimated Cost})}{(\text{Cost Index for Known Cost})}$$

Let's look at an example.

EXAMPLE 1-2

The cost for constructing a new hotel in New York in 1998 was $25 million. What is the estimated cost for constructing a similar hotel in Chicago in 2002?

From Figure 1-5, we can determine that the index number for New York in 1998 is 51, and that the corresponding index number for Chicago in 2002 is 47. Using these two index numbers and the cost for constructing the hotel in New York in 1998, we can estimate the cost for constructing the hotel in Chicago in 2002 to be

$$\frac{(\$25 \text{ million})(47)}{(51)} = \textit{\$23 million}$$

Semi-Detailed Cost Estimates

Semi-detailed cost estimates are developed while basic design decisions are being made to verify that the project can be constructed at its intended scope within the owner's budget. Some aspects of the project may be completely designed—the foundations for example—while some of the architectural features are yet to be determined. Detailed estimating methods can be used to estimate the cost of project components that have been designed, and conceptual estimating methods are used to estimate the cost of those components that remain to be designed. This means that databases are used to estimate the cost of components for which the design is not complete, and project data are used to estimate the cost of components for which the design is complete. Therefore, these estimates are known as semi-detailed cost estimates. An example of a semi-detailed estimate is shown in Figure 1-6. In this example, detailed estimating methods were used to determine the estimated costs for the foundations, substructure, superstructure, exterior closure, roof, and sitework. Conceptual estimating methods were used to estimate the costs for interior construction, mechanical, and electrical.

Detailed Cost Estimates

Detailed cost estimates are prepared once the design has been completed and all construction documents prepared. The estimator divides the project into individual elements of work and estimates the quantities of work for each element. Dividing the proj-

Cost Estimate				
Project: Central High School Estimator: Todd Jones Date: March 25, 2003				
Description	**Material**	**Labor**	**Equipment**	**Total**
Foundations	$150,000	$107,000	$116,000	$373,000
Substructure	$124,000	$116,000	$107,000	$347,000
Superstructure	$268,000	$114,000	$106,000	$488,000
Exterior Closure	$175,000	$134,000	$65,000	$374,000
Roof	$350,000	$165,000	$103,000	$618,000
Sitework	$256,000	$480,000	$360,000	$1,096,000
Subtotal				$3,296,000
Description	**Quantity**	**Unit**	**Unit Price**	**Total**
Interior Construction	50,000	sf	$18.00	$900,000
Mechanical	50,000	sf	$17.50	$875,000
Electrical	50,000	sf	$10.50	$525,000
Subtotal				$5,596,000
Project Overhead (10%)				$559,600
Subtotal				$6,155,600
Company Overhead (5%)				$307,900
Total				**$6,463,500**

FIGURE 1–6   Example semi-detailed cost estimate.

ect scope into elements of work is known as the *work breakdown,* and estimating the individual quantities of work is known as the *quantity take-off (QTO).* Next the individual elements of work are priced to determine an estimated cost for each one. The estimated costs are summed, and overhead costs are added to cover the contractor's cost of managing the work. The estimated costs of constructing the project are known as the *direct costs,* and the *overhead costs* are known as the *indirect costs.* Two formats are commonly used in developing detailed cost estimates. The first is a systems format, known as the *Uniformat,* that was developed by the U.S. General Services Administration; it is illustrated in Figure 1-7. An enhanced version known as Uniformat II has been developed by the American Society for Testing Materials. The other is the *MasterFormat,* developed by the *Construction Specifications Institute (CSI),* which is illustrated in Figure 1-8. The Uniformat is organized by building components or systems while the MasterFormat is organized similar to the technical specifications used in most construction contracts. Both formats are shown in more detail

Project: Southside Middle School
Estimator: Sally Jackson
Date: June 18, 2003

Estimate Summary

Uniformat Division	Description	Labor	Material	Suppliers & Subcontractors	Total
1	Foundations	$40,000	$74,100	$30,000	$144,100
2	Substructure	$49,800	$60,000	$28,000	$137,800
3	Superstructure	$50,000	$0	$150,000	$200,000
4	Exterior Closure	$2,500	$1,500	$187,700	$191,700
5	Roofing and Insulation	$2,500	$4,300	$125,400	$132,200
6	Interior Construction	$23,750	$10,375	$377,600	$411,725
7	Elevators	$0	$0	$30,000	$30,000
8	Mechanical				
	Plumbing	$0	$0	$66,200	$66,200
	HVAC	$0	$0	$155,200	$155,200
	Fire Protection	$0	$0	$56,800	$56,800
9	Electrical	$0	$0	$205,600	$205,600
10	Jobsite General Conditions	$130,000	$42,200	$5,800	$178,000
11	Specialties	$3,500	$2,255	$46,000	$51,755
12	Sitework	$13,300	$26,600	$345,000	$384,900
	Subtotal	$315,350	$221,330	$1,809,300	$2,345,980
	Labor Burdens		45% of labor	$141,908	$2,487,888
	Liability Insurance		1%	$24,879	$2,512,767
	Builders Risk Insurance		0.20%	$5,026	$2,517,793
	State Excise Tax		1%	$25,178	$2,542,971
	Home Office Overhead and Profit		5%	$127,148	$2,670,119
	Total Estimate:				**$2,670,119**

FIGURE 1–7 Example Uniformat detailed cost estimate.

in Appendix C. We will use the MasterFormat for preparing detailed estimates in this text. Which format is used on a particular estimate generally is based either on the policy of the company or the personal choice of the estimator. Some estimators use a systems format for early budget estimates to assess the estimated cost of major building components and then use the MasterFormat for the final detailed cost estimate once the design is completed.

Project: Southside Middle School
Estimator: Sally Jackson
Date: June 18, 2003

Estimate Summary

CSI Division	Description	Labor	Material	Suppliers & Subcontractors	Total
1	Jobsite General Conditions	$130,000	$42,200	$5,800	$178,000
2	Sitework	$13,300	$26,600	$345,000	$384,900
3	Concrete	$99,800	$134,100	$58,000	$291,900
4	Masonry	$0	$0	$37,000	$37,000
5	Structural Steel	$50,000	$0	$150,000	$200,000
6	Carpentry	$10,000	$7,800	$26,700	$44,500
7	Roofing and Insulation	$2,500	$4,300	$125,400	$132,200
8	Doors and Glazing	$2,500	$1,500	$139,600	$143,600
9	Finishes	$0	$0	$306,000	$306,000
10	Specialties	$3,500	$2,255	$21,000	$26,755
11	Audio-Visual Equipment	$0	$0	$25,000	$25,000
12	Furnishings	$3,750	$2,575	$56,000	$62,325
13	Special Construction	$0	$0	$0	$0
14	Elevators	$0	$0	$30,000	$30,000
15	Mechanical				
	Plumbing	$0	$0	$66,200	$66,200
	HVAC	$0	$0	$155,200	$155,200
	Fire Protection	$0	$0	$56,800	$56,800
16	Electrical	$0	$0	$205,600	$205,600
	Subtotal	$315,350	$221,330	$1,809,300	$2,345,980
	Labor Burdens		45% of labor	$141,908	$2,487,888
	Liability Insurance		1%	$24,879	$2,512,767
	Builders Risk Insurance		0.20%	$5,026	$2,517,793
	State Excise Tax		1%	$25,178	$2,542,971
	Home Office Overhead and Profit		5%	$127,148	$2,670,119
	Total Estimate:				**$2,670,119**

FIGURE 1–8   Example MasterFormat detailed cost estimate.

1.5   TYPES OF CONSTRUCTION CONTRACTS

There are several methods for pricing construction *contracts*. The project owner selects the method for a particular project based on the risks associated with the project, deciding how much risk to assume and how much to impose on the construction contractor. The amount of risk borne by the contractor varies depending on the pricing method selected by the

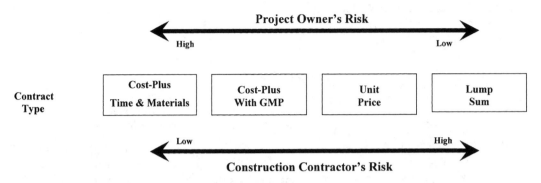

FIGURE 1–9 Owner's and contractor's risk based on contract pricing method.

owner. Figure 1-9 shows the relative risk the owner and the contractor assume for each of the alternative pricing methods. Since contractors want compensation for risks they assume, it is important to perform a thorough risk analysis when developing a cost estimate for a particular project.

Lump-sum contracts are used when the scope of work can be defined. The owner provides a set of drawings and specifications (either in paper or electronic form), and the contractor agrees to complete the project for a lump sum. An example might be a city fire station or a public high school. In this type of contract, the contractor assumes all risk associated with constructing the project in accordance with the plans and specifications, except unusually adverse weather. The risk of subsurface conditions that are more adverse than those described in the project documents or of inadequate or defective design documents is borne by the owner. Lump-sum contracts also are used for design-build projects where the owner specifies design criteria, and the contractor agrees to design and construct the project for a single price. While the exact scope of work is not defined in a design-build project, the contractor controls the design process and produces a design that can be constructed within the contract price. In a lump-sum contract, the contractor is responsible for determining all the material, labor, equipment, and subcontract costs to establish the project cost.

Unit-price contracts are used when the exact quantities of work are not known at the time the contract is signed. The designer provides an estimate of the material quantity of each element to be constructed, and the contractor determines the unit price for each element. The actual contract value is not determined until the project is completed. In this type of contract, the contractor bears the risk of properly determining the unit prices, but the owner bears the risk related to the specific quantities of work required. The actual quantities of work are measured during the completion of the project, and the cost is determined by multiplying the actual material quantity by the unit price established by the contractor. Unit-price contracts are used extensively on highway or environmental clean-up projects where exact quantities of work are difficult to define. Unit-price and lump-sum methods can both be used in the same contract. Sometimes the foundation of a building is unit price, and the rest of the building is lump sum.

Cost-plus contracts are used when the scope of work cannot be defined. They are sometimes referred to as *cost-reimbursable contracts*. All the contractor's project-related costs that are identified in the contract are reimbursed by the owner, and a fee is added to cover profit and company overhead. The fee may be a fixed amount or a percentage of project costs, or it may be an *incentive fee.* In this type of contract, the contractor bears the risk of determining an appropriate fee to cover overhead costs, but the owner bears the risk related to the actual cost of constructing the project. Cost-plus contracts typically are awarded based on an agreed-upon fee structure, since project costs are not known until the project has been completed. Cost-plus contracts generally are used when the construction contract is awarded prior to the completion of the design. An example might be a new office building for which the owner wants the construction contractor to participate in the design process.

Cost-plus contracts with guaranteed maximum price (GMP) are special types of cost-plus contracts in which the contractor agrees to construct the project at or below a specified cost (the GMP). Any cost exceeding the GMP would be borne by the contractor. Some of these contracts have a cost-sharing provision that provides for sharing of cost savings between the owner and the contractor, if the final project cost is less than the GMP. For example, the contract may state that 25% of the savings would go to the contractor and 75% to the owner. In other cases, the contracts indicate that all savings return to the owner.

Time-and-materials (T&M) contracts are used when the specific scope of work is not defined. In this type of contract, the owner and contractor agree to specific labor rates for each classification of work to be performed. The labor rate includes the contractor's overhead and profit. The contractor's payment is based on the actual cost for materials used on the project and the agreed-upon labor rates multiplied by the actual hours that each individual worked on the project. In this type of contract, the contractor bears the risk of determining appropriate labor rates, but the owner bears the risk relating to the scope of work and material costs. Time-and-materials contracts generally are used only on small projects, on specialized industrial projects, or for consultant services.

1.6 PROCUREMENT METHODS

Owners use either a bid or a *negotiated procurement process* to select a construction contractor for a project. Public owners, such as government agencies, use public solicitation or procurement methods. These owners may require prospective contractors to submit documentation of their qualifications for review before being allowed to submit a bid or proposal, or the owners may open the solicitations to all qualified contractors. Requiring contractors to submit their qualifications prior to being allowed to submit a bid or proposal is known as *prequalification of contractors.* Private owners can use any method they wish to select contractors, but most use contractors with whom they have had a good experience in the past. Private owners might ask only a select few or even one contractor to submit a bid or proposal.

Bid Method

The *bid procurement process* is illustrated in Figure 1-10. Bid contracts generally are awarded solely on price. The owner defines the scope of the project, usually with a detailed set of plans and specifications, and contractors submit lump-sum bids, unit-price bids, or a

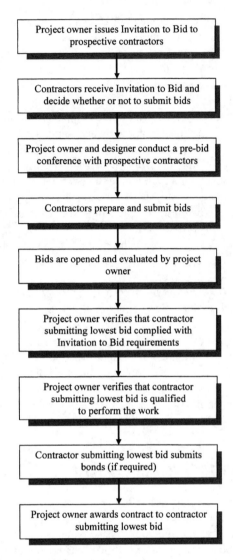

FIGURE 1–10 Bid procurement process.

combination of both. The owner then awards the contract to the contractor submitting the lowest bid that conforms to all contractual requirements. The owner may or may not require *performance* and *payment bonds* from the contractor submitting the lowest bid before awarding the contract. On unit-price contracts, the actual quantities of work are not known for unit-priced items so the contractors' unit prices are multiplied by the estimated quantities provided on the bid form and summed. The contractor with the lowest sum is selected for award.

Owners sometimes include alternate bid items on their bid forms that they may or may not choose to award to the successful bidder. An example of a completed lump-sum

> **BASE BID**
>
> Pursuant to and in compliance with the Advertisement for Bids and Instructions to Bidders, the undersigned hereby certifies having carefully examined the Contract Documents entitled
>
> Market Street Sewage Treatment Plant,
> prepared by Stellar Engineers, Inc.
>
> and conditions affecting the work, and is familiar with the site; and having made the necessary examinations, hereby proposes to furnish all labor, materials, equipment, and services necessary to complete the work in strict accordance with the above named documents for the sum of
>
> _Ten Million Three Hundred Seventy-Eight Thousand Nine Hundred_ Dollars ($ _10,378,900_)
>
> which sum is hereby designated as the Base Bid.
>
> **ALTERNATES**
>
> The undersigned proposes to perform work called for in the following alternates, as de-scribed in Section 01030 and the drawings of the Contract Documents, for the following resulting additions to or deductions from the Base Bid.
>
> Alternate #1: Delete Selected Landscaping
>
> _Fifty Thousand Eight Hundred_   Dollars ($ _50,800_)
>
> Alternate #2: Delete Paved Parking Lot
>
> _Sixty Thousand Two Hundred_   Dollars ($ _60,200_)
>
> Alternate #3: Add Second Floor Upgrade
>
> _One Hundred Twenty-Five Thousand Five Hundred_   Dollars ($ _125,500_)

FIGURE 1–11 Lump-sum bid form with alternate bid items.

bid form with alternate bid items is shown in Figure 1-11, and a completed unit-price bid form is shown in Figure 1-12. The *pre-bid conference* usually is held in the designer's office or at the job site to resolve any questions prospective contractors and subcontractors may have relating to contract or project requirements.

Negotiated Method

Negotiated contracts are awarded based on any criteria the owner selects. This method is used more often by private owners than it is by public owners. Typical criteria include cost (or fee in the case of cost-plus contracts), project duration, expertise of the project management team, contractor's plan for managing the project, contractor's safety record, contractor's existing work load, and contractor's experience with similar projects. Rather than require just total project cost, such as a lump-sum amount, owners may require that detailed cost estimates be submitted as part of the contractors' proposals.

The undersigned proposes to perform the work called for in the Contract Documents, for the following schedule of prices. Exact quantities will be determined upon completion of the work.

Work Items	Unit of Measure	Estimated Quantity	Unit Price	Bid Amount
1. Mobilization	lump sum	1	$16,000	$16,000
2. Traffic Control	lump sum	1	$3,800	$3,800
3. Erosion Control	lump sum	1	$7,000	$7,000
4. Clearing and Grubbing	lump sum	1	$16,000	$16,000
5. Embankment in Place	cubic yards	5,000	$12.50	$62,500
6. Culvert Pipe	feet	600	$70.00	$42,000
7. Aggregate Base	square yards	2,000	$12.50	$25,000
8. Asphalt Pavement	square yards	7,000	$52.50	$367,500
9. Seeding	square yards	4,000	$2.50	$10,000
10. Signage	each	5	$120.00	$600

Total Bid Price:

Five Hundred Fifty Thousand Four Hundred _____ Dollars ($ _550,400_)

FIGURE 1–12   Unit-price bid form.

Most negotiated contracts are awarded using the two-step process illustrated in Figure 1-13. First, prospective contractors are invited to submit their qualifications for the project. After review of their prior work experiences and safety records, the most qualified contractors (usually four to six) are *short listed* and invited to submit proposals containing specific project information requested by the owner. Since the contractors may suggest design modifications in their proposals, the owner usually discusses each proposal with the contractor who submitted it. Based on this discussion, the owner may issue an *addendum* clarifying any issues and then ask each proposer to submit a *best and final proposal.* As a part of the evaluation process, owners may require each contractor to make a presentation explaining its plans for managing the project.

The owner then selects the contractor submitting the proposal that is ranked highest based on the owner's evaluation criteria and negotiates a contract price, and maybe a project duration. The *pre-proposal conference* is similar to the pre-bid conference used in the bid method. Once the negotiations are completed, the owner may or may not require the successful proposer to submit performance and payment bonds before awarding the construction contract. The major difference in a negotiated procedure is the opportunity for the owner to discuss the contractors' proposals, modify contract requirements, and clarify any issues before requesting best and final proposals.

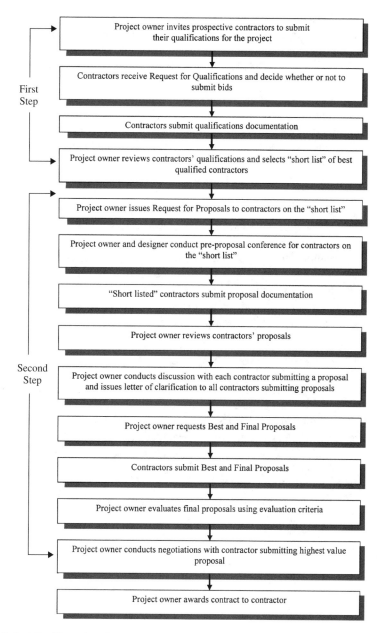

FIGURE 1–13 Negotiated procurement process.

1.7 PRECONSTRUCTION SERVICES

The project owner may choose to select the construction contractor during the design process, as shown in Figure 1-1, and ask the contractor to perform *preconstruction services*. These services may include consultation, budget cost estimating, preliminary project scheduling, constructability analysis, value engineering, or site planning. Consultation involves participating in design coordination and review meetings and providing advice regarding material, system, and equipment selection. Budget estimates are developed using the conceptual cost estimating techniques discussed in Section 1.4 and refined as the design evolves to ensure that the estimated cost of the project is within the owner's budget. A preliminary schedule may be developed to assess the time impacts of design alternatives. *Constructability analysis* is reviewing the proposed design for its impact on the cost and ease of construction. *Value engineering* is identifying the most economical project components from a life-cycle cost perspective. Site planning involves analysis of site restrictions, and organization to support construction operations.

Preconstruction services are more prevalent on privately funded projects than they are on publicly funded projects. This is because private owners are not restricted to the public bidding procedures that many public owners are required to use. Some public agencies are beginning to award cost-plus contracts early in design development so they can use the construction contractors to perform preconstruction services. Contractors may negotiate lump-sum, cost-plus, or time-and-materials contracts with owners for preconstruction services. The owner defines the scope of preconstruction services desired and then negotiates a contract with the construction contractor. A preconstruction services contract may be a separate contract between the owner and the construction contractor, or it may be included as a portion of the overall contract for the construction of the project.

1.8   RISK ANALYSIS AND CONTINGENCIES

As mentioned at the beginning of Section 1.5, the estimator must perform a thorough risk analysis when developing a cost estimate for a project. Some sources of risk on a project might include unusually adverse weather, labor and material cost inflation, owner's inability to finance the project, bankruptcy of subcontractors, incomplete design documents, project size, project location, labor shortage, labor productivity, and project constructibility and complexity. The estimator needs to forecast the likelihood of such risks, the range of possibilities, and the impact of each on the firm's ability to complete the project profitably. This is particularly true of constructability risks identified during analysis of the *soils report* for the project site. Many *general contractors (GC)* subcontract most or all of the scope of work to specialty contractors to reduce risk and provide access to specialized, skilled craftworkers and equipment. By subcontracting, the general contractor transfers the risk related to his or her own workforce to the subcontractors, but incurs the risk of subcontractor bankruptcy and/or poor subcontractor workmanship.

The estimator must understand the risk associated with each project and include adequate contingencies for risk mitigation. *Contingencies* are added to cost estimates to allow for changes resulting from conditions different from those that were originally assumed. The level of contingency is a measure of the degree of uncertainty on a project.

The general categories of contingencies that may be used by project owners are as follows:

- Design contingencies are used in budget estimates because final design decisions have not been made and appropriate drawings and specifications prepared. The contingency size would be reduced as the design is developed. For example, a larger contingency would be used for schematic design budget estimates than would be used for design development budgets.

- Document contingencies are used to cover the risk associated with potential conflicts among contract documents. Any contract document discrepancies usually result in change orders.
- Permit contingencies are used to cover the permitting risk prior to the receipt of the building permit and any permit agency comments.
- Scope contingencies are used to cover the cost of owner-directed changes in project scope after the drawings and specifications are completed, and construction has been initiated.
- Unforeseen conditions contingencies are used to cover the risk of unknown site conditions. This can be a major cost item on renovation projects or where the site subsurface conditions materially differ from the conditions described in the soils report.

The general categories of contingencies used by construction contractors are as follows:

- Design contingencies to cover the risks associated with elements of the design that have not been completed. This contingency is most common in budget estimates.
- Escalation contingencies are used early in the design process to cover the risk associated with material and labor inflation.
- Estimating contingencies are used when estimators have not completely taken off the entire project and have not obtained material and subcontractor pricing. This contingency is most prevalent in GMP estimates.

It is common to see contingencies added to early budget estimates that are reduced as the design progresses. Common contingencies as they relate to design completion are shown in Figure 1-14. Figure 1-15 shows typical contingency values for the three types of

---

Contingency Values

- **20%:** A substantial contingency is applied to very early schematic design budgets due to the lack of *design definition.*
- **10%:** This amount will be applied to fairly well-defined budgets or early GMP estimates for *design completion,* such as at the completion of the design development stage. Some public owner's may also include a 10% contingency for change orders due to *unforeseen conditions* or *document discrepancies* after a project is lump-sum bid.
- **5%:** This would be the appropriate *design contingency* applied to guaranteed maximum price estimates that were developed before the 90% construction document stage. Most lump-sum bid owners would also put at least a 5% contingency for *discrepancy change orders* or *scope changes* on their side of the ledger.
- **2% or 3%:** This amount would be consistent with an *escalation allowance.* Even if the GMP estimate was prepared with complete documents, the owner should retain at least this amount on his or her side of the ledger for *document inconsistencies.*
- **1/2% or 1%:** Estimators may try to include a stated *estimating contingency* with minimal percentage value in their estimates. If the owner were to negotiate this out, most estimators have at least this much also added into line items (hidden) throughout open book estimates. A minimal contingency such as this may also be included for potential *municipality issues* if the estimate is developed before the permit is received.

FIGURE 1–14 Typical contingency amounts.

Appropriate Contingency Values

Type Contingency	Estimate Type		
	Budget	**GMP**	**Lump-Sum**
Owner Contingencies			
Design Contingency	10–20%	5–10%	N/A
Document Contingency	N/A	10%[1]	5–10%[1]
Permit Contingency	N/A	1%	1–3%
Scope Contingency	5–10%	5%	0–2%
Unforeseen Conditions Contingency	N/A	10%[1]	5–10%[1]
Contractor Contingencies			
Escalation Contingency	N/A	2–3%	included in costs
Estimating Contingency	5%	½–1%	included in profit
Total Contingency	[2]	[2]	[2]

Notes:
[1]*Unforeseen conditions and document contingencies combine to make 10%, not 10% each.*
[2]*Most of these percentages are not cumulative. For example, if 20% design contingency were added to a budget estimate, the other contingencies would not be added on the assumption that the 20% would cover the other contingencies. In a similar manner, if 10% contingency were added to a lump-sum bid by the owner, it would be presumed to be adequate to cover the other issues as well.*

FIGURE 1–15 Typical contingencies for budget, GMP, and lump-sum estimates.

estimates that are the focus of this text. These values are shown for comparison purposes to indicate the relative accuracy of budget, GMP, and lump-sum estimates.

1.9 SUMMARY

Cost estimating is the process of analyzing a specific scope of work and predicting the cost of performing the work. The accuracy of the estimate will depend on how well the specific scope of work is defined and the amount of time available to the estimator. Cost estimates are developed and updated throughout the design and construction of a project. They are used by the following:

- The owner to establish a project budget and determine project feasibility
- The designer to ensure the estimated construction costs do not exceed the owner's budget
- The construction contractor to prepare a bid or negotiate a contract price

There are three major types of cost estimates:

- Conceptual cost estimates are developed to determine approximate project costs when the projects have not been designed. The three types of conceptual cost estimates are rough-order-of-magnitude, assemblies, and cost indices.

- Semi-detailed cost estimates are prepared when parts of the project have been designed, while other components remain to be designed.
- Detailed cost estimates are developed based on completed project plans and specifications.

There are several methods for pricing construction contracts. Lump-sum contracts are used when the scope of work can be defined. The contractor submits a single price for each bid item or for the entire scope of work. Unit-price contracts are used when the exact quantities of work are not known. The contractor submits a unit price for each of the quantities listed on the bid form. Cost-plus contracts are used when the scope of work cannot be defined. The contractor submits a fee proposal and project-related costs are reimbursed. Time-and-materials contracts also are used when the scope of work is not defined. Labor costs are reimbursed at an agreed-upon rate, and materials are reimbursed at cost.

Owners use either a bid or negotiated procurement process to select a construction contractor for a project. Bid contracts generally are awarded solely on price, while negotiated contracts are awarded based on criteria the owner selects. The project owner may choose to select the contractor during the design process and ask the contractor to perform preconstruction services.

The estimator must perform a thorough risk analysis when developing a cost estimate for a project. The sources of risk, the range of possibilities, and the potential impacts must be understood by the estimator to ensure that adequate contingencies are included for risk mitigation.

1.10 REVIEW QUESTIONS

1. What are the major factors in determining the accuracy of a cost estimate?
2. What are four reasons why a construction contractor might prepare a cost estimate?
3. What are the three major types of cost estimates? How do they differ?
4. What are rough-order-of-magnitude cost estimates and how are they developed?
5. What are assemblies cost estimates and how are they developed?
6. What are cost indices and how are they used?
7. What are the basic steps in developing a detailed cost estimate?
8. What are lump-sum contracts and when are they used?
9. What are unit-price contracts and when are they used?
10. What are cost-plus contracts and when are they used?
11. What is a guaranteed maximum price and how is it determined?
12. What are time-and-materials contracts and how are they priced?
13. What are the primary differences between the bid and the negotiated methods of contract procurement?
14. What is meant by preconstruction services and how are preconstruction services contracts usually priced?
15. Why must estimators conduct a thorough risk analysis when preparing a cost estimate for a project?
16. Why are contingencies included in some cost estimates? How is an appropriate contingency amount determined?

1.11 EXERCISES

1. You have been asked to prepare an assemblies estimate for the construction of a 2-story office building. What assemblies would you use to prepare the estimate?
2. What project risks does a construction contractor assume when receiving a lump-sum contract for the construction of an office building?
3. Using Figure 1-2, what is the typical range of conceptual cost estimates for a manufacturing facility that has an actual construction cost of $15 million?
4. Using Figure 1-2, what is the typical range of semi-detailed cost estimates for a manufacturing facility that has an actual construction cost of $15 million?
5. Using Figure 1-2, what is the typical range of detailed cost estimates for a manufacturing facility that has an actual construction cost of $15 million?
6. Using Figure 1-3, develop a rough-order-of-magnitude cost estimate for the construction of a 20,000-square foot fire station.
7. Assume that the estimate developed in exercise 6 was for construction in Dallas in 2002.
   a. Using Figure 1-5, what do you estimate the cost would be for a similar fire station constructed in New York in 2002?
   b. Using Figure 1-5, what do you estimate the cost would have been if the fire station had been constructed in Dallas in 1997?

2

CASE STUDY: TRAINING CENTER

2.1　INTRODUCTION

Now that we have discussed the types and uses of cost estimates and reviewed the procurement processes and methods for pricing construction contracts, we will discuss a construction project that will be used as a case study throughout the remainder of the book. This project will be used as the context for illustrating the concepts addressed in each chapter and for many of the exercises provided at the ends of the chapters. The project selected has sufficient attributes to illustrate the major teaching points, yet is not so complex that students would get lost in the details.

2.2　PROJECT DESCRIPTION

The project selected as the case study in this book is a 2-story structural steel building with tilt-up concrete exterior wall panels. Only a third of the second floor was constructed, but the building foundation was built to support future construction of the remainder of the second floor. Some of the materials and systems used in the project include spot footings, continuous footings, cast-in-place concrete slabs and walls, composite second-floor deck, built-up roofing, a bridge crane, punch windows, aluminum storefront, an elevator, electrical, mechanical, and plumbing. Finishes included carpet, vinyl tile, millwork, and paint. Sitework included water, storm and sanitary sewers, landscaping, asphalt paving, concrete curbs, and sidewalks. These systems are represented in the estimates produced as examples throughout this book. The estimating systems and processes used for these materials can be applied to other materials and systems on other projects.

FIGURE 2-1 Completed Training Center.

The $2.5-million, 35,000-square-foot facility was constructed in Kent, Washington, for the Carpenters-Employers Apprenticeship and Training Trust Fund of Western Washington. The mixed-use project includes office, warehouse, computer laboratory, and classroom space; a welding shop; and unfinished shell space for future tenants. Figure 2-1 shows an artist's rendering of the completed project, which was named the Kent Specialties Training Center. Throughout this text, we will refer to this project as the Training Center project. A site plan and selected construction drawings are shown in Appendix H. We will develop a budget estimate for the project in Chapter 4, a lump-sum bid estimate in Chapters 6 through 11, and a guaranteed maximum price estimate in Chapter 18.

2.3   PROJECT EXECUTION STRATEGY

The owner of the project chose to use a negotiated procedure for selecting the construction contractor. The procedure was similar to that illustrated in Figure 1-13. First, interested contractors were invited to submit their *statements of qualification* for the project. The statements of qualification were reviewed, and a request for proposal was issued to each contractor considered qualified. A request for proposal describes the specific information requested by the project owner and the criteria that will be used to evaluate the information and select the contractor for the project. The request for proposal for the Training Center is shown in Appendix D. Proposals were to consist of resumes of project team members, cost information for the base bid, a summary schedule, and a listing of work to be self-performed. After negotiations were concluded, a cost-plus contract with a guaranteed maximum price was awarded to the successful construction contractor, who in this book we will identify as Western Construction Company. Western was selected for the project because its proposal provided the best value to the owner—reasonable price, experienced project management team, and timely completion. The details of the negotiating process used for the Training Center will be discussed in Chapter 19.

While a negotiated procurement process was used for the Training Center, a lump-sum bid process could have been used if the owner had wanted to select the contractor solely on contract price. An Invitation for Bid for this process is shown in Appendix E. Chapters 6 through 15 will discuss the preparation of a bid in response to this Invitation for Bid.

2.4   PROJECT PARTICIPANTS

The owner chose to hire a construction management consultant for the project who acted as the owner's advisor throughout the design and construction of the project. Preconstruction services were performed by the consultant rather than by the general contractor, who was selected near the end of design development (documents were about 90% complete). An organization chart for the project delivery team for this project is shown in Figure 2-2.

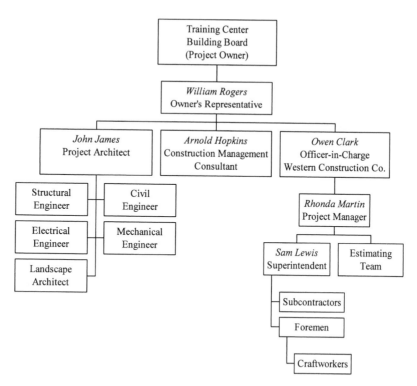

FIGURE 2-2   Project organization.

II

BUDGET ESTIMATING PROCESS

CHAPTER 3
BUDGET ESTIMATES

CHAPTER 4
BUDGET ESTIMATES FOR THE TRAINING CENTER

CHAPTER 5
ESTIMATES FOR PRECONSTRUCTION SERVICES

3

BUDGET ESTIMATES

3.1   INTRODUCTION

As shown in Figure 1-1, *budget cost estimates* are developed throughout the design process of a construction project. Early in the programming phase, the owner usually establishes a tentative project scope and a preliminary budget. The project budget includes both the estimated construction cost and other estimated owner costs. As design decisions are made and drawings created, additional budget estimates are prepared to ensure that the project being designed can be constructed within the owner's established budget. If the budget estimates indicate that the construction costs will exceed the owner's budget, the owner has two choices: either reduce the project scope or increase the budget. These budget estimates may be prepared by the designer, by a cost consultant, by a construction management consultant, or by the general contractor (as one of the preconstruction services discussed in Chapter 1). The accuracy of these estimates is a function of the degree of design completion. Because there is considerable uncertainty in preparing budget estimates, the final estimate value should be rounded to the nearest hundred or thousand dollars. Presenting a budget estimate that shows dollars and cents may create a false impression regarding the accuracy of the estimate. In this chapter, we will discuss the types of budget estimates, when they are prepared, and the level of detail involved.

3.2   PROGRAMMING BUDGET ESTIMATES

Programming budget estimates are prepared during the programming phase to assess the financial feasibility of the project and to identify anticipated funding requirements. The construction cost estimates typically are developed using historical cost data for similar projects that may be adjusted using cost indices similar to those shown in Figure 1-5 or square-foot cost factors similar to those shown in Figure 1-3. Other owner costs are estimated as percentages of the construction cost estimate or as allowances. These costs typically include the following:

- Fees
- Permits
- Taxes
- Owner-furnished Furniture, Fixtures, and Equipment (FF&E)
- Other owner soft costs (interest, etc.)
- Potential land mitigation costs
- Contingencies

Figure 3-1 shows an example programming budget estimate that was developed for the construction of a new university classroom building. First the construction costs are es-

---

Western Construction Company
550 South 7th Avenue
Kent, Washington 98002

Project: New Classroom Building, State University, Olympia, Washington
Estimator: Jerry Jackson
Estimate Date: January 15, 2003

Programming Budget Estimate

	Scope	Unit Price	Total
Building Construction	50,000 sq ft	$110/sq ft	$5,500,000
Site Development	200,000 sq ft	$5/sq ft	$1,000,000
Subtotal (Construction Costs)			$6,500,000
Programming Fees	Allowance		$50,000
Design Fees	6% of Construction Cost		$390,000
Geotechnical Investigation	Allowance		$100,000
Testing & Inspection Fees	3% of Construction Cost		$195,000
Permits & Fees	2% of Construction Cost		$130,000
Insurance	2% of Construction Cost		$130,000
Owner-Furnished Furniture, Fixtures, & Equip	Allowance		$1,500,000
Owner Soft Costs	Allowance		$2,000,000
Subtotal (Costs)			$10,995,000
Sales Tax	8% of Subtotal		$880,000
Owner Contingency	20% of Subtotal		$2,200,000
Total Budget Estimate			$14,075,000

FIGURE 3–1   Programming budget estimate.

timated using square foot cost factors. The $110 per square foot cost factor came from Figure 1-3. The other owner costs are then estimated as percentages of the estimated construction cost, and an appropriate contingency is added for risk mitigation. Note that a 20% contingency was added to ensure adequate resources were programmed to address possible unknown project site conditions and cost escalation, as suggested in Figure 1-15.

Once the programming budget has been approved by the owner, the design team proceeds with the development of preliminary design concepts. The design concepts are then reviewed by the owner and, if approved, the design team initiates the preparation of the schematic design.

3.3 SCHEMATIC DESIGN BUDGET ESTIMATES

During schematic design, the construction cost estimate is transformed from a gross square-foot estimate into a systems or assemblies estimate. The design team makes decisions regarding major design features and project layout. Schematic design budget estimates are based primarily on assemblies or composite systems, such as steel frame, foundation, and substructure. During the design of each system, the design team considers the cost implication and net effect on the estimated construction cost of the total project. The owner and designer consider the potential cost implications when selecting individual design features and project components.

The following assemblies or systems typically are used when preparing schematic design construction cost estimates:

- Foundations
- Substructure
- Superstructure
- Exterior closure
- Roofing and sheet metal
- Interior construction and equipment
- Mechanical
- Electrical
- Sitework

Once the construction cost estimate has been developed, the schematic design budget estimate is prepared by adding the owner's costs that were discussed in Section 3.2. An example of a schematic design budget estimate for the university classroom building introduced in Figure 3-1 is shown in Figures 3-2 through 3-4. Figure 3-2 shows the analysis of each building system. Historical square foot cost factors should be used if they are available. If not, cost reference books such as those published by R. S. Means can be used. The contractor's indirect costs (general conditions, insurance, and fee) are added to cover the cost of managing the project, to cover a portion of the cost of the construction firm's overhead, and to provide a profit. As suggested in Figure 1-15, a 10% construction contingency was included to address possible design enhancements, unknown site conditions, and cost escalation. A construction contingency was not included in the programming budget estimate shown in Figure 3-1, because the design had not been initiated, and the construction cost estimate was based on gross square feet of building. The systems estimates are summarized in Figure 3-3 and summed to

Foundations

Description	Quantity	Unit	Unit Price	Total	Cost/sf
Conventional spread footings	50,000	sf	$2.00	$100,000	
Subtotal				$100,000	$2.00

Substructure

Description	Quantity	Unit	Unit Price	Total	Cost/sf
Reinforced slab-on-grade (6 inch)	50,000	sf	$7.00	$350,000	
Subtotal				$350,000	$7.00

Superstructure

Description	Quantity	Unit	Unit Price	Total	Cost/sf
Concrete support walls (1,000 ft × 50 ft × 20 ft)	42,000	sf	$5.50	$231,000	
Roof structure	50,000	sf	$4.00	$200,000	
Subtotal				$431,000	$8.62

Exterior Closure

Description	Quantity	Unit	Unit Price	Total	Cost/sf
Exterior walls—masonry (60%)	30,000	sf	$4.50	$135,000	
Exterior doors & windows (40%)	20,000	sf	$2.00	$40,000	
Subtotal				$175,000	$3.50

Roofing and Sheet Metal

Description	Quantity	Unit	Unit Price	Total	Cost/sf
Roofing & sheet metal	50,000	sf	$5.00	$250,000	
Architectural metals (allowance of 300 ft by 12 ft)	3,600	sf	$10.00	$36,000	
Subtotal				$286,000	$5.72

Interior Construction & Equipment

Description	Quantity	Unit	Unit Price	Total	Cost/sf
Finishes	50,000	sf	$11.50	$575,000	
Special construction & equipment	1	allowance	$500,000	$500,000	
Subtotal				$1,075,000	$21.50

Mechanical

Description	Quantity	Unit	Unit Price	Total	Cost/sf
Mechanical	50,000	sf	$18.50	$925,000	
Fire protection	50,000	sf	$2.00	$100,000	
Subtotal				$1,025,000	$20.50

FIGURE 3–2 Schematic design systems cost estimate.

Electrical					
Description	Quantity	Unit	Unit Price	Total	Cost/sf
Electrical	50,000	sf	$10.00	$500,000	
Subtotal				$500,000	$10.00

Sitework					
Description	Quantity	Unit	Unit Price	Total	Cost/sf
Sitework	200,000	sf	$5.00	$1,000,000	
Subtotal				$1,000,000	$20.00

FIGURE 3–2 Continued.

Western Construction Company
550 South 7th Avenue
Kent, Washington 98002

Project: New Classroom Building, State University, Olympia, Washington
Estimator: Jerry Jackson
Estimate Date: April 10, 2003

Schematic Design Construction Cost Estimate

Building System	Total	Cost/sf
Foundations	$100,000	$2.00
Substructure	$350,000	$7.00
Superstructure	$431,000	$8.62
Exterior Closure	$175,000	$3.50
Roofing & Sheet Metal	$286,000	$5.72
Interior Construction & Equipment	$1,075,000	$21.50
Mechanical	$1,025,000	$20.50
Electrical	$500,000	$10.00
Sitework	$1,000,000	$20.00
Subtotal	$4,942,000	$98.84
General Conditions, Insurance, & Fee (15%)	$741,300	
Subtotal	$5,683,300	$113.67
Construction Contingency (10%)	$568,300	
Subtotal	$6,251,600	$125.03
State & City Excise Tax (1.6%)	$100,000	
Total	$6,351,600	$127.03

FIGURE 3–3 Schematic design construction cost estimate.

Western Construction Company
550 South 7th Avenue
Kent, Washington 98002

Project: New Classroom Building, State University, Olympia, Washington
Estimator: Jerry Jackson
Estimate Date: April 10, 2003

Schematic Design Budget Estimate

	Scope	Unit Price	Total
Building Construction & Site Development	50,000 sq ft	$127.03	$6,351,600
Subtotal (Construction Cost)			$6,351,600
Programming Fees	Allowance		$50,000
Design Fees	6% of Construction Cost		$381,100
Geotechnical Investigation	Allowance		$100,000
Testing & Inspection Fees	3% of Construction Cost		$190,500
Permits & Fees	2% of Construction Cost		$127,000
Insurance	2% of Construction Cost		$127,000
Owner-Furnished Furniture, Fixtures, & Equip	Allowance		$1,500,000
Owner Soft Costs	Allowance		$2,000,000
Subtotal (Costs)			$10,827,200
Sales Tax	8% of Subtotal		$866,200
Owner Contingency	5% of Subtotal		$541,400
Total Budget Estimate			$12,234,800

FIGURE 3–4   Schematic design budget estimate.

develop the estimated construction cost, which is the first entry on the schematic design budget shown in Figure 3-4. Next the owner's cost items are added as percentages of the estimated construction cost. Finally an appropriate contingency is added as a risk mitigation measure. As suggested in Figure 1-15, the owner's contingency was reduced to 5%, because some major design decisions had been made.

The individual assembly cost estimate starts as a rough-order-of-magnitude value based on square-foot or composite cost factors. As design details are selected, the costs are revised based on material selections. Alternative designs may be considered, and the cost implication of each design evaluated. Design documents typically are about 30% complete at the end of schematic design, and *schematic cost estimates* generally include narratives prepared by the estimator similar to the one shown in Figure 3-5. This narrative is used to identify any assumptions made when developing the estimate and is a good management tool for owners and designers.

Western Construction Company
550 South 7th Avenue
Kent, Washington 98002

Project: New Classroom Building, State University, Olympia, Washington
Estimator: Jerry Jackson
Estimate Date: April 10, 2003

Schematic Design Budget Estimate Narrative

Qualifications and Assumptions:
- This estimate assumes a basically flat site without export of soil.
- Building will be founded on conventional spread footings without pile supports and will have a 6-inch concrete slab on grade.
- The exterior walls will be cast-in-place concrete clad with masonry at the following ratio: 60% cladding and 40% to be painted aluminum and tinted glazing.
- Roof structure will be structural steel and deck supported by tube columns and ledger angles, all with one-hour rated fireproofing.
- Roofing will be either a mechanically adhered single ply or 4-ply built-up with cap sheet over R-30 semi-rigid insulation.
- The interior clear height will be 15 feet.
- An estimate of $11.50 per square foot has been used since finishes are not shown.
- Mechanical estimate assumes natural gas air handling units with constant air volume.
- All areas will be fully sprinklered with a standard wet-type system.
- Four restrooms that meet disability requirements are included.
- Classroom lighting will be drop-in indirect and laboratory lighting will be pendant indirect.
- Allowance for fire alarm, clocks, security, and closed-circuit television are included.
- Sitework is an allowance, since it is undefined.

Exclusions:
- Window treatments
- Telephone and data systems
- Building signage
- Furniture and fixtures
- Demolition of existing structures on site
- Soil remediation or removal of underground structures

FIGURE 3–5 Schematic design budget estimate narrative.

3.4 DESIGN DEVELOPMENT BUDGET ESTIMATES

Design development construction cost estimates usually are prepared using an assemblies or systems format similar to that used for schematic design budget estimates. The primary difference is the amount of detail supporting the estimated cost for each assembly or system. The value for some items will be based on quantity take-off with associated labor and material costs.

It generally is accepted practice to estimate the cost of several design options during design development. For example, during schematic design, the exterior cladding may have been envisioned as a composite system. As design development is initiated, the concept has changed to 40% glazing, 40% metal panels, and 20% stone or precast concrete. Later as more design decisions are made, specific materials are selected for the exterior cladding system. Now more accurate cost estimates can be prepared and contingency amounts reduced, because some construction materials have been identified, which can be used as a basis for preparing the estimate. A revised systems construction cost estimate for the classroom building at about 60% design completion is shown in Figure 3-6. Just as with the schematic design estimate, a narrative, similar to the one shown in Figure 3-5, should be maintained identifying all assumptions made when preparing the cost estimate.

Design development is the stage when all assemblies become clearly distinguishable as individual construction elements; for example, a slab on grade is detailed as six inches thick with a specific reinforcing scheme and a specified finish. The previously priced assembly cost estimate can now be quantified and priced in more detail.

Foundations					
Description	**Quantity**	**Unit**	**Unit Price**	**Total**	**Cost/sf**
Conventional spread footings	465	cy	$260.00	$120,900	
Subtotal				$120,900	$2.42

Substructure					
Description	**Quantity**	**Unit**	**Unit Price**	**Total**	**Cost/sf**
Reinforced slab-on-grade (6 inch)	50,000	sf	$7.00	$350,000	
Subtotal				$350,000	$7.00

Superstructure					
Description	**Quantity**	**Unit**	**Unit Price**	**Total**	**Cost/sf**
Concrete support walls (1,000 ft × 50 ft × 20 ft)	850	cy	$300.00	$255,000	
Roof structure	230	tons	$1,000.00	$230,000	
Subtotal				$485,000	$9.70

Exterior Closure					
Description	**Quantity**	**Unit**	**Unit Price**	**Total**	**Cost/sf**
Exterior walls—masonry and precast sills (60%)	38,000	sf	$4.00	$152,000	
Exterior doors & windows (40%)	20,000	sf	$2.00	$40,000	
Subtotal				$192,000	$3.84

FIGURE 3–6   Design development systems cost estimate.

Roofing and Sheet Metal

Description	Quantity	Unit	Unit Price	Total	Cost/sf
Roofing with R-30 insulation & sheet metal	50,000	sf	$8.00	$400,000	
Architectural metals (allowance of 100 ft by 12 ft)	1,200	sf	$10.00	$12,000	
Subtotal				$412,000	$8.24

Interior Construction & Equipment

Description	Quantity	Unit	Unit Price	Total	Cost/sf
Finishes	50,000	sf	$11.50	$575,000	
Special construction & equipment			with FF&E	$0	
Subtotal				$575,000	$11.50

Mechanical

Description	Quantity	Unit	Unit Price	Total	Cost/sf
Plumbing	20	fixtures	$3,000.00	$60,000	
Laboratory piping	10,000	lf	$8.00	$80,000	
HVAC & controls	50	zones	$3,000.00	$150,000	
HVAC roof equipment	25	tons	$30,000.00	$750,000	
Fire protection	50,000	sf	$2.00	$100,000	
Subtotal				$1,140,000	$22.80

Electrical

Description	Quantity	Unit	Unit Price	Total	Cost/sf
Switch gear and transformers	1	lump sum	$20,000.00	$20,000	
Distribution wiring and electrical devices	50,000	sf	$4.00	$200,000	
Lighting	50,000	sf	$5.00	$250,000	
Low voltage (security, clocks, fire alarms, CCTV)	50,000	sf	$3.00	$150,000	
Site lighting	150,000	sf	$1.00	$150,000	
Subtotal				$770,000	$15.40

Sitework

Description	Quantity	Unit	Unit Price	Total	Cost/sf
Clearing & earthwork	200,000	sf	$1.50	$300,000	
Storm sewer with catchbasins	1,000	lf	$25.00	$25,000	
Sanitary sewer (12 inch)	150	lf	$35.00	$5,250	
Water (potable) (12 inch)	175	lf	$75.00	$13,125	
Water (irrigation) (6 inch)	185	lf	$55.00	$10,175	
Paving & sidewalks	7,500	sf	$7.50	$56,250	
Landscape & irrigation	140,000	sf	$4.50	$630,000	
Subtotal				$1,039,800	$20.80

FIGURE 3–6 Continued.

Western Construction Company
550 South 7th Avenue
Kent, Washington 98002

Project: New Classroom Building, State University, Olympia, Washington
Estimator: Jerry Jackson
Estimate Date: July 15, 2003

Design Development Construction Cost Estimate

Building System	Total	Cost/sf
Foundations	$120,900	$2.42
Substructure	$350,000	$7.00
Superstructure	$485,000	$9.70
Exterior Closure	$192,000	$3.84
Roofing & Sheet Metal	$412,000	$8.24
Interior Construction & Equipment	$575,000	$11.50
Mechanical	$1,140,000	$22.80
Electrical	$770,000	$15.40
Sitework	$1,039,800	$20.80
Subtotal	$5,084,700	$101.69
General Conditions, Insurance, & Fee (15%)	$762,700	
Subtotal	$5,847,400	$116.95
Construction Contingency (5%)	$293,400	
Subtotal	$6,140,800	$122.80
State & City Excise Tax (1.6%)	$98,300	
Total	$6,239,100	$124.78

FIGURE 3–7 Design development construction cost estimate.

Another approach to estimating during design development is to employ *specialty contractors* for pricing individual elements. For instance, the architect may know he or she wants to use metal panels, but may not have selected patterns, textures, colors, or even materials. By contacting a *subcontractor* or even several suppliers, the estimator can secure relevant pricing of various combinations. He or she might also compare different materials from other projects to determine the cost implications of various design alternatives.

A sample construction cost estimate at about 60% design completion is shown in Figure 3-7. The systems cost estimate data in Figure 3-6 is used to estimate the direct construction costs. Next, the contractor's indirect costs—general conditions, insurance, and *fee*—are added as a percentage of the estimated direct construction cost. Finally, an appropriate contingency was added to mitigate risks. Note that the construction contingency was reduced to 5% because more design features have been identified. Appropriate owner's

Western Construction Company
550 South 7th Avenue
Kent, Washington 98002

Project: New Classroom Building, State University, Olympia, Washington
Estimator: Jerry Jackson
Estimate Date: July 15, 2003

Design Development Budget Estimate

	Scope	Unit Price	Total
Building Construction & Site Development	50,000 sq ft	$124.78	$6,239,100
Subtotal (Construction Costs)			$6,239,100
Programming Fees	Allowance		$50,000
Design Fees	6% of Construction Cost		$374,400
Geotechnical Investigation	Allowance		$100,000
Testing & Inspection Fees	3% of Construction Cost		$187,200
Permits & Fees	2% of Construction Cost		$124,800
Insurance	2% of Construction Cost		$124,800
Owner-Furnished Furniture, Fixtures, & Equip	Allowance		$1,500,000
Owner Soft Costs	Allowance		$2,000,000
Subtotal (Costs)			$10,700,300
Sales Tax	8% of Subtotal		$856,000
Owner Contingency	3% of Subtotal		$321,000
Total Budget Estimate			$11,877,300

FIGURE 3–8 Design development budget estimate.

costs were added next as percentages of the estimated construction cost, and an owner contingency was added for risk mitigation. Note that the owner's contingency was reduced to 3% because most design decisions had been made. The resulting design development budget estimate is shown in Figure 3-8.

As shown in Figure 1-1, a design development budget estimate is not the same as a lump-sum bid. The contract documents (drawings and specifications) are not complete at the end of design development, so conceptual cost estimating techniques must be used for some project components. The lump-sum bid is prepared from completed project drawings and specifications.

3.5 SUMMARY

Budget estimates are developed throughout the planning and design phases to ensure that the project being designed can be constructed within the owner's desired budget. The accuracy of these estimates is a function of the degree of design completion. Programming budget estimates are prepared early in the planning process to assess the financial feasibility of the project and to identify funding requirements. The programming construction cost estimate typically is developed using historical cost data or gross square-foot cost factors. Estimated owner costs are added to produce the programming budget estimate. Schematic design budget estimates are developed as preliminary design decisions are made, and the designer develops conceptual drawings. The construction cost estimate for these budget estimates is developed based on project systems or assemblies. Again estimated owner costs are added to produce the schematic design budget estimate. Design development budget estimates are prepared as the designer completes the design. The construction cost budget estimate contains some systems that are estimated based on gross square feet, while others are estimated based on quantity take-off and pricing. Specialty contractors may be used to assist with pricing selected systems. Contingencies are included in budget estimates to mitigate risks, but are reduced as design decisions are made.

3.6 REVIEW QUESTIONS

1. Name and describe the three primary types of budget estimates.
2. What are four owner costs that typically are included in a budget estimate?
3. Why are construction contingencies used on early budget estimates?
4. Why are budget estimate narratives prepared, and what do they describe?
5. What are five building systems that typically are used for both schematic design and design development construction cost estimates?
6. Should the construction contingency for a schematic design construction cost estimate be greater or less than the construction contingency for a design development construction cost estimate for the same project? Why did you make this selection?
7. What choices does the project owner have if the budget estimate is greater than the amount of funding available for the project?

3.7 EXERCISES

1. Develop a programming budget estimate for a 100,000 square-foot warehouse, assuming a square-foot cost factor of $60 per square foot. The site will be about 200,000 square feet with a site development cost of $3 per square foot. Use the same factors as shown in Figure 3-1 for other owner costs, except assume owner-furnished FFE will be about $1,000,000 and owner soft costs will be $800,000.

2. Develop a schematic design construction cost estimate for the warehouse described in exercise 1. Use the unit prices shown in Figure 3-2, except the exterior doors and windows will be only 10% of the exterior closure, architectural metals is estimated to be 1,000 square feet, finishes will be $5.00 per square foot, and mechanical will be $10.00 per square foot. Use the same mark-up for general conditions, contingency, and tax as shown in Figure 3-3.

3. Without reading ahead, what do you think will happen to the construction contingency as the design progresses? What contingency would you forecast a competing general contractor will place on a competitive lump-sum bid based on a completed set of construction documents?

4

BUDGET ESTIMATES FOR THE TRAINING CENTER

4.1 INTRODUCTION

As indicated in Chapter 3, construction budget estimates are prepared at different times during the development of the project design. Although the development of budget estimates is introduced early in this text, the development of such estimates usually is reserved for experienced estimators. The architect for the Training Center developed the programming construction budget estimate well before the construction contract was awarded. The Building Board (see Figure 2-2 for the project organization chart) authorized purchase of the property and initiation of schematic design based upon this budget estimate. The Board also hired a construction management consultant to act as the owner's advisor. The consultant prepared a schematic design construction budget estimate at completion of schematic design. Western Construction Company prepared a third construction estimate, which was used to develop the guaranteed maximum price, at the time the proposal was requested.

4.2 DESIGN STATUS

The programming construction budget estimate was prepared based upon a general description of a mixed-use building with approximately 30,000 square feet of space. Some of the floor area was to be office, some open workspace similar to a warehouse, and some unfinished shell space. The estimate was developed without any drawings. The architect is experienced in tilt-up, mixed-use buildings and provided a rough verbal estimate of $70 per square foot, or a total cost of $2,100,000 (30,000 square feet times $70 per square foot). The 30,000 square feet was an early estimate from the architect regarding the size of the building that could be placed on the lot, which was being evaluated for purchase. The $70 per square foot budget unit price was derived from the square-foot database shown in Figure 1-3. About 20% of the completed facility was estimated to be office space, and the remaining 80% warehouse space. The cost factor for office space (office building, 2–5 story) from Figure 1-3 is $107 per square foot and for warehouse space is $60 per square foot. By weighting the square-foot data, a composite cost factor was determined as shown:

Office area: $0.2 \times \$107$ per square foot $= \$21$ per square foot

Warehouse area: $0.8 \times \$60$ per square foot $= \$48$ per square foot

Total: $21 per square foot $+$ $48 per square foot $= \$69$ per square foot,

rounded to $70 per square foot

No additional clarifications or detail were provided with the estimate. Budget estimates such as this are commonly requested by owners but are risky due to the lack of design information. If the estimate is too low, the owner may proceed with the project and run short of funds when the design is complete and bids are received. If the estimate is too high, the project may be canceled or scaled back before the budget can be validated. The architect should have added a contingency, but did not. Adding a 20% contingency would have increased the estimated construction cost to $2.5 million.

Employment of a general contractor during the preconstruction phase is beneficial to both the designer and the owner. The contractor is well versed in current construction costs and can provide a better construction budget estimate, assuming the design has progressed enough to support that effort. However, many estimating firms and estimating consultants can provide a similar service. Many of these people are former contractors and have current pricing available. The Building Board chose to employ a construction management consultant to act as their advisor.

As indicated in the introduction to this chapter, the consultant prepared a construction budget estimate after the architect finished schematic design documents. A rough floor plan similar to the one shown in Figure 4-1 and the rendering shown in Figure 2-1 were available. The consultant met with the architect to understand his intentions based on other similar projects. The schematic design budget estimate was prepared in a systems or assemblies format, as shown in Figure 4-2, and was more expensive than was anticipated in the architect's programming budget estimate of $2.1 million. Note that a 10% construction contingency was used (as discussed in Chapter 3) because many design issues were yet to be resolved. The unit price data used to prepare an estimate like this should come from an historical cost database that the estimator maintains. The *estimating database* is created by updating unit price cost data with actual costs at the completion of each construction project. If such a database is not available, the estimator can use published unit cost data.

When the consultant completed the schematic design construction budget estimate, it was apparent that the building was slightly larger than originally anticipated and would include some specialty items such as a second floor mezzanine, bridge crane, and welding shop. The owner also made it apparent that the interior finishes should display the capabilities of the carpenter trade and would include upgraded finishes and millwork.

It should be noted that these early budget estimates are presented in rounded figures. In the schematic design budget estimate, the consultant adjusted the figures to provide a

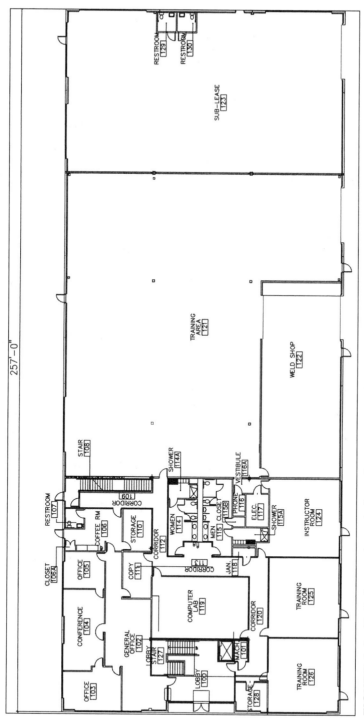

FIGURE 4-1 Preliminary schematic floor plan.

45

Cascade Consulting Services
100 South 10th Avenue
Kent, Washington 98002

Project: Training Center
Estimator: Arnold Hopkins
Estimate Date: January 28, 2003

Schematic Design Construction Budget Estimate

System	Quantity	Units	Unit Price	Budget
Sitework (including sidewalks and landscape)	120,000	sf of site	$3	$360,000
Substructure (foundations and concrete slab)	27,000	sf footprint	$5	$135,000
Superstructure (tilt-up concrete panels and steel)	35,000	sf of floor	$8	$280,000
Enclosure (including windows and roof)	35,000	sf of floor	$6	$210,000
Finishes	35,000	sf of floor	$10	$350,000
Premium for welding shop	2,000	sf of floor	$25	$50,000
Bridge Crane	1	allowance	$70,000	$70,000
Elevator	2	stops	$15,000	$30,000
Mechanical	35,000	sf of floor	$7	$245,000
Electrical	35,000	sf of floor	$5	$175,000
Subtotal				$1,905,000
Contractor Markups (general conditions, fee, insurance, and taxes)			15%	$285,800
Subtotal				$2,190,800
Construction Contingency			10%	$190,500
Subtotal				$2,381,300
Rounding Adjustments				$18,700
Total				$2,400,000

FIGURE 4–2 Schematic design construction budget estimate.

round estimate of $2,400,000. Early budget estimates should be presented in round figures, as they are only approximate, and using more significant digits may create an impression that the estimate is more accurate than it is. For example, if a budget was presented as $2,399,347.32, it may cause the owner to believe that it is accurate to the last two digits, which are 32 cents. Even if the information used to prepare the figure was approximate, the addition of several approximate numbers might result in such a detailed number. This second construction budget estimate was presented and explained to the Building Board and approval was granted to proceed to design development. As the design proceeded, the owner intentionally added scope and improved materials and finishes. These were conscious decisions on their part. This is one of the reasons that detailed bid breakdowns would eventually be requested from proposing contractors.

4.3 TAKE-OFF OF SUBSTANTIAL AREAS

An estimator prepares as accurate a budget estimate as possible. The structural work is usually designed first. The general contractor may use his or her own crews to perform the structural construction. If this is the case, the contractor would perform detailed quantity take-offs for whatever design is completed at the time the estimate is prepared. The quantity take-off is measuring the length, area, or volume of specific elements of work, such as 500 lineal feet of steel column. Some contractors will prepare sketches for work that has not yet been defined, or may provide extensive lists of assumptions and clarifications to define the basis for the estimate. Contractors and estimators do not want to be embarrassed later by a grossly erroneous budget estimate. As discussed in Chapter 3, the more complete the design and detailed the estimate, the greater the accuracy.

In the case of the Training Center, the programming construction budget estimate prepared by the architect was not based on take-offs. The schematic design construction budget estimate prepared by the consultant broke the project down into systems and included initial system take-off amounts. This information is shown in the quantity and units columns in Figure 4-2. Western Construction Company eventually divided the entire project into measurable items according to a very detailed work breakdown structure.

4.4 PRICING DATA

In addition to using quantity take-offs, the estimator also uses the most current and accurate pricing data available. Most contractors have in-house electronic databases or the ability to access a published estimating database. Even more relevant pricing resources are actual material unit prices obtained from suppliers, current local wage rates for craftworkers, and subcontractor pricing from experts in these specialty areas. For the Training Center, the construction management consultant used his own database to prepare the budget estimate shown in Figure 4-2.

4.5 BUDGET ESTIMATE ACCURACY

As discussed in Chapter 3, a budget estimate is only as accurate as the information used to develop it. Figure 4-3 shows the evolution of the various budget estimates for the Training Center and their respective accuracies. Even though the guaranteed maximum price eventually came in higher than either of the two previous budget estimates, the increase was being tracked by the architect and owner and was anticipated because of design decisions. Even with these increases, the guaranteed maximum price fell within the anticipated budget range shown in Figure 1-2, albeit on the high end. A lump-sum estimate requires more accurate documents and, therefore, has less need for a contingency. The amount of contingency needed on any project is directly related to the anticipated risk. Site conditions, weather, economy, low bids, availability of subcontractors, or lack of design completion can create risk. With respect to budgeting, the percentage of contingency applied usually is directly related to the stage of design completion. The various types of contingencies were discussed in Chapter 1.

During schematic design and design development, it is important to monitor scope and cost changes to ensure that the project remains within the owner's established budget. The most

	Accuracy	Budget Range	Contingency Included
Programming Budget Estimate $2,100,000	±20%	$1,680,000 to $2,520,000	none
Schematic Design Budget Estimate $2,400,000	±10%	$2,160,000 to $2,640,000	10%
Western Construction's GMP $2,612,807	±5%	$2,482,167 to $2,743,447	3%

FIGURE 4–3 Budget estimate accuracy.

common technique for doing this is to create a *budget control log*. Such a log provides both the owner and the designer with a record of design and cost decisions made during the design of a project. This will be discussed in more detail as a preconstruction service in the next chapter.

4.6 SUMMARY

Some projects have many budget estimates. The architect developed the programming construction budget estimate for the Training Center. Sometimes owners, construction management consultants, general contractors, or even real estate agents will prepare early budget estimates as well. During the design phases of this project, the scope increases resulted in budget estimate increases and eventually a guaranteed maximum price, which exceeded the budget estimate but was within the budget estimate accuracy range given the state of the design documents. Estimators attempt to provide estimates that are as accurate as possible as decisions regarding project scope are made during the development of the design. They perform detailed quantity take-offs and use current pricing data for work that has been defined. Contingencies are applied to estimates based on the level of detail of the design documents. The more complete the documents, the less contingency needed.

4.7 REVIEW QUESTIONS

1. What are some of the issues that create risk and subsequently the need for contingency in a project?
2. Who prepares budget estimates?
3. What are budget estimates used for?
4. Why do estimators want to be accurate with their budget estimates?
5. What could happen if a budget estimate were too low?
6. What could happen if a budget estimate were too high?

7. Why were the Training Center's early budget estimates too low?
8. Why might a lump sum estimate be less than a budget or a guaranteed maximum price estimate?
9. When would an estimator present an exact figure for an estimate rather than a rounded figure?

4.8 EXERCISES

1. Using the unit price recommended by the architect in the programming construction budget estimate presented in this chapter, what would the budget estimate have been if the anticipated size of the project were 35,000 square feet?

2. Using a unit price of $85 per square foot, what would the Training Center programming construction budget estimate have been?

3. What are some of the tools an estimator could use to track changes in design that could affect early budget estimates and ultimately the cost of the project?

5

ESTIMATES FOR PRECONSTRUCTION SERVICES

5.1 INTRODUCTION

The concept of the construction contractor providing preconstruction services to the owner was introduced in Chapter 1. Use of these services is more prevalent in the private sector than it is in on public projects. Some public agencies, however, also are employing contractors to provide these services, particularly on large, complex projects. Some of the activities that may be performed by a general contractor as a part of preconstruction services include the following:

- Budget estimating
- Prequalifying subcontractors and suppliers
- Constructability analysis
- Planning and scheduling
- Assistance with permits
- Budget control
- Value engineering
- Early submittals
- Release of early bid packages for long-lead materials

The purpose of this chapter is to describe the process used to estimate the cost for providing preconstruction services, not to provide a comprehensive discussion of preconstruction services. Owners may choose to select the general contractor early in the design process to provide a constructor's perspective and to perform some or all of these preconstruction services. The owner may request an early proposal from a contractor to provide preconstruction services. Because the contractor is paid a fee for this service, the owner is not committing to the contractor for construction services. Sometimes a construction management consultant is selected in lieu of a general contractor to perform these services. Some owners prefer using a consultant to eliminate any pressure to negotiate a follow-on contract for construction services. The advantage to both the owner and the design team of adding construction expertise is to provide input regarding cost, schedule, and constructability during design development.

5.2 MARKETING FOR THE GENERAL CONTRACTOR

The general contractor usually views the preconstruction process as an opportunity to negotiate a contract for construction of the project. The contractor's ultimate goal is to build the project. At a minimum, the general contractor would like to get on a select list of general contractors, if not for this project, then for another one with either the owner or the designer. Most contractors believe that if they perform well during the preconstruction phase, they may get an opportunity to negotiate a guaranteed maximum price contract without any competition.

5.3 THE REQUEST FOR PROPOSAL

An example *Request For Proposal (RFP)* for preconstruction services is shown in Figure 5-1. The RFP identifies the documents that are to be submitted in the proposal and the specific preconstruction services that are to be performed. The RFP may ask for the firm's experience on similar projects and may request resumes for the proposed key project management and supervisory personnel.

The Training Center
20474 72nd Avenue South
Kent, Washington 98032

February 6, 2003

To: Selected Contractors

Request for Proposals for Preconstruction Services

Thank you for your expressed interest in the Training Center. We are requesting proposals for preconstruction services. Some of the considerations for your proposal are as follows:

1. The project consists of sitework, shell, and phase one tenant improvements. Some of the **specifics** of the project include

   - Tilt-up concrete shell.
   - Structural steel second floor and roof structure.
   - Bridge crane.
   - Weld-exhaust booths.
   - Elevator.
   - Complete tenant improvements for phase one.
   - Design-build fire protection system is the responsibility of the general contractor.
   - Mechanical, plumbing, and electrical systems will be designed by the owner's engineers.
   - All civil, landscape, on-grade parking, and sitework is in the general contractor's scope of work.

FIGURE 5–1 Request for proposals for preconstruction services.

2. The preliminary **schedule** for the project is
   - Design has been completed through the schematic design phase.
   - Permit will be requested at the 60% construction document stage.
   - Preconstruction proposals are due on Friday, February 21, 2003. Interviews will be scheduled for the following week.
   - Selection of the preconstruction consultant will occur before the end of February.
   - Construction is scheduled to start on June 21, 2003.
   - Six-month construction duration is anticipated, but we will be looking to the preconstruction consultant to validate that assumption.

3. The following documents are attached to this Request for Proposals: floor plan, architectural rendering, soils report, and topographic survey.

4. The following **documents** are required to be submitted with your proposal
   - Experience with similar types of projects.
   - Prior experience with the owner or the design team.
   - List of proposed personnel and their resumes.
   - Proposed preconstruction fee.

5. It is anticipated that the construction contract will be the 1997 version of the AIA A111 (cost of the work plus a fee with a guaranteed maximum price) and the AIA A201 general conditions. We anticipate the preconstruction consultant providing input regarding the final construction contract documents.

6. The preconstruction firm will be expected to work with the owner and designer teams throughout the completion of the design. The **preconstruction services** to be performed are
   - Budget control.
   - Constructability reviews.
   - Cost estimating.
   - Prequalification of subcontractors.
   - Scheduling.
   - Value engineering.

7. A copy of the preconstruction services contract to be executed is attached for your review.

8. Thank you again for your interest in the Training Center. We look forward to receiving your proposal on February 21, 2003.

Sincerely,

William Rogers

Owner's Representative

Attachments

cc: John James, Project Architect

FIGURE 5–1 Continued.

The RFP also may request an early construction budget estimate for the project based on schematic design documents. This budget estimate will be prepared as discussed in Chapters 3 and 4. If a budget estimate is not requested from the contractors, the owner or design team may inform the contractors of an approximate budget to assist with the preparation of their fee proposals.

5.4 DEVELOPMENT OF THE PRECONSTRUCTION SERVICES ESTIMATE

Designers refer to the cost of their contributions as design fees. The design firm's profit and general overhead costs are added to the cost of preparing the design to determine the design fee. For contractors, this preconstruction phase may be referred to as a cost rather than a fee. Very few contractors earn any profit on the preconstruction phase; again, they are usually simply trying to get the contract to build the project. The general contractor is not in the business of performing preconstruction services as a sole pursuit.

It is more difficult for a general contractor to determine a firm estimate for preconstruction services than it is to prepare a construction estimate. There is little that she or he can measure and apply historical unit prices against to develop a lump-sum value. The RFP may request a set of hourly rates, a guaranteed maximum price, or a lump-sum price. Many intangibles such as market condition, prior relations with the design and owner teams, experience on this type of project and in this location, and availability of personnel are considered. The most common situation is for a contractor to request a minimal fee that will cover her or his estimated actual costs without profit.

Assume that the Training Center owner has requested a lump-sum preconstruction services fee proposal from Western Construction Company for the Kent facility. The design team will have informed Western about the stage of design, permits, and financing. They will have indicated that Western is expected to participate for three months, performing standard preconstruction services that include weekly meetings. Western can then develop a lump-sum fee as shown in Figure 5-2 based on an estimate of the personnel required, the amount of time that will be spent by each individual, his or her salary, and any material costs. In this example, the owner would only be providing the lump-sum of $25,000 for preconstruction services.

As indicated earlier, an alternative to the lump-sum fee is an hourly fee that includes home office overhead and that covers anticipated material expenses. This type of fee proposal is more common with design professionals or consultants than it is with general contractors. A "multiplier" is used to convert anticipated in-house wages to an outside billing rate, which is intended to cover all expenses. This sort of fee is also referred to as time and materials, which may or may not include a "not to exceed amount." There is not a fixed amount charged to the owner as there is with the lump-sum fee. Figure 5-3 is an example of this type of hourly preconstruction services estimate. Columns 1, 5, and 6 would be provided to the owner in this example.

On more complicated projects, subcontractors may also contribute to the preconstruction estimate. Seldom will subcontractors offer to perform their share of the work below cost. Subcontractor requests for compensation generally will be higher than the general contractor's estimate. Subcontractors generally are not as driven by marketing to owners as is the general contractor and will not perform work without an opportunity for profit, or guarantee for construction services.

Western Construction Company
550 South 7th Avenue
Kent, Washington 98002

Project: Training Center
Date: February 12, 2003

Lump-Sum Cost Calculation

Description	Estimated Duration	Units	Unit Price	Direct Cost
Labor:				
Project Manager	100	hours	$42	$4,200
Chief Estimator	20	hours	$44	$880
Chief Scheduler	20	hours	$40	$800
Staff Estimator	200	hours	$25	$5,000
Officer-in-Charge	8	hours	$75	$600
Superintendent	20	hours	$40	$800
Administrative	100	hours	$20	$2,000
Subtotal Labor:				$14,280
Labor Burdens			30%	$4,284
Total Labor with Burden:				$18,564
Material Costs:				
Travel	3000	miles	$0.30	$900
Blueprints	1	allowance	$350	$350
Copies	1	allowance	$175	$175
Schedule Plots	1	allowance	$500	$500
Photographs	2	sets	$100	$200
Consumable Materials	1	allowance	$750	$750
Subtotal Materials:				$2,875
Subcontractors and Consultants:			allowance	$1,500
Subtotal Anticipated Costs				$22,939
Contingency			10%	$2,294
Adjustment				−$233
Total Anticipated Preconstruction Services Cost:				$25,000

FIGURE 5–2 Lump-sum preconstruction services fee.

Western Construction Company
550 South 7th Avenue
Kent, Washington 98002

Project: Training Center
Date: February 12, 2003

Labor Unit Cost Calculation

Description	(1) Estimated Hours	(2) Actual Wage $/hour	(3) Direct Cost	(4) Multiplier	(5) Billable Wage $/hour	(6) Total Estimate
Personnel						
Project Manager	100	$42	$4,200	1.75	$74	$7,350
Chief Estimator	20	$44	$880	1.75	$77	$1,540
Chief Scheduler	20	$40	$800	1.75	$70	$1,400
Staff Estimator	200	$25	$5,000	1.75	$44	$8,750
Officer-in-Charge	8	$75	$600	1.75	$131	$1,050
Superintendent	20	$40	$800	1.75	$70	$1,400
Administrative	100	$20	$2,000	1.75	$35	$3,500
Subtotal			$14,280			$24,990
Adjusted Estimate:						$25,000

Multiplier includes labor burdens, materials, travel expenses, incidental expenses, home office overhead and profit, outside consultants if needed.

FIGURE 5–3 Hourly preconstruction services fee.

5.5 PRECONSTRUCTION SERVICES CONTRACT

If Western is successful with their preconstruction services fee proposal, they may be awarded a contract similar to the one shown in Figure 5-4. Many owner and contractor teams do not feel that a preconstruction contract is necessary, however, it is strongly recommended that one be executed. This short agreement will define the scope of work and the roles of the parties and will indicate that no additional commitments have been made.

The preconstruction costs may be recovered with monthly payment requests during the preconstruction phase, similar to construction pay requests during the construction phase. This is the preferred method. Sometimes the *preconstruction agreement* will indicate that the preconstruction costs will be rolled into a construction contract, should one be awarded. In this situation, the general contractor cannot recover its wages and expenses for an extended time period.

PRECONSTRUCTION SERVICES AGREEMENT

This agreement made this 1st day of March, 2003 between

the **Owner:**
Training Center
20474 72nd Avenue South
Kent, Washington 98032

and the **Contractor:**
Western Construction Company
550 South 7th Avenue
Kent, Washington 98002

for the following project:
The Kent Training Center

The **Owner** and the **Contractor** agree as follows:

1. That during the development of the design and prior to the start of construction, the Contractor will provide preconstruction services as follows:
   - Attend weekly coordination meetings.
   - Prepare budget estimates at the completion of conceptual documents, and design development documents during construction document development and as otherwise required.
   - Develop cost analyses of design options.
   - Conduct value engineering studies as necessary to achieve budget goals.
   - Develop and maintain preconstruction/construction schedule.
   - Develop site logistics plan.
   - Meet with consultants and/or subcontractors and suppliers, as necessary, to assist in the development of the design.
   - Conduct constructability review at completion of design development documents, 90% construction documents, and as otherwise required.

2. That preconstruction services will be billed at the following rates:

Administrative/clerical	$35 per hour
Chief estimator	$77 per hour
Chief scheduler	$70 per hour
Officer-in-charge	$131 per hour
Project manager	$74 per hour
Project superintendent	$70 per hour
Staff estimator	$44 per hour

3. That all cost of materials and equipment associated with providing preconstruction services shall be borne by the **Contractor.**

4. That all costs incurred by the **Contractor** prior to construction will be billed on a monthly basis for payment, by the **Owner,** by the 10th of the following month.

5. That it is the **Owner's** intent to enter into an agreement with the **Contractor** for the construction of the project assuming that:
   - The negotiated guaranteed maximum price meets the **Owner's** budget.
   - The final construction schedule meets the **Owner's** occupancy requirements.
   - Contractual terms and conditions can be negotiated to mutual agreement.

FIGURE 5–4 Preconstruction services contract.

6. That the **Owner** has the right to terminate this agreement at any time prior to start of construction. In the event of termination, all charges incurred or committed to date of termination will be reimbursed.

7. That the above agreement is hereby acknowledged and shall serve as the preconstruction services agreement between the **Owner** and the **Contractor.**

Western Construction Company   **Training Center**

Owen Clark   William Rogers
Officer-in-charge   Owner's Representative

5.6 BUDGET CONTROL LOG

One tool used by the estimator to manage the estimating process during preconstruction and to control the budget is a control log. This document may be referred to as a value-engineering log or a budget control summary. In some instances owners receive cost input on an ongoing basis as the design progresses. The purpose of this document is to track changes made, options proposed, and the anticipated cost impact of design decisions. It will help minimize surprises if the final estimate differs from the early schematic budgets. An example budget control log is shown in Figure 5-5. The initial log entry is the schematic design budget estimate. Subsequent entries show the anticipated cost impact of individual design decisions, which may be additive or deductive. The log should be maintained until the design is complete and the final cost estimate is prepared.

Any member of the owner-contractor preconstruction team may propose a change in the design or option to be considered. The estimator then adds these items to the project control log and prepares an estimate for each change. This is similar to estimating bid alternatives and change orders, except that it is prepared during the early design/preconstruction phase.

5.7 SUMMARY

Preconstruction services may be performed either by general contractors or by consulting firms. Such services include a variety of functions involving estimating, scheduling, and value engineering. Contractors often see the preconstruction phase as an opportunity to market themselves to the owner and the design team and to either negotiate a construction contract for the project or be added to a short list of potential contractors. The RFP for preconstruction services will identify the scope of preconstruction services that are to be provided and the specific documentation that is to be included in the proposal. A time-and-materials method or a lump-sum method may be used to determine the estimated fee. A short contract should be executed to define scope, establish relationships, and indicate that no commitments are implied regarding award of a construction contract. The preconstruction contractor or consultant performs many services that help control the budget and integrate the services provided by the design professionals and the builders.

Western Construction Company
550 South 7th Avenue
Kent, Washington 98002

Project: Training Center

Date: March 25, 2003

Budget Control Log

Line Item	Activity Description	$ Potential	$ Accepted	$ Rejected	Comments
	Original Budget Estimate		$2,400,000		
1	Increase electrical budget for shop equipment		$13,000		
2	Delete east end rest rooms			−$7,500	Carry as an alternate on the bid form
3	Change from steel to wood roof structure			$15,000	
4	Delete motorized overhead doors	−$2,500			
5	Add weld shop to scope		$50,000		Excludes welding equipment—by owner
6	Upgrade wood finishes in lobby and stair		$25,000		
7	Shell east end except rest rooms	−$12,000			
8	Include contingency for poor soil	$75,000			Need additional soils test
9	Schedule extension if permit not available	$35,000			
10	Add audio-visual equipment to Western's scope		$12,500		Shift from owner's FF&E budget
11	Occupancy separation wall track revision		$27,500		Required by city
12	Reduce landscape scope			−$14,200	Full scope required by city
	Current Budget Estimate		$2,528,000		

FIGURE 5–5   Budget control log.

5.8   REVIEW QUESTIONS

1.   What is the difference between "preconstruction cost" and "fee"?
2.   Why is it advantageous to the owner to employ a contractor to perform preconstruction services?
3.   Why is it advantageous to the owner to employ a third-party consultant rather than a general contractor to perform preconstruction services?
4.   Why should a contract be executed for preconstruction services?

5. Name three items of work that may be performed by a general contractor during the preconstruction phase.

6. In addition to fee, name three other items an owner may request in a preconstruction services RFP.

5.9 EXERCISES

1. Using the labor rates that follow, prepare a preconstruction services estimate for a 5-month preconstruction phase. Assume the contractor charges an hourly rate that has a 2.0 multiplier (billing rate of 2.0 times the actual hourly rate to cover corporate costs). Assume the following team members and durations:

   - Project Manager: 1 day per week
   - Chief Estimator: 8 hours (assume 120% wage of project manager)
   - Chief Scheduler: 8 hours (assume 80% wage of project manager)
   - OIC: No cost
   - Superintendent: 12 hours
   - Project Engineer: 2 hours per week
   - Company Labor Rates: Project Manager—$25 per hour
                             Superintendent—$30 per hour
                             Project Engineer—$20 per hour

2. Draft a lump-sum preconstruction services contract for the amount indicated in exercise 1.

3. Draft a time-and-materials preconstruction services contract for exercise 1.

4. Prepare a letter addressed to the Training Center offering to perform preconstruction services for their project. Explain the advantages of employing a construction team member during the schematic design phase. Explain why your firm is the best to perform this task. Explain to the owner why your choice of fee approach is the most appropriate for this relationship and their project.

6
PRE-ESTIMATE ACTIVITIES

7
QUANTITY TAKE-OFF

8
PRICING SELF-PERFORMED WORK

9
ESTIMATING SUBCONTRACTOR WORK

10
ESTIMATING GENERAL CONDITIONS

11

COMPLETING THE ESTIMATE

12

UNIT PRICE ESTIMATES

13

PRE-BID DAY ACTIVITIES

14

BID DAY ACTIVITIES

15

POST-BID DAY ACTIVITIES

6

PRE-ESTIMATE ACTIVITIES

6.1 INTRODUCTION

Lump-sum contracts were introduced in Chapter 1. They are used when the scope of work can be defined and described by the project drawings and specifications. Most lump-sum contracts are awarded using the bid procurement process that also was introduced in Chapter 1. In Chapters 6 through 15, we will discuss the process for developing a detailed cost estimate and ultimately a lump-sum project bid.

Certain basic skills are required to complete a lump-sum bid. These include knowledge of construction processes, the ability to read specifications and drawings, and basic mathematical skills for measuring and calculating the quantities of work. It is also helpful if the estimator is able to visualize the construction process of the project being estimated.

When starting to work on a bid, two things may seem somewhat overwhelming. First, the volume of work may seem daunting; second, some parts of the project may seem complex. The estimator has to take the time to review the work and develop an estimating plan. It is helpful if he or she realizes that approximately 20% of the work will account for about 80% of the cost. By concentrating on this 20%, the bulk of the estimate will be completed. An estimator who takes the time to plan and organize the work is better prepared to complete the bid.

Teamwork is another asset in the lump-sum bid process. There is always an estimating team, even if only one person is actually doing the estimating. He or she usually consults with more experienced estimators, superintendents, and project managers during the process. On bid day, several people are members of the bidding team. The *chief estimator* (or lead estimator) will be responsible for assembling the required team and instructing them on duties and expectations. In other words, the lead estimator is not just an estimator. He or she is also a manager whose success will be measured by tendering a bid on time and by winning a reasonable share of the projects bid.

As an estimator gains experience, he or she starts to realize that there are certain traits that improve one's skills. Consistency of methods makes it easier to plan and execute the process and assures that all parts of the specified work will be included in the bid. There are many places where inadvertent errors can occur such as incorrectly transferring numbers from one page to another, adding columns incorrectly, and transposing figures. Consistent procedures should be established to double check for these errors and thus minimize the likelihood of winning a bid by making the biggest mistake. Finally, estimating skills improve as the estimator gains experience.

Some general contractors perform portions of the project scope of work and execute the remainder with subcontractors, while other general contractors may perform the entire scope of work with subcontractors. For purposes of this text, we will assume that Western Construction will perform the following work on the Training Center:

- Structural excavation and backfill
- Concrete construction
- Structural steel erection
- Rough and finish carpentry
- Installation of the doors and hardware

The remaining elements of work will be performed by subcontractors. A different general contractor may perform other elements of the work, but the estimating process described in this text would still be used to develop a bid. The only difference would be in the elements of work that would be priced with detailed quantity take-offs and those that would be priced based on subcontractor quotations.

6.2   ESTIMATING PROCESS

The basic lump-sum estimating process is shown in Figure 6-1. Starting at the bottom, the invitation for bid is collected and reviewed. The estimating strategy includes reviewing the documents, visiting the site of the project, determining roughly the size of the project, and assessing the competition. This leads to a decision regarding whether or not to tender a bid.

A positive decision to tender a bid leads to the detailed work of the estimating process, which includes quantity take-off, recapitulation, pricing, developing order-of-magnitude estimates for subcontractors and major suppliers, creating a summary schedule of the project, and estimating the general conditions. This will produce an approximate price that validates the initial assessment of the project. On bid day, subcontractor quotations are received and evaluated, and the final bid is tendered. Successful completion of this process results in a competitive bid that in turn may reward the general contractor with a contract to perform the work. The steps of the estimating process will be discussed in Chapters 6 through 15. Steps 1 and 2 are discussed in this chapter.

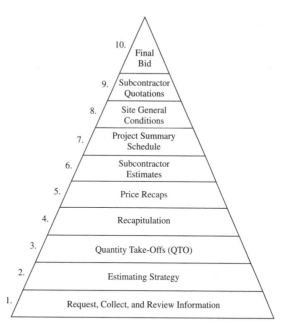

FIGURE 6–1 The estimating process.

6.3 SOLICITATION OF LUMP-SUM BIDS

It is important for the estimator to understand the role of the various parties in the solicitation of lump-sum bids. For the experienced general contractor, these roles may be a factor in deciding whether or not to tender a bid.

Owners are responsible for providing and dispersing funds for their projects and for obtaining building permits. They have the ultimate authority for all decisions regarding the work. Some owners, such as fast food or home improvement store companies, may complete and open as many as 300 stores in a year. They usually are deeply involved in the construction process and often have their own representatives to oversee their projects. On the other hand, a few doctors may decide to build a medical clinic. This is a one-time project for them, and they may not understand the construction process or have any interest in it other than getting their building completed so that they can set up their individual practices. Owners like these doctors usually hire a consultant who is qualified and willing to be their representative to manage the project. No matter how a project is managed, the general contractor usually executes a contract directly with the owner.

The architect for a project prepares the design documents for the owner. The design must be of a quality that can be submitted to the local building authorities for review and issuance of a building permit. Usually on lump-sum contracts, the architect submits the drawings for review and correction prior to the owner's solicitation of a bid. It is also possible for the general contractor to pick up the building permit and include its cost in the bid.

An owner who desires not to be involved in the management of the construction process will sometimes retain the architect to be his or her representative. This usually means that the architect has sole responsibility of approval of the general contractor's work and applications for payment. While the construction contract is executed between the owner and the general contractor, the architect may be designated to act as the owner's representative.

The general contractor is responsible for seeing that the project is built within the parameters defined by the contract. This includes complying with building codes and inspections. The general contractor hires all of the forces necessary to do the work, including material suppliers and subcontractors, and is responsible for their management. After completion of the project, the general contractor continues to serve the owner for warranties, usually for a period of one year, unless a longer period is required by the contract specifications.

In addition to the relationship of the contracting parties, the estimator must be aware of the risks of a lump-sum contract. Perhaps the most important risk is that the general contractor must perform the work as specified within the price of his or her bid and within the schedule indicated in the *bid documents.* Any cost or schedule overruns that result in costs beyond the contract amount must be absorbed by the general contractor. Conversely, if the general contractor can save money and deliver the quality of project specified within or ahead of schedule, any resulting savings goes to the general contractor unless stated otherwise in the contract.

In some cases, the schedule is very important to the owner. If the owner is moving from a rented facility to the new one, he or she may have terminated his or her lease by a certain date. An overrun of the construction schedule may cause the owner to incur extra costs in additional rent. Retail stores usually must be completed in time for the owner to stock the store for a holiday event, which is a large part of their annual sales. Many times, in an effort to emphasize the importance of the schedule and to help defray costs due to delays, the owner may include a liquidated damages clause in the contract. This basically is a statement of a financial penalty to be paid by the contractor to the owner for every day that the contractor is late completing the project. The amount of liquidated damages will vary from project to project and in some cases can be very significant. The estimator must be aware of this when the project is discussed with the *officer-in-charge* (OIC) and when determining the desired profit.

A second risk that the estimator must consider is the payment schedule of the owner and his or her historical compliance. The billing schedule is usually specified in the general conditions section of the bid documents; however, the estimator must look to see if it has been modified, which will usually be noted in the supplemental conditions. If an owner is new to the general contractor, the estimator should determine its payment history and solvency. Sources of this information include the owner's creditors, Dun & Bradstreet, and the Better Business Bureau to name a few. A late remittance by an owner costs the contractor and can thus affect the profitability of a project.

The owner's representative can also pose a risk. In some cases, the representative may be slow in approving applications for payment and change orders and, in some cases, may suggest holding approval of change orders until the end of the project. If the representative has a history of this behavior, the project manager knows that payments for portions of the work may be delayed and that some changes may not be approved until after the work has been completed, if at all.

6.4   INVITATION FOR BID

A solicitation for a lump-sum bid will have a cover document that may have any one of several titles. Most commonly, they are designated a *Request for Quotation* or an *Invitation for Bid (IFB).* For purposes of this discussion, the term Invitation for Bid will be used. Appendix E is an example of an IFB for the Training Center.

A typical bid package will contain (1) a cover letter addressed to the general contractor, (2) a project manual, and (3) drawings. A typical project manual contains the following documents:

- Table of contents
- List of bidding general contractors (optional)
- Invitation For Bid that lists when and where the bids are to be tendered and a brief scope of the work. In addition it may list the type of bid opening (public or private), what documents are issued to each general contractor, where documents may be viewed, and a right to reject any and all bids.
- Instructions to bidders that detail some of the requirements of bidding. Typical items include instructions to examine the bid documents before tendering a bid, interpretations of the drawings, how to submit the bid, substitution of specified materials, alternate bids, bond requirements, withdrawal of bids, evidence of qualification, any bid proposal supplemental information requirements, and submission of a project schedule by the winning bidder.
- Bid form upon which the bid is to be tendered. This *bid form* may also indicate any liquidated damages to be levied on the general contractor for not meeting the schedule dates. An important part of this form is the recognition of receipt and inclusion of the provisions of any addenda that have been issued during the bidding period.
- A contract agreement that is usually included so that the bidding contractor can review the terms prior to submitting a bid. The submission of a bid signifies acceptance of the terms of the owner's contract. In some cases, the owner will require that the bid price be entered onto the contract document and a signed copy be submitted with the bid.
- General conditions of the contract for construction that may be either a standard document produced by a professional association such as the AIA, or a customized document, which is part of an owner's contract.
- Specifications that define the material standards and quality, and installation methods required to complete the project. The most common format for the specifications is the MasterFormat that was developed by the Construction Specifications Institute (CSI). Sample specifications for the Training Center are shown in Appendix G.
- Drawings that are a graphical representation of the work that is to be accomplished. They may be either a complete set that describes in detail all of the work, or they may be abbreviated. An example of an abbreviated set may be one that describes the civil, architectural, and structural work in detail but requests that the electrical and mechanical subcontractors submit design-build bids for the electrical and mechanical work. In other words, as part of their bid they will design their work to meet the requirements of the specifications and develop a price based on their own design. Sample drawings for the Training Center are shown in Appendix H.

6.5 PRE-BID MEETING

One of the early requirements for most construction projects is that the bidders attend a pre-bid meeting and site inspection. The date and time of these meetings is usually indicated in the IFB or the instructions to bidders. It is imperative that the estimator attends this meeting even if he or she is familiar with the site. Much can be learned at these meetings, including who the potential competition is. The owner may hand out additional information and may point out restrictions or hazards at the work areas, indicate locations for trailers, and suggest *laydown areas.* In addition, the estimator will learn the location of utilities and will be able to assess what environmental controls are needed.

A little preparation work will help the attendees get the most out of a pre-bid meeting. First is a review of the drawings, especially those for the site and civil work. A basic review should be made of the IFB, including general and *special conditions,* and any other area that may pose some questions. Estimators should be especially cognizant of items that subcontractors may question during the proposal period.

During the site inspection, the estimator should look for conditions that may not be readily evident on the drawings. For example, the drawings may show a clear site with easy access. However, the site inspection may reveal that the site is bordered on three sides by residences, and that the fourth side poses difficulties in maneuvering for large trucks and hoisting equipment.

A pre-bid meeting usually has a period in which to ask questions. Keep in mind that these questions and their resulting answers are made available to all bidding parties. Care should be taken not to ask questions that may tip the competition to some innovative ideas that could provide a competitive advantage in bidding. Also listen carefully to questions from competitors for the same reason. A good posture regarding questions is to ask only those necessary for clarification of the scope of work. Some estimators may interpret an item as being part of the contract while others may not, so they may tender a lower bid. This is a way of making sure all bidders are assessing the work the same way.

The estimator should ascertain either in the pre-bid meeting or privately from the owner's representative how questions during the bidding process will be handled. It is common for the owner to issue one or more addenda during the bid period that addresses everyone's questions. This is their effort to make sure that all bids are consistent in covering the required work. Some owners, however, will keep a bidder's questions confidential, especially if they regard innovative ideas. The bidder needs to be judgmental regarding the owner's integrity.

Finally the estimator should look at the competition that is present at the pre-bid meeting. An ideal bid list is five bidders who are regular competitors and who seem to win an equal share of the projects by submitting quality bids. Two conditions can be a cause of concern when deciding whether or not to bid the project. If the bid list is open to any bidder or is an excessively long list, there is a good chance that the winner will be the one who makes the largest mistake in favor of the owner. Also if the bid list is made up of contractors who do not normally compete on the same type of work, for example, residential and commercial builders, the quality of the bids can be affected.

6.6   BID DATE AND TIME

As discussed previously, the bid date and time are stated in the IFB. The significance of this date and time is that it is the latest time that a bid can be tendered and still be considered valid. A late bid is usually considered nonresponsive. A significant effort goes into preparing a bid, and to tender it late means that all of this work was a waste of time.

One common question heard in a pre-bid meeting is a request for an extension in the bid time. This tells the owner that this contractor is busy bidding other work and, if he or she needs extra time for this bid, there is no assurance that the project will be completed on time. About the only time bid extensions are granted is if there have been significant changes to the design so that bidders have had to re-estimate portions of work. In this case, the remaining bid time may be insufficient.

6.7 BID DOCUMENT REVISIONS

During the course of the bidding, there are times when revisions need to be made to the bid package. These changes to the bid package are known as *addenda*. They may be due to on-going design work, changes requested by the owner, building department corrections, or questions asked by the bidders. Bidder's questions typically focus on incorrect or non-existent sections or details, conflicting dimensions, and other remedial information. When the estimator encounters a need for clarification and the project manual does not define procedures for obtaining it, a request for information (RFI) form (Form F-10 in Appendix F) is a good communication tool to use. As questions arise, the RFI is filled out and transmitted to the owner's representative. The representative will issue one or more addenda that specifically address the questions of all of the bidders.

It is always tempting to pick up the telephone and ask a question directly; however, this can pose a risk. If a bid is tendered based on a verbal answer given by either the architect or owner's representative, it is not considered part of the bid package. If the contractor wins the bid, he or she is solely responsible for the consequences of bidding to a verbal answer that may be in direct conflict with the project documents. The person who provided the answer is not liable because the change was not properly issued in writing to all bidders.

6.8 PERSONAL ESTIMATING NOTEBOOK

An experienced estimator usually has in his or her possession a library of cost information based on historical data collected from projects completed by his or her company. Upon completion of a project, the estimator should review and collect actual cost data that can be used in future estimates. A suggested table of contents for the notebook is shown in Appendix C. The estimator must, on occasion, take the time to discard out-of-date information and replace it with more current data. While this updating takes considerable effort, it is more than offset by having current historical information that may provide the edge over competitors.

A new estimator is encouraged to start an estimating notebook the day he or she begins estimating. In the early stages, a good source of information may come from more experienced estimators. With time, actual project information will be obtained, which will quickly fill a notebook. Keeping the data current and organized makes it more reliable and easier to use.

6.9 ORDER-OF-MAGNITUDE ESTIMATES

Once the bid package has been reviewed and the pre-bid meeting attended, the estimator should determine the approximate cost of the project. This is known as an order-of-magnitude estimate. Its purpose is to provide a reasonable estimate of what a given type of project should cost. This estimate becomes a discussion point when deciding whether or not to tender a bid, and later will be used to compare against the detailed estimate.

There are basically two kinds of order-of-magnitude estimates, the rough-order-of-magnitude (ROM) and the *order-of-magnitude (OM) estimate.* The ROM estimate for the entire project generally is determined from minimal design information and is based on published and/or historical data from similar projects, as discussed in Chapter 1. To develop a ROM estimate for a medical clinic, for example, look at the basic building and determine its *footprint* area, number of stories, and general construction such as concrete, steel frame, brick veneer, etc. Using published and historical data for similar projects, a quick determination of the cost per square foot of footprint area can be made. Most published data requires the use of size and location correction factors, which are explained in the reference source. The extended cost will then represent a reasonable estimate of what the particular type of building should cost in the area in which it is being constructed. An experienced estimator can develop a ROM estimate quickly.

The OM estimate for a specific element of work is based on more complete information but not necessarily the detailed design. Within a building, the estimator may want to determine an OM estimate for the plumbing. It is easy to count the number of fixtures, water heaters, drinking fountains, etc., and to use unit cost data to develop the cost estimate. This would then be considered a reasonable price for the plumbing work given a typical routing of the piping and other standard details. The estimator must be aware of what the data include and exclude. Some cost factors may be listed for labor and material costs only, while other data may be shown as a subcontract cost that includes all markups and a profit.

ROM and OM estimates are commonly used in developing various types of budget estimates and have been discussed previously in Chapters 3 and 4. When making an order-of-magnitude estimate, the estimator must look for significant differences between the project currently being bid and those used in the database. For example, if the project is a medical center, it may be found when surveying published and historical data that the reference information includes one x-ray room. The specific project for which the ROM estimate is being developed, however, may have three x-ray rooms. Since these require lead shielding and related special construction, they will cost more per square foot than an exam room. The estimator must try to determine what the unit cost is for an x-ray room and make adjustments accordingly. Sometimes this is difficult, but discussions with other experienced estimators and industry specialists can be helpful.

The ROM and OM estimates serve different purposes in the lump-sum bidding process. The ROM estimate provides a cost range that the estimator can use to evaluate the desirability of tendering a bid. OM estimates are developed for the subcontractor and major supplier work and are used to check the reasonableness of subcontractor and supplier quotations on bid day. They also are used to develop the first-run estimate bid total before subcontractor quotations have been received. The bid total is then compared against the ROM estimate to determine if they are within a reasonable range of one another.

Training Center ROM Estimate

When generating a ROM estimate, only very basic information is used. Quickly scanning the drawings, the estimator can determine the building footprint area, number of stories, general type of construction and proposed use. Let's look at the example of the Training

Center. Selected drawings are shown in Appendix H. The building basically is a two-story warehouse building with approximately a 27,000-square-foot building footprint. Only a third of the second floor is to be constructed, which will contain partially finished space. The first floor offices are to be finished. The building is to be equipped with a passenger elevator and two 5-ton bridge cranes. Using the technique discussed in Chapter 4 (Section 4.2), the estimator developed a square foot cost factor for the basic building of $70 per square foot. Referring to the personal estimating notebook, the estimator determined that the finished offices would cost about $40 per square foot and that the unfinished second floor would cost about $10 per square foot. If the estimator could not find relevant cost factors from the personal estimating notebook, a commercial cost reference could be used. The estimator contacted an elevator supplier and determined an estimated cost of $40,000 for the elevator. The cost of the bridge cranes involved estimating the cost for the crane and the cost for the rail to support each crane. Again, a supplier was contacted, and the estimated cost for one crane and its supporting rail was determined to be $50,000. The estimator now is ready to produce the ROM estimate for the Training Center shown in Figure 6-2.

6.10 DECIDING WHETHER OR NOT TO TENDER A BID

Once a project has been reviewed, the pre-bid meeting attended and a ROM estimate developed, it is time to decide whether or not to bid the project. While this is the job of the officer-in-charge, the estimator must review conditions with the officer so that an informed decision can be made. Factors to be considered include the following:

- Is this the type of project that the company normally does or has the capability of doing?
- Is the company's workload such that the company has available resources to perform the work?
- How many competitors are bidding? Are they similar types of contractors or are there some that are notably more difficult to win against? For example, have nontraditional builders been included on the bid list for a substantial commercial project?
- If it is decided not to tender a bid and this is a valued client, should a courtesy bid be tendered to show interest in maintaining a business relationship? By not wanting to be the low bidder, the courtesy price may end up being embarrassingly high. Conversely, there also is the risk that the owner may be offended if a bid is not received.
- Can the company obtain performance and payment bonds for this size project?

6.11 WORK BREAKDOWN STRUCTURE

When the officer-in-charge decides to bid a project, the first job of the estimator is to plan the estimating process. One of the best organizational tools is the *work breakdown structure (WBS)*. This is simply an outline of the activities necessary to construct the project. The benefit of the WBS is that it takes a seemingly large, complex project and turns it into many easy to manage segments. The WBS will be used, upon winning the project, for planning and scheduling, which in turn influences many of the project management activities. Making a comprehensive outline at this point is thus beneficial to later operations, as well as to the estimating process.

Project: *The Training Center*
Location: *Kent, WA*
Arch./Engr.:: *LM*

Date: *May 15, 2003*
Estimator: *P. Jacobs*
Estimate #: *TTC ROM*

Division		1 Story Factory										
Code	Sec/Det	Description	Qty	Unit	UMH	Man Hours	Wage Rate	Unit L Cost	Labor Cost	Unit M Cost	Material Cost	Total Cost
		Voc. Training Facility	*25,000*	*sf*						*$70*	*$1,750,000*	*$1,750,000*
		Shop	*2,000*	*sf*						*$70*	*$140,000*	*$140,000*
		Offices										
		1st floor	*9,000*	*sf*						*$40*	*$360,000*	*$360,000*
		2nd floor	*9,000*	*sf*						*$10*	*$90,000*	*$90,000*
		Add										
		Elevator	*1*	*ea*						*$40,000*	*$40,000*	*$40,000*
		Bridge Cranes	*2*	*ea*						*$50,000*	*$100,000*	*$100,000*
												$2,480,000

Notes:
1. *The training facility is basically a tall, one-story factory*
2. *The shop is one story with some facilities for equipment*
3. *The first floor office is furnished*
4. *The second floor office is open area with ceiling, plumbing, mechanical, fire protection, and electrical. There are no partitions or finishes.*

FIGURE 6–2 ROM estimate for the Training Center.

As a prelude to discussing the WBS, the following terms need to be defined.

- Element or activity—A description of work such as concrete footings, steel erection, structural excavation, etc.
- Task—Specific tasks that need to be done to complete an activity. Form, fine grade, install reinforcing steel, place concrete, finish, and strip forms are six tasks that are required to complete the activity called concrete footings.
- Basic outline—The basis of the WBS is the CSI numbering system. The basic outline is therefore the CSI division numbers.
- First level expansion—The WBS expanded to show activities within a CSI division.
- Second level expansion—A second expansion of the WBS to task level.

Further expansions of the WBS beyond the second level results in such incremental detail that it is not useful. The first two levels are used when planning and scheduling a project, thus their use in estimating helps to prepare the project team for the work after winning the bid.

When creating a WBS, a good approach is to visualize how the project will be built. The CSI MasterFormat (shown in Appendix C) that is used for most estimating and specifications provides the general order of the work. For example, the first activities might be to clear, grade, and install site utilities, which is shown in CSI division 2. The substructure, which encompasses the structural excavation and concrete foundations, is found in CSI divisions 2 and 3. The superstructure activities can be found in divisions 3 through 6. Divisions 7 through 14 are basically nonstructural items such as thermal and moisture protection, finishes, and various equipment and specialties, while 15 and 16 cover the mechanical and electrical work, respectively. This basically is the order of construction of most projects. Figure 6-3 shows the basic WBS for the Training Center.

When starting on a WBS for a new building, look at it in four major divisions: (1) *substructure,* which includes site work; (2) *superstructure;* (3) finishes; and (4) miscellaneous. These are shown in Figure 6-3, with the various CSI divisions that may apply listed under each major division. This WBS was constructed from a template, and those divisions that do not apply have been lined out indicating that these sections were not found within the scope of work. If they were deleted from the listing, it would not be known if they were purposely left out or whether they were forgotten.

Figure 6-3 can now be expanded to the activity level. Only division 2, which represents subcontractor work, and division 3, which represents work performed by the general contractor, are shown in Figure 6-4. Note that the contractor-performed work is shown in bold.

The substructure includes the cast-in-place concrete footings, foundation walls, pits, machine foundations, and any other concrete that is generally below the ground level of the building. For a simple warehouse, the WBS may show footings as a single activity that needs to be accomplished. Structural excavation is the excavation and backfill done after site grading that is necessary to build the footings and foundations. On this project, there are no precast concrete elements in the substructure, and therefore none are shown in the expansion.

Division 3 under the substructure includes the slab-on-grade (SOG). On a pre-engineered steel warehouse, the SOG is commonly placed prior to the steel erection, thus giving the ironworkers a stable working platform. Where very heavy equipment is needed

---

Work Breakdown Structure

Project: The Training Center   Date: May 16, 2003
Estimator: Paul Jacobs   Est. # TTC-1

Substructure

Division 2, Earthwork
Underground Utilities (Divisions 2, 15, & 16)
Division 3, Concrete
Division 7, Thermal and Moisture Protection
~~Division 4, Masonry~~

Superstructure

Division 3, Concrete
~~Division 4, Masonry~~
Division 5, Metals
Division 6, Wood and Plastics
Division 7, Thermal and Moisture Protection
Division 15, Rough-in Mechanical
Division 16, Rough-in Electrical

Finishes

Division 6, Wood and Plastics
Division 7, Thermal and Moisture Protection
Division 8, Doors and Windows
~~Division 9, Finishes~~
~~Division 10, Specialties~~
~~Division 11, Equipment~~
~~Division 12, Furnishings~~
~~Division 13, Special Construction~~
~~Division 14, Conveying Systems~~
Division 15, Mechanical Trim
Division 16, Electrical Trim

Miscellaneous

Division 2, Sitework
Division 3, Concrete
Division 1, General Requirements

FIGURE 6–3   Work breakdown structure for the Training Center.

for steel erection, the SOG may be placed after the framing and roof panels are in place. Buildings of tilt-up construction usually need the SOG as a place on which to cast the panels. A closure strip for the SOG is then placed after the panels have been set and secured. Therefore, it can be argued that the SOG may be either part of the substructure or the superstructure. It doesn't matter as long as there is consistency from project to project. On this project, the estimator considered the SOG as part of the substructure.

Work Breakdown Structure

Project: The Training Center   Date: May 16, 2003
Estimator: Paul Jacobs   Est. # TTC-1

Substructure
Division 2, Earthwork
    Site Grading
    Subsurface Drainage
    Underground Utilities and Containment
        Plumbing
        Electrical and Telephone
        Containment
    Subgrade
    Structural Excavation

Division 3, Concrete
    Structural Concrete
        Footings
        Slab on Grade (SOG)

FIGURE 6–4 Partial WBS expansion to activity level.

The superstructure is all of the structural work above the ground. This includes structural concrete and steel from the foundation to the roof, elevated floor slabs, and precast concrete items. The roofing system usually is considered to be part of the superstructure because inside finish work cannot begin without overhead protection.

Precast concrete elements can be either constructed by the general contractor or purchased from a supplier. Either way, the general contractor usually installs them. Most precast elements are purchased, but tilt-up walls, such as those used for the Training Center, are constructed on the project site and lifted into place. The WBS for the Training Center, therefore, will show all cast-in-place concrete, tilt-up walls, and steel erection in bold to indicate contractor-performed work, but the roofing system will be shown as subcontract work.

A miscellaneous category may be included in division 3 to list activities for exterior concrete work. This includes sidewalks, extruded curbs, the curbs and gutters along pavement, as well as concrete pavement. Depending on the work specified, these activities may be self-performed by the general contractor or subcontracted. Subcontractors frequently have specialty equipment for doing these curbs and therefore may be more cost effective than the general contractor. If, however, the work is only flat work such as pavement and sidewalks, the general contractor may be able to do the work more efficiently.

In Figure 6-3, division 15 is listed under both the superstructure and finishes. This is the mechanical portion of the project and consists primarily of the plumbing, HVAC, and fire sprinklers. Rough-in is done during the superstructure construction, while the installation of fixtures and diffusers, setting the sprinkler heads, etc.—commonly known as trim work—are activities and tasks of the finish phases. The activities for bringing the utility services to the building are part of CSI division 2.

Some subcontractors perform all of the division 15 work while others specialize in only one set of activities. It is common for the mechanical contractor to do the plumbing and HVAC, while a separate subcontractor does the fire sprinklers. All three activities should be listed on the WBS. Underground utilities frequently are done by a second tier subcontractor to the mechanical subcontractor.

Electrical, division 16, includes two types of work: (1) power, distribution, and lighting and (2) controls, alarms, and data. It is common for a single subcontractor to perform all of these activities, but on larger projects, two or even three different subcontractors may be employed. The estimator needs to review the specifications to determine the extent of the work and list each major activity regardless of whether the work will be done by one or several subcontractors.

Figure 6-5 is a task level expansion of Figure 6-4 showing the specific work items required to complete an activity. While the experienced estimator already knows what tasks are needed, this level provides a checklist to ensure that all work has been quantified. After winning the project, this is used for the detailed planning by the construction team.

Excavation and backfill are each shown as activities under division 2 in Figure 6-5. Since these are done at different times and may require different equipment, they cannot be lumped as a single task. Division 3 shows tasks that are required to construct the footings. While it may be argued that the fine grade is part of the excavation, this task is done after the forms are set and before the reinforcing steel is installed, therefore it is part of the footing construction.

The completed WBS now shows the estimator which work will be performed by the general contractor (bold type) and which will be performed by subcontractors (standard type). Expansion to the task level provides a comprehensive guide and checklist for the estimating process and should be referred to frequently to ensure that all items have been quantified and priced.

Figure 6-6 is a project item list (Form F-1 in Appendix F) as used by the estimator to list work activities and indicate whether an activity is to be done as direct work or subcontracted. A separate column under each heading indicates whether the work is labor and/or material. From this, the estimator can tell if a subcontractor is really a subcontractor or a major material supplier. For example, the line item structural steel is checked as labor for the general contractor and material for a subcontractor. This delineates that the material is furnished by a supplier to the job site for installation by the general contractor's own forces. In another instance, such as reinforcing steel, a supplier may furnish the material, and a subcontractor may be hired to install it. This is then listed as two line items—one for furnishing material and the other for installation—indicating that two different contracting parties are involved. A single line item such as electrical with both the subcontractor labor and material spaces checked means that the same subcontractor will furnish and install the materials. The project item list is similar to the WBS, but this list identifies who supplies the material and labor for each work activity. It is used later during selection of subcontractors and suppliers.

Work Breakdown Structure

Project: The Training Center   Date: May 19, 2003
Estimator: Paul Jacobs   Est. # TTC-1

Substructure
Division 2, Earthwork
    Site Grading
    Subsurface Drainage
    Underground Utilities and Containment
        Plumbing
        Electrical and Telephone
        Containment
    Subgrade
    Structural Excavation
        Excavate Footings
        Backfill Footings
        Dispose of Excess Excavation

Division 3, Concrete
    Footings
        Form Footings
        Fine Grade
        Reinforcing Steel
        Place and Rod Off
        Strip Forms
    Slab on Grade (SOG)
        Fine Grade for SOG
        Edge Forms
        Reinforcing Steel
        Place SOG Sections
        Finish SOG Sections
        Strip and Clean Forms for Reuse

FIGURE 6–5   Partial WBS expansion to task level.

6.12   ESTIMATING TEAM

Once the WBS has been developed and the project item list completed, the estimator is ready to assemble an estimating team and make assignments. This team may be composed of only one person in the case of a relatively straightforward project, or it may have several members for more complex ones. Each project will have different requirements for the makeup of an estimating team. Typical team members may include the following:

- Officer-in-charge (OIC)—a company executive who has overall responsibility for seeing that a viable bid is tendered. This person usually has a financial stake in the company.

PROJECT ITEM LIST

Project: The Training Center   Date: May 19, 2003
Estimator: Paul Jacobs

| | | | Provider | | | |
| | | | General Contractor | | Subcontractor | |
Line #	CSI Div	Cost Item Description	Materials	Labor	Materials	Labor
1	2	*Structural Excavation*	X	X		
2	3	*Form, Place, and Finish Concrete*	X	X		
3	3	*Reinforcing Steel Supply*			X	
4	3	*Reinforcing Steel Installation*				X
5	4	*Masonry Walls*			X	X
6	5	*Structural and Miscellaneous Steel Fabrication*		X	X	

FIGURE 6–6   Project item list.

The OIC generally delegates the responsibility for forming a team to either a project manager or the chief estimator. The OIC usually makes the final decision whether or not to tender a bid and the amount of profit to include in the price, and may also make a final adjustment to the price at the last minute depending on the quality of the subcontract bids and market conditions. The OIC is ultimately responsible for the successful completion of the project if the company wins the bid. He or she usually takes no part in the day-to-day work of developing the bid price.

- Project manager—oversees the entire bid process. Some companies select a project manager at the time the Invitation for Bid is received. It then becomes his or her responsibility to do much of the work of the chief estimator. This person will be responsible for making sure that a viable bid is ready to be tendered on time. If the project is won, the project manager then assumes all duties of managing the project to a profitable completion. In cases where only one or two people are needed to develop the bid, the project manager often does the majority of the estimating work.
- Project superintendent—available for consultation on construction procedures, crew sizes, and productivity issues, and to assist in developing a project summary schedule. Even if a project superintendent is not on the team, the estimator will benefit by consulting with any *superintendent* experienced in similar projects.
- Chief estimator—oversees the estimating effort and may estimate some of the more complex portions of the project. This person is responsible for reviewing all work, assembling the estimate sections, summarizing the costs on the bid summary, estimating the general conditions, and determining necessary markups. The chief estimator reviews the work and the estimate with the officer-in-charge and/or project manager and discusses factors that affect the amount of profit to be included in the bid price. This person is the most experienced estimator on the team and is well versed in factors that make a successful bid.

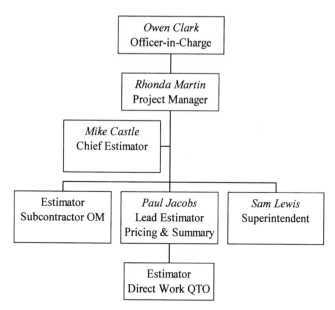

FIGURE 6-7 Estimating team organization chart.

- Lead estimator—in the absence of a chief estimator, the lead estimator takes on the duties of the chief estimator for most items. Major decisions will be deferred to the project manager, or in his or her absence, to the officer in charge. The lead estimator is the most experienced estimator on the team below the chief estimator or project manager.
- Estimator(s)—perform the quantity take-off of all of the work that will be done by the general contractor's own forces. Estimators generally will be assigned a particular discipline of work such as concrete, structural steel, or rough carpentry. The more experienced estimators will also summarize and price the work. On larger projects, some estimators may continue on as project engineers if the contract is won.
- Subcontract estimator—prepares OM estimates for the work that will be subcontracted. This person usually is an experienced estimator.

For the most part, the project manager and the chief estimator's duties and responsibilities are the same except possibly for a level of decision-making. The lead estimator is not necessarily empowered to perform some of the duties of the project manager and/or chief estimator and, therefore, must be fully instructed on his or her limits of responsibility. Figure 6-7 shows the estimating team used for the Training Center. Individual team member responsibilities are shown in Figure 6-8.

TEAM RESPONSIBILITY LIST

Project: **The Training Center**   Date: May 19, 2003

Line #	CSI Div	Work Item	Resp. Person	Due Date
1		Develop ROM estimate	MC	5/15/03
2		Attend pre-bid meeting and site inspection	MC, RM	5/16/03
3		Work breakdown structure	MC	5/19/03
4		Schedule the estimating work	MC	5/19/03
5	3	QTO footings and foundations	PJ	5/20/03
6	all	Call subcontractors	PJ, RM	5/21/03
7	3470	Tilt up concrete	RM	5/22/03
8	5	Structural and miscellaneous steel	PJ	5/22/03
9	7	Rough carpentry	RM	5/23/03
10		Summarize and price all divisions	RM, PJ	5/27/03
11		Subcontract OM estimates	RM, PJ	5/27/03
12		Project summary schedule	SL	5/28/03
13	1	General conditions	RM	5/29/03
14		First run bid estimate	RM	5/30/03
15		Determine fee	OIC, MC	5/30/03
16		Prepare for bid day	PJ	6/2/03
17		Bid day	RM, PJ	6/3/03

FIGURE 6–8 Team responsibility list.

6.13 SCHEDULING THE ESTIMATING WORK

When assembling an estimating team and performing the various estimating duties, it is important to keep track of the progress of the overall work. To do this, the chief estimator should generate a simple bar chart schedule that is easily understood. It becomes effective when it is prominently posted and progress is shown and updated. Estimators will strive to do their part on time, but if some tasks show signs of lagging, the chief estimator can adjust workloads accordingly. This assures the officer-in-charge that the bid will be ready to tender on time.

The schedule for the estimating work does not need to be elaborate. Several basic electronic scheduling programs are available; use the one that is simplest to operate. A time-scaled, horizontal, relational bar chart provides team members with a feel for the overall duration and how their work affects that of other team members. It is also recommended that open bars be used so that progress can be noted using a yellow or pink highlighter— yellow representing work that is on time or ahead of schedule and pink to show that which is falling behind. Figure 6-9 shows the *estimate schedule* for the Training Center.

Figure 6-9 has a typical number of activities that is adequate for most schedules. Ten or fewer activities will not show sufficient detail and, except for very complex projects, more than twenty activities probably show too much detail. The number of activities should conform to the number of items on the team responsibility list. A schedule of fifteen or so activities is very easy to create, use, and maintain.

6.14 SUBCONTRACTORS AND MAJOR SUPPLIERS

One of the first things the estimating team needs to do is start contacting subcontractors and *major suppliers* to see if they are aware of the job and if they will be furnishing quotations for their areas of work. The time needed to do this can easily be underestimated, so calls to preferred subcontractors should be made first; that is, those that consistently furnish good bids for projects and who work well with the general contractor. Priority should also be given to those whose contracts are relatively large and/or are bidding risky items of work. It is important to keep track of who was called and what their responses were. Figure 6-10 is an example of a subcontractor call log (Form F-2 in Appendix F) that can be used for recording subcontractor and supplier responses.

The estimator must be aware that not all of the subcontractors who say they will respond will actually tender a bid, so several bidders in each category need to be contacted. Ideally, receiving at least three bids will validate the price of the low bidder. Only one or two bids in each category does not assure that the lowest and most complete bid has been received. More than three bids improves the price coverage of a particular category. There may be cases where no bids are received, so the estimator must include an estimated amount that he or she believes is reasonable and competitive so that the bid can be completed and tendered to the owner on time. This is the subject of OM estimates, which will be discussed in Chapter 9.

Some estimators prefer not to solicit bids from subcontractors, but will estimate the work themselves. If the project is won, the general contractor offers the work to a select list of subcontractors at specific prices, at or below the price he or she put into the bid. If the general contractor's estimate is too low and no subcontractor agrees to do the work for that amount, the general contractor has to fulfill his or her obligation to the owner and will probably be forced to perform the work at a loss. Soliciting subcontractor prices for a bid significantly reduces the risk in the performance of the contract.

Another bidding method is for the general contractor to team up with certain key subcontractors who have major portions of the work, such as electrical, mechanical, and fire protection. In this instance, the general contractor is obligating himself or herself to use these subcontractor's prices, and the subcontractors are indicating that they will give the general contractor a preferentially low price. If a general contractor has a good working relationship with subcontractors and pays obligations on time, some subcontractors are more willing to provide discounted pricing in appreciation for this relationship. This can provide a definite bidding edge for the general contractor.

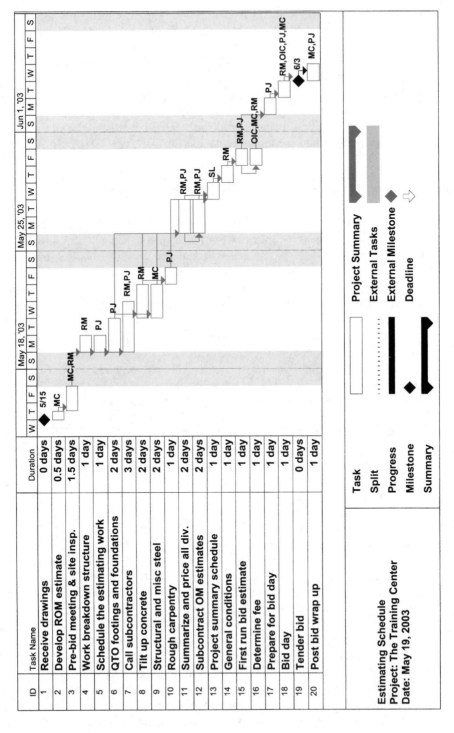

FIGURE 6-9 Estimating schedule.

SUBCONTRACTOR CALL LOG

JOB: **The Training Center**   DATE: May 21, 2003

Firm	Contact	Phone Number	WILL BID (yes/no)
ABC Painting	John	(206) 555 4576	yes
Fumerole Coatings	Jim Keenan	(206) 555 8781	yes
Don Jones Painting	Don	(253) 555 7746	too busy
Coatings by DB	Jill	(206) 555 1041	yes
Spiffy Finishes	Rachael or Sam	(253) 555 6647	maybe

SUBCONTRACT/SUPPLY ITEM: Painting

SPECIFICATION SECTION(s):   09900, Painting

GENERAL SCOPE OF WORK:

Interior and exterior painting

SPECIFIC INCLUSIONS:

Doors, trim, registers, and grills

Iron handrails

All staining and coating of woodwork

SPECIFIC EXCLUSIONS:

Prepainted metal toilet partitions

Anodized aluminum

Prefinished wood surfaces

OTHER NOTES:

All work shall be done in accordance with the general contactor's schedule

FIGURE 6–10   Subcontractor call log.

6.15   PLAN CENTERS AND ROOMS

Owners sometimes elect to put the bid documents in *plan centers*. This usually is done when the owner does not have a preferred contractor list and is willing to accept bids from any contractor who wishes to submit one. In plan centers, a room is made available for bid documents to be inspected and used by both general contractors and subcontractors. Some plan centers also provide their services electronically. Members can download the projects' plans and specifications from the Internet.

Contractors should similarly have a plan room, containing a complete set of all of the documents, to be used primarily by subcontractors from whom they are soliciting bids. Typically, the plan room has a listing of each project that is currently bidding along with the date the bid is due and the person responsible for the project. All of the addenda that have been issued to date are listed, and copies are included with the documents of the respective project. Keeping a complete and up-to-date set of documents in the plan room makes subcontractors cognizant of all contractual obligations and minimizes claims due to lack of available information.

The chief estimator should make it his or her duty to check the company's plan room at the end of each day. Frequently several jobs are bidding at the same time, and documents can easily be misplaced. On projects where a very large amount of subcontractor activity is expected, it may be prudent to put two sets of documents in the plan room.

6.16   DATA RESOURCES

Many resources are available for the estimator to use when developing a lump-sum bid. There is a myriad of published data, which is available to anyone who wants to purchase them. One must be aware of two things regarding published estimating data. First, the data is a nationwide average and index factors must be used for a specific location; second, being an average, the data will usually have higher or lower prices and productivity rates than those in your particular location.

Most general contractors, unless they are doing a new category of work, will have their own database of historical productivity rates and cost factors based on previous projects. If a formal database does not exist, the more experienced estimators will have their own historical files. Estimates that did not win a bid, but were a very close second also can be a source of data. These are the best sources of information for the estimator to use.

Another valuable source of information is an experienced superintendent or specialty person such as a carpenter or ironworker foreman. These people usually are willing to give advice and often provide some innovative ideas. Good foremen will also know the most cost-effective way of performing work.

6.17   ESTIMATING FORMS

A key to developing reliable estimates is consistency of process. By performing the same tasks the same way in all estimates, the estimator knows that his or her procedures are correct. A simple way to do this is to use the same forms for all estimates. Many estimating forms have been developed over the years and are fairly consistent with one another. With electronic spreadsheets, it is worth the time to make up a set of templates to be used for all estimates. Typical forms, shown in Appendix F, include the following:

- *Quantity Take-off* Forms (QTO) F-3 and F4 sometimes are referred to as the quantity survey forms or quantity sheets. Measurements and related data for the detail work items are recorded and calculations are then made to determine quantities such as area, volume, and weight.
- *Recapitulation* (Recap) F-5 is the form onto which the totaled quantities for a given item of work are transferred to determine productivity and pricing of labor and materials. This form is also used as a summary recapitulation to consolidate several activities of one CSI division to a single set of totals.
- *General Conditions* Form F-6 is used to determine the cost of the field overhead and related items such as certain equipment rental, cleanup, and trash hauling.
- *Bid Proposal* Form F-7 is used by bid takers on bid day to record subcontractor and major supplier bids.
- *Subcontractor* List F-8 is the summary sheet that lists the lowest subcontract bid for each category of work from the bid evaluation sheets.
- *Bid summary* F-9 is the form onto which all of the recaps, summary recaps, and general conditions are transferred. Eventually the total of the subcontractor list is also entered; various markups are then calculated and the sheet is totaled to a final bid amount.

A summary recap sheet and bid evaluation worksheets should be added when appropriate. They will be discussed in later chapters.

6.18   ESTIMATE FILES

In addition to using standard estimating forms, the estimator must also organize and keep track of all sheets during the estimating process. Imagine the horror of turning in a bid and learning afterward that a critical sheet was lost, causing an omission. While it is true that a contractor can claim a bid error, the consequences of doing so are usually not favorable. The owner may make the contractor do the work for the bid amount or in the future may not include the contractor's name on a select bid list.

A first step in organizing the estimate is to properly title and number all pages. The title should include the project name, the estimator's name, the date that the page was completed, an estimate number, the work classification, and the page number. If another estimator removes a page from a file for his or her use, then he or she will be able to return it to its proper place in the estimate file. Also as a later check, the estimator should make sure that all pages are in the file and that information has been properly transferred onto the succeeding pages. On electronic spreadsheets, using page numbers with the number of pages in each section can be helpful. Knowing what the last page number is, the estimator can make sure a particular section is complete.

The second step in organizing the estimate is to properly file it as various sections of the work are completed. Different people have different ways of organizing the file, but a system should be used that is understandable to anyone who accesses the file. One way is to use a manila folder with inside clips on each side for two-hole punched pages, as illustrated in Figure 6-11. As a CSI section of the estimate is done, it is arranged in the folder

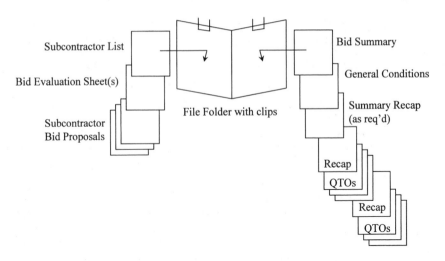

Subcontractor List

Bid Evaluation Sheet(s)

Subcontractor
Bid Proposals

File Folder with clips

Bid Summary

General Conditions

Summary Recap
(as req'd)

Recap

QTOs

Recap

QTOs

FIGURE 6–11 Typical estimating file organization.

with its summary recap sheet on top, the system or assembly pricing recap sheets behind it, and the QTO sheets that feed each system pricing recap behind the pricing sheets. These section packages are then filed in order of their CSI number on the right-hand side of the folder. Subcontractor bid pages, the evaluation worksheets, and the subcontractor list are then filed respectively from bottom to top on the left side of the folder. As the bid summary is completed and the bid is tendered, it is filed on top of the recaps on the right side with a copy of the signed and filled-in bid form on top of it. This provides a concise file with the complete bid in one folder. For larger jobs, it may be necessary to use two folders, one for the direct work and one for subcontractor bids. An alternative is to use a three-ring binder.

It is important to make sure all pages are clipped into the folder as soon as they are completed. If a file is dropped or jostled, there will be no loose pages to fall out. Once the pages are clipped into the folder, all members of the estimating team should leave them there, if at all possible, to avoid inadvertently losing pages by not returning them to the folder. Adhering to these two organizing steps will help the chief estimator to keep control of the estimate during the bidding process, especially as the deadline approaches.

6.19 ELECTRONIC SPREADSHEETS

Computers have had a major impact on the efficiency of estimating. Setting up form templates and automatic calculations has taken a lot of the busywork out of the process, thus allowing the estimator to think more about how to apply innovations that may increase the odds of winning. It is very easy for an estimator to set up the spreadsheets with the calculations. For the QTO sheets, apply the calculation formulae as the work is done, because operations vary depending on what is being quantified. The recap sheet uses standard calculations based on quantity, productivity factors, labor rates, and material prices. A single recap template can be set up to use for all situations. The bid summary and subcontractor list can similarly be set up as universal templates.

Some standard procedures should always be used when setting up and using templates. The estimator should always do a spot check to ensure that the calculations are being performed correctly. Secondly, whenever a spreadsheet has been modified, such as by deleting or adding a line, a check of all calculations is warranted, especially those that perform operations on a column basis. A common error occurs when lines have been added or deleted thereby altering the range of a summation operation such that all lines are not included in the total. One common accounting type check should always be used for the recap and bid summary sheets. First the rows are spot checked for proper calculation and addition to a total on the right-hand side. Next the column summation operation should be checked. The final check is to make sure that the total of the total column on the right-hand side is the same as the row total of the row containing the totals of the labor and material columns. An easy comparison formula can be used to do this on electronic spreadsheets.

When working with electronic spreadsheets, the estimator may be tempted to put in automatic links that will transfer totals from one page to another. While this is handy, it can defeat the checking process, thus increasing the possibility for error. If, for example, a page is deleted or another page is inserted, it will affect how the transfer is made, and the final total may not reflect all of the work. If several pages are added and/or deleted, the transfer process can be invalidated. Performing hand transfers, as discussed in Section 6-20, is a very reliable way of minimizing errors and omissions.

In situations where a long page is needed, it is tempting to use two standard template pages and link them. A better method is to use a single long page, set up the print titles on each page, and number them in sequence. This avoids a possible transfer error, and the estimator only has to make sure all the pages are present. To make this even more professional, find where the print page break is and make the line before the break a carry-forward total to the next page. Then make the first line on the following page the brought-forward total from the previous page. The two numbers will be the same and when looking at the printed pages, it is easy to keep track of their order and know if a page is missing. A check should be done to make sure the summation operator ranges are correct for each page.

Chapter 20 covers computer-estimating programs. Electronic spreadsheets discussed here are only an enhancement of the same operation that traditionally has been done with pencil and paper.

6.20 ACCURACY AND ERROR PREVENTION

Bids may be won in an undesirable fashion when errors and/or omissions are made in an estimate. Conversely, other mistakes can cause a general contractor to submit a bid that is embarrassingly high. While the latter is not as damaging as the former, neither case is a desirable result. Error prevention should be the estimator's foremost concern throughout the estimating process. Common estimating errors include the following:

- Incorrectly adding a column of numbers
- Incorrectly calculating the prices
- Incorrectly transferring numbers from one page to another
- Making errors in dimensional conversions
- Omitting a page of the estimate
- Misplacing decimals

An underlying theme throughout the lump-sum bid process is error prevention. By setting up certain automatic checks on electronic spreadsheets and using additional spot checks, an estimator can significantly reduce their occurrence.

There is always a question of what significant figures to use when estimating. Even though an estimate can be prepared to the nearest penny on electronic spreadsheets, such detail does not add to the accuracy of the estimate. Proper rounding off to the nearest significant figure does not deteriorate the accuracy of the estimate. In the end, the OIC may cut several thousand dollars out of the bid to increase the odds of winning, thus negating the careful attention to penny and small dollar amounts. Exact figures create a false impression regarding the accuracy of the estimate.

An estimator must also be aware of significant figures used in the quantity take-off. Too much detail of measurements decreases estimating efficiency and not enough detail decreases accuracy. As a general rule, measurements are expressed to the nearest inch. Measurements to the nearest ¼ of a foot can cause major errors. All measurements should be converted and recorded on the QTO sheets in feet. For example, 13 inches is expressed as 1.08 feet; 39 inches is 3.25 feet; and 4 feet 7 inches is 4.58 feet. Lineal measurements should be expressed to two decimal places.

Using decimals of feet eliminates a potential error by not making length, area, and volume conversions that involve compound numbers of feet and inches. Extensions will automatically be in feet, square feet, and cubic feet. After extending the calculations, decimals are dropped in favor of the nearest foot, square foot, or cubic foot. Larger units, such as cubic yards are shown to one decimal place. There is a significant difference between 4.6 cubic yards and 5 cubic yards when it comes to certain costs.

When rounding numbers, it may be tempting to round up all decimals (or down if one has a mind to get the job). The best practice is to apply standard mathematical rounding off procedure, which rounds up decimals of 0.5 or greater and rounds down those below 0.5. This method is self-compensating in that there likely will be about the same number of figures rounded up as down in the overall estimate. Figure 6-12 is a general guide to the use of significant figures used in lump-sum estimates.

Probably one of the most important error prevention procedures is used in transferring figures from one page to another. A recommended technique is to mark checked values with a red pencil. When a column of numbers is summed and has been checked, the total would be double underlined with a red pencil. This signifies that the number has been checked and is ready to be transferred to the next page. When transferring the number to the next page, it is double-checked to make sure the number is exactly the same on both pages; then the double underlined total that has been transferred is circled in red. The transferred number in the new location is not circled because it will be used in the next phase of the process. This procedure is used for all numbers that are transferred regardless of what page they are transferred from or to. Just before bid day, the estimator reviews each page of the estimate to make sure that all totals used for determining the cost have been double underlined. He or she will then make sure all double underlined numbers have red circles around them to show that they were transferred to the next page. A final spot check will also be made to assure that numbers were not transposed during transferring. This process consumes very little time and yet can expose errors, which can be quickly corrected prior to tendering a bid.

Guide to Significant Figures	
Item	**Nearest Figure**
Linear measurements	0.01 feet
Area and volume measurements	1 sf or 1 cf
	0.1 cy
Unit prices	$0.01
Wage rates	$0.01
Unit man hours	0.01
Man hours small quantities	0.1
over 100	1
Extended costs	$1
Final bid amount	$100

FIGURE 6–12   Guide to significant figures.

As an estimator is pricing the work on recap sheets, it is wise to keep only one type of work on a particular recap sheet. For example, one recap sheet may be for footings, another for walls, and a third for the slab-on-grade. At the bottom of the recap sheet, the estimator should make unit price calculations for the assembly on the recap. For example, if a job has 150 cubic yards of concrete in the footings, the man hours and total cost should be divided by the cubic yards of concrete in the footings. This will provide the man-hours per cubic yard of concrete placed as well as the total cost. By comparing this with similar projects, the estimator can quickly determine whether or not the estimate is within an expected range. This is commonly called the assemblies analysis, which will be discussed in Chapter 8.

When the estimate is nearing completion, the estimator should perform two additional accuracy checks. A first-run bid total should be compared to the ROM estimate developed at the beginning of the process. The first-run total uses subcontractor OM estimates or any bids that have been received. All direct work numbers and the total from the first run subcontractor page is entered onto the bid summary. If the first-run total is within a reasonable range of the ROM, the estimate is reasonably accurate. Large discrepancies should be investigated to see what has caused such a wide variance. It may be some complicated construction within the project that significantly increases the cost. Lacking evidence of any such situation, a review should be made of various sections of the estimate until the source of the difference is discovered and reconciled. Lastly, the estimator should make a comparison of the total or unit costs of the project against similar projects done by the company. As before, careful attention should be given to variations between similar projects and how they affect the overall cost. The experienced estimator will be able to reconcile differences relatively quickly and make any necessary adjustments to the estimate. These two checks will greatly increase the confidence of the estimating team as they approach bid day.

6.21   SUMMARY

Pre-estimate activities significantly influence the efficiency with which the estimating work is done. When a general contractor is asked to furnish a bid for a project, he or she receives a Request for Quotation or an Invitation for Bid (IFB), which defines the scope of work and the relationship of the contracting parties. These documents define a specific date and time that the bid is due. The universal rule of lump-sum bidding is that a late bid is considered nonresponsive, and the bidder has no chance of being awarded the contract.

An owner or his or her representative notifies a general contractor of an upcoming bid. Upon receiving the documents, there are three important items that need to be completed.

1. The documents need to be reviewed in preparation for attending the pre-bid meeting.
2. The pre-bid meeting, which usually includes an inspection of the job site, must be attended.
3. A rough-order-of-magnitude estimate needs to be generated so that a decision of whether or not to tender a bid can be made.

The chief estimator or project manager will then review the project with the OIC who will make the decision whether or not to tender a bid. After deciding to bid the project, the chief estimator organizes the work, assembles an estimating team, and assigns responsibilities. A key to the organizing process is the work breakdown structure (WBS), which outlines the construction process. The WBS is also used as a basis of organizing the estimating work, which generally follows the order of construction. Creating a schedule of the estimating work aids in tracking its progress so that the chief estimator can allocate resources where needed to assure that the bid will be tendered on time. This process helps promote a winning attitude, which in turn can increase the chances of winning the project. Finally, some things that will aid a person in becoming a good estimator are a personal notebook of valid historical data, consistent procedures, and a winning attitude.

6.22   REVIEW QUESTIONS

1. What would you conclude is the most important item specified in the bid documents in relation to creating a lump-sum bid?
2. What happens to a contractor's bid if the owner receives it five minutes after the time it is due?
3. What is the WBS used for?
4. Who has the ultimate responsibility for tendering a viable bid?
5. For most projects, 20% of the work items represent what percentage of the cost?
6. What are two sources of common errors in the estimating process?
7. Two terms for the bid package of documents issued to a general contractor are the invitation for bid and _____?
8. What is the best way to request a clarification of the bid documents?
9. When should verbal answers to questions to the owner or architect be accepted?
10. What are three factors that the OIC will consider in deciding whether to tender a bid?
11. What is the difference between a subcontractor and a major supplier?
12. Besides being a factor in deciding whether to bid a project, what else is the ROM estimate used for?

6.23 EXERCISES

Using the Training Center project and considering that it is impractical to attend a pre-bid meeting, complete the following pre-estimate activities.

1. The OIC has decided to bid the project. Prepare two work breakdown structures for the project as follows:

   a. Your company is a general contractor who self-performs all the concrete work, structural steel erection, and rough carpentry, and installs all doors and toilet accessories.

   b. Your company is a general contractor who subcontracts all of the work in the project and therefore serves only as a construction manager.

2. From the date that the IFB has been issued until the date the bid is due is three weeks and one day. Develop a simple schedule of the estimating activities using two people to do all of the work. A project manager will oversee your work but he or she is currently closing out another project and only has time for periodic review with the estimating team until the day before bid day.

3. Create electronic estimating templates for the quantity take-off sheet, recapitulation sheet, subcontractor list, and commercial project bid summary. Do not put in formulas at this time, as they will be discussed in later chapters.

7

QUANTITY TAKE-OFF

7.1   INTRODUCTION

This chapter addresses the third level of the lump-sum estimating process shown in Figure 6-1; the quantity take-off (QTO) process. During the QTO, work tasks are defined and measured, and the quantities are calculated. In this chapter, we will focus on the elements of work that will be performed by the general contractor's crews. As discussed at the beginning of Chapter 6, we are assuming that Western Construction Company will perform the following work on the Training Center:

- Structural excavation and backfill
- Cast-in-place (CIP) concrete
- Tilt-up concrete
- Structural steel erection
- Rough and finish carpentry
- Installation of the doors and toilet accessories

All other work will be subcontracted, and order-of-magnitude (OM) estimates for these activities will be discussed in Chapter 9.

The first thing an estimator does is review the specifications thoroughly and look at each drawing that applies to the work that has been assigned. All other drawings must be examined for information pertinent to the work being taken off. Mechanical and electrical drawings frequently have items like concrete equipment pads or other structural supports that are part of the general contractor's work.

The QTO is the most tedious and time-consuming part of the lump-sum estimating process. An extensive search is made for the measurements needed to calculate the various quantities that will be used for pricing in a later phase of the estimating process. Considerable time is spent reviewing the drawings to determine how something is built and finding applicable information. It is also necessary to look at some not-so-obvious details to make sure the estimator understands how the construction is to be performed. There will be places where something seems to be missing or details are confusing. In most cases, the information is shown somewhere on the drawings, just not where it is convenient for the estimator's use. This can become frustrating, but it must be done to complete the bidding process.

Architects typically show dimensions for an item only once on a set of drawings. If a dimension is changed, it only needs to be corrected one place on the drawings. This is a way to minimize errors. At times it appears that a dimension is completely nonexistent, but with further study, it will be found on a section or detail view. In rare instances, a dimension will be missing, and it will then be necessary to obtain a clarification. Scaling of drawings is discouraged because of resolution errors introduced when reproducing the drawings. However, as a last resort it can be done if the architect does not furnish the information in a timely manner. Always measure a shown dimension that is similar, determine the variation between what the drawing shows and what it actually measures, and adjust any scaled dimensions accordingly.

The inexperienced estimator may be tempted to group items that are similar but do not have the same dimensions to make the work easier. This can introduce significant errors into an estimate, which may be detrimental to the accuracy of the process. The estimator must take time to record each item of work accurately. For this reason, the time needed to complete a QTO can easily be underestimated.

Sometimes an estimator quantifies smaller items such as installing doors or toilet accessories first. These are easy to count, and there is little calculation required. Remember the *eighty-twenty rule*—that 20% of the work accounts for about 80% of the cost. By doing the smaller items first, an estimator is quantifying the 80% of the work that accounts for only 20% of the cost. The irony is that the 20% of the work that accounts for 80% of the cost can also account for 80% of the estimating effort. Keeping this in mind helps in planning the QTO work.

An estimator needs to pay attention to the units in which the work is being quantified. Errors occur when incorrect units are used and when they are converted to other units. Also using incompatible units when calculating extensions can cause problems. An estimator should adopt the habit of checking both calculations and units. Treat the units basically the same as if they were fractions. For example:

$$(3\ \mathrm{cf})(150\ \mathrm{lb/cf}) = (3\ \mathrm{\cancel{cf}})(150\ \mathrm{lb/\cancel{cf}}) = 450\ \mathrm{lb}$$
$$(4\ \mathrm{lb/cf})(27\ \mathrm{cf/cy}) = (4\ \mathrm{lb/\cancel{cf}})(27\ \mathrm{\cancel{cf}/cy}) = 108\ \mathrm{lb/cy}$$

This practice assures that the calculations result in the correct units.

7.2   BASIC PROCEDURES

An estimator needs to develop consistent procedures for quantifying and pricing work. This section describes suggested procedures that can help develop consistency in estimating.

Document Review

The first step is to review the complete bid package. This does not mean to read the documents in detail, but to make a thorough review of the important parts of the package. Any supplemental and/or special conditions should be reviewed. Modifications of the general conditions are of little concern when developing the estimate, but special conditions that affect the design or construction process may affect the estimate.

A review of the drawings prior to starting the work provides the estimator with a general understanding of how the architect has prepared them, which will help when searching for information. For example, the architect might show certain dimensions on the plan and elevation views, and others on the sections and details. Or there might not be any particular procedure for the location of dimensions. The sections and details should be examined to determine how they apply to the project. Mechanical and electrical drawings may have support information that the steel fabricator needs and that the estimator must include in the general contractor's installation labor costs.

Specifications may be either on the drawings or in a separate manual. Generally they are in a manual and are supplemented with notes on the drawings. An estimator does not need to read specifications on a particular section until he or she is working on it. For example, the concrete and reinforcing steel specifications should be read early, since this is some of the first work that will be quantified. The sections that cover the construction of walls and partitions do not need to be reviewed until it is time to perform an OM estimate for the subcontract work. Many specification manuals are made up of *boilerplate* sections, that is, sections that are written with the intent that they apply to most projects. Drawing notes usually are specific to the project being bid, and it is important for the estimator to read each one before starting work.

Request for Information

When an estimator encounters items that need clarification, two things must be done. First, a thorough review of all drawings including the applicable sections and details should be made in an attempt to locate the needed information. If further information is needed, a request for information (RFI) form should be submitted.

Form F-10 in Appendix F is a sample RFI form. The information to be provided is well defined, but a couple of spaces need emphasis. Always provide the project description and the name of the person to whom the question(s) is addressed. Most important is to indicate the date when a response to the RFI is needed. The architect may answer the RFI and send it back to the bidder, but usually the architect prefers to answer all clarification questions via an addendum issued to all bidders. This reduces the possibility of someone claiming impropriety of the bid process. The key point is to always submit questions and requests for clarifications in writing and to state when a reply is needed.

Measurement

An estimator will search for and record many measurements and convert them from one set of units to another. It was recommended in Chapter 6 that lineal measurements be shown as decimal feet instead of feet and inches. This eliminates one conversion from the QTO sheet, thus reducing the chance for errors. An estimator should make a table in her or his personal estimating notebook showing the decimal equivalents of inches in terms of feet. A good rule of thumb is that ⅛ inch is approximately 0.01 feet.

Another handy table to generate is a list of common units used in QTO work. Many beginning estimators use one set of units when quantifying only to convert them to another set of units to make them usable. For example, if an estimator takes off structural steel in terms of length, but labor productivity is estimated in terms of pieces, and the steel fabricator prices in terms of weight, the information will have to be converted to number of pieces and weight. Using published estimating references, a list of units for QTO work can be generated and put into the estimator's personal notebook.

Marking the Drawings

As an estimator proceeds with the QTO work, he or she can become confused about which information has already been taken off making it necessary to stop work and recheck previously quantified items before proceeding further. While checking is good, there is an easier way. When taking off information, an estimator should list it and then go back and make sure that what was taken off is complete and correct. A slash line is then made with a highlighter through the item on the drawing that has been quantified to show that the QTO work is done.

The estimator should look at sections and details that relate to the item taken off for any other information that may be needed, and then draw slashes through them also. When all QTO work is complete, every direct work item on the drawings should have a slash through it, including applicable sections and details. When checking to see if something was quantified, the estimator only has to scan the drawings looking for the slash.

Exercise caution when marking drawings. Certain views will be used for more than one part of the estimate. For example, a footing on a structural drawing may also show a steel column. When marking the work, only the footings or only the columns will show a slash depending on which has been taken off. Upon completion of the estimate, both the footings and the columns will have a slash through them. Another method is to use different colors for different work activities, thus the footing might be marked in yellow and the steel column in green.

When doing a concrete QTO, multiple work tasks such as form construction, reinforcing steel placement, concrete placement, and surface finishing are needed. It is not necessary to mark a footing for each task. This would result in four slashes, and it would be difficult to determine which item had not been quantified if only three slashes were seen. The better way is not to draw the slash on the item until all tasks have been taken off. Concrete and structural steel, however, are quantified in different parts of the estimate, so a slash through each is necessary to make sure both items are accounted for.

An estimator may be tempted to mark one of a group of identical items to represent the group. For example, on the Training Center, there are two F.9.5 footings on drawing

S-2.0, and two should be listed on the QTO sheet. An estimator may elect to only mark one to show that the F.9.5 footings as a group have been taken off. However, the estimator did not see that the perimeter contains F.9.5 footings in the corners so four were not counted. When checking, the estimator sees the slash through the one F.9.5 footing and assumes that all six were taken off. An error has now occurred, which means that the bid will be short the cost of these footings. Each footing should be marked when it is counted and included in the quantity on the QTO sheet, leaving no doubt as to whether or not it has been taken off.

Sections and Details

Upon completion of the QTO and before transferring information to a recap page, an estimator needs to perform a series of checks. The first is to scan the drawings looking for any items that have not been highlighted. Even though all items are marked on the plan and elevation drawings, every section and detail needs to be checked also. When working under pressure, the sections and details may not have been marked. Look at each one and determine if the information was quantified. If so, put a slash through it and, if not, take the information off and then mark it. Do not just assume that the information was taken off; verify it and then mark the drawing accordingly.

An estimator must also be aware that some details are generic and may not apply to the project being bid. In such a case, the detail should be marked with "NIC," which shows that the work is not in the contract. At least two people should make sure the detail does not apply, as this can also be a source of inadvertent omission.

After all sections and details have been checked and marked, go back through the entire set of drawings and look for items that do not have slashes. If some are still not marked, put notes on the items stating why they are not marked. When others check the work, they will quickly see that the item has been looked at and can then determine its status.

Checking the QTO Sheet

As QTO sheets are finished for each activity of work, time should be taken to check them for completeness before moving on to the next activity. First the drawings are rechecked for any unmarked items. Each QTO sheet is examined to see that there is a quantity and appropriate dimensions for each line item. Lines are then reviewed for extensions, and summation ranges for the columns are verified. The estimator should do a manual check on one or two of the line items and add one of the extension columns to verify that the calculations are correct.

Once a quantity sheet is finished and all checks have been performed, the totals are double underlined to show that they are ready to be used in the next part of the estimating process. This double underlining is very important later on when performing a final check of the entire estimate. Do not skip this step; to do so can cause items to be missed when being transferred from one sheet to another resulting in winning a bid by an omission.

Setting Up and Completing the Quantity Sheet

Quantity measurement and calculations are recorded and performed on a quantity sheet. Page F-3 in Appendix F is a typical form on which the QTO is performed. While these forms are commonly found on 8 ½ × 11 sheets, an estimator can customize them as necessary. When planning where to start the QTO, an estimator should refer to the WBS discussed in Chapter 6. Because the project will be estimated generally in the order of construction, the first work to be estimated is typically the substructure. A quick review of the WBS shows which activities are essential to the construction of the substructure.

Activities and tasks to be done by the general contractor's own forces have been shown in bold. The first task is structural excavation; however, since these quantities depend on the volume of the concrete, the concrete QTO should be done first. The WBS shows that the footings will be the first concrete to be quantified and that form construction, fine grade, reinforcing steel placement, placing and leveling the concrete, and stripping forms are the tasks for which quantities are needed.

The first thing to do on every quantity sheet is to fill in the title and page numbering. Just above the description column is a place to put the CSI division number and a description of the activity being quantified. The first six columns are used from left to right as follows:

- Reference a drawing number where the information was acquired
- Description of the work being quantified
- The quantity counted
- Dimensions (3 columns) with units

The remaining columns are blank so that they can be customized to produce the desired calculations.

7.3   SUBSTRUCTURE CONCRETE
Footings

An estimator must keep in mind certain properties of concrete and how they affect cost. The cement component in concrete hardens by a chemical reaction. The environment within which concrete is placed affects the reaction rate and therefore its final properties. In hot weather, water will evaporate from the concrete before the reaction can be completed, thus reducing its strength. In very cold weather, the water may freeze, which also reduces strength. Methods can be used to counteract these conditions, but at a cost. In addition, rain on a slab during the early stages of curing may affect its finish, so extra protection may be required. Concrete generally is placed within acceptable environmental conditions, but an estimator must be aware of when protective measures are needed.

Figure 7-1 is a completed quantity sheet for the interior spot footings for the Training Center. The title and page numbers have been filled in, and the columns have been set up for the concrete and structural excavation since these activities are related. Division 3 concrete is entered above the description box. The first line shows a reference to drawing S-2.0 and the description "Spot footings." Below, interior spot footings of each designation are listed, and the number of each is recorded in the quantity column. Dimensions shown in the footing schedule on drawing S-3.0 are entered as decimal feet in the next three columns. At this point, the estimator should recheck the dimensions as entered and then go back to the drawing to recount each footing and highlight the concrete. A quick check will show that eleven footings have been marked on the drawings and that the total of the quantity column, while not shown, also equals eleven.

Quantity Sheet

Project: *The Training Center*
Location: *Kent, WA*

Date: May 20, 2003
Estimator: *P. Jacobs*
Est #: *TTC-1*

Division 3 Concrete

Ref	Description	Qty (ea)	L (ft)	W (ft)	H (ft)	Forms (sfca)	Fine Grade (sf)	Concrete (cf)	Concrete (cy)	Rod Off[1] (sf)	Excavation Depth (ft)	Excavation (bcf)	Backfill (cf)
S-2.0	Spot footings												
	F 8.5	2	8.5	8.5	1.5	102	145	217		145	1.42	444	227
	F 9.5	2	9.5	9.5	1.67	127	181	301		181	1.59	580	279
	F 10	5	10	10	1.75	350	500	875		500	1.67	1,637	762
	F 10.5	2	10.5	10.5	1.83	154	221	404		221	1.75	736	332
	Subtotal Concrete & Excavation					733	1,047	1,797		1,047		3,396	1,600
							divide by 27 =		66.5		divide by 27=	125.8	59.3
											Cross check		OK
											Swell	x 1.35 =	80.0
											Backfill	divide by 0.95 =	84.2
											Disposal—haul off		85.6

Backfill (lcy) = [excavation (bcy) - concrete volume (cy)] x swell factor (1.35) / compaction factor (0.95)

Backfill = [125.8 bcy - 66.5 cy] x 1.35 / 0.95 = 84.2 lcy

Disposal (lcy) = [excavation (bcy) x swell factor (1.35)] - backfill (lcy)

Disposal (lcy) = [125.8 bcy x 1.35] - 84.2 lcy = 85.6 lcy

Anchor bolts are 5/8 inch diameter expansion anchors—see structural steel.

[1] Rod Off is a type of finish that levels the concrete to the top of the forms.

bcy = bank cubic yards; lcy = loose cubic yards

FIGURE 7-1 QTO form for spot footings.

Showing a total-of-the-quantity column can be confusing when listings include other items that are not quite the same. For example, this page may eventually include the continuous footings, which may need to be taken off in sections for ease of quantifying. There will then be several identical sections to be counted that are all part of a single footing. Therefore, their count is useful only for calculating purposes and has no meaning in a summation of the number of footings.

To illustrate how a quantity sheet can be used, this page has five blank columns for the concrete work first and then three for the structural excavation and backfill. Note that the order of the columns generally follows the order of work within the concrete. The excavation is listed separately because its calculations depend on the concrete quantities.

The first blank column is used to calculate the area of the formwork. Note that the unit designation "sfca" has been entered in the column heading under forms. This stands for square feet of contact area. Estimating formwork by estimating all the materials used in their construction is difficult and usually does not prove to be worth the effort to do so. Most data, whether published or company historical, unitizes formwork costs per the area that is in contact with the concrete. For the spot footings, this is the area of the vertical sides only as the bottom is formed by the earth.

When setting up the calculations for the listed footings, the area of one side can be computed and then multiplied by four. If, however, the page were to include footings with a rectangular footprint, this calculation would not work. If the estimator sets the calculations to compute the area of a side and multiply it by 2, add the end area multiplied by 2, and then multiply the result by the quantity of footings, it will not matter whether the footing has a square or rectangular footprint. Other shapes will require unique formulas depending upon their configuration.

Fine grading is done whenever concrete is placed onto the earth or a granular base. When setting forms, the base or earth gets disturbed and may have rocks, trash, or other items that are not desired. Fine grading levels and cleans the area within the perimeter of the forms to provide a good surface for the concrete. While this seems like a minor operation, the cost becomes significant for all of the footings or for a slab-on-grade (SOG).

The next two columns are used to quantify the concrete to be placed into the footings. The volumes are calculated in cubic feet (cf), totaled, and then converted to cubic yards (cy). Cubic foot units are used for the excavation and backfill quantities also, and their conversions to cubic yards are done only as totals. Not making the conversion to cubic yards on each line item is an error control procedure. The more calculations that are done, the more chance there is of an error occurring. Converting only the total minimizes the number of computations that need to be performed.

The fifth column for the concrete is the finish area. Footings do not require a specified finish as does, say, a SOG. However, a finish operation of scraping the excess concrete off is necessary so that the top of the footing will be level. The common term for this is "rodding off" and it does require the expenditure of labor. Therefore, the column is titled accordingly. The finish area for footings is usually the same as the fine grade area but not always, so calculate it separately as some foundation elements may not require a fine grading operation.

Footings and foundations other than the spot footings appear to be more complicated. If an estimator keeps in mind that large problems are no more than an aggregate of several smaller problems, he or she will realize that breaking them down will make them easier to estimate. Perimeter footings can be sectionalized and quantified similar to the spot footings. The operations are basically the same as described previously.

Once the footing quantification is complete, a search is made of the drawings, including the sections and details, for any footing or foundation that may have been missed. Sometimes an estimator will make a mental note to pick up a particular footing at a later time and, without checking, this could be missed completely. More commonly, a foundation such as a pad for a transformer or a heat pump may be shown on another drawing that is not in the structural set. These may be on the electrical or mechanical drawings but must still be constructed by the general contractor.

Structural Excavation

When an estimator is calculating the structural excavation, the first thing to determine is the depth of the footing. In the Training Center drawings, there are different depths depending on the specific footing and the adjacent ground elevations. Detail D-1.0 shows the top of the spot footings to be 8 inches below the floor surface. The SOG is 5 inches thick and the soils report requires a 4-inch granular base on the subgrade. When the footings are constructed, the ground will have been leveled to the subgrade so their top surface will actually be 1 inch above it. The depth of excavation will therefore be one inch less than the depth of the footing. It has been specified that the footings may be placed on undisturbed earth, unless deemed otherwise by an inspector. A backhoe and a little handwork will provide an undisturbed surface.

On some projects, the concrete specifications state that footings can be earth-formed. This means that instead of building forms, the contractor can dig a neat hole and place the footing directly into it without further forming. The specifications often call for the footings to be increased in size, typically by about 6 inches in the length and width to compensate for dirt contamination at the sides. To determine which is more economical, an estimator must compare the cost of building forms against the cost of purchasing, placing, and finishing the extra concrete. This is not an issue for the Training Center. Since the top of the footings are one inch above the subgrade, a form has to be constructed.

It is difficult to anticipate situations where an inspector finds that the soil is not suitable and must be overexcavated and filled with an engineered material to provide adequate bearing. At the beginning of the project, it is difficult to anticipate what the conditions of the earth will be unless a soils report specifically addresses each footing location, which would be very expensive. A search of the geotechnical data may show test borings in two or three different locations within the building perimeter. These may or may not help guide the estimator on the work that has to be done. If conditions are other than what have been indicated, the contractor will negotiate any added cost with the owner for any required work beyond the defined scope.

The sixth blank column on the quantity sheet is used to enter the depth of the excavation. In this case, subtracting 1 inch from the footing depth will determine the depth. The estimator may want to use the formula (depth of footing − 0.08 foot) to automate this calculation.

During structural excavation, construction equipment is removing undisturbed earth, and the quantity is designated as either bank cubic feet or bank cubic yards; that is, the volume of the undisturbed bank or ground. Soil swells upon excavation. Some estimating references discuss swell and suggest swell factors to use for various types of soil. The geotechnical data will, on occasion, indicate a swell factor for a given test bore, but this is relatively rare, and the estimator needs to make an informed judgement as to what to use.

Many terms are used for the volume of soil after it has been excavated, such as truck cubic yards or loose cubic yards. These can cause some confusion, as there is no standard term for this other than cubic yard. Assuming that the soil at the location of the Training Center typically swells about 35%, the estimator will then multiply bank cubic yards by 1.35 to get the volume of earth that has to be handled when backfilling or disposing of spoils.

When working with any below-grade concrete, at least 2 feet must be left clear beyond each side so that workers have room to set and brace the forms. The excavation volume is

$$(\text{length} + 4 \text{ feet})(\text{width} + 4 \text{ feet})(\text{depth})$$

The results of the excavation at the spot footings are shown in the excavation column on the quantity sheet. The units are kept as bank cubic feet, and only their total is converted to *bank cubic yards* to keep conversion calculations to a minimum.

Backfill is calculated by subtracting the volume of concrete from the excavation volume. Units are still in bank cubic feet as shown in the backfill column heading. After summing the columns, the totals are multiplied by the swell factor to determine the volume in loose cubic yards. An accounting crosscheck that compares the total backfill to the result of the excavation minus the concrete is made to assure all calculations are correct.

$$\text{total excavation} - \text{total concrete volume} = \text{total backfill}$$
$$\text{or } 125.8 \text{ bcy} - 66.5 \text{ cy} = 59.3 \text{ bcy}$$

Earthwork volumes can be rounded to the nearest cubic yard because the costs of fractions are insignificant.

Next, the backfill has to be converted into a usable quantity. First the swell factor is applied, then a compaction factor. Once the soil is backfilled and compacted, its volume shrinks to less than it was in its natural state or bank volume. Let's assume that the amount of shrinkage for the compactive effort will be 5%. The compacted volume will then be 95% of the bank volume. It must be remembered, however, that the earth swelled and that the swelled amount is being handled by the equipment. Figure 7-1 shows the accounting for swell and compaction as it is applied to the backfill. What is not as clear is the amount to be disposed of. For this, an estimator needs to do the following calculation:

$$[(\text{excavated material})(\text{swell})] - \text{backfill} = \text{disposal}$$
$$\text{or } [(126 \text{ bcy})(1.35)] - 84.2 \text{ lcy} = 85.6 \text{ lcy}$$

A note can be put on the QTO sheet stating whether the excess material is to be disposed of by spreading on the site or by being hauled away.

The common error regarding excavation and backfill is the state of the material during the various calculation processes. Special care needs to be taken to assure that they are all made in terms of bank cubic yards or in the swelled volume. A mixup will result in a major error in earth volumes, which can have a significant affect on the bid price.

When footings are fairly deep, for example 5 feet below the subgrade, an estimator has to consider safety issues. A vertical trench wall is very dangerous and generally illegal due to the possibility of collapsing. The geotechnical data will frequently provide information for safe slopes for trenches depending on the soil type. If nothing is shown, the estimator should use slopes no steeper than 1 to 1. This greatly increases the amount of excavation and backfill.

On deeper excavations, an estimator may encounter some figures that do not seem correct. The concrete volume is small in relation to the total volume of soil to be backfilled and, when the swell factor is applied, it is common that the swelled backfill quantities will be larger than the amount excavated. When this happens, all calculations should be verified.

Reinforcing Steel

A separate QTO sheet is used to quantify the footing reinforcing steel. This is necessary because the work is measured differently and is done by a different crew. Figure 7-2 is a completed quantity sheet for the reinforcing steel that is in the footings shown in Figure 7-1.

An estimator should read and understand the notes in the specifications and on the drawings prior to starting this quantification. Perhaps the two most important items are (1) clearance to the edge of the concrete and (2) how much the bars will lap each other. This information is needed to determine the length of the reinforcing steel.

When reinforcing steel is specified on a spacing basis, instead of the specific number of bars, one more bar must be added to the number of spaces. For example, if a given footing is 10.34 feet wide and bars are to be on 1-foot centers, calculate that 10 bars are required, which will leave 2-inch clearance. On this basis, the first bar would actually be located at 1 foot 2 inches when the intent is for a bar to also be located at 2 inches from the beginning edge; therefore, one additional bar is required. When setting up the QTO sheet, only the first two dimensional columns are used for reinforcing steel. The first blank column calculates the total length of the reinforcing steel. Each layer, along with the size of bar, has been listed in the description column. The next column lists the unit weight for the designated bar size, and the following column calculates the total weight of the line item. The weights are then summed, and the total is converted to tons. Published estimating references usually have a table of unit weights for reinforcing steel. An example is shown in Appendix C.

Taking off reinforcing steel for an entire project can be very time consuming. If the bidding time is short, a reasonable estimate may be made by determining the unit weight of steel per cubic yard of concrete for a given item. In Figure 7-2, the unit weight is shown on the lower part of the page. Representative unit weights can be calculated from portions of the perimeter footings, SOG, and most CIP walls within a reasonable accuracy to use for labor costing. Unit weights determined for concrete members on one project must not be used on any other project, because of differing engineering requirements.

Embedded Steel

Embedded steel is placed such that it becomes an integral part of a concrete member. It usually is supplied by the structural steel fabricator. The most common embedded items are anchor bolts used to secure structural steel columns and some equipment. An anchor bolt is either hooked on the end or has a washer to secure it into the concrete to anchor the member to which it is bolted. Other embedded items include trench or pit edge angles, weld plates in walls, tilt-up connection angles, and lifting anchors.

Quantity Sheet

Project: The Training Center
Location: Kent, WA

Date: May 20, 2003
Estimator: P. Jacobs
Est #: TTC-1

Division 3200 Reinforcing Steel

Ref	Description	Qty (ea)	L (ft)	W (ft)	H (ft)	Total Len. (ft)	Unit Wt (lb/ft)	Total Wt (lb)	
S-2.0	Spot footings								
S-3.0	F 8.5								
	(8) # 6 E.W. Bottom	8	8			64	1.502	96	
		8	8			64	1.502	96	
	F 9.5								
	(7) #7 E.W. Bottom	7	9			63	2.044	129	
		7	9			63	2.044	129	
	F 10.0								
	(8) #7 E.W. Bottom	8	9.5			76	2.044	155	
		8	9.5			76	2.044	155	
	F 10.5								
	(9) #7 E.W. Bottom	9	10			90	2.044	184	
		9	10			90	2.044	184	
	Total reinforcing steel							1,128	
							=	0.56	Ton
	Unit reinforcing steel (lb/cy)							17	lb/cy

FIGURE 7-2 QTO form for reinforcing steel.

Carpenters install embedded steel as part of the formwork. Looking at the interior spot footing for the Training Center, a pattern can be seen for column anchor bolts, and detail D-1.0 indicates that these are expansion bolts. They are installed after the concrete has cured rather than being cast into the footing. The trade that uses them for securing their material or equipment typically installs these types of bolts. Bolts used for the structural steel will be installed by ironworkers. Similarly, a plumber will install ones that are used to hold piping, and electricians those for securing conduit.

Embedded steel should be shown on a separate quantity sheet that becomes part of the concrete QTO. In cases such as the Training Center where the anchor bolts will be installed during structural steel erection, the anchor bolts should be quantified for inclusion into the structural steel portion of the estimate. The bolt supply can cause problems for the estimator. If one assumes that a supplier will furnish a large number of bolts and they do not, there is a significant material omission in the estimate. For example, the structural steel fabricator will furnish all steel-to-steel bolts and those that are embedded into concrete. Bolts for any other connection, such as steel to wood, are to be furnished by the general contractor. The wise estimator will make sure to determine who is furnishing the bolts when doing the QTO.

Cast-in-Place Concrete Walls

Three walls for the elevator pit for the Training Center are of CIP concrete, while the fourth wall is a tilt-up panel. Cost factors for CIP walls are different than for other concrete sections, so an estimator will quantify them on a separate QTO sheet. The quantity sheet is set up essentially the same as for other concrete members but will have a column for de-fin and patch and, since the structural excavation has been done as part of the foundation, these columns will not be needed. In general, two finish items must be considered when constructing walls—wall tops and the vertical surface. On the Training Center, both of these will be covered, so finish other than leveling the tops, de-fin, and patching of rock pockets is not required.

Slab-on-Grade

The last concrete to be placed in the substructure is the SOG. The type of building will determine how the SOG is placed. For example, the Training Center is to be constructed with tilt-up wall panels, which defines a particular way in which the SOG is placed. The drawings show a 5-foot closure strip (CS) around the perimeter. This section of concrete is not placed until after the panels have been set and the structural steel has been erected and aligned. All other SOG concrete will be constructed and prepared for use as a casting slab for the wall panels. Other types of construction, such as a pre-engineered steel building, may dictate that the entire SOG be placed before erection of the steel. However, a building with CIP concrete walls may not have the slab placed until after the walls have been constructed.

Drawing S-1.0 shows the layout of *construction joints (CJ)* and *control joints (SJ)* in the SOG. Construction joints are formed edges that, in this design, are running along the longitudinal column lines. The control joints are put into the slab to control where the SOG cracks as it shrinks during curing. The designed control joints are shown as 1 inch deep saw cuts, which will be made after the initial curing of the concrete. Control joints will be quantified for pricing but otherwise do not affect the placement of the SOG concrete.

The construction joint layout indicates that there are three placement lanes running the length of the building. The estimator should determine the approximate amount of concrete in the widest lane to see if it is of reasonable size for a single placement. On the Training Center, the quantity is approximately 136 cubic yards, which can easily be placed. The finish area is about 8,800 square feet, which will require about eleven cement finishers, assuming a productivity of 800 square feet per man-day.

A generally accepted placement method for concrete is to use a concrete pump. Some superintendents will place all concrete with a pump regardless of the size or location. Part of a winning attitude is to decide if there is a more economical way to place concrete in various applications. The SOG is one place that should be studied, and discussions with a superintendent may be helpful for determining whether it is more cost effective to use a pump or to place the concrete directly from the truck chute. Generally pumping is the most cost effective way of placing large quantities of concrete when compared with all other methods, except placement from the truck chute.

Preparations for the SOG include laying down a base layer of aggregate and installing a vapor barrier. Edge forms are then set, reinforcing rod or wire mesh is installed, and the slab is ready to place. It is the superintendent's job to select placement methods that can be done within the cost parameters of the estimate. Edge forms for slabs and other thin sections are constructed from dimensioned lumber such as 2×6 or 2×8, and quantified as lineal feet. When edge forms are higher than 12 inches, they are made from a sheet-type form material such as plywood or Medium Density Overlay (MDO) board. These are quantified on a square foot basis as has been done for the footings. Some estimators prefer to quantify all form material by the square foot, but most published and historical estimating databases use lineal feet and square feet. An estimator should review the units prior to quantifying these forms to minimize dimensional conversions.

There are several configurations of construction joints between slab sections, and most are designed to minimize vertical movement between them. Some joints are keyed either with a preformed metal form or with wood. Dowels of smooth reinforcing rod are inserted through the forms to keep adjacent slab sections aligned. These are furnished as part of the reinforcing steel package. Both the construction joints and the dowels are cost factors that an estimator must consider.

An estimator needs to look for variations in the SOG that will affect the cost. On the Training Center, the office area has an additional 2 inches of sand over the aggregate below the vapor barrier. Portions of the slab are thicker at the columns and in some other areas. These will require additional concrete and a little extra effort when fine grading.

Closure strips and column block-out fillers will be placed after the wall panels are set and the structural steel has been erected. The work includes backfilling between the placed SOG and the wall panels, forming the backfill material for the thickened slab, placing a few end forms for sectionalizing the closure strips, and placing and finishing the concrete. Column block-outs will be filled when the closure strip is placed, and only a reasonable cleaning of the top of the footing and the installation of isolation material around the edges are required. This work is still part of the substructure, and the estimator should do the QTO work in that section lest it be forgotten.

Control joint sawing may be done by the general contractor's own forces, but it is more likely to be done by a concrete sawing subcontractor. Sometimes a bid price for the sawing will be forthcoming on bid day, but many times no bids are received. The estimator should quantify the length of the control joints, obtain a unit price from a subcontractor and develop an independent estimate. This will then be used as an OM estimate in Chapter 9.

With the completion of the foundations and the SOG, the substructure concrete has been quantified. Referring to the expanded WBS shown in Figure 6-4, the next construction work is the tilt-up concrete walls. Although the order of work is to construct and set the wall panels first, erect the structural steel, then place the mezzanine floor, this is where a little variation in the order of estimating is justified. An estimator may want to complete the mezzanine slab first to finish all of the interior CIP concrete and then do the wall panel estimate. This is the order that will be discussed in this chapter.

Elevated Concrete

Mezzanine and elevated floor slabs for offices are relatively simple structures. For a structural steel framed building such as the Training Center, structural steel members support fabricated metal joists on which a metal decking is welded. Steel erection includes installation of angles to be used as slab edge forms that become permanently embedded in the concrete. There may be some places where wood edge forms are required to have a clean concrete edge showing. An estimator needs to pay particular attention to the type of edge forms and make sure that they are all covered within the estimate.

The volume of concrete placed on a corrugated metal deck is less than the equivalent thickness placed on a flat surface. There are many configurations for decking that affect the concrete volume, and an estimator needs to use those for the specified decking. Some estimating references have quantities or formulas for representative shapes of decking, but manufacturer's data for the specified product will provide more accurate information.

Estimating elevated structural slabs and beams present some different estimating techniques. Both require bottom forms, which are of heavier construction and therefore more costly. The difficult item is the support of the forms. Concrete weighs approximately 150 pounds per cubic foot or more than 4,000 pounds per cubic yard. An elevated beam that is 12 inches wide by 2 feet deep then weighs 300 pounds per foot of beam length, and if it is 20 feet long, the total weight is 6,000 pounds. The forms alone will not hold this weight, and supplemental supports are required. The size and type of support depends on the location of the concrete element. A beam that is 6 feet above a ground surface may only need pole jacks placed at selected intervals, but an elevated floor slab 20 feet up will require a system of heavy-duty scaffolding. The ability of an estimator to determine the support system for elevated concrete depends on experience. There is an extreme risk associated with these support systems, and the estimator should seek engineering help to determine the correct system.

Concrete Finishing

The estimator should pay particular attention to concrete finishes. Types of finishes include leveling to the top of the forms (rodding off), float finish, steel trowel finish, and broom finish. In addition, there are several surface treatments such as a curing compound that retards water evaporation, spray-on hardeners, and the seeding of aggregates for architectural or wearing purposes. An estimator needs to note on the QTO sheet which type finish is specified. On quantity sheets where several different concrete types are likely to be listed, a separate column should be shown for each type of finish.

Tilt-Up Concrete

An economical method for constructing a building such as the Training Center is the use of *tilt-up concrete walls*. Panels are cast on a flat slab, such as the SOG, and after curing are lifted and set (tilted up) onto the foundations. The economics is in the forming. Since only edge forms are required, less form material is needed. In addition, the workers are always at ground level. These savings more than offset the cost of the equipment and manpower used to lift and set the panels, and the construction is much faster.

When starting the tilt-up QTO, an estimator should discuss the project with an experienced superintendent. Together they can determine if the SOG is suitable for the work and what has to be done to prepare for it. If the SOG is not suitable, they will need to determine where a casting slab can be constructed. It is common for panels to be cast one on top of another. Methods and material only as they relate to costs are the estimator's immediate concern.

Information about the tilt-up panels for the Training Center is shown on drawing S-6.1. While this is the primary detail drawing for the panels, there is some architectural information on other drawings. An estimator must look at all drawings and note where different information is located. For example, drawing S-6.1 indicates that there is a ¾-inch reveal but its location is not shown. These are found on the wall sections of the architectural set (Drawing A4.1). The location of the reveal is important only as it affects its length.

Of particular concern to an estimator are the embedded items. Angles and plates are shown for the joints between panels and for connecting the structural steel to the concrete. One significant item that is not shown is the lifting hardware. There are companies that supply all sorts of concrete accessories from form ties to tilt-up anchors; a product catalog should be in every estimator's library. The responsibility of engineering the sizing and placement of the lifting anchors lies with the contractor doing the work—in this case the general contractor. The estimator is not an engineer. Therefore, he or she should seek professional help for sizing and locating the lifting anchors. Contractors who do tilt-up work usually have a structural engineer available for this. The engineer, ironworker foreman, and anchor supplier can usually determine the number, size, and location of the anchors that are needed. Locations at this point are not important, but the estimator must add cost for the panel engineering and detailing work to the estimate.

When quantifying tilt-up work, an estimator will want to look for panels that are basically the same. For example, on the Training Center, panels #1 and #2 are dimensionally the same with the only difference being the imbedded connection steel. These can be quantified on the same line as long as the different types of embeds are quantified separately. Most embedded steel is relatively similar in size, and it takes about the same effort to install each one. Unless there is an unusually large piece of embedded steel that takes more effort to install, they may be grouped together on a single line. Figure 7-3 shows how a typical tilt-up panel QTO sheet might look for the Training Center.

Figure 7-3 demonstrates a feature that is helpful in the QTO. Simple panel sketches have been drawn so that someone else knows exactly what is being quantified. This is a good practice for items that are difficult to visualize such as specially bent reinforcing steel or some odd-shaped cast-in-place concrete. Sketches add pages to the estimate, but provide clarity to those who will use the estimate after the project is won.

Quantity Sheet

Project: *The Training Center*
Location: *Kent, WA*

Date: May 21, 2003
Estimator: *P. Jacobs*
Est #: *TTC-1*

Division 3470 Tilt-Up Concrete

Ref	Description	Qty (ea)	L (ft)	W (ft)	H (ft)	Edge Forms (lf)	Chamfer (lf)	Concrete (cf)	Concrete (cy)	Finish (sf)	Embeds (ea)	Anchors (ea)
S-6.1	Panels #1 & 2	2	29.98	31.56	0.60	246	120	1,143		1,892		16
	Block outs (2/panel)	4	20.00	3.00	0.60	184	184	(145)		(240.0)		
	Embeds											
	Panel connections A & B										12	
	Steel connections										2	
	Panel 3	1	29.98	31.56	0.60	123	60	572		946		8
	Step	1	15.5	2	0.60	2		19		31		
	Block outs - window	1	20	3	0.60	46	46	(36)		(60.0)		
	Doors	2	7.17	3.34	0.60	42	35	(29)		(47.9)		
	Embeds											
	Panel conn. A, B & C	9									9	
	Steel connections	1									1	
	Carry forward to page 2					643	445	1,524		2,521	24	24

Eight anchors for each full-size panel have been assumed pending further research.

scaled dimension

FIGURE 7–3 QTO sheet for tilt-up concrete panels.

As an estimator becomes more experienced, he or she looks for ways to save time and effort. The quantification of the tilt-up panels is just such a place. A QTO for the embedded steel will need to be made for developing an OM estimate later on for the fabricated steel material supply. While the panels are being quantified, the estimator can start a separate sheet for the embedded steel and list such pertinent information as the quantity, dimensions, weights, and materials. Extensions need not be made at this time, and the sheet can be put into a file for OM estimates to be completed later. This saves time by not having to review the drawings again to search for the information.

Panel formwork for the perimeter and blockouts is quantified as edge forms similar to the SOG. The estimator will note the architect's use of feature strips and chamfers. Some of the information is shown on the structural details, but some is also on the architectural wall sections. All drawings must be reviewed to make sure the information quantified is complete. Reinforcing steel cannot be typified for all of the panels as it was in the footings. Panels have different engineering requirements depending on their configuration; therefore, the unit weight of reinforcing will also be different. Figure 7-4 shows a reinforcing steel QTO sheet for panels #1, 2, and 3.

Once the tilt-up panels have been cast and cured, they are ready to be tilted up and set in place. Labor cost factors include attaching the braces, rigging the panel for lifting, breaking the panel loose as lifting tension is applied, guiding it into place, securing the bracing, patching, and grouting the base. Material and equipment cost will include the cost of the crane, rental of braces, shim packs, and patching material and grout.

Cranes are rented by the hour, day, or month and their rate usually includes the rigging for hoisting and setting the panels. There are, however, two additional cost items associated with them: (1) the travel time to and from the job, sometimes referred to as "in and out" time, and (2) the cost of mobilizing the crane on site. Mobilizing a crane includes assembling and rigging the boom for lattice-boomed cranes and installing rolling outriggers. One tank of fuel is furnished, and if more is needed, the general contractor will furnish it. Cranes used for relatively heavy lifting typically will come to the job site with a trained operator; if it is a very large crane, it will also have an oiler. An estimator must call the crane rental company to get the hourly rate, in and out cost, and mobilization costs. The general contractor furnishes the labor to supplement the crane crew during mobilization, so the estimator needs to find out from the vendor about how long the operation takes.

The erected panels need to be supported until the structural steel is installed. Braces usually are rented from the same accessories vendor who furnishes the lifting embeds discussed earlier. The estimator must determine how many are needed and how long they will be required. A superintendent and the vendor can help with this. The braces for all panels of the building need to be rented for the entire time until the steel erection is completed.

Grout

Grout is a cementitious compound applied under the base of some elements to provide full bearing surfaces. It is applied in two places on the Training Center—under the tilt-up panels and under the structural steel columns. The drawings indicate the approximate gap under the members of each application in which the grout is to be installed. Cement finishers install grout and, although amounts are small, the cost can be significant.

Quantity Sheet

Project: *The Training Center*
Location: *Kent, WA*

Date: May 21, 2003
Estimator: *P. Jacobs*
Est # *TTC-1*

Division *3200 Reinforcing Steel*

Ref	Description	Qty (ea)	L (ft)	W (ft)	H (ft)	Total Length (lf)	Unit Wt (lb/lf)	Total Wt (lb)			
S-6.1	*Tilt-up panels #1 & 2*										
	#4 vertical bars	*16*	*29.88*			*478*	*0.668*	*319*			
		28	*2.875*			*81*	*0.668*	*54*			
		28	*8.875*			*249*	*0.668*	*166*			
		28	*5.875*			*165*	*0.668*	*110*			
	#5 horizontal bars										
	Under openings	*6*	*29.80*			*179*	*1.043*	*186*			
	Between openings	*14*	*29.80*			*417*	*1.043*	*435*			
	Above openings	*10*	*29.80*			*298*	*1.043*	*311*			
	Each side of openings	*24*	*4.90*			*118*	*1.043*	*123*			
	Chord steel, #6	*6*	*29.80*			*179*	*1.502*	*269*			
	Side reinforcing, #5	*56*	*29.88*			*1,673*	*1.043*	*1745*			
	Opening reinforcing										
	Horizontal, #7	*8*	*24.67*			*197*	*2.044*	*403*			
	Vertical	*8*	*see side reinforcing*								
	Diagonal, #4	*16*	*2.5*			*40*	*0.668*	*27*			
	Note: #7 bars over and under the openings are not dimensioned and were scaled at 24' 8"										
	Carry forward to page 2							*4,148*			

FIGURE 7-4 QTO sheet for tilt-up panel reinforcing steel.

Quantity Sheet

Project: *The Training Center*
Location: *Kent, WA*

Date: May 21, 2003
Estimator: P. Jacobs
Est # TTC-1

Division 3200 Reinforcing Steel

Ref	Description	Qty (ea)	L (ft)	W (ft)	H (ft)	Total Length (lf)	Unit Wt (lb/lf)	Total Wt (lb)
	Brought forward from page 1							4,148
	Panel #3							
	#4 Vertical bars							
	West side	3	29.88			90	0.668	60
		1	22.88			23	0.668	15
	Under top opening							
	Between doors	7	17.88			125	0.668	84
	East of doors	6	25.88			155	0.668	104
	Over door	2	10.88			22	0.668	15
	Over top opening	12	5.875			71	0.668	47
	West side	4	31.88			128	0.668	85
	Under one door	2	1.875			4	0.668	3
	#5 Horizontal bars							
	Above top opening	5	29.85			149	1.043	156
	Each side of opening	10	4.85			49	1.043	51
	Below top opening	8	29.85			239	1.043	249
	West of doors	5	3.35			17	1.043	18
	Between doors	5	10.04			50	1.043	52
	East of doors	5	9.52			48	1.043	50
	Below doors	2	14.88			30	1.043	31
	West reinforcement, #5	22	29.88			657	1.043	686
	East reinforcement, #5	14	29.88			418	1.043	436
	Top opening horiz., #7	2	24.67			49	2.044	101
	Door horiz., #7	3	8.00			24	2.044	49
	Door vert., #7	1	17.88			18	2.044	37
		2	19.88			40	2.044	82
	Diagonals, #4	9	2.50			23	0.668	15
	Carry forward to page 3							6,574

FIGURE 7-4 continued.

An estimator should set up a separate QTO sheet for all the grout on a project. There are only two cost items in the grouting operation—the grout material and installation labor. It is quantified in cubic feet, and most estimating references have productivity rates that are reasonably accurate.

7.4   STRUCTURAL STEEL

Structural and miscellaneous steel components are produced by a steel fabricator and delivered to the job site ready to be installed. Structural members include beams, columns, and joists that are usually rolled shapes produced by a steel mill. Miscellaneous steel includes stairs, handrails, and other components that are not part of the main structural support.

A review of the structural drawings for the Training Center shows simple steel framing and a modest amount of miscellaneous steel: primarily stairs, railings, and mechanical supports at the roof. A common point of confusion for the beginning estimator is cold-formed metal framing used to frame walls and partitions. This light-gage framing is found in CSI division 5400 but is furnished and installed by the subcontractor who does the gypsum wallboard.

Structural steel is quantified by the number of pieces for the installation labor, and by weight for the OM estimate of the fabricator. Miscellaneous steel is taken off in various units depending on the application. An estimator may find it easier to use one set of quantity sheets for structural items, and a different set for the miscellaneous steel.

Figure 7-5 is a quantity sheet for structural steel. Columns have been set up to calculate the weight and piece count. The columns have connection plates shop-welded to their tops and bottoms. These plates reduce the length of the tube steel slightly but add weight. Usually this difference is insignificant, unless unusually large mounting plates are used. The estimator must be sure to quantify all bracing, special connections, and any other items that are shown. Most estimating references list weight data for basic structural steel shapes.

All bolts used in the steel erection must be counted. Quantities can be difficult to determine, and the work is very tedious. An estimator needs to develop a method for keeping track of the bolts as they are taken off. A common way is to determine the number of similar connections and note the number of bolts in one. Once the number of connections is determined, a simple multiplication will calculate the number of bolts for all connections of that type. Bolts are quantified by number for labor productivity. Material pricing is included in the unit price of the fabricated steel.

Open-web steel joists are furnished by a different vendor. They are quantified by length for each designation shown on the drawings. Both material and labor costs may be determined by lineal foot of joist. Unless a catalog from the joist supplier or complete joist design data is available, quantifying the weight of joists is difficult and unnecessary. Bridging and bracing are loose items that come with the joists and should also be listed on the joist quantity sheet.

Joists are quantified on a separate set of QTO sheets. On the Training Center, there are joists of the same designation that are different lengths, and, conversely, joists of different designations that are the same length. An estimator needs to quantify joists by specific designation and length. Rolled steel sections may also be used as joists and should be quantified as part of the structural steel, rather than with the fabricated joists. Figure 7-6 shows the beginning of a typical listing of joists for the Training Center.

Quantity Sheet

Project: *The Training Center*
Location: *Kent, WA*

Date: May 21, 2003
Estimator: P. Jacobs
Est #: TTC-1

Division 5 *Structural and Miscellaneous Steel*

Ref	Description	Qty (ea)	L (ft)	W (ft)	H (ft)	Pieces (ea)	Base Pl Area (sf)	Col Length (ft)	Unit Wt		Total Wt (lb)
S-2.0	*Columns¹*										
	TS 10×10×5/16	3	31.8			3		95	40.35	lb/lf	3,849
		3	30.82			3		92	40.35	lb/lf	3,731
	Baseplate—1 1/4" Plate	6	1.34	1.34			11		51.05	lb/sf	562
	Top plate—7/8 plate	6	1.34	1.00			8		35.74	lb/sf	287
	TS 8×8×5.16	1	31.8			1		32	31.84	lb/lf	1,013
		1	30.82			1		31	31.84	lb/lf	981
	Baseplate—1 1/4" Plate	2	1.17	1.17			3		51.05	lb/sf	119
	Top plate—7/8 plate	1	1.34	1.00			1		35.74	lb/sf	48
		1	0.92	1.00			1		35.74	lb/sf	33
	TS 8×8×3/8	2	31.8			2		64	37.69	lb/lf	2,397
		2	30.82			2		62	37.69	lb/lf	2,323
	Baseplate—1 1/4" Plate	4	1.17	1.17			5		51.05	lb/sf	239
	Top plate—7/8 plate	4	0.92	1.00			4		35.74	lb/sf	132
	TS 8×8×1/4	2	31.8			2		64	25.82	lb/lf	1,642
		2	30.82			2		62	25.82	lb/lf	1,592
	Baseplate—1 1/4" Plate	4	1.17	1.17			5		51.05	lb/sf	239
	Top plate—7/8 plate	2	1.17	1.00			2		35.74	lb/sf	84
		2	0.92	1.00			2		35.74	lb/sf	66
	Total Columns					16					19,337

¹8" deleted at the top for joist thickness and add 8" at the base of columns for footing elevation.

FIGURE 7-5 QTO sheet for structural steel.

113

Project: *The Training Center*
Location: *Kent, WA*

Date: May 20, 2003
Estimator: *P. Jacobs*
Est #: *TTC-1*

Division 052500 *Steel Joists*

Ref	Description	Qty (ea)	L (ft)	W (ft)	H (ft)	Total Joists (ea)	Total Length (ft)							
	Girder Joists													
	RG 6	*2*	*26.83*			*2*	*54*							
	RG 5	*2*	*58.83*			*2*	*118*							
	Joists													
	26K255/141	*4*	*35.00*			*4*	*140*							
		4	*36.75*			*4*	*147*							
		4	*35.25*			*4*	*141*							
	25K240/150	*9*	*35.00*			*9*	*315*							
		9	*36.75*			*9*	*331*							
		9	*35.25*			*9*	*317*							
	Bridging													
	Bracing													

FIGURE 7-6 Partial joist QTO.

114

Decking is installed on top of the joists and is simple to quantify. It is measured in square feet. The estimator should note the lap requirements in order to calculate a percentage to add to the area measured on the drawings for an OM material estimate. Installation of the decking involves two operations—laying the sheets in position and welding. An estimator should consult with a superintendent or an experienced ironworker foreman for assistance in estimating decking. He or she must also be aware of what work is included in the labor productivity factors that will be used in the pricing process. Some factors include the welding, and some do not. If welding productivity is separate from the deck placing, the welds must be counted and listed by type. If the productivity factor is for placing and welding the sheets, the estimator should compare the number of welds per square foot in the factor with those shown on the drawings and, if different, make necessary adjustments.

Miscellaneous steel includes prefabricated stairs, handrails, and other nonstructural items. The handrails generally are shipped loose and installed after the stairs are in place. Stair sections are quantified by the number of flights, number of landings, or length. Other items, such as mechanical equipment supports, are quantified similar to the structural steel. When an estimator finishes with the miscellaneous steel, a complete review of the drawings is performed. He or she should ensure that all bolts have been counted and that the welds have been quantified, not only by type and length but also by welding position, as productivity varies accordingly.

Now the entire set of project drawings, including all details, are reviewed for any steel items not marked. The estimator should look for various braces, metal edge forms, embedded plates, and bridging. Some items may be shown on the mechanical or electrical drawings that are not shown anywhere else. Especially troublesome is where the drawings indicate that support steel is to be installed in the roof for mechanical equipment, but there is no designation of the size, shape, or location for it. The estimator should discuss these situations with the superintendent, and then include an allowance quantity for them in the QTO. When finished, every item of steel on the project shown on the drawings should be highlighted.

7.5 ROUGH CARPENTRY

Rough carpentry can constitute either a significant amount of work or a relatively small amount. For the Training Center, the majority of the rough carpentry is in the coping at the top of the tilt-up wall panels. Miscellaneous blocking may be required around some of the door and window jambs and as supports for toilet room fixtures and accessories. The general contractor may perform this work with its own forces.

When a significant amount of wood wall framing is required, the general contractor may solicit bids from a framing subcontractor. While the general contractor's own carpenters can do the work, they may be efficient in constructing concrete forms but may not be cost effective on framing. An estimator should develop a cost for the wood framing as a separate OM estimate to compare against subcontractor bids. When quantities are small, such as is the case on the Training Center, the framing work can be estimated as direct work, because there is a good chance that no subcontractor bids will be received.

Wood is quantified in two basic categories—lumber and sheet material. Lumber is planed or rough-sawn boards while sheet material is plywood, particleboard, or oriented strand board (OSB). Both categories can be listed on the same quantity sheet for small amounts of work, but it may be simpler to use separate sheets for projects involving significant quantities. Lumber is taken off by the lineal foot for a listed size and then converted to board feet. Sheet material is quantified by the square foot of each material of a specified thickness. One board foot of lumber is equivalent to a board that is 12-inches long by 12-inches wide and 1-inch thick. To convert lumber to board feet, multiply the width in inches by the thickness in inches by the length in feet. Divide the answer by 12 inches per foot to determine the number of board feet. A table of conversion factors is shown in Appendix C.

The estimator should review all architectural drawings and details for lumber usage. Some places, such as the coping detail on the Training Center, show lumber and sheet material used in combination. Blocking occasionally is shown, but many times the amount needed for paper towel holders, mirrors, or toilet paper holders is left to the contractor to determine and install. Miscellaneous blocking quantities typically are minor (belonging to the 20% of cost category), and only a small amount of time should be spent on it.

One item that the estimator must look at specifically is the cant strip on flat-roofed buildings. The Training Center has an insulation board cant strip, which is installed by the roofer. Some roof systems are not insulated, and a wood cant strip is then installed by the general contractor prior to the installation of the roofing.

Some commercial projects have a significant amount of wood wall framing. Walls commonly are constructed with a bottom plate, double top plate, and studs on 16-inch centers. Considerable small blocking and bracing may be required, which is difficult to quantify. A common practice is to quantify the walls based on studs located on 12-inch centers, which will then automatically account for blocking and bracing.

An option to counting each stud and measuring each plate and header is for the estimator to take a representative wall section constructed of a given lumber size and calculate the board feet, unitize it to board feet per square foot of wall, and then use this as a multiplier to determine the quantity for the entire section. This way the walls are taken off in square feet instead of counting studs and plates.

7.6   DOORS

Doors are relatively simple to quantify. There are three basic components to a door—the door leaf, frame, and hardware. Doors usually are either metal or wood and may be solid core, hollow core, insulated, security type, or fire-rated. They come in various standard sizes and can be ordered in custom sizes. Frames are made of either wood or metal. Metal doors and frames are commonly referred to as hollow metal. The most commonly used door/frame combinations are metal doors in metal frames, wood doors in wood frames, and wood doors in metal frames. Prices will be received on bid day for wood doors and/or frames from one supplier, and metal doors and/or frames from a different supplier. A different vendor may furnish the hardware. However, on occasion a single vendor may furnish a combined price that includes all doors, frames, and hardware.

Specific door requirements are shown on a door schedule in the architectural set of drawings. This schedule lists the door type and size and will include separate columns for the frame and hardware. Doors that are pre-hung include the hinges but no other hardware. The installation crew will install them as a single unit. Commercial metal doors usually are not pre-hung, and frames may be either welded assemblies or knocked down for assembly on site.

Columns are designated on the QTO for each type and size of door and frame listed. Welded frames are quantified separately from knock-down units, as their installation labor is different. Specialty doors, such as fire doors, sound doors, or security doors, need to be listed separately even though they may look similar to some of the more common doors. If sound doors are specified, the estimator needs to look for sound testing requirements, which can be expensive. Also, if grouting of the doorframes is specified, the estimator needs to be sure it is included on the grout quantity sheet.

Hardware is defined in the specifications by groups. A hardware group may be as simple as a single latch set or may contain hinges, closers, match-keyed locksets, panic bars, thresholds, and/or kick plates. The group will represent all of the hardware that is to be installed on a particular door and may be used on more than one door in the project. The estimator can extend the door quantity page to show the applicable hardware group. A column for each group number should be shown. One may also want to make a separate sheet listing each group and its contents for pricing purposes later on. Each door, frame, and hardware group is highlighted when it is taken off. When finished, the estimator should check the drawings to ensure that there are no unmarked items.

7.7 TOILET ACCESSORIES

The toilet accessories are usually in the 80% category of the work that represents only 20% of the cost. An estimator should learn to quantify these items quickly. They include mirrors, soap dispensers, toilet paper holders, and towel bars. Toilet partitions are furnished and installed by a subcontractor, and are quantified only for OM purposes. The toilet accessories can quickly be taken off by type. Suppliers will furnish a price on bid day, but the general contractor will install them. The estimator will use these same quantities later on for an OM estimate.

7.8 FINISH CARPENTRY

Finish carpentry includes moldings, paneling, cabinetry, and architectural woodwork. An estimator needs to determine which of these items are to be installed by the general contractor's own forces and which are to be installed by the vendor. As a rule, the general contractor installs moldings and paneling as well as prefabricated cabinetry. Custom cabinets and case goods generally are manufactured and installed by a vendor. Consultation with a superintendent will help to determine who is responsible for the installation of various finish items. Some millwork is prefinished and some is not. The estimator should determine which will be finished at the job site and use the quantities later on for the OM estimate for the painting subcontractor. Estimating references serve as guides to estimate labor productivity for finish carpentry.

7.9 COMPLETING AND CHECKING THE QUANTITY TAKE-OFF

As each subsection of a QTO has been finished, it should be checked for completeness and accuracy. For example, the footings are a subsection of the concrete, as are the SOG, mezzanine slab, and tilt-up walls. All items that belong in these subsections should be highlighted in yellow on the drawings indicating that they have been quantified. Dimensions, extensions, and summation calculations should be checked. A manual spot check of column addition is done along with a crosscheck, and totals are double underlined. Only the information that will be used on succeeding pages should be totaled, checked, and underlined.

When all of the QTO for the self-performed work is completed, the estimator should scan all of the drawings to look for any items that are not subcontract work that may have been missed. Every QTO page should be examined to ensure that all totals that will be transferred to another sheet have double underlines. At this point, the estimator is ready to start the pricing recapitulation process, which we will discuss in Chapter 8.

7.10   SUMMARY

The QTO can be tedious but should not be difficult. An estimator must look at the construction process and determine how the work is to be quantified in preparation for pricing. Published estimating references can be a guide to determine units for the materials. An estimator must understand that the QTO is the most time-consuming part of the process. Using the WBS helps focus on the 20% of the work that represents 80% of the cost. Quantities of work are measured and entered on the quantity sheets. As elements of work are taken off, they should be marked with a highlighter. Before proceeding to the next phase, the estimator should check the drawings to ensure that all major items have been taken off. This checking of the QTO for completeness and accuracy is one of the most important parts of the work.

7.11   REVIEW QUESTIONS

1. What is the purpose of the QTO?
2. What is the first thing an estimator must do when starting the QTO?
3. How does an estimator request information and/or clarifications about the drawings?
4. How does the estimator keep track, on the drawings, of what work has been quantified?
5. What is the first information that should be entered on every quantity sheet?
6. The estimator may plan his/her approach to the QTO work by creating what?
7. The structural excavation and backfill quantities are dependent on what other quantity?
8. How much room should be excavated beyond the sides of subgrade concrete to allow for workers to set and brace forms?
9. What is embedded steel?
10. In what units is structural steel quantified?
11. Who furnishes embedded anchor bolts used to secure structural steel?
12. Who installs the slab edge forms for the mezzanine slab on the Training Center?
13. How is a QTO checked to ensure it is complete?
14. In what units is dimensional lumber quantified?
15. Who installs wood doors that are in metal frames?

7.12 EXERCISES

1. Quantify the following for the CIP concrete walls of the elevator pit shown for the Training Center:

   - Form area
   - Concrete volume in cubic feet, converted to cubic yards
   - Rod-off area
   - Reinforcing steel weight in pounds, converted to tons, assuming 2-inch clearance

2. Calculate the following excavation quantities for the Training Center elevator pit assuming that the excavation will be 2 feet beyond the elevator pit slab and that 1:1 slopes are required for safety:

   - Structural excavation in bank cubic yards
   - Backfill in cubic yards after swell
   - Excess excavation to be disposed of

   It is suggested that a simple sketch be made prior starting this quantification.

3. The SOG of the main floor of the Training Center is specified as 5-inches thick. A 2×6 that can be used as an edge form is 5½ inches wide. Quantify the total form length and comment on the following:

   - Do you think it is worth ripping a 2×6 down to 5 inches for the edge form? Why or why not?
   - Using a full width 2×6 for the edge form, how much more concrete is used in the 5½-inch thick floor than in the 5 inches specified? At a material cost of $60 per cubic yard for the concrete, how much will this add to the cost of the SOG? Does this have any bearing on the consideration of ripping a 2×6 down to 5 inches?
   - How can a 5-inch floor be placed without ripping down a 2×6 or incurring the additional cost for the extra concrete?

4. What is the unit weight of the following structural steel members:

   - W10×12
   - W18×40
   - W21×44
   - TS10×10×⁵⁄₁₆
   - TS8×8×¼
   - Plate ½ × 12

8

PRICING
SELF-PERFORMED
WORK

8.1 INTRODUCTION

Recapitulation (recap), the fourth level of the lump-sum estimating process shown in Figure 6-1, is a summarizing process that follows the QTO work. Quantity totals are used as the basis of the tasks listed on the recap sheets. These tasks are then priced and totaled. In some cases, the amount of work requires several recap sheets, and a summary recap is used to consolidate them. The recap process involves transferring numbers from the quantity sheets; consequently, errors are likely to occur. An estimator should make it a habit to implement error prevention procedures to minimize the potential for making errors in the estimate.

Along with error prevention, the estimator should apply good organizational skills. Attaching the recap to the top of a group of QTO sheets from which data has been transferred completes a package of information that can be easily checked and used later by the project team. If a summary recap is necessary, it should be attached to the corresponding groups of recap/QTO packages used to generate it. These should then be filed in a manila folder or in a three-ring binder as discussed in Chapter 6.

8.2 RECAPITULATION SHEET

The recap sheet is used to gather the quantified data, apply pricing factors, and perform calculations that result in the various costs that make up a bid. It is also used as a summary recap to consolidate several priced work activities into a single line item cost for a particular group of work. In Chapter 11, we will see how this number is then entered onto the bid sum-

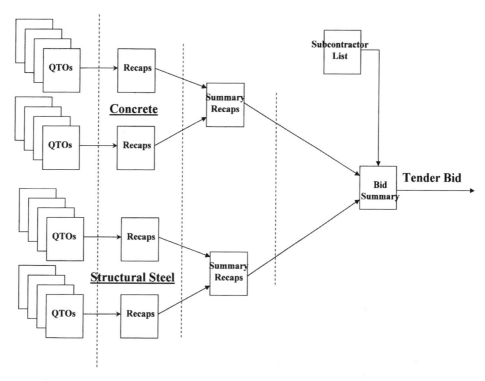

FIGURE 8–1 Recapitulation flow chart.

mary form to complete the estimate. Figure 8-1 is a flow chart that illustrates the recapitulation process. Standard recap Form F-5 is shown in Appendix F.

The recap sheet is a relatively standard form. The title area is essentially the same as that on the quantity sheet, except that the recap has a line for the name of the architect or engineer. This item is optional and may be more useful for historical purposes, but an estimator is encouraged to always fill it in. All other information must be filled in for the same reasons as discussed in Chapter 7.

Starting at the left, the first column is primarily for a cost code. It can be left blank or used for custom information, such as a drawing or addendum reference. After the job is won, the project manager may want to use this column for designating cost codes. The sec/det column may be used to reference a particular section or detail from the drawings.

The description column on the quantity sheet lists the items being quantified. On some recap sheets, the tasks shown will be the same as the column headings on the quantity sheet. For example, on the QTO sheet for the spot footings (Figures 7-1 and 7-2), the columns were forms, fine grade, concrete, rod off (finish), excavation and backfill, and reinforcing steel. Figure 8-2 shows a completed recap for the interior spot footings. Note that the line item descriptions are basically the same as the column headings on the quantity sheet. The two columns following the description are the quantity and units columns. The quantities to be entered are the double underlined totals from the quantity sheet with the units always shown.

Recapitulation

Project: The Training Center
Location: Kent, WA
Arch./Engr.: LM

Date: May 26, 2003
Estimator: P. Jacobs
Estimate #: TTC-1

Division 3 Concrete

Code	Sec/Det	Description	Qty	Unit	UMH	Man Hours	Wage Rate	Unit L Cost	Labor Cost	Unit M Cost	Material Cost	Total Cost
		Interior spot footings										
23440	2035	Structural excavation	125.8	bcy	0.178	22.4	28.56	5.08	640	5.05	635	1,275
31430	5050	Form footings (2 use)	733	sfca	0.086	63.0	28.58	2.46	1,802	3.23	2,368	4,169
		Fine grade	1,046	sfca	0.04	41.8	24.71	0.99	1,034	–	–	1,034
		Reinforcing steel	0.56	ton	15.238	8.5	28.22	430.02	241	–	–	241
		Purchase concrete[1]	68.5	cy						63.00	4,315	4,315
		Transport concrete[2]	0	cy						–	–	–
		Place concrete	66.5	cy	0.4	26.6	26.58	10.63	707	–	–	707
		Rod off concrete	1,046	sf	0.01	10.5	26.58	0.27	278	–	–	278
2315	2020&11	Backfill	84.2	cy	0.009	0.8	27.34	0.25	21	1.37	115	136
	2020	Dispose of excess excav matl	93.8	cy	0.012	1.1	28.56	0.34	32	0.70	66	98
		(spread on site)									–	–
		Nail, form oil etc,[3]	1	lot							118	118
		Reinforcing steel accessories[4]	1	lot							30	30

1 Includes 3% waste
2 Footing concrete is placed from chute in back of mixer truck
3 5% of form material cost
4 10% of reinforcing steel cost based on $550/ton

Page Totals (to bid summary)   175 $4,754 $7,647 $12,401
Add labor burden @ 45% of labor   2,139   2,139
Add reinf. steel mat'l @ $560/ton (major supply item not included above)   314
Total Cost $14,854
Assembly Check/(cy of concrete) =   2.63 $ 223

FIGURE 8–2 Recap sheet for interior spot footings.

A consistent procedure should be used when transferring information from the quantity sheets to the recap sheet to minimize the chance of errors. When the quantity from the QTO is transferred to the recap sheet, the estimator should make sure that the number has been entered on the recap sheet exactly as it is shown on the quantity sheet along with the correct units. A common error is transposing numbers within the quantity being transferred.

Once it has been verified that the quantity shown on the recap sheet is exactly the same as on the quantity sheet, the double underlined total on the quantity sheet is circled. This indicates to others that the checked total has been used on the next sheet in the sequence, in this case the recap. Circling should always be done when the quantity is transferred instead of waiting until later. Time constraints as bid day gets closer may affect the thoroughness of checking. Figure 8-3 is a repeat of Figure 7-1, but it shows that the transferred totals of Figure 7-1 have been circled.

The estimator is encouraged to group only like items on a recap sheet. Figure 8-2 shows the interior spot footings and may eventually include the perimeter footings as well. The totals then will reflect the man-hours and the labor and material costs for all of the building footings. The SOG, mezzanine slab, and miscellaneous concrete will each be on separate recap pages. Totals from all of these pages will be consolidated onto a summary recap whose totals will then represent the cost for all cast-in-place (CIP) concrete work. Later the CIP concrete will be entered as a line item on the bid summary.

8.3   MATERIALS

Material pricing is straightforward when done on the recap sheet. The material unit price is entered in the column headed Unit M Cost. It is then multiplied by the quantity to get the total material cost in dollars. An estimator must ensure that the units of the unit price are the same as those of the quantity.

Unit prices can be obtained in several ways. The first is to use published estimating reference data. Current pricing also is available through some subscription services. Most estimating references are published annually, and their prices have been updated during the previous year. They are representative of a nationwide average and may not reflect the prices of a particular location. A second source is from historical data maintained by the estimator. Data may come from cost reports of previous jobs or from recent estimates. The age and verifiability of these prices must be kept in mind if the estimator decides to use them. Prices that are a year or more old should, at a minimum, be adjusted for inflation. The best way to obtain unit prices is to solicit them from vendors. The estimator can explain to them what the job is and when it is expected to be performed. As a result, the vendors will usually honor their pricing throughout the duration of the work.

An estimator must understand that some material prices can be solicited during the estimating process, but others will not be received until bid day. Vendors that are major material suppliers, such as reinforcing steel and structural steel fabricators, will submit their prices as complete bids on bid day. Materials that are priced by the unit, such as concrete and lumber, can be priced by calling the vendors during the course of the estimating process. In some cases, bid prices also may be received from them on bid day, which may require the estimator to make a last-minute adjustment to the over-all bid.

Quantity Sheet

Date: May 20, 2003
Estimator: P. Jacobs
Est #: TTC-1

Project: The Training Center
Location: Kent, WA

Division 3 Concrete

Ref	Description	Qty (ea)	L (ft)	W (ft)	H (ft)	Forms (sfca)	Fine Grade (sf)	Concrete (cf)	Concrete (cy)	Rod Off[1] (sf)	Excavation Depth (ft)	Excavation (bcf)	Backfill (cf)
S-2.0	Spot footings												
	F 8.5	2	8.5	8.5	1.5	102	145	217		145	1.42	444	227
	F 9.5	2	9.5	9.5	1.67	127	181	301		181	1.59	580	279
	F 10	5	10	10	1.75	350	500	875		500	1.67	1,637	762
	F 10.5	2	10.5	10.5	1.83	154	221	404		221	1.75	736	332
	Subtotal Concrete & Excavation					733	1,047	1,797		1,047		3,396	1,600
							divide by 27 = 66.5			divide by 27 = 125.8			59.3
										Cross check			OK
										Swell	x 1.35 =		80.0
										Backfill	divide by 0.95 =		84.2
										Disposal—haul off			85.6

Backfill (lcy) = [excavation (bcy) - concrete volume (cy)] x swell factor (1.35) / compaction factor (0.95)

Backfill = [125.8 bcy - 66.5 cy] x 1.35 / 0.95 = 84.2 lcy

Disposal (lcy) = [excavation (bcy) x swell factor (1.35)] - backfill (lcy)

Disposal (lcy) = [125.8 bcy x 1.35] - 84.2 lcy = 85.6 lcy

Anchor bolts are 5/8 inch diameter expansion anchors— see structural steel.

[1] Rod Off is a type of finish that levels the concrete to the top of the forms.

bcy = bank cubic yards; lcy = loose cubic yards

FIGURE 8–3 Circling of transferred totals.

Concrete

Concrete is priced by the cubic yard delivered to the job site. The vendor needs to know the concrete specifications and the approximate quantity of each type being used. For example, the Training Center specifications call for 2,500 pound per square inch (psi) concrete for the footings and SOG, 3,000 psi for the mezzanine slab and 4,000 psi for the tilt-up walls. Exterior paving is to be air entrained to 6% and maximum slump for all concrete is 4 inches. The *project manual* should be checked to see if superplasticizers or other additives that aid in the placing, finishing, or curing of the concrete can be used. The estimator should send the specifications to concrete suppliers and then follow up for pricing.

Lumber suppliers tend not to furnish prices on bid day. They prefer to have the estimator determine the approximate quantity of lumber and sheet goods required, and then they will furnish prices over the telephone. Some vendors price lumber according to each size, while others group certain sizes and price the group. Sheet material is priced according to type and size. The estimator should talk to a lumber supplier prior to estimating the work to learn how the pricing will be received. He or she can then set up the estimating sheets accordingly.

One item that deserves special attention is concrete form material. There are different ways to build forms depending on the type and size of the concrete elements being constructed. To price forms by the materials used is very time-consuming and not necessary on small projects. Construction firms generally have historical records that provide data on the cost of the material per square foot of contact area. This cost includes all lumber and sheet material, bracing, kickers, and form ties. Items such as nails and form oil are priced separately.

If the estimator does a study of concrete construction, he or she will see that for many elements, such as walls, elevated slabs, and elevated beams, the forming is the most expensive of all of the tasks. A contractor, in an effort to reduce this cost, will buy material that can be used more than once. For example, forming material will be purchased for only 1/4 of a long wall section. After the first placement, the forms will be stripped, cleaned, patched, and reused. Since the forms do not have to be built from scratch, a major cost reduction is realized in both the material and labor. It is common to use forms up to four times, and on occasion, five or six times.

When pricing form material, an estimator must have a good idea of how many times the forms will be used. There are eleven interior spot footings in the Training Center, and the estimator may look at the form material and decide that all of the footings will be placed at one time. Knowing that there will be multiple placements of the perimeter footings, the estimator can anticipate that the superintendent will place some of the spot footings with the placement of each perimeter footing. For example, the superintendent may construct two sets of forms for the F10.5 footings and two for the F10.0 footings. These will be placed at the same time as the first length of perimeter footings. After stripping, the F10.5 footing forms will be removed and cut down to form the F9.5 footings. On the next perimeter footing placement, two more F10.0 footings and the two F9.5 footings will be placed. The F9.5 footing forms will then be cut down and used on the F8.5 footings, and one set of the F10.0 forms will be used for the last footing of that size.

The estimator has a slight dilemma now in that most forms were used three times but one set was used only twice. This can be resolved by keeping in mind that two sets of forms have been modified after each concrete placement, which takes a little more labor than just cleaning and patching them. Using unit costs for two uses of forms will provide reasonable savings over single use and will eliminate the need for more complex calculations. With a little study, it can be seen that the largest benefit generally occurs when forms are used twice and that each additional use produces smaller savings.

In other situations in which forms are used more than once, the savings are more substantial than for footings. Walls require working at elevated levels, which reduces efficiency and increases costs. Multi-use forms, therefore, generate substantial savings over single use. The same is true for many elevated structures, such as beams, columns, and structural slabs.

Prefabricated metal forms can be rented for some common shapes, such as columns and beams. On some heavy construction projects, form costs can be reduced by having custom metal forms made and using them an indefinite number of times. Prefabricated forms are usually made of steel and are strong enough to minimize the need for any extra bracing that might be required for wood forms. If prefabricated forms are more economical, the estimator needs to obtain a quote from a form-rental supplier.

Occasionally the specifications will prescribe how long forms are to be left in place. Most superintendents remove forms as quickly as possible, so they can be reconditioned and set up for the next placement. The estimator must be aware of anticipated form use and concrete curing requirements before pricing them.

Other material prices that need to be determined are fasteners, bonding agents and curing compounds, chairs and tie wire, lifting inserts, and any other similar items. For nails and bonding agents, the estimator should use a percentage of the total form material cost, showing it as a line item on the recap sheet. Curing compound is applied only to flat slab surfaces, elevated slabs, and tilt-up panels. It is priced by the area of coverage. Tie wire and chairs are classed as reinforcing steel accessories and are calculated as a percentage to the reinforcing steel costs.

The estimator also needs to consider any hoisting equipment that may be required to lift forms into place. In some situations, the forms can be handled by a jobsite forklift. Multi-story projects will require a crane to lift the forms and set them. If a tower crane is to be used, it will be priced separately and does not need to be included in the concrete work. However, if a 20-ton crane is to be brought onto the jobsite just for handling the forms, its cost needs to be included in the concrete section of the estimate.

Steel

Structural steel material prices are furnished as competitive bids by fabrication shops. It is important for the estimator to know what is included and what is not. Bolts were discussed in Chapter 7, but as a reminder, the fabricator furnishes all steel-to-steel connecting bolts and all anchor bolts embedded in concrete. The general contractor will furnish all other bolts.

Another small item that is often overlooked is shim material. Shims are small pieces of steel plate that are placed under column base plates to set them to the proper elevation. The fabricator does not furnish shims, and the estimator must determine their cost and include them as a line item on the recap. Some companies have historical data that allows a percentage of the steel cost to be used to cover shims. The estimator must include the cost of shims and the grout under the base plates.

All structural steel needs hoisting equipment to handle it. This can be anything from a forklift to a heavy lift crane or traveling derrick. Equipment selection and costing can pose difficulties for the estimator. He or she should consult with a superintendent and an iron-worker foreman to determine the type and size of equipment that is best suited for the project. It is also important to discuss operating personnel and mobilization costs. Additional consultation with a company that rents hoisting equipment will provide rental rates, travel times and costs, and fuel and maintenance requirements.

Equipment

Equipment that is used for a specific set of activities of work is referred to as direct equipment. A crane brought on site specifically to hoist structural steel is a piece of direct equipment, because once this work is done, it will be removed from the site. The cost of this piece of equipment is charged only to the structural steel. Another example is a concrete pump that is used only for concrete work. On the other hand, a tower crane or jobsite forklift is used for many work activities for most of the duration of a project. Its cost is difficult to apportion to specific tasks and is therefore considered part of the jobsite overhead. This will be discussed in Chapter 10.

The estimator needs to understand the characteristics of hoisting equipment when sizing it for a particular job. A forklift has a rated capacity based on the load being a certain distance from the backstop and with the forks positioned near the ground. Once the load is elevated or a boom is extended, the lift's capacity is reduced due to an increased tendency of tipping. This is basically true for cranes also. An accurate determination of the weight of a load and equipment rating tables will provide information on sizing the equipment to the job. The estimator should always discuss hoisting with a superintendent so that properly sized equipment is priced.

Concrete pumps can be a source of confusion for the estimator. Many estimators will price pumping at a historical rate such as $9.00 per cubic yard for all concrete. This is satisfactory as long as the estimator understands what makes up the pumping cost and what affects the rate. A concrete pump carries a minimum charge for just showing up at the site plus a rate per cubic yard for pumping. For most quantities to be pumped at a given time, the rate used by the estimator is usually fairly accurate. If a small quantity is to be pumped, the pumping unit cost will be much higher, because the minimum pumping charge is applied to the small quantity of concrete. Large placements will have a lower pumping unit cost. If the pumping costs are high, the estimator should identify another more economical means of placing the concrete.

Concrete pumps come in various sizes, and the estimator must anticipate a placement rate. Pumps that are too large are more expensive, and those that are too small will affect the placing labor cost. Another item to consider is the amount of time a concrete truck is at the job site. The price of the concrete typically includes transportation to and from the site and 20 minutes for standby and placement time. A small pump can cause additional costs by keeping the concrete truck on site too long.

8.4   LABOR

General contracting is a challenge because a contractor bids to perform work for the lowest price with a temporary workforce. The key to being effective is to have key field personnel who can direct and perform the work efficiently and correctly. Direct labor is a general contractor's own labor force that does the construction work. It also represents his or her firm's greatest risk. Labor costs are determined in one of several ways. An estimator must be aware of these methods, because some bids may ask for labor rates, and he or she should know the proper way to determine them. Some of the factors of labor pricing are as follows:

Productivity Factors vs. Labor Unit Prices

Labor costs can be determined by using either labor unit prices or productivity factors and wage rates. Labor unit prices are expressed as dollars per unit of the quantity being priced—for example, dollars per square foot—and are subject to revision due to a change in the wage rate, fringe benefits, and/or tax rates. Productivity, on the other hand, is expressed as man-hours per unit and is constant over time for a given work task.

Figure 8-2 shows columns for both unit man-hours and labor unit prices. Labor costs are calculated by entering the unit man-hours and the current wage rate without fringe benefits or labor taxes. The unit man-hours are multiplied by the quantity to get the man-hours, which in turn are multiplied by the wage rates, with the result being the labor costs. Labor cost can then be divided by the quantity to get the unit labor cost, which can be used as a check against historical information. Using current wage data, this process eliminates the need to make adjustments in labor costs over time. Fringe benefits and labor taxes are accounted for at the end of the estimating process and will be discussed in Chapter 11.

An estimator should always calculate the unit labor cost and use it as a checking tool. For example, if unit man-hours times the wage rate equals a unit labor cost of $10 per board foot, and $0.10 per board foot is more in line with historical costs, the estimator knows there is an error.

Productivity

Productivity is the amount of time it takes a person to do a unit of work. Examples of productivity factors are man-hours per square foot of contact area for concrete forms or man-hours per ton of steel. They are entered in the unit man-hours (UMH) column on the recap. When multiplied by the quantity, the result is the man-hours needed to complete the line item. Most published estimating references show productivity factors and will delineate the crew that does the work and the daily output for the crew. The productivity in man-hours per unit and the crew makeup are important. Daily output is used in planning and scheduling after the project has been won.

Many contractors record cost information based on unit labor costs and do not bother with productivity factors. Cost accounting systems in use today can determine historical productivity factors and provide the estimator with a wealth of information. The practice of using productivity factors helps to produce good estimates and reduces the amount of work by eliminating the need to adjust for inflation. Consider the following:

(quantity)(unit labor cost) = total cost,
which must be adjusted for inflation for future use,

whereas:

(quantity)(productivity factor)(wage rate) = total cost.
For future use, only the wage rate needs to be updated.

Adjusting for inflation can be done, but judgment must be exercised to estimate how it has affected construction costs. Conversely, updating a wage rate does not require judgment.

The Cost of Labor

Three basic elements that make up the cost of labor are wages, fringe benefits, and payroll taxes. Other elements that may be part of the cost are travel, per diem, and overtime. Projects performed by local contractors seldom need to account for travel and per diem, and most commercial projects tend not to require overtime.

Of the three basic elements, two are negotiable, and one is mandated by the government. Wages are paid based on hours worked with straight time generally being the first 8 hours worked per day up to 40 hours per week. Overtime comes generally in two multiples, time-and-a-half (wages × 1.5) or double time (wages × 2). All time over the base wage rate is classified as *premium time* because it represents the premium cost of working a person beyond the agreed-upon normal pay period.

Fringe benefits are items such as health and welfare, pension, apprenticeship fund, and in some cases, dental insurance and/or annuity. Benefits are paid based on each hour worked and are not subject to the effects of premium time.

Payroll taxes are government-mandated taxes and are based on the amount of total wages paid. They consist of FICA (social security), state unemployment insurance, federal unemployment insurance, and *workers' compensation insurance*. The first three are calculated as a percentage of the actual wages paid. Workers' compensation may be either a percentage calculation or a specified hourly deduction depending on the state. It is important for the estimator to know how the fringe benefits and payroll taxes are calculated, because they will affect the labor burden percentage used later on the bid summary sheet.

Another item for the estimator's personal notebook is a sheet of local wage rates and fringe benefits. The information should be available from the company payroll department. Figure 8-4 is an example of the cost for union carpenters at the location of the Training Center. This example also shows the payroll taxes and a hypothetical workers' compensation rate.

The combination of fringe benefits and payroll taxes are commonly referred to as *labor burden*. This burden can vary widely from one trade to another, and the estimator can spend an inordinate amount of time calculating them for each crew. It is common to determine an average labor burden based on the overall makeup of all tradespersons employed by the company. This average can then be used for most estimating purposes. To keep things simple, only the base wage rate is used on the recap sheets, and the labor burden is then calculated from the total direct work labor cost and inserted as a line item on the bid summary.

Occasionally the estimator will encounter a project in a remote location. The work force has to travel to the site and stay there for certain periods of time. The travel and per diem costs have to be included in the bid. These, like the labor burden, are shown as a line item on the bid summary.

Subcontractors and some general contractors use a taxable wage on the recap sheet. This wage includes the base wage rate plus those fringe benefits that are subject to payroll taxes. Wages for apprentices are variable depending on the workers' training time and progress. An estimator should not use apprentice wage rates for any pricing, unless specifically requested by the project owner.

Western Construction Company

Labor Burden Detail						
Western Washington State CARPENTERS	Journeyman			Foreman		
	Straight Time	**Time & a Half**	**Double Time**	**Straight Time**	**Time & a Half**	**Double Time**
Rates	$27.95	$41.93	$55.90	$30.47	$45.71	$60.94
Health & Welfare	2.90	2.90	2.90	2.90	2.90	2.90
Pension	3.87	3.87	3.87	3.87	3.87	3.87
Apprentice	0.35	0.35	0.35	0.35	0.35	0.35
Total Fringes	7.12	7.12	7.12	7.12	7.12	7.12
Taxable Wage Rate	35.07	49.05	63.02	37.59	52.83	68.06
FICA @ 7.65%	2.14	3.21	4.28	2.33	3.50	4.66
State Unemployment @ 5.42%	1.51	2.27	3.03	1.65	2.48	3.30
Federal Unemployment @ .8%	0.22	0.34	0.45	0.24	0.37	0.49
Workers' Comp. @ $2.0859 per Hr.	2.09	2.09	2.09	2.09	2.09	2.09
Total Payroll Taxes & Insurance	5.96	7.91	9.85	6.31	8.44	10.54
Labor Burden (total fringes + total labor taxes and insurance)	13.08	15.03	16.97	13.43	15.56	17.66
Total Labor Rate (wage rate + fringes + payroll taxes & insurance)	$41.03	$56.96	$72.87	$43.90	$61.27	$78.60

Labor Burden [(fringes + payroll taxes + insurance) divided by base wage rate]	46.80%	35.85%	30.36%	44.08%	34.04%	28.98%

Companies typically use a calculated average labor burden based on the manpower used during a given year. For example, a company that uses carpenters, some ironworkers, and laborers may have an overall average labor burden of 49%.

FIGURE 8–4 Labor rates.

8.5 APPLYING PRICING FACTORS

In illustrating how the recap sheet is used, reference will be made to the quantity sheets developed in Chapter 7.

Concrete

Referring to Figure 8-2, the application of the pricing factors are shown in the Unit M Cost column. The estimator should make sure that the units of the unit prices match the units shown after the quantity unit column. As long as the units of the quantity and the material unit price match, it is not necessary to indicate units anywhere but in the designated column after the quantity.

The unit prices and quantities are extended (multiplied) to determine material cost of the line item. Note that the figures to the right of the decimal point are insignificant and are not shown. There are some spaces in the unit M cost column for which no cost is entered. A zero or dash should always be entered, so that others will know that there is no material and that a cost was not accidentally omitted.

Two line items are shown that were not quantified on the quantity sheets. These are accessory items that are priced by calculating them as a percentage of some other cost. Nails and form oil are noted as 5% of the form material costs. There is no unit price, because this line item is shown as an undefined quantity. The space in the material cost column is a formula that calculates 5% of the total form material. If the form material cost is changed, this line will automatically be adjusted.

The second accessory line item is miscellaneous material needed for installing the reinforcing steel. This cost covers the purchase of the tie wire, chairs, doby, or other supports specified to give the proper spacing to the bars. The note indicates that the cost is calculated as 10% of the cost of the reinforcing steel material. The actual price for the reinforcing steel will not be known until bid day, but it has been quantified by weight so a simple extension will determine a cost. Unless there is a wide variation in the weight shown on supplier's bid and that quantified, an adjustment in the calculation of the reinforcing steel accessories on bid day will not be necessary.

Labor productivity in unit man-hours (UMH) and wage rates have been used in Figure 8-2 to determine the labor cost of each line item. The estimator may question what wage rate is the correct one to use for composite crews. Some will pick a rate that is representative of all work and use it throughout the entire estimate. A better approach is to determine a composite wage rate based on the type of work being done. Where a crew is one foreman and a crew of three or four carpenters, the composite wage rate is relatively easy to determine. When it comes to a concrete placing crew, several trades are involved, and the calculation is more complex.

Figure 8-5 shows a calculation sheet that can be used to determine the composite wage rate for crews being used to perform a given task. Several crews have been shown. The calculations on this form are simple, and an estimator can quickly set it up so that it only needs to be updated annually for the current wage rates. Only the base wage rates are used in the form, but taxable rates can be substituted if this is what is being used in the estimate.

Each column pair on the form is headed with a name for a particular crew. The current wage rates for the journeyman, foreman, and general foreman are entered for each trade. The number of individuals are entered into the proper column and multiplied by the wage rates to get the total cost of the line item. The columns are summed, and the total cost is divided by the size of the crew to determine a composite wage rate. The cost column can be set up with a formula that calculates the cost only if a number has been entered into the No. column, which makes the work go a little faster. These composite wage rate calculations should be filed with the estimate as supplemental information.

The estimator should determine composite wage rates for the several crews that will do most of the work on a project. Slight variations will make little difference in costs, unless the work extends over a long period. For example, one form-building crew might be made up of three journeymen and one foreman, another might be one foreman and one journeyman, and a third might be five journeymen and one foreman. These variations make little

Project: *The Training Center*
Location: *Kent, WA*

Date: *May 26, 2003*
Est. #: *TTC-1*

Trade/Rank	Base Wage	Forming		Conc. Placing		Concrete Finishing		Steel Erection		Tilt-Up Const	
		No.	Cost	No.	Cost	No.	Cost	No.	Cost	No.	Cost
Carpenter											
Journeyman	$27.95	3	$83.85							5	$139.75
Foreman	$30.47	1	$30.47	1	$30.47					1	$30.47
General foreman											
Cement mason											
Journeyman	$28.05			2	$56.10	10	$280.50			2	$56.10
Foreman	$29.30					1	$29.30				
General foreman											
Ironworker											
Journeyman	$27.22			1	$27.22			7	$190.54	2	$54.44
Foreman	$29.22							2	$58.44		
General foreman	$30.22										
Laborer											
Journeyman	$24.71			4	$98.84					4	$98.84
Foreman	$26.49										
General foreman											
Total No. in Crew		4		8		11		9		14	
Composite Wage		**$28.58**		**$26.58**		**$28.16**		**$27.66**		**$27.11**	

Notes:
1. *Base wage is the base hourly rate without fringes and payroll taxes.*

FIGURE 8–5 Composite crew rate calculations.

difference because the foreman might run slightly different crew compositions than what can be anticipated. They do, however, take into account the cost of foremen.

When all recap entries have been completed and the extensions made, the man-hour, labor cost, material cost, and total cost columns are summed to totals at the bottom of the page. Two checks should be made at this point. First, the page should be scanned to make sure it is complete and that every line item has the entries and appropriate calculations. The summation ranges should also be checked. The format of the page is such that the line items are totaled to the total cost column, which is then summed to a total at the bottom of the page. A crosscheck now should be made. This check adds the totals of the labor cost and material cost columns to make sure that the result equals the sum of the total cost column. If it does not, there is an error on the recap sheet.

When completed, the estimator may wonder whether the cost is competitive or not. A quick assemblies check, as shown at the bottom of Figure 8-2, will provide a unit cost that can be used as a check against other estimates or data. An assemblies check unitizes certain figures to a common quantity on the recap sheet. In this case, the man-hours per cubic yard of concrete placed and the total cost per cubic yard placed are calculated. The first figure shows 2.63 man-hours per cubic yard to construct the spread footings including the excavation and backfill. The second figure is the total cost of $223 per cubic yard. If the estimator has done several estimates, he or she will attain a level of comfort with these figures.

The estimator should also check the wage rate for the entire recap sheet. This is done by dividing the total labor cost by the total man-hours. The result should approximate that of the various wage rates used on the sheet. If there is a wide variation, the estimator knows that there is an error in the labor cost calculation and must devote the time to find it.

The recapitulation of the tilt-up panels will be similar to that of other concrete except that it will also include the hoisting, shimming, bracing, and grouting of the panels. Figure 8-6 is a recap sheet for the three panels quantified in Figures 7-3 and 7-4. The same checking and circling procedure is used on the tilt-up quantity sheets as was done for the spread footings.

Published references provide varying data on tilt-up wall panels. Some give a detailed account of the items that make up the construction costs, and others only give an average price per square foot of panel. If the estimator lacks a good sample estimate to use as a model for his or her work, it is worthwhile to find an estimating reference that provides details of the various costs. These details can then be used as a guide to obtain local pricing.

The estimator may not be able to find good reference information for the tasks required to construct tilt-up panels. A little thought about what they are similar to will be helpful. For example, thinking about a slab on grade, the slab preparation is similar to fine grading, and applying bonding agent is similar to a sprayed membrane curing compound. Edge forms are similar to SOG forms, and placing and finishing of the concrete are also similar to a SOG. Reinforcing steel is a little heavier, but labor productivity is based on weight so this task is easily defined. This leaves only the inserts, hoisting, and setting of panels as the unknowns. Grouting is given in most estimating references. Backfilling in preparation for the closure strip has already been accounted for in the SOG section of the estimate. This analogy will aid in developing most of the costs of the tilt-up panels, and consulting with a knowledgeable superintendent or ironworker foreman will provide the rest.

Note that Figure 8-6 shows a detailed task listing of the work required. The first item, "Prepare pouring slab," has been noted to include the application of a bond breaker to the slab.

Recapitulation

Project: *The Training Center*
Location: *Kent, WA*
Arch./Engr.: *LM*

Date: *May 26, 2003*
Estimator: *P. Jacobs*
Estimate #: *TTC-1*

Division 3 Concrete

Code	Sec/Det	Description	Qty	Unit	UMH	Man Hours	Wage Rate	Unit L Cost	Labor Cost	Unit M Cost	Material Cost	Total Cost
		Tilt-up Wall Panels #1, 2, 3										
		Prepare pouring slab[1]	2,522	sf	0.004	10.088	28.58	0.11	288	0.02	50	339
		Form wall panels	643	lf	0.03	19.29	28.58	0.86	551	0.75	482	1,034
		Reinforcing steel	3.285	tons	0.027	0.0887	27.66	0.75	2	550.00	1,807	1,809
		Embeds	24	ea	0.25	6	28.58	7.15	171	5.00	120	291
		Hoisting anchors	24	ea	0.25	6	28.58	7.15	171	2.25	54	225
		Purchase concrete	58.1	cy				–	–	63.00	3,663	3,663
		Pump concrete	56.444	cy				–	–	9.00	508	508
		Place concrete	56.444	cy	0.492	27.771	26.58	13.08	738	–	–	738
		Finish panels (steel trowel)	2,522	sf	0.015	37.83	28.16	0.42	1,065	–	–	1,065
		Curing compound	2,522	sf	0.0017	4.237	28.16	0.05	119	0.04	101	220
		Hoist and set panels	3	ea	1	3	27.11	27.11	81	–	–	81
		Braces	9	ea				–	–	5.00	45	45
		Shims	267	lb				–	–	0.65	174	174
		Grout	3	cf	2.9	8.7	28.16	81.66	245	125.40	376	621
		185-ton crane	1	hr				–	–	215.00	215	215
		in & out & mobilization	1	l/s	8	8	27.66	221.28	221	1,500.00	1,500	1,721
		Detail lift points	3	pnls						25.00	75	75
		Weld joints	24.67	lf	0.2	20.58	27.66	23.07	569	2.13	53	622
		(incl mat'l & equip.)										
		Grout—see misc concrete										
	1	*Building SOG, includes cleaning, layout, and bond breaker.*										
						152			$4,225		$9,222	$13,447
						0.06			$1.68		$3.66	$5.33

Assembly Check/sf =

FIGURE 8–6 Recap of tilt-up wall panels.

This is done after the forms are in place and is the only material cost in the slab preparation process. The form material was quantified in lineal feet similar to that of a slab on grade.

The number of hoisting anchors and their placement was determined at the time of the panel detailing. The estimator can determine how many will be needed by first, consulting with a superintendent or ironworker foreman to determine what type of anchor is preferred. The estimator will also want to have a catalog of concrete accessories that shows hoisting anchors and their load data. He or she should also have some basic knowledge of structural properties.

To determine the number of lifting inserts in panel #1 for the Training Center, the weight of the panel is calculated by multiplying the concrete volume in cubic feet by a unit weight of 150 pounds per cubic foot. This results in a panel weight of approximately 85,950 pounds. Typical vendor data recommends that even though the sizing information incorporates a 2:1 safety factor, 33% should be added to allow for the extra tension required to break the bond between the panel and the forming slab. Adding 33% to the calculated weight results in a total weight of 114,305 pounds. A data table for the inserts may show one capacity figure for face tension and one for face shear. The face tension is the critical one, since it is experienced in the bond-breaking process. An insert is selected and its capacity is divided into the total weight. Using a 16,000-pound capacity face tension insert:

$$114,305 \text{ pounds} \div 16,000 \text{ pounds per insert} = 7.14 \text{ inserts required.}$$

The estimator should use 8 inserts for this panel. Always have the vendor's sales engineer verify these calculations, and use the results only for pricing purposes. The final panel detailing may cause a variation in the number and type of inserts, but the cost difference is generally insignificant.

Some items on the tilt-up recap are unique to this particular type of construction. These include braces, shims, and grout. When a panel is installed, it needs to be leveled and set at the proper elevation. Tops of footings are designed to be slightly low so the panel can be set on shim packs. This does two things: (1) allows adjustment so the panel can be set to the proper elevation and (2) provides a space in which grout will be inserted so the panel will have full bearing on the footing. Once the panels are in place, they need to be braced until the structural steel and/or roof system is completed. A concrete-accessories vendor will provide shim packs and grout, and rent braces to the job. This vendor is a good source of pricing information. From a labor standpoint, the installation of the shims and all the work involved with the braces is included in the panel hoisting and setting cost. Grouting is a separate operation and needs to be priced accordingly.

Near the end of the listing on the recap are two line items for the crane that will be used to hoist the panels. Assuming that panel #1 is the heaviest, its calculated weight including the 33% for bond breaking is approximately 57 tons. The estimator must have someone who is knowledgeable about cranes and their operation select the crane required or he or she must learn to use crane rating tables that are available from vendors who rent cranes. Remember that crane capacity drops off very fast from their nominal rating, and the last thing an estimator wants is for the job to experience a financial loss or, worse yet, have an accident caused by selecting too small a crane.

Some estimators like to show the crane in the general conditions section of an estimate; however, this is incorrect. The crane for hoisting the panels is used only for that purpose and should be included with the recap that shows the tilt-up work. By contrast, if the building were constructed with a stucco finish or a brick veneer, the crane would not be required. Also, the estimator must include the transportation to and from the site and, if a lattice boom unit is being used, the mobilization costs. Mobilization will include the cost of renting the unit for the mobilization time and the cost of the general contractor's ironworkers who will assemble the boom and thread the cabling. There will also be a similar cost at the end of the work to prepare the crane for transportation back to its base. If a hydraulic crane is being used, there is only the transportation charge because the onsite mobilization is very short and can be considered part of the operation.

Two miscellaneous items need to be added to the tilt-up recap sheet. The first is the detailing of the lift points, which must be done by a qualified structural engineer. This cost is the responsibility of the general contractor and is to be included in the estimate. The estimator needs to find out who his or her company regularly employs for panel detailing and have them provide an estimated cost for the work.

The second miscellaneous item is patching the lifting and bracing points after the panels have been set and the structural steel erection has been completed. The patching is a cement-based material, and the work usually is done by the general contractor's own forces. The estimator can determine the labor and material cost of doing a single patch and multiply the answer by the number of places that require patching. Some estimators will use a historical percentage for the patching work in lieu of quantifying the number required. This is one of the items that belongs in the 80% of the work that is only 20% of the costs, and an established percentage is usually accurate enough for an estimate. When finished, the estimator must do the operational and accounting checks as discussed for footing recaps. The assemblies check is done on a square foot basis for a given thickness of wall. In Figure 8-6, the labor cost is $1.68 per square foot, which may be a little low, and the cost for the material and equipment is $3.66 per square foot, which may be a little high. The overall total is reasonable, so one would go back and look for adjustments in the material and labor columns. This is important because of the way the labor burden will be applied on the bid summary.

Structural Steel

A recap for structural and miscellaneous steel erection contains tasks that are not necessarily shown as columns on the quantity sheets. The examples shown in Figures 7-5 and 7-6 were only a part of all of the items that need to be taken off. Figure 8-7 shows a typical listing of work that is required for the structural steel erection.

This recap sheet is straightforward, but there are a few items that need to be addressed. Estimating references commonly provide productivity in terms of man-hours per ton of steel. If the estimator has not quantified the steel by weight, this productivity factor is of no use. A more accurate way to perform the labor estimate is to know the crew size and capabilities. For most projects, structural steel will be erected with a five-person crew commonly called the raising gang. This crew should be capable of installing forty pieces of steel a day for most of the structural members. Once the steel is plumbed and aligned, a two-person bolt crew will install the remaining bolts. This is done on a mechanical lift, and a good crew should be able to install and tighten a bolt every 2 minutes. This time includes required inspections by the building department.

Joists and decking are installed relatively quickly. Estimating references show joists installed by the lineal foot. The estimator should talk to an ironworker foreman to deter-

Recapitulation

Project: *The Training Center*
Location: *Kent, WA*
Arch./Engr.: *LM*

Date: *May 27, 2003*
Estimator: *P. Jacobs*
Estimate #: *TTC-1*

Division 5 Metals

Code	Sec/Det	Description	Qty	Unit	UMH	Man Hours	Wage Rate	Unit L Cost	Labor Cost	Unit M Cost	Material Cost	Total Cost
		Structural and Misc. Steel										
		Unload and shakeout	1	l/s	8	8	27.66	221.28	221			221
		Erect columns	16	ea	1	16	27.66	27.66	443			443
		Erect beams	20	ea	1	20	27.66	27.66	553			553
		Plumb and align	1	l/s	20	20	27.66	553.20	553			553
		Install end braces	18	ea	1	18	27.66	27.66	498			498
		Install slab edge forms	435	lf	0.022	10	27.66	0.61	265			265
		Welding	62	lf	0.267	17	27.66	7.39	458	0.74	46	504
		Bolt up framing	840	bolts	0.07	59	27.66	1.94	1,626			1,626
		Install girder joists	686	lf	0.044	30	27.66	1.22	835			835
		Install deck joists	5,215	lf	0.04	209	27.66	1.11	5,770			5,770
		Install bridging	3,100	lf	0.01	31	27.66	0.28	857			857
		Install mezzanine deck	8,010	sf	0.009	72	27.66	0.25	1,994			1,994
		Install roof deck	270	sq	0.7	189	27.66	19.00	5,228			5,228
		Shear studs	8,010	ea	0.016	128	27.66	0.44	3,545			3,545
		Install stairs and railings	52	risers	1.17	61	27.66	32.36	1,683			1,683
		Column shim packs	32	pks						2	64	64
		Expansion anchors	64	ea	0.2	13	27.66	5.53	354	3.29	211	565
		Manlifts	2	un/wk						2,500	5,000	5,000
		35-ton crane	12	hrs						105	1,260	1,260
		in & out (crane)	1	l/s						500	500	500
		Impact wrench	1	un/wk						125	125	125
		Welding machine	1	un/mo						210	210	210
		Stud welder	1	un/wk						400	400	400
						901			$24,883		$7,816	$32,699

FIGURE 8–7 Structural steel recap.

mine the time it will take to install the joists and related bracing. Bridging for the joists is listed and priced as a separate line item. Decking is priced by the square foot for slab form and by the square (100 sq ft) for roofs. Productivity includes its welding to the support structure. Shear studs are shown separately on the page and include the labor to weld them as well as the material cost of the studs and special welding equipment.

The estimator will see on the steel drawings that there is a requirement for two cement-based items—the grout under the column base plates and the fill and slab for stair treads and landings. Both of these should be quantified and recapped as miscellaneous concrete.

No assembly check is shown on the structural steel recap. If the estimator spent the time to quantify the steel in weight as well as number of pieces, an assembly check could be made based on tons of steel. A more common assembly check would be to unitize the man-hours and total cost in terms of square foot of the building footprint. This can be checked against other square foot cost data in either published or historical references.

Other Items

The general contractor who does some rough carpentry and finish carpentry, and who installs doors and toilet accessories will have QTO sheets and recaps for each of these. These are relatively simple and straightforward. Since the Training Center has no wood framing and little other rough carpentry, relatively little time will be spent on it. Material pricing is solicited from the lumber supplier, and published or historical productivity factors are commonly available. Doors and toilet accessories need only be priced for the installation labor in the direct work estimate. OM estimates for material will be done at a later time and bids will be received on bid day.

8.6   SUMMARY RECAP

A summary recap is an extra sheet on which to consolidate several recaps, as might be the case for the CIP concrete. The commercial bid summary that will be used in Chapter 11 is limited in the number of line items that can be used for direct work. Using a summary recap on some work allows more concise information to be entered onto the bid summary.

CIP concrete frequently is recapped on several sheets. There may be one for footings and foundations, one for floor slabs, one for CIP walls, and one for miscellaneous concrete, among others. The totals of these are listed as line items on a summary recap sheet, and then summed to a bottom line total for all CIP concrete activities. These totals are then ready to be transferred to the bid summary as a single line item. Figure 8-8 represents the start of a summary recap as it might appear for the Training Center. Tilt-up panels will not be included on the CIP concrete summary recap, because of the hoisting and setting operations that are unique to that work.

It should be noted that the summary recap does not contain all the information that is on a recap. It is only necessary to show the man-hours, labor cost, material cost, and total cost. After checking for transposition errors and range summations, and doing an accounting crosscheck, the totals on the summary recap are double underlined to show that they are ready to be transferred to the bid summary.

Recapitulation

Project: *The Training Center*
Location: *Kent, WA*
Arch./Engr.: *LM*

Date: *May 27, 2003*
Estimator: *P. Jacobs*
Estimate #: *TTC-1*

Division 3 CIP Concrete—Summary Recap

Code	Sec/ Det	Description	Qty	Unit	UMH	Man- Hours	Wage Rate	Unit L Cost	Labor Cost	Unit M Cost	Material Cost	Total Cost
		Interior Spot Footings	66.5	cy		175			$4,758		$7,643	$12,401
		Perimeter Footings										
		Elevator Pit Walls										
		SOG										
		Composite Floor Concrete										
		Total CIP Concrete	67						$4,758		$7,643	$12,401

FIGURE 8–8 Summary recap for Division 3.

Not all work activities will use a summary recap. Only those that require several re-caps for sub-activities, such as the CIP concrete, structural steel, and possibly the rough carpentry, will have them. Smaller items such as door installation, toilet accessories, and minor amounts of finish carpentry will have single page recaps.

8.7 SUMMARY

The recap process is the listing and pricing of the items that have been quantified. Some work activities, such as CIP concrete, require summary recap pages, which consolidate the totals of several recaps into a single total. This total is then entered as a single line item on the bid summary. During the recap process, quantities are transferred from the QTO sheets to the recap sheet. This operation can be a source of error, and the estimator needs to be dili-gent in following procedures for reducing them. Circling the totals on the QTO after they have been transferred eases the checking process later on.

Pricing of materials is a straightforward process. Data may be available from past projects the construction company has done. Published data also is available. Vendors pro-vide the most current unit prices for many materials. Labor pricing can be more difficult, especially if unit labor costs are used. These have to be adjusted for inflation. Productivity factors, which are man-hours per unit, are easier to use. They seldom change for a work ac-tivity, unless there is a new and innovative way of working more efficiently. Determining labor costs using productivity factors only necessitates the use of current wage rates, which are commonly available. This eliminates the need to apply inflation judgments to the cost-ing process. The estimator may then calculate the unit labor cost, if so desired, to use as a check against other similar projects.

There are two ways to use the wage rates in determining labor costs. The estimator can develop an average wage for all work of a class of activities and use it throughout those activities or he or she can develop a composite wage for crews used on particular activities. While the latter may be slightly more accurate, the average wage method is sufficient for most work and is easier to use.

The estimator needs to think about where the cost of certain equipment will go in the estimate. Some equipment is unique to certain activities, and the cost should be included in the direct work part of the estimate. A concrete pump, for example, is used only for the con-crete work and is a direct cost to those activities. The cost of a crane to hoist tilt-up wall pan-els should be shown on the recap for the panels. Equipment that is used throughout the job is considered an overhead cost and will be discussed in Chapter 10. Proper placing of equipment cost will have an effect on the checking procedures done as the estimate is completed.

8.8 REVIEW QUESTIONS

1. What is the purpose of a recapitulation sheet?
2. When is a summary recap page used?
3. What is a productivity factor and what are its units?
4. How is a crosscheck performed?
5. What can an assemblies check indicate?

6. What can a wage rate check indicate?
7. Where is the rental shown for equipment that is specific to an activity of work such as concrete tilt-up or structural steel?
8. Who are good resources for the estimator to consult with?
9. What is one of the best sources of information for pricing and productivity factors?
10. Is it necessary to check work once the recap sheets are started?

8.9 EXERCISES

1. Make a recap sheet for the concrete walls quantified in exercise 1 of Chapter 7. Using a current published estimating reference, price the material using the unit material prices shown. Price the labor costs using the productivity factors from the reference and current wage rates for the trades in your area. How do the labor costs calculated from the local wage rates differ from those using the published unit labor prices? What is the cause for the differences? Hint: What is included in the published costs?

2. Create a recap for the excavation and backfill in exercise 2 of Chapter 7. Price the work similar to exercise 1 above.

3. Perform assembly checks at the bottom of the recaps created in exercises 1 and 2. Using published assemblies estimating data, how do your costs compare? What might be the reason(s) for significant differences?

9

ESTIMATING SUBCONTRACTOR WORK

9.1   INTRODUCTION

Much of the work required to complete a project involves subcontractors and major material suppliers. Some general contractors estimate this work in detail and plan, upon winning the project, to solicit subcontractor/supplier quotations. This is risky and may not always prove to be the best method of doing business. A more common practice is for general contractors to solicit quotations from subcontractors and suppliers while preparing their bids. The advantage is that the general contractor, upon being awarded the contract, can immediately enter into agreements with the subcontractors and vendors knowing their final prices. The general contractors in this scenario, however, do not know the subcontractors' and suppliers' prices until near the time that bids must be submitted to the owner. To protect themselves, the contractors prepare OM estimates for the subcontractors' scope of work and the major suppliers' materials.

The sixth step in the lump-sum estimating process shown in Figure 6-1 provides a way to determine an approximate estimate of the cost of the overall project. In this step, the estimator creates OM estimates for the work that will be done by subcontractors and for the material furnished by major suppliers. OM estimates are a determination of the expected range of subcontractors' or major suppliers' quotations. The method for developing these estimates is not as detailed as was used for self-performed direct work, but is based on historical or published reference data. Since these estimates are based on averages for several projects, they do not consider some of the unique aspects of the project being bid. Architects and owners use similar approaches to estimate the construction costs of designs as discussed in Chapter 3.

Some categories of subcontract work, such as mechanical and electrical, represent significant portions of the project cost but are based on information that may not be completely detailed in the bid documents. It is difficult for an estimator to anticipate all of the work, because such things as routing of pipes, ducts, and wiring are left up to the subcontractor to determine. These OM estimates should not be used to complete the contractor's bid to the owner. Some of the smaller OM estimates, however, can be used in cases where no vendor quotations are received. OM estimates are useful in completing the first-run bid estimate so that various markups can be determined. The first run bid estimate will be discussed in Chapter 11.

9.2 SUBCONTRACTOR WORK

In Chapter 6, the estimator determined what portions of the project would be performed by subcontractors and what materials would be provided by major suppliers or fabricators. Form F-8 in Appendix F is a subcontractor list that can be used to show the work that will be done by these vendors. When listing them on the form, the estimator must be aware that some direct work sections will also be listed. For example, the general contractor may install the reinforcing steel, but a fabricator supplies it. The same usually is true for the structural steel. On bid day, the general contractor may receive bids for the reinforcing steel installation and for the structural steel erection. Figure 9-1 is a subcontractor list completed for the Training Center.

Subcontractor List

Project: The Training Center, Kent, WA   Estimator: Paul Jacobs   Est. #: TTC-1

Bin	Spec	Description	Bid	+ or −	Revised	Subcontractor
	02200	Earthwork				
	02215	Finish grading				
	02515	Exposed agg./conc. paving				
	02618	Pavement marking				
	02620	Concrete curbs				
	02621	Foundation drainage syst.				
	02711	Chain link fences & gates				
	03200	Reinforcing steel supply				
	03210	Reinforcing steel install				
	05100	Structural steel supply				
	05150	Structural steel install				
	05200	Metal joists and girders				
	05300	Metal decking				
	06240	Plastic laminates				
	06410	Cabinet work				
	07120	Fluid membrane waterproof				
	07210	Building insulation				

(continued)

FIGURE 9–1   Subcontractor list for The Training Center.

Bin	Spec	Description	Bid	+ or −	Revised	Subcontractor
	07270	Firestopping				
	07510	Built-up bituminous roofing				
	07600	Flashing and sheet metal				
	07810	Skylights				
	07830	Roof hatches				
	07900	Joint sealants				
	08110	Steel doors & frames				
	08330	Coiling doors				
	08670	Vertical lift doors				
	08410	Aluminum storefront syst.				
	08710	Finish hardware				
	09250	Gypsum wallboard				
	09310	Ceramic tile				
	09511	Acoustical panels				
	09540	Acoustical suspension syst.				
	09560	Resilient flooring				
	09681	Carpet cushion				
	09682	Carpeting				
	09900	Painting				
	10110	Markerboards & tackboards				
	10161	Toilet part. & urinal screens				
	10440	Signs				
	10445	Building ID numbers				
	10500	Metal lockers				
	10800	Toilet accessories				
	10905	Misc specialties				
	12501	Blinds & shades				
	12676	Recessed foot grills				
	12695	Entrance mats				
	14200	Elevator				
	15500	Fire sprinklers				
	15550	Fire extinguisher				
	15400	Plumbing				
	15500	HVAC				
	16000	Electrical				

Total Subcontracts _____ _____ _____

FIGURE 9–1 Continued.

When completing the subcontractor list, the estimator uses the WBS as a guide. This list is used more than once in the bid completion process. Each time it is used, it should be prominently identified, as OM Estimates or Final Run, so that the wrong version will not be used in the final bid.

As a reminder, not all materials are on this list. Only those that are procured from major suppliers, such as reinforcing steel and structural steel, are listed. Direct work items for which the estimator expects to receive subcontract bids should be broken out of the direct work estimate and listed on the subcontractor list. This is done by taking the total cost for the work, including labor taxes, and treating it as a vendor bid with the general contractor being the vendor. This price is then used in the first-run estimate and entered as one of the subcontractor prices on the bid evaluation worksheet on bid day. The estimator must make sure that the cost of these work items is eliminated from the direct work portion of the estimate. If the subcontractor's quotation is lower than the estimated cost of self-performing the work, the general contractor may choose to execute a contract with the subcontractor.

The procedure for generating an OM estimate is to perform a simple quantification of the work to be done and then apply unit prices. Sources of unit price data include published estimating references, historical databases, and the estimator's personal notebook. Prices for OM work do not need to be broken down into labor and material. Most references will show an overall unit price that includes a reasonable overhead and profit for the subcontractor. If productivity information is available, it can be entered on the recap sheet and extended to provide the total man-hours for the work. This information will be helpful when generating the project summary schedule discussed in Chapter 11.

After the bid has been tendered, the estimator should compare the OM estimates with the vendor prices. If there is a wide variation, it is useful to determine the reason. Performing this post-bid analysis will increase an estimator's skill in developing more realistic OM estimates in the future.

9.3 ESTIMATING SUBCONTRACTOR WORK FOR THE TRAINING CENTER

Several techniques are used to create OM estimates for the work that is to be subcontracted on the Training Center project. Most of the finishes are defined and can be quantified readily. The fire sprinklers are bidder design meaning that the subcontractor bidding the work will design the system and then furnish a price based on his or her design. The following discussion will cover the process of OM estimates for work that is easily quantified and items for which little information is available.

A typical example of an OM estimate is the floor covering specified for the Training Center. The estimator should review the finish schedule to determine what materials are required for each room. Figure 9-2 shows how a QTO might be set up for the floor covering, with extended quantities shown for carpeting.

When taking off the quantities for OM estimates, an estimator often encounters fractional dimensions. These should be rounded up to the nearest reasonable unit (inch or foot). The estimator, in the interest of improving efficiency, may want to make a template QTO that lists all the rooms and their dimensions. It can then be copied and used for most of the room finishes as well as walls, floors, and ceilings by delineating the work item being estimated and labeling the columns accordingly. When listing the room dimensions, any fractions should be rounded up to the nearest inch. The complete OM estimate would include the second floor as well.

On Figure 9-2, columns are shown for resilient base, which is quantified in lineal feet, and for resilient flooring with units of square feet. These are two different specifications because the resilient base may be used with resilient flooring, vinyl tile, or carpeting. Base for

Quantity Sheet

Date: *May 27, 2003*
Estimator: *P. Jacobs*
Est #: *TTC OM-1, Carpeting*

Project: *The Training Center*
Location: *Kent, WA*

Floor Covering —Carpeting

Room #	Description	Qty (ea)	L (ft)	W (ft)	H (ft)	09310 Ceramic Tile Base (lf)	Floor (sf)	09330 Quarry Tile Base (lf)	Floor (sf)	09651 Resilient Base (lf)	09658 Resilient Flr'g (sf)	09680 Carpet Area (sy)
100	Lobby	1	25	11	18							31
102	General Office	1	6.5	12.5	9							9
	+	1	16.5	10.5	9							
	+	1	24.5	17	9							
	+	1	17.5	6	9							
	Total General Office											218
103	Office	1	16.25	22	9							40
104	Office	1	28.25	15.25	9							48
105	Office	1	13.83	15.25								23
106	Corridor	1	15.5	13.5	9							
	+	1	8	8	9							
	Total Corridor											56
108	Stairs	1	10.5	5	9							6
109	Corridor	1	33.25	5.5	8.5							20
110	Storage	1	15.5	10.5	9							18
111	Copy	1	17	10.5	9							20
112	Corridor	1	35.5	5.5	9							22
113	Corridor	1	31	7	9							
	+	1	10.42	5	9							
	Total Corridor 113											55
119	Computer Lab	1	36	22.5	9							90
120	Corridor	1	45.5	7	9							35
124	Training Room	1	27.5	28.34	10							87
125	Training Room	1	27.5	29.46	10							90
126	Training Room	1	27.5	27.67	10							85
127	Stairs	1	12.42	5.25	9							7

Total 1st Floor Carpeting   959

FIGURE 9–2 Floor covering QTO.

ceramic or quarry tile, on the other hand, is used primarily with their respective floor systems and are shown in the same specifications as the flooring. Since floor covering is unitized in square feet and base in lineal feet, two columns are required. If conversion to square yards is required, it can be done after the area has been totaled.

The template with the room dimensions can be used for other finishes. Ceilings are nearly always the same as the floor area, and columns are set up for the different types that may be used, such as acoustical and drywall. Another copy will be used to quantify the walls by type and finish, and yet another for paint and wall covering.

The experienced estimator will do two things to enhance his or her ability to efficiently prepare OM estimates. First, he or she will use assemblies or systems pricing whenever possible or reliable unit prices that include all related costs. Second, the estimator will make sure that he or she understands what quality level the system or unit price represents. For example, an interior partition will include framing, wallboard on both sides, and one of four quality levels of taping finish. Adjustments may also have to be made for such things as ⅝-inch wallboard in lieu of ½-inch or fire-rated board instead of standard board. Quantities are transferred to the recap sheet using the same error control procedures that were discussed in direct work estimating in Chapter 7. For OM estimates, several changes are made to the recap sheet. The material unit cost and cost columns are changed to read S/C (subcontract) unit cost and subcontractor cost. Since these are subcontract/major supplier OM estimate sheets, the labor and total cost columns are not used, and the headings are deleted. Figure 9-3 shows an OM recap for the carpet quantities shown in Figure 9-2.

Recapitulation

Project: *The Training Center*
Location: *Kent, WA*
Arch./Engr.: *LM*

Date: *May 27, 2003*
Estimator: *P. Jacobs*
Estimate #: *OM-1, Carpeting*

Division 09682 Carpeting

Code	Sec/ Det	Description	Qty	Unit	UMH	Man Hours	Unit S/C Cost	Subcontractor Cost
9680		Carpeting, 1st floor	959	sy			22.05	$ 21,146
		40 oz commercial grade						
		Cushion, fiber	959	sy			3.00	2,877
		Subtotal carpeting						$ 24,023
		Locale correction factor						x 1.057
		Kent, WA x 105.7%						
		Total carpeting						$ 25,392

FIGURE 9–3   OM recap for floor covering.

Sitework

Sitework includes earthwork, underground utilities, paving, sidewalks, and curbs as well as landscaping, which are all listed in division 2. An estimator must determine which of these apply to a particular project from the WBS. The first ten items on the subcontractor list for the Training Center shown in Figure 9-1 relate to the sitework. Earthwork is probably the most difficult of all sitework items to estimate. It is the mass excavation and backfill that is required to level the site and prepare it for the building. Earthwork subcontractors commonly quote unit prices for the cut, fill, and hauling. Thus, they transfer the risk of estimating the quantities of work to the general contractor. The general contractor should accept only bids for the total cost of the work from subcontractors.

Earthwork can present many problems, and subcontractors generally will disclaim responsibility for unforeseen conditions. Even though a soils report is part of the project manual, it cannot predict everything that might be encountered. For example, a shallow rock outcropping or submerged spring may be discovered so that special work will be required to make the area suitable for the building. The subcontractor has a right to file a claim for more money for rock removal, to stabilize the ground at a spring, or for any other hidden condition. They cannot be responsible for unanticipated or undefined conditions.

To estimate earthwork, an estimator can use a basic grid system to determine the cut and fill. Identical rectangular grids are set up on the existing and proposed contour drawings. By determining the difference of the average elevations for a given grid, the cut and fill can be calculated. Grids used for calculating cut and fill can be any size that the estimator finds convenient; however, a little forethought can simplify the work. A large grid size can be used for a relatively flat site, but not for a sloped hill. Very small grids increase accuracy but are time-consuming to use. A grid system that is simple to use is one whose area equals 270 square feet. This may be squares of 16.43 feet, rectangles of 10 feet by 27 feet, or any other convenient size that equals 270 square feet. The key, though, in selecting the grid size is that with a 270 square-foot grid, each foot of cut or fill equals 10 bank cubic yards.

Once a grid has been established, the estimator finds the elevation change of a given grid on the existing and proposed contour drawings. The average elevation of a grid is determined by averaging the elevations at the four corners. The average elevation on the existing grid is subtracted from the corresponding elevation on the proposed grid. A negative answer represents a cut, and a positive answer represents a fill. Earthwork measurements are the same as for structural excavation and backfill discussed in Chapter 7.

Other sitework items cannot be estimated the same as those for the building. Unit prices are hard to determine on an average basis due to variations of conditions from one project to another.

Building Substructure and Superstructure

Most of the work in division 5 involves materials furnished by fabricators and installed by other subcontractors or the general contractor. The major variation is cold-formed metal framing, which usually is furnished and installed by a subcontractor as part of the wall systems. A few other minor work items will also be subcontracted, and a thorough review by the estimator will pick these up.

Masonry (division 4) is one of the few major work items in the substructure or superstructure that is done by a subcontractor. There is none in the Training Center. When encountered, it is relatively easy to develop an OM estimate. Most estimating references have good information for doing this and often company historical data can be used. Units generally are square foot measure or piece count.

Division 6 covers wood and plastics. Rough carpentry is commonly used for the superstructure of various housing projects, but its use in commercial and institutional buildings is limited. It is common to find rough carpentry for accessory items such as canopies and soffits in commercial projects. In general, an OM estimate would be similar to that for direct work, and the estimator should use reference data for unit prices or contact lumber brokers to determine current prices.

Most projects will have some architectural wood such as moldings, base, and other types of trim. Using the room finish templates discussed earlier, the estimator should be able to quantify the items and complete the OM estimate. Some cabinets and all of the plastic and specialty items will be furnished and installed by subcontractors. The estimator should use published or company data sources as a guide for quantifying and pricing.

Division 7 covers items that provide thermal and moisture protection for the building structure. The main items are foundation moisture proofing, insulation, roof systems, fire stopping, and caulking and sealing. Most quantities are either square foot or lineal foot, and dimensions previously determined in other parts of the estimate can be used for these also.

Doors and Windows

Doors and hardware are furnished by vendors and may be installed by the general contractor. The estimator already has prepared an installation estimate when estimating the direct work. The OM material estimate is prepared based on the QTO made for the labor estimate. Windows, glass, and glazing usually is furnished and installed by a subcontractor. This includes storefronts and curtain walls. Estimating guides will provide the units and unit prices for most of these items. Perhaps the most difficult will be the curtain walls. Many variants can affect costs of the curtain walls, and the type and height of the building will also make a difference.

Finishes

Division 9 covers finishes throughout the building. Most of this work involves dimensions and quantities that have been determined for other items. Floors, walls, ceilings, tile, painting, and wall coverings as well as floor coverings are shown on the finish schedule. In most cases, the unit prices can be determined from published estimating databases or historical records.

When doing the OM estimate for walls and partitions, an estimator should be aware of different construction methods and how they affect cost data. Two-sided partitions will be priced per square foot for a complete wall system, which includes framing, wallboard on both sides, and taping. Perimeter walls may be listed as a system, but more commonly the estimator will have to price the framing and the wallboard separately, which is based on the lineal feet of framing and the area of the wallboard installed.

Specialties, Equipment, and Furnishings

Divisions 10, 11, and 12 contain many items that may be specified for a given project. The estimator needs to be sure how they are specified in relation to the general contractor's direct work estimate. Some will be purchased and installed by the general contractor, some furnished by the contractor for installation by a subcontractor, some furnished by a supplier to be installed by the general contractor, and some furnished and installed under a separate contract. Because there are no general procedures for OM estimates of such items, the estimator should consult references to determine the best way to determine unit costs. Many items, such as signage, fire extinguishers, and whiteboards, are straightforward. Others, such as projection or sound equipment, are more complex.

Conveying Equipment

Division 14 has two items that are of interest in the Training Center, elevators and bridge cranes. There is substantial published estimating data on elevators, but the estimator has to fully understand the specifications. For the Training Center, the elevator is a 2,000-pound capacity hydraulic unit. A quick review of the specifications will determine that there is nothing unusual about it, and no adjustments to the costs will be necessary. Looking at some typical estimating references, installed costs can be found in the range of $35,000 to $40,000 for the unit specified.

Elevators used in high-rise buildings have more extensive controls due to their coordinated operation with other units and for some of the life-safety issues. The estimator needs to understand what is specified in order to find the costs in published or historical reference data. As the complexity increases, the estimator may have to build the unit pricing from the data given. For example, one may encounter a two-car electric passenger elevator system with a capacity of 3,500 pounds. The base price is found in reference data but adjustments may have to be made for travel of more than 40 vertical feet and for the number of stops over four. Other add-ons may include two-car group automatic controls, automatic emergency power switching, and special cab finishes.

The Training Center shows two 5-ton bridge cranes. An effective way to develop an OM estimate for special items and equipment such as the bridge cranes is to have one or more suppliers look at the requirements and ask them for help in determining the costs. Many times they will provide a budget price based on their experience and may guide the estimator on related costs. In many cases, a supplier will budget with specific qualifications and may be willing to commit to it. If his or her system appears to meet the owner's intent, the budget can be considered a substantiated allowance. More than one supplier should be solicited, and each should know that others are looking at it so the best quotation will be received.

Mechanical

Mechanical work for a project can be broken down into four basic areas: service piping, plumbing, HVAC, and sprinklers. The service piping is perhaps the most difficult to estimate. It is the piping from the nearest utility connections offsite to approximately 5 feet outside of the building perimeter. The estimator should note pipe size, length, and depth of burial and then consult published costing data to obtain an anticipated unit cost. Most data will not include excavation and backfill, so the estimator will need to add these as well as any special valves and fittings. For most installations, the estimator should be able to estimate an installed unit cost per 100-foot section with minimal fittings, and extend it to the length of line shown on the drawings. A reasonable allowance for connection and metering fees should be included also. Relying on the advice of vendors will greatly aid in developing a reasonable OM estimate for the service piping.

Regarding plumbing, the Training Center project is somewhat of a hybrid building. It has an office area and a large training room with bridge cranes. This is not a typical situation that can be found in reference books. In most cases, however, plumbing unit costs are based on one fixture per a given number of square feet of floor area. For the Training Center, the estimator can determine the floor area per fixture by looking for a similar project in one of the estimating references.

When doing a fixture count, some confusion can occur about what is and is not a fixture. Most fixtures have a supply and drain connection, and some have a hot water connection. Water heaters have a water supply, possibly a fuel connection, and an exhaust (unless electric). They can be considered the same as a fixture as far as installation and rough-in are concerned. However, the estimator should look at its size and check costs in relation to that of a fixture and make any adjustments accordingly.

The plumbing drawings for the Training Center show that there are thirty-two fixtures and two water heaters for a total of thirty-four fixtures. The building floor area, including the second floor office, is approximately 35,610 square feet. Dividing this area by thirty-four fixtures equals 1,056 square feet of floor per fixture. The estimator can then look for a unit cost of a representative building with approximately 1,000 square feet per fixture.

As the estimator peruses unit price data for plumbing, he or she will find that several types of structures show 1,000 square feet per fixture. Some, such as community centers, will include kitchen equipment, which adds to the cost, while the unit cost for a convenience store is low. A one-story factory of about 30,000 square feet shows one fixture per 1,000 square foot and an installed cost of $3.08 per square foot of floor area. Entering the data on an OM recap and extending the information produces a plumbing OM estimate of $109,695.

Figure 9-4 shows an abbreviated fixture count QTO, and Figure 9-5 shows a recap based on building size for the plumbing OM estimate. The water heaters are relatively small and have been assumed to be about the same price as any other fixture. Therefore, they are included in the fixture count. This particular estimate does not include the outside service piping.

HVAC estimates are more dependent on the type of system specified. The Training Center only shows gas-fired unit heaters. The estimator can use only basic unit price information to develop the OM estimate. Looking again at the factory building used for estimating the plumbing work, the estimator should use an estimating reference or database to find a listing for gas-fired hot water and unit heaters. It does not matter whether these are oil or gas fired; the cost difference will not be a factor for the OM estimate. A price of $5.19 per square foot is listed for the heating system and water heater fuel connections, and a slightly higher rate for a system that includes cooling. The HVAC OM estimate would be as follows:

(35,610 square feet) ($5.19 per square foot) = $184,816, or about $185,000

Project: *The Training Center*
Location: *Kent, WA*

Date: *May 27, 2003*
Estimator: *P. Jacobs*
Est #: *TTC OM-1, Plumbing*

Division *15400 Plumbing*

Ref	Description	Qty (ea)	L (ft)	W (ft)	H (ft)	Area (sf)	Total Fixtures (ea)	Water Heaters (ea)	
	1st floor office								
	fixtures—north						3		
	—central						13		
	2nd floor office								
	fixtures						11	2	
	water heaters						1		
	Training area								
	fixtures						4		
	Building area								
	footprint	1	257	105		27,000			
	+ 2nd floor offices	1	105	82		8,610			
	Totals					35,610	32	2	
							2	←	
							34		

FIGURE 9–4 Plumbing OM estimate QTO.

The fire sprinkler specifications state that the system is to be bidder designed, and only general information has been provided. The main concern for the estimator is the hazard classification, as this is the major cause of cost variations. Notes on the drawings indicate the NFPA specification for the system and there are no extraordinary hazards noted within the structure. Both published and historical data on fire sprinkler systems usually are quite representative of actual costs. The Training Center is mostly similar to an open warehouse without racks and with some office area. The one-story factory used previously is not used for the sprinklers because the systems are more extensive, thus raising the unit cost. Typical unit price data for a wet pipe ordinary hazard system will range from about $1.60 per square foot for the warehouse to about $1.50 per square foot for offices. By contrast, a one-story factory will have unit prices that are 10% to 15% higher. Using an adjusted cost of $1.55 per square foot, the estimate would be as follows:

(35,610 square feet)($1.55 per square foot) = $55,196, or about $55,200

Project: *The Training Center*
Location: *Kent, WA*
Arch./Engr:: *LM*

Date: *May 27, 2003*
Estimator: *P. Jacobs*
Estimate #: *TTC OM-1 Plumbing*

Division *15400 Plumbing*

Code	Sec/Det	Description	Qty	Unit			Unit S/C Cost	Subcontractor Cost
		Unit price based on 1 fixture per 1,000 sf floor area for a 1-story factory						
		Total floor area	*35,610*	*sf*			*$3.08*	*$109,695*

FIGURE 9–5 Plumbing recap.

153

Subcontractor List

Project: The Training Center, Kent, WA   Estimator: Paul Jacobs   Est. #: TTC OM-1

Bin	Spec	Description	Bid	+ or −	Revised	Subcontractor
	02200	Earthwork	178,400			
	02515	Conc. paving	48,920			
	02618	Pavement marking	2,000			
	02620	Concrete curbs	17,300			
	02711	Chain link fences & gates	9,400			
	02900	Landscaping	34,150			
	03200	Reinforcing steel supply	33,000			
	03210	Reinforcing steel install	17,650			
	05100	Structural steel supply	54,150			
	05150	Structural steel install	50,400			
	05200	Metal joists and deck	79,000			
	05300	Stainless steel handrail	4,000			
	06240	Architectural woodwork	12,800			
	07120	Fluid membrane waterproof	500			
	07210	Building insulation	16,300			
	07270	Firestopping	2,000			
	07510	Built-up bituminous roofing	90,000			
	07600	Flashing and sheet metal	17,200			
	07810	Skylights	3,250			
	07830	Roof hatches	500			
	07900	Joint sealants	2,500			
	08110	Steel doors & frames	24,890			
	08670	Vertical lift doors	23,000			
	08410	Aluminum storefront syst.	75,000			
	08710	Finish hardware	16,500			
	09250	Gypsum wallboard	156,200			
	09310	Ceramic tile	32,000			
	09511	Acoustical ceiling system	18,000			
	09560	Resilient flooring	1,750			
	09682	Carpeting	25,392			
	09900	Painting	55,000			
	10110	Markerboards & tackboards	3,500			
	10161	Toilet part. & urinal screens	4,450			
	10440	Signs	2,500			
	10500	Metal lockers	4,000			
	10800	Toilet accessories	5,600			
	10905	Misc specialties	1,000			
	12501	Blinds & shades	4,750			
	12676	Recessed foot grills	1,200			
	12695	Entrance mats	1,500			
	14200	Elevator	35,000			
	15500	Fire sprinklers	55,200			
	15400	Plumbing	109,695			
	15500	HVAC	185,000			
	16000	Electrical	253,864			
		TOTAL SUBCONTRACTS	1,768,411	———	———	

FIGURE 9–6 Completed OM subcontractor list.

Electrical

Electrical work generally is divided into three categories: service, distribution, and security. Service is the power from the utility connection to and through the main service panel. Distribution is the wiring, switches, receptacles, and connections within the building, and security includes alarm systems and emergency lighting. Unit prices for each of these categories can be found in estimating references. The Training Center can be interpreted as being similar to a one-story manufacturing building. The range for a single story manufacturing building might be as follows:

Service including a 600 amp main panel	$0.80 per square foot
Distribution	$5.98 per square foot
Security	$0.35 per square foot
Total	$7.13 per square foot

This total is then multiplied by the overall building floor area to calculate an OM estimated cost.

OM estimates for division 15 and 16 are developed similar to the ROM estimates discussed in Chapter 6. The difference is that they are for specific divisions rather than the entire project. Since these are listed only for the first-run bid determination, this type of OM estimate is adequate.

9.4 COMPLETING THE SUBCONTRACTOR LIST

As the OM estimates are completed, they are entered onto the subcontract list that is marked OM ESTIMATE. Once all line items have been filled in, the OM estimating work is complete and ready to use in determining the first-run bid total as will be discussed in Chapter 11. Figure 9-6 shows a completed OM subcontractor list for the Training Center

9.5 SUMMARY

OM estimates are developed for all subcontracted work items to have a means of preparing a first-run bid total and to have a basis for comparing subcontractor quotations on bid day. For most of a project, OM estimates can be developed by making simplified QTOs and applying either assembly costs or unit prices per square foot of building floor area. When taking off building dimensions, an estimator can set up a QTO sheet for the flooring, one for the ceiling and one or two for the framed walls, using the same data. Mechanical and electrical OM estimates are more difficult to determine. The best source of information is unit prices from references based on a similar type of project. Sitework includes items from mass excavation to special foundation work to landscaping. In developing an OM estimate, these items range from relatively straightforward for paving and curbs to difficult for earthwork and landscaping. For much of the sitework, the estimator usually has to perform a semi-detailed estimate and use published references for costing.

9.6 REVIEW QUESTIONS

1. What work should OM estimates be done for?
2. What are two purposes for developing OM estimates?
3. Where are the results of the OM estimates listed?
4. What type of data source material is good to use for pricing OM estimates?
5. If subcontractor prices are received for work usually done as direct work, how should these be handled?
6. How can the estimator make his or her work easier when doing OM estimates?
7. Why is the resilient base estimated separately from the resilient flooring?

9.7 EXERCISES

1. Determine an OM estimate for a 2,500-pound capacity hydraulic passenger elevator for a two-story office building. Use commonly available estimating references.

2. Determine a reasonable unit price for HVAC of a two-story fire station. What kind of system is this?

3. How does the cost of the HVAC for the fire station compare with a two-story medical office building both in unit price and percentage of total building cost?

10

ESTIMATING
GENERAL
CONDITIONS

10.1 INTRODUCTION

The general conditions section of the lump-sum estimate is represented by step 8 of the lump-sum estimating process shown in Figure 6-1. Before determining the general conditions requirements, it is usually necessary to prepare a summary schedule for the project (step 7 in Figure 6-1) so that the duration of the project can be estimated. General conditions costs are the jobsite overhead and the indirect project costs that are not attributable to specific work activities, but occur during the completion of the project. Estimating references commonly refer to these costs as CSI division 1 or general requirements costs. The general conditions cost estimate may or may not relate to the project manual (or contract) general conditions section, which defines many contractual aspects of the project.

Indirect labor and materials are those not used directly in the performance of the construction activities on the project. For example, the labor of the superintendent and the project management staff are not attributable to any of the work but are necessary for the execution of the project. Similarly a jobsite pickup truck or forklift is used for many tasks, but to prorate its cost to each construction activity is difficult and meaningless. Some other general conditions items include trash hauling, taxes and insurance, jobsite office, and utilities.

The general conditions should be thought of as the jobsite or project overhead. It delineates costs associated with administration of the project, indirect equipment usage, temporary construction, and certain miscellaneous items. This is different from the contractor's company overhead and profit. The jobsite overhead pertains strictly to the project while the contractor's company overhead and profit relate to the home office operation of the construction firm. Home office overhead and profit will be discussed in Chapter 11.

10.2 PROJECT SUMMARY SCHEDULE

In order to develop a general conditions estimate, an estimator must know the project duration. This may be determined in more than one way. The duration may be defined in the contract, or an owner might ask bidders to submit a price and schedule. In either case, the estimator should develop a project summary schedule prior to completing the general conditions estimate. A project summary schedule differs from a project schedule in its level of detail. It is a summary of the work required to complete the project and shows only gross activities, such as major concrete elements, structural steel, drywall and painting, mechanical, and electrical. It does not show any breakdown of these activities. A project summary schedule should exhibit twenty to thirty activities for the project. Several formats are available for creating a project summary schedule. The format that is easiest to create and understand is the horizontal time scaled bar chart. Figure 10-1 is an example of a project summary schedule that might be proposed for the Training Center.

Man-hours can be used as a guide to determine activity duration. For example, suppose that the summary recap for substructure concrete shows that it will take 2,115 man-hours to complete. The estimator determines that the crew will consist of four carpenters, two laborers, one ironworker, and one concrete finisher. The crew makeup will vary depending on the specific task being done at a given time, but in general there will be an eight-person crew for this work. The duration calculations are

$$(8 \text{ workers})(8 \text{ hours per day per worker}) = 64 \text{ man-hours per day}$$
$$2,115 \text{ man-hours} \div 64 \text{ man-hours per day} = 33 \text{ days duration}$$

This then becomes the length of the bar on the summary schedule, and the procedure is repeated for the remainder of the direct work.

Duration of subcontract activities is more difficult to determine. The estimator must use either published estimating references, similar projects, or potential subcontractors to determine typical durations for subcontracted activities. The estimator must also be aware of any unusual or difficult situations that may affect crew productivity.

10.3 ALTERNATIVE TECHNIQUES

There are two methods for developing a general conditions estimate. The first is to do a detailed estimate for all items that will be required. This is the method that is discussed in this chapter. A QTO is not required, because the quantity being used is the project duration, or in some cases a portion of the duration. Some items, such as the building permit, business taxes, or insurance, may be prorated as a percentage of the overall cost of the contract.

A second method is to calculate jobsite overhead based on a historical percentage of the total direct costs prior to the addition of the final fee (overhead and profit), for example 10%. While this is used in developing budget estimates, as discussed in Chapter 3, it is not recommended for lump-sum bidding, because it may not account for some items that will affect general conditions costs. For example, estimates for industrial projects tend to have high general conditions costs because of more field supervision, additional jobsite

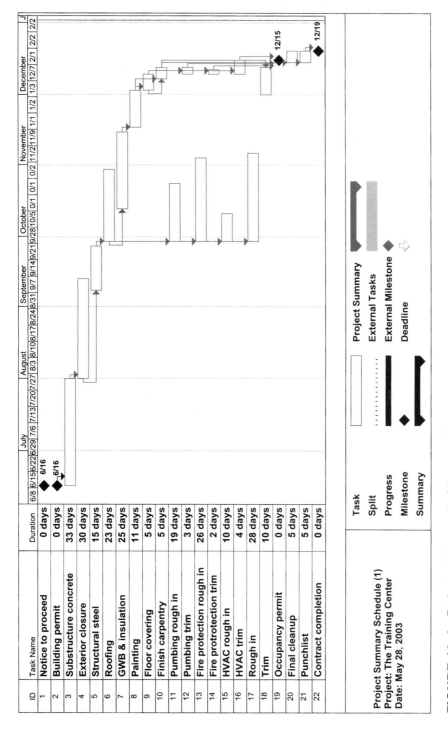

FIGURE 10–1 Project summary schedule.

equipment, and the use of small precision tools. Doing a detailed estimate allows the estimator to analyze the needs of a specific project and estimate costs accordingly.

A good use of historical percentages in lump-sum estimating is to check the magnitude of the general conditions estimate to the bid amount. If one would expect the general conditions to be approximately 8% of the subtotal prior to the fee and it turns out to be 11%, the estimator should determine why such a variation exists.

10.4 ELEMENTS OF THE GENERAL CONDITIONS ESTIMATE

The general conditions estimate is divided into four parts: administrative expense, equipment, temporary construction, and general operations. Form F-6 in Appendix F is a four-part form that lists items that might be included as costs to a project. For most projects, only a portion of the line items are used, but other items might need to be added for some special requirements or to satisfy company policies. The form also serves as a checklist to ensure that nothing has been overlooked.

Before proceeding with the general conditions estimate, an estimator should thoroughly review division 1 of the specifications and any supplemental or special conditions to look for specific requirements or limits that will affect how the costs are determined. As previously discussed, the estimator also needs to determine the project duration. The owner of the Training Center specified a twenty-eight-week duration. This defines the duration of several line items within the general conditions estimate, such as the field supervision and staffing, job offices, and temporary utilities. It also establishes the start and finish of the project summary schedule shown in Figure 10-1.

When developing the general conditions estimate, an estimator should keep in mind that jobsite overhead must be kept reasonably low so that the final bid is competitive. Each of the pages of the general conditions estimating form should be carefully examined to select a winning strategy for this part of the bid. Figure 10-2 is a condensed form of the four-page general conditions estimate for the Training Center. All of the unused line items have been deleted to save space.

Administrative Expense

The administrative expense page contains the field supervision and will reflect the most labor. An insufficient amount of supervision will be detrimental to the project, and too much promotes inefficiency. The estimator should consult with a project manager to determine the most efficient manning that will ensure continuity of the project. The administrative expense sheet prices the field management and supervision, office and field support personnel, and material that are required to run a project field office efficiently. The first section, Management & Supervision, lists the supervisory staff required for a project. Principal line items include the following:

- Project manager
- Project superintendent
- Assistant superintendents
- Field survey/engineer

GENERAL CONDITIONS

PROJECT: The Training Center
OWNER: Trust Fund of Western Washington

DATE: May 29, 2003

ESTIMATOR: P. Jacobs
ESTIMATE #: TTC-1

Code	Description	Qty	Unit	Labor Unit Price	Labor Cost	Material Unit Price	Material Cost	Total Cost
Administrative Expense MANAGEMENT & SUPERVISION								
	Project manager	10	wks	1,000	10,000			10,000
	Project superintendent	28	wks	1,200	33,600			33,600
	Field survey/engr	1	wks	800	800			800
ENGINEERING & SAFETY								
	Project engineer	28	wks	700	19,600			19,600
	Plan & schedule	1	ls			5,000	5,000	5,000
	Blueprinting	1	ls			250	250	250
	Safety/medical	1	ls			500	500	500
OFFICE								
	Office utilities	7	mos			250	1,750	1,750
	Job telephone/fax	14	un/mo			150	2,100	2,100
	Set up telephones	1	ls			1,500	1,500	1,500
	Office supplies	6	mos			50	300	300
	Public relations	1	ls			300	300	300
ADMINISTRATIVE EXPENSE TOTALS					**$64,000**		**$11,700**	**$75,700**

Code	Description	Qty	Unit	Labor Unit Price	Labor Cost	Material Unit Price	Material Cost	Total Cost
Equipment								
	Pickup truck	7	un/mo			650	4,550	4,550
	Forklift	6	un/mo			3,000	18,000	18,000
	Torch set	1	ea			500	500	500
	Saw sharpening	1	ls			200	200	200
	Small tools	3%	dl	(based on $123,353)			3,700	3,700
	Consumables	15%	eq				75	75
	Equipment fuel & maint.	15%	eq/rnt				3,458	3,458
EQUIPMENT TOTALS				$	—		**$30,483**	**$30,483**

FIGURE 10–2 General conditions estimate.

(continued)

				Labor		Material		Total
Code	Description	Qty	Unit	Unit Price	Cost	Unit Price	Cost	Cost
Temporary Construction								
	BUILDINGS							
	Job office	7	un/mo			350	2,450	2,450
	Dry shacks	7	un/mo			75	525	525
	Trailer transportation	4	trips			150	600	600
	Trailer setup	1	ls	400	400	100	100	500
	INSTALL UTILITIES							
	Temp power hookup & dist	1	ls			1,000	1,000	1,000
	Project sign	1	ls			500	500	500
	Layout & batter boards	1	ls	400	400	50	50	450
	PROTECTION							
	Fences						-	-
	Fire protection	1	ls			300	300	300
TEMPORARY CONSTRUCTION TOTALS					**$800**		**$5,525**	**$6,325**
General Operations								
	UTILITIES							
	Drinking water	28	wks			50	1,400	1,400
	Chemical toilet	24	un/mo			95	2,280	2,280
	TESTING & INSPECTION							
	Testing lab	1	ls			3,500	3,500	3,500
	CLEANUP							
	Final cleanup	1	sub			5,600	5,600	5,600
	OTHER							
	Trash hauling	7	mo			150	1,050	1,050
GENERAL OPERATIONS TOTALS					$ _		**$13,830**	**$13,830**

FIGURE 10–2 Continued.

Projects such as the Training Center typically will have the part-time services of a project manager and a full-time superintendent. Assistant superintendents usually are necessary only on large projects. Field survey is a company person who lays out the building and property lines.

The project manager's effort will be needed full-time at the beginning of the project when planning and controls are being developed and project management procedures are being established. Monitoring the controls and administering the change order process takes less time. Also, if a project engineer is on the staff, that person will perform the day-to-day administrative duties, and the project manager may be needed for only one day a week. At the end of the project, the project manager will be busy with closeout activities. The estimator, after talking with others, may determine that the project manager will only be required for ten of the twenty-eight weeks.

The superintendent is a full-time supervisor and the chief safety officer for the project. He or she will be on the project for its entire duration. For the Training Center, this means that the superintendent's time is twenty-eight weeks. Field surveying is the work of laying out the building. Some additional minor locations might need to be established in conjunction with the layout. The duration of the field surveying will be short, generally a few days, and any assistance will be provided by other personnel already working on the jobsite.

The second section, Engineering & Safety, lists items primarily for site engineering staffing, scheduling, quality control, and safety. A project engineer is commonly used to perform the day-to-day functions of contract administration. These include estimating change order proposals; monitoring cost controls; preparing status reports; conducting meetings with the owner, design team, and subcontractors; and handling detailed duties relating to closing out the project. The estimator may decide that this is full-time work, and that the duration will be twenty-eight weeks. Project close-out usually extends beyond the contract completion date, but the project manager and engineer will manage their time to cover this period.

Three other line items used on most projects are plan and schedule, drawing reproduction, and safety/medical. Plan and schedule can be done either in-house or by a consultant, which would result in both labor and material costs. An owner usually furnishes one set of reproducible drawings, and the general contractor makes sufficient copies for the direct work and management duties. Subcontractors purchase the sets they need. Safety and medical supplies are required for every job. The company safety department should be able to provide guidelines about what is needed, and historical data will help to determine typical costs for similar types of projects. Job size and type will dictate whether or not items such as additional engineers, form detailing, and professional surveying will be required. Safety training for the Training Center will be in the form of a weekly toolbox safety meeting, which is usually recorded as regular work time on a construction activity so there will be no entry on the safety training line. Some projects have special safety requirements, and the cost will be included in this section.

The final section of the administrative page deals with the field office and some miscellaneous items. Typically on lump-sum projects, the owner allows the contractor to determine what is necessary to administer a project and to include the costs in the bid. The estimator should plan for the smallest staff that can do the work effectively. Certain items are required for running the field office, which may include utilities, telephones, a facsimile machine, and some office supplies. Home office personnel may perform some of the duties listed in this section, but no cost is estimated for them, as they are included in the company overhead. Some estimators include a small amount for public relations, which is used at the discretion of the field supervisors to enhance relationships with the owner or architect.

Several line items on the administrative page are not used for projects like the Training Center. Some of them, such as a field secretary, would be nice to have but represent an unnecessary expense on a project of this size. Lump-sum projects need to be staffed lean, so that the final bid is competitive.

Quantities used on the administrative page are in units relative to the overall project rather than to construction activities. Productivity factors are not an issue for project administration labor. Units are listed in weeks, and the labor unit price is the weekly pay of the position of the line item. Many of the material items are one-time costs with units shown as ls, which is an abbreviation for lump sum. Some items, such as telephone are quantified as unit months, which means the number of telephones onsite for the number of months. If three telephone lines will be used for six months, the quantity is eighteen unit months, and the material unit price will be the anticipated monthly bill per telephone line per month.

Equipment

The equipment page is used to list any equipment that is not specific to a given activity but will be needed on the project. This includes a jobsite pickup truck and often a forklift truck that is used for general purposes throughout the work. Equipment owned by the general contractor is rented to the job just as if it were acquired from a rental company. It was discussed in Chapters 7 and 8 that equipment used for specific activities, such as hoisting tilt-up panels or structural steel erection, are priced as part of those activities and not shown on this equipment page.

Indirect equipment is equipment used for multiple activities on a project, such as a jobsite forklift. The estimator determines the number of indirect units required and their duration. Extension is then a simple multiplication of the quantity by the rental rate. Some items, such as a welding torch, may be purchased, and the units are then lump-sum.

General contractors have found that for certain sites, a tower crane is needed. While these cranes typically do not have the capacity to lift heavy items, they do most of the lighter hoisting and can prove to be more economical than other equipment. The estimator should include all costs associated with the tower crane on the equipment sheet, and price it for the duration of the general contractor's direct work. It may be advantageous for subcontractors to do hoisting, but this is an item to be negotiated after the project is won. Because of its use for multiple work activities, the tower crane is considered a piece of indirect equipment to be used throughout a major portion of the project.

The lines in the center of the equipment page pertain to both tower cranes and labor and material hoists. The estimator should make a special QTO and recap page for these items. There are costs associated with constructing a base and erecting and dismantling the equipment. The estimator needs to do a detailed estimate on this type of equipment so all costs are included. A question arises many times regarding who furnishes the heavy hoisting, such as lifting air conditioning units to the top of a roof. On a lump-sum bid, subcontractors usually are responsible for their own hoisting as well as any other equipment and tools needed to perform their work.

The last four line items on the equipment page are difficult to quantify but, historically, their costs are relatively consistent for most projects. Saw sharpening is a necessity for carpentry work and, although it could be attributed to concrete form construction, many jobs involve other rough and/or finish carpentry. Saw sharpening is, therefore, considered an indirect job cost.

Small tools are those that are not furnished by the workers but that are required for them to complete the construction work. As a general rule, these tools are ones that cost less than a prescribed amount, commonly $500 apiece. An example would be a portable power circular saw, which is used to build forms as well as for rough and finish carpentry. Being of minor cost and used throughout the project, it is not practical to assign the cost of hand tools to specific work activities. For this reason, small tool costs are estimated as a percentage (commonly 3%) of the direct labor cost for the project. Most companies have good historical guidelines for determining this cost. The estimator should review the specification's general conditions regarding small tools. Most commercial projects do not designate a maximum value for an individual small tool but some do. If a contractor estimates this cost based on a $500 maximum cost for a small tool, and the owner specifies that the maximum cost is $250 or $1,000, a different percentage should be used.

Consumables cover miscellaneous items like welding supplies that are used for general purposes. The type of project will influence this cost, and the estimator must be aware of what they are. Discussions with superintendents will help in determining an amount to be used for consumables. Equipment fuel and maintenance is an easy item to estimate. A generally accepted method is to use 15% of the equipment rental cost as the amount needed for fuel and maintenance. Most projects have spill containment requirements, and these costs also need to be added.

Temporary Construction

Temporary construction includes the office and site facilities that will be used during the construction process, and then removed once the project is complete. These include the field office trailers, tool trailers, utilities installation, temporary roads, rubbish chutes, fences, and signs. The costing is straightforward, and the estimator only needs to find out what the rates are, or anticipate monthly bills, in the case of utilities. Most line items will have only material costs, but there is labor for some things, such as setting up trailers. Looking at the Training Center, the cost of some items were based on the following:

- Job office—The rental of a single trailer or other structure for the duration of the project. It should have adequate office space for the superintendent and project manager (or engineer).
- Owner/arch office—This cost is not included unless specifically stated in division 1 of the contract specifications.
- Dry shacks—These are very simple trailers or rooms where the workers can hang up wet clothes overnight to dry.
- Warehouse—This is not required on this project.
- Tool shed—This may be combined with the dry shack or portion of the office trailer.
- Trailer transportation—The cost to move the field office and dry shack to and from the jobsite.
- Trailer setup—The labor needed to set the trailer on blocks and to make the inside usable for the field staff. This might include building plan tables and structures on which to put a facsimile machine.
- Saw line—This will not be required. These usually are employed on large projects where considerable production sawing is required. The cost is the labor and materials to set up a large saw and build tables for it.

Not all line items on this page will be used in an estimate. The estimator needs to determine which ones will be required and develop typical costs for them according to the job parameters. For example, large projects will require a sizeable telephone system and possibly jobsite radios. Renovation of a major high-rise building may require a rubbish chute, and certain tilt-up projects may require a separate precast yard other than the building floor slab. Some typical items that will be required for the Training Center are

- Temporary power hookup and distribution
- Temporary lighting—In winter, to support second shift, or to allow interior construction on cloudy days
- Project sign
- Layout and batter boards—The markers that show the location of the building
- Signs and barricades—For open trenches and pits
- Fire protection—Fire extinguishers placed throughout the jobsite

The estimator needs to pay particular attention to the utilities. Projects that are built on a new site usually have no available services (water, electricity, sewer, or communications), and the general contractor must provide them. Temporary power is an expensive item. Electrical subcontractors usually do not include this in their bid, and the estimator should consult with one to determine what a typical temporary installation will cost. Temporary lighting and heating systems are weather related; the estimator needs to anticipate their use. Job communications, such as radios, are determined by the size of the project and company policy.

Telephone installation is an item of concern. The cost will depend on how extensive a system is needed and where the lines are coming from. If the telephone lines will be used for data transmission, the systems will be more extensive and expensive. Wireless telephones have helped reduce this cost, but high-speed data landlines may still be needed.

Many of the listed site facilities are not needed on a project the size of the Training Center. The estimator, however, must understand the conditions that may require them. For example, if a project is being built on a site that retains a lot of surface water during a rainy season, some temporary roads may be needed. Most sites will have a project sign. The layout and batter boards item contains the labor and minor materials that the carpenters will use to help the surveyor lay out the building. Erosion control materials will be needed to prevent surface water from leaving the project site and should be included in the general conditions estimate. The jobsite may need to be fenced to keep the public from entering the construction site. The cost of installing and removing the fence should also be included in the general conditions estimate.

An item in the protection category that is required on all project sites is fire protection. This covers the material cost of supplying fire extinguishers at various locations on the jobsite. Usually state safety requirements will dictate how many and what sizes are needed. The cost is relatively modest, but necessary for a complete estimate. All other protection items are dependent on the jobsite conditions and owner's requirements.

General Operations

The general operations includes items that are specified by the owner to be furnished by the general contractor and those that are required to maintain the temporary facilities and other parts of the site. The first section pertains to permits, licenses, and taxes. An estimator needs to determine whether the building permit will be paid for by the general contractor and the cost included in the bid or whether it will be furnished by the owner. It is common for the owner to submit for the building permit but may require the contractor to pay for it. A call to the local building department will provide the estimator with parameters for determining what the permit will cost. Some cities have a published rate schedule, and others simply use a percentage calculation. Most other permits, such as plumbing and electrical, are furnished by the respective subcontractors, and the cost is included in their bids.

There can be other permits, such as jobsite environmental, grading, and foundation permits. Some are part of the building permit requirements, and others may be in addition to them. The estimator should become familiar with all of the permitting requirements and make sure that he or she knows who will pay for them and whether or not the owner requires these costs to be included in the bid.

The lines below the building permit pertain to various taxes. An estimator must understand which taxes are applicable to a project and how they are calculated. Usually a contractor's accounting department will have this information or be able to determine it. Perhaps the most difficult tax to determine is the sales tax. There are state sales taxes and local sales taxes, and they will vary from one location to another. Some laws require that sales tax be included in the bid price, while others forbid including the sales tax in the price. No universal procedure can be applied to sales taxes, so the estimator must know which ones apply to the specific location of the work. The Training Center is located in a state that does not include sales tax in the bid price, so the owner must determine and add this cost to the bids. Whenever a street is blocked off for construction purposes, a street use permit must be obtained. The estimator must find out what the unit cost is, extend it by the anticipated duration, and include it in the estimate.

Information regarding specific building permit rates, taxes, insurance, and bonds should be kept in the estimator's personal notebook. Time can be saved by using the notebook and avoiding the need to call various agencies and companies each time an estimate is prepared. This information should be updated annually.

A bond is a requirement that may be stated in the bid documents. Owners may request separate quotes for bonds and decide at the time of award whether or not they wish to purchase them. Bonds are obtained through contractors' bonding agents, and estimators can obtain rates from them.

Insurance is a requirement on most construction projects. Many owners are specific about coverage, and the contractor's insurance agent will provide either a quote or a method for calculating the cost. Two similar line items are shown in this subsection—broad form and liability insurance. They are essentially the same but with different terminology. Both cover personal liability and *property damage*. Earthquake and flood insurance is a specific choice of either the owner or general contractor, and in most cases is not included in the price.

The estimator has a choice of how to calculate items that are dependent on the contract amount. One way is to use a first-run estimate as a basis amount for the calculation. The first-run estimate will be discussed in Chapter 11. Permits, taxes, and insurance costs will be calculated and entered on the appropriate lines of the general operations page. These costs can be combined and divided by the bid subtotal to get a percentage of the total. As subcontractor bids are received and the summary page is completed, the difference between the first-run and the final bid subtotal prior to the adjustment line is multiplied by this percentage to calculate an adjustment factor to be added to or subtracted from the subtotal. An alternative method is not to fill in the items on the operations page but to determine their value and add them after the last subtotal of the bid summary (adjustments section).

The general operations page is used for the building permit calculation. Its basis amount can be the first-run bid total, which can later be adjusted to the final bid subtotal. Generally any adjustment to the final amount will be insignificant unless there is a wide variation between the first-run and the final bid. If necessary, an adjustment can be made on the bid summary.

The estimator can determine most material pricing by getting quotes from suppliers and/or using historical information. Items to pay particular attention to are drinking water and chemical toilets. A jobsite should have a good source of clean cool drinking water. One or two insulated containers filled with ice water each day usually will be sufficient. While this is minor, it is a cost and should be included in the bid. The estimator must establish the average number of persons that will be on the job to determine the number of chemical toilets required. Many state laws are very specific about this. If there are no state laws, some basic guidelines can be determined from suppliers. On most projects, the general contractor furnishes chemical toilets for the subcontractors' use as well.

Specifications will dictate what inspections and testing are required. A general contractor may be contractually responsible for all inspections and tests required by a building department. If the owner's requirements are more than those of the building department, the contractor must satisfy the contract requirements. Inspections usually are not a cost item if they are done by the building department, but they must be accounted for if done by an independent agency and not paid for by the owner. An estimator must review the general and special conditions of the contract to determine who furnishes the testing for concrete and structural steel. Some owners assign the testing to the general contractor, but some municipalities consider it is a conflict of interest to do so. All other inspections are part of subcontract work, and costs are included in their contract price. The owner of the Training Center has not specified any tests beyond what is required for the building department. The estimator needs to research what these requirements are and obtain unit prices or quotes from a testing agency. Company historical data may be helpful for this also.

Each of the four sections of the general conditions are summed on their own page but are not consolidated to a single total until after they are transferred to the bid summary. This allows for easier checking for errors.

10.5 SUMMARY

The general conditions estimate defines and prices the jobsite overhead (indirect work) for a project. It lists all the indirect labor and material required to manage, supervise, and complete work activities. When developing the jobsite overhead costs, the estimator must be aware of what the contract requires. For example, a full-time superintendent may be required to be on the job for its duration. Other items, such as the jobsite pickup, will not be defined; they are left up to the bidder to determine whether or not they are needed. Form F-6 in Appendix F lists numerous indirect work items. For a typical project, only some of them will be necessary. This listing can be used as a checklist as well as a costing form. An estimator is encouraged to use these forms and modify them as needed. For example, a contractor may be more inclined to use an extending boom forklift rather than a boom truck or light crane. The rental rates are different, and the estimator may want to add a specific line item to the template for this equipment to make sure it is not forgotten on future projects.

10.6 REVIEW QUESTIONS

1. What does the general conditions section of the estimate represent?
2. What are indirect work items?
3. What are the titles of each of the four pages of the general conditions estimate?
4. How does the general conditions section of the estimate relate to the general conditions of the specifications?
5. What is another name for the general conditions part of the estimate?
6. Why should the general conditions be estimated in detail rather than using a percentage of the project costs?
7. How are taxes and insurance commonly estimated?
8. What is the basis of costing of the building permit? Bonds?
9. Each sheet is totaled within itself. Where are these totals consolidated?

10.7 EXERCISES

1. Develop an administrative estimate for a project involving two buildings similar to the Training Center. Both are being constructed at the same time but on opposite ends of a large site. Project duration for both buildings is twenty-eight weeks, and they will be done concurrently.

2. Make an equipment estimate of a six-story high-rise building that uses a tower crane. Assume the project will be completed in one year.

3. Obtain the building permit rates from the nearest major city and determine the permit cost for a building with an estimated construction contract amount of $2,840,000.

11

COMPLETING THE ESTIMATE

11.1 INTRODUCTION

The estimating work has progressed from initial document review to the QTO, recap, and pricing of the self-performed work. OM estimates have been developed for subcontractor work, and the project summary schedule and general conditions estimate are complete. This concludes the first eight steps of the lump-sum estimating process shown in Figure 6-1. The two remaining steps represent work that is done on bid day. It is now time to complete the estimate and determine a first-run total based on the information developed thus far. The completion process is an excellent time to review the work, not only for completeness, but to check transferred numbers. Even though an estimator has diligently performed all reviews and error checks during the development of the estimate, a final review and check is needed.

11.2 FINAL DOCUMENT REVIEW

The first step in completing the estimate is to conduct a thorough review of the bid documents, including all addenda. They should be read in the same order as before beginning the estimating work; that is, the invitation for bid, instructions to bidders, the bid form, and any supplemental and special conditions. The bid form is especially important because it defines what pricing is required and how it is to be tendered. Procedures for sales tax should also be reviewed.

Frequently the owner will ask what markups the general contractor intends to use for change orders. This can become an issue when the owner assumes that the stated markup includes those of subcontractors, while the general contractor assumes that it does not. If there is a question, an estimator should submit a request for information to get a clarification. Sometimes an owner also will require markups that the general contractor plans to use for subcontractors. The estimator must ensure that he or she understands the markup structure before finalizing the bid as it can have an effect on how the final fee is determined.

Unit pricing may also be requested for a given list of work activities. These are more common for industrial and heavy construction, but occasionally an owner of a commercial project will request them. Unit price determination will be discussed in Chapter 12, but the estimator should know that if requested, its inclusion is required in order to tender a qualified bid.

The second part of the document review is looking at the drawings that were used for estimating—the ones that were marked up as items were quantified. The estimator should verify on each drawing which items are self-performed work and which are subcontract work. It is very important to look at the mechanical, electrical, and civil drawings as they may have items, such as concrete pads for transformers or air conditioning units, that the general contractor is to construct that are not shown on the architectural and structural drawings. During the drawing review, the estimator should ensure that all items of direct work have been marked. It is not necessary to perform another dimensional check of the quantities, but simply to make sure that all items of work have been quantified. Items not marked should be verified as not having been estimated, and a miscellaneous QTO and recap sheet should be prepared for them. All of the sections and details should be reviewed thoroughly. Sometimes an element on a plan has been marked as taken off, but the section or detail has not. While the information in the estimate may be correct, the detail may show things that are different than the estimator thought. When finished, all sections and details that pertain to self-performed work should have been marked. This is an especially important check.

Some additional items in the specifications should be verified. Typically specification sections are basic standards that have been modified for a specific project. Additional specifications are included on some drawings, and the estimator must determine which ones take precedence. Many of the specifications concern standards to which the work is to be performed and the methods to be used to accomplish it. For most projects, the productivity used in the estimate is adequate to cover most variations in the specifications. A quick scan will verify this. The estimator should pay more attention to the material specifications. For example, 3,000 psi concrete may be required for footings and slabs, while 4,000 psi may be required for some other sections, and the estimator must ensure that the proper quantities have been priced.

Once the document review has been completed and any miscellaneous items have been identified, it is time to review the estimate sheets. Every sheet should be scanned to see that the totals to be used are double underlined. The estimator should ensure that each double underlined total has been circled, signifying that it has been transferred to the next applicable sheet in the estimate and then check that sheet to make sure the number was transferred correctly. A spot check should be done on the summation of some columns to make sure the spreadsheet formulas are working properly. Finally, the unit costs at the bottom of the recap sheets should be checked to determine if they are within a reasonable range for the work to be performed.

At this point, the estimate should be ready for the final summarization. All totals on the recaps and summary recaps should be double underlined, and those that have been transferred from a recap to a summary recap should be circled. The estimator should make sure that the estimate sheets have been properly filed as discussed in Chapter 6. There should be files for the major work activities, such as foundations, slabs, and tilt-up walls. The estimator then submits the estimate to the project manager for review. A properly prepared file makes it easier to see errors or anomalies that may need to be corrected. The reviewer can spot other items that the estimator may have overlooked or work procedures that may not have been considered.

11.3 COMPLETING THE BID SUMMARY

The bid summary, Form F-9 in Appendix F, is used for summarizing the work and producing the bid. Figure 11-1 is an example bid summary form for the Training Center with all of the self-performed work and general conditions amounts filled in.

The bid summary is laid out in five sections. Starting at the top, the first section is for entering the totals from the general conditions estimate. The lines are already labeled to conform to each of the four pages of the general conditions estimate. The second section is for listing the amounts from the various self-performed work packages. The line descriptions are blank. This is where the estimator enters appropriate descriptions, as numbers are ready to be transferred. Different projects may have different descriptions, but general CSI categories or assemblies should be used whenever possible. The third section is for making adjustments to the labor. The fourth section lists the total from the subcontractor list and any necessary adjustments, and the final section is for determining markups. The total bid shown on the bottom line is the one that will be tendered to the owner.

The estimator may fill in the bid summary in any manner that he or she chooses. Some will start the sheet at the beginning of the estimating process and fill it in as various sections are completed; others will wait until all self-performed work and general conditions have been estimated and fill it in all at once. Whatever system the estimator chooses, consistency should be used for all estimates. In Figure 11-1, the estimator has filled in the general conditions and self-performed work amounts, and subtotals are shown after the first and second sections. It should be noted that the subtotal of each section includes the subtotal of the previous section.

When transferring numbers from the recap or summary recap pages to the bid summary, only the total man-hours, labor, and material amounts are transferred. A summation formula in the far right column will calculate the total cost. This total is then checked against the total on the recap sheet to make sure they match. This serves as an additional guard against transposing numbers when transferring. The transferred numbers on the recap sheets are circled, and the total is also circled when it has been verified that it is correct.

The third section of the bid summary serves to add necessary adjustments to the direct labor. Labor burden is a cost that is in addition to the base wage rate being earned by employees. It includes fringe benefits and payroll taxes. Contractors have different ways of accounting for labor burden, and it is the estimator's responsibility to know the basis of his or her company's calculations. A common way is to cost all labor within the estimate, both direct and indirect (overhead), using unburdened base wage rates; that is, those without

Bid Summary

Project: *The Training Center*
Owner: *Carpenters Trust Fund*

Bid Date & Time: *June 3, 2003, 2:00 P.M.*
Estimator: *P. Jacobs   Est. #: TTC-1*

CODE	PAGE	DESCRIPTION	MAN-HOURS	LABOR	MATERIAL	TOTAL	
		Administrative		$64,000	$11,700	$75,700	
		Indirect Equipment		–	30,483	30,483	
		Temporary Construction		800	5,525	6,325	
		General Conditions		–	13,830	13,830	
							OK
		Total Job Overhead		$64,800	$61,538	$126,338	27%
		Demolition	125	1,890	0	1,890	
		Sitework	595	8,988	9,793	18,781	
		Concrete	3,618	54,680	118,754	173,434	
		Tilt-up Walls	2,904	43,885	72,322	116,207	
		Wood & Plastics	920	13,910	9,511	23,421	
		Subtotal	8,162	$188,153	$271,918	$460,071	OK
		Labor Burden					
		Trade Travel & Subsistance					
		Labor Increase					
		Contingency					
		Subtotal		$188,153	$271,918	$460,071	OK

Subcontracts		
Subcontractor Bonds		
Adjustments		
	Subtotal	$460,071
Fee		
	Subtotal	$460,071
Business Taxes &		
Insurance		
	Subtotal	$460,071
Adjustments		
	TOTAL BID	$460,071

FIGURE 11–1   Partially complete bid summary.

173

fringes and payroll taxes. Labor burden can range from 30% for open shop (non-union craftworkers) and administrative personnel to as much as 80% for certain union trades. Some companies calculate a percentage markup to be used for all work, which is based on an average crew mix throughout the company. This percentage is used for the overhead labor as well as for the trades, and the entire labor burden is considered a material item. Other companies treat labor burden differently. Some consider the fringe benefits as a labor cost and add it to the base wage rate. This rate is commonly known as the *taxable wage rate,* because it is the rate upon which payroll taxes are calculated. Only the payroll taxes are then considered a material item. Still other companies consider the base wage plus benefits and payroll taxes to be labor costs and set up their cost systems accordingly.

Understanding how labor burden is calculated is crucial for the estimator because it affects what wage rates are used throughout the estimate. Western Construction Company has chosen the method of treating fringes and payroll taxes as a material item and has determined a company-wide average that is 45% of the direct and indirect labor. Their calculation of labor burden is

$$(\$188,153)(0.45) = \$84,669$$

This figure is then entered in the material column and summed to the total column.

Other lines in the labor section apply to special situations. If a jobsite is at a remote location, travel and subsistence costs will be incurred. The estimator needs to calculate these costs for any affected direct labor. If the project is in a city where labor is readily available, there are no additional costs. Travel and subsistence for the management and supervision is in the general conditions estimate and is not included in this section of the bid summary. Some projects use labor whose wage rates will increase during construction of the project. The estimator needs to determine the increase and add it in on the appropriate line. The project summary schedule should be reviewed to determine how much of the work will be done prior to the increase and how much will be done after award. Figure 11-2 shows the bid summary with the labor burden calculated and also indicates that the estimator sees no need for any other labor adjustments.

11.4 FIRST-RUN BID ESTIMATE

An important part of estimating is to compare the first-run bid estimate with the ROM estimate that was made in Chapter 6 (see Figure 6-2). If there is a wide difference, the estimator needs to compare the components of the ROM against like components of the first-run bid to determine where differences exist. Totals that are within a reasonable variance (±10%) validate the estimate as being within an expected range.

When creating a first-run bid estimate, the estimator should prominently mark the top of the bid summary "FIRST RUN." This is extremely important so that it doesn't get used for the final bid. In addition, after the first run is made and used for validation purposes, it should be filed and not used on bid day. If the first run does not validate the ROM and more work is done on the estimate, the procedure should be repeated and the next version should be marked "SECOND RUN." This process should be repeated until the differences are reconciled, with each succeeding bid summary marked in the next sequential run number. Figure 11-3 shows a bid summary marked as a first-run estimate.

Bid Summary

Project: *The Training Center*
Owner: *Carpenters Trust Fund*

Bid Date & Time: *June 3, 2003, 2:00 P.M.*
Estimator: *P. Jacobs   Est. #: TTC-1*

CODE	PAGE	DESCRIPTION	MAN-HOURS	LABOR	MATERIAL	TOTAL	
		Administrative		$64,000	$11,700	$75,700	
		Indirect Equipment		–	30,483	30,483	
		Temporary Construction		800	5,525	6,325	
		General Conditions		–	13,830	13,830	
							OK
		Total Job Overhead		$64,800	$61,538	$126,338	23%
		Demolition	125	1,890	0	1,890	
		Sitework	595	8,988	9,793	18,781	
		Concrete	3,618	54,680	118,754	173,434	
		Tilt-up Walls	2,904	43,885	72,322	116,207	
		Wood & Plastics	920	13,910	9,511	23,421	
		Subtotal	8,162	$188,153	$271,918	$460,071	OK
		Labor Burden	45%		$84,669	$84,669	
		Trade Travel & Subsistance					
		Labor Increase					
		Contingency					
		Subtotal		$188,153	$356,587	$544,740	OK
		Subcontracts					
		Subcontractor Bonds					
		Adjustments					
		Subtotal				$544,740	
		Fee					
		Subtotal				$544,740	
		Business Taxes & Insurance					
		Subtotal				$544,740	
		Adjustments					
		TOTAL BID				$544,740	

FIGURE 11–2   Bid summary with labor adjustments.

Bid Summary

Project: *The Training Center*
Owner: *Carpenters Trust Fund*

Bid Date & Time: *June 3, 2003, 2:00 P.M.*
Estimator: *P. Jacobs   Est. #: TTC-1*

CODE	PAGE	DESCRIPTION	MAN-HOURS	LABOR	MATERIAL	TOTAL	
		Administrative		$64,000	$11,700	$75,700	
		Indirect Equipment		–	30,483	30,483	
		Temporary Construction		800	5,525	6,325	
		General Conditions		–	13,830	13,830	
							OK
		Total Job Overhead		$64,800	$61,538	$126,338	5%
		Demolition	125	1,890	0	1,890	
		Sitework	595	8,988	9,793	18,781	
		Concrete	3,618	54,680	118,754	173,434	
		Tilt-up Walls	2,904	43,885	72,322	116,207	
		Wood & Plastics	920	13,910	9,511	23,421	
		Subtotal	8,162	$188,153	$271,918	$460,071	OK
		Labor Burden	45%		$84,669	$84,669	
		Trade Travel & Subsistance					
		Labor Increase					
		Contingency					
		Subtotal		$188,153	$356,587	$544,740	OK

Subcontracts		$1,768,411
Subcontractor Bonds		
Adjustments		
	Subtotal	$2,313,151
Fee	6%	$138,789
	Subtotal	$2,451,940
Business Taxes &		
Insurance	1.6%	$39,231
	Subtotal	$2,491,171
Adjustments		
	TOTAL BID	$2,491,171

FIGURE 11-3   First-run bid estimate.

176

The first-run estimate is created from the information that has been developed to this point. The self-performed work and the jobsite overhead already have been transferred from their corresponding estimate pages, and labor burden calculations and adjustments made. These parts of the estimate will remain on all bid summary pages, unless the first run is not validated. Subcontractor and major supplier pricing usually have not been received when the first run is generated. The estimator should use the total from the subcontractor list on the OM estimates developed in Chapter 9 (see Figure 9-5). The total from that list is transferred to the appropriate line in the fourth section of the bid summary.

Two other lines in this section are not used for the first run, but may be required in the final bid. On bid day, a very low bid may be received from a subcontractor with whom the general contractor has not worked. There may be a tendency to disregard this bid as being unrealistically low, but it must be considered that the general contractor's competitors have also received this bid and may use it. The greatest risk to the contractor is that the bid was made in error, and that the subcontractor may either decline to do the work or go bankrupt while work is in progress. The general contractor might decide to require the subcontractor to furnish performance and payment bonds as financial protection. The anticipated cost of these bonds would then be entered on the subcontractor bond line.

The subcontracts section is subtotaled and, as before, includes the subtotal of the previous section. This completes all of the self-performed work, jobsite overhead, and subcontracts, and the estimate is now ready for the final markups.

11.5 FINAL MARKUPS

Final markups are items that pertain to the overall total, which will be the contract amount if the project is won. These include the general contractor's fee, certain business taxes, and liability insurance. The fee represents a portion of the *home office overhead* and the profit (OH&P) for the project. Some like to call it overhead and profit, and others like to call it the fee; but they are the same. Home office overhead covers the basic services provided to each project by the company's home office. This includes accounting services, sales, estimating, home office facilities, cost of project managers and superintendents between jobs, and salaries of the home office personnel including the officers.

Fee Determination

Home office overhead for general contractors varies depending mostly on the contractor's size and work backlog. For small to medium-size contractors, it typically ranges from about 3% to 7% of the contract cost. Larger general contractors have a home office overhead as low as 1%. If the company is doing one very large project along with its normal work, the overhead for the project may be as low as 0.5%. This is because most of the staff that would normally be at the home office are stationed in the field for this project and charged directly to the job.

There are several considerations for determining the amount of profit to include in the project bid. The first priority of the general contractor is to limit the risk of losing money. The biggest single operations risk for the general contractor is whether or not the direct labor will achieve the productivity that was used in the estimate. Some general contractors limit this risk by subcontracting all of the work and then managing the subcontractors. The risk then becomes the general contractor's management capabilities, and the technical capabilities and financial condition of the subcontractors. The downside is that a contractor who is innovative in performing direct work benefits by generating savings, which are added to the profit. When all of the work is subcontracted, the contractor will not realize such a savings.

There are several factors to consider in calculating an appropriate fee (OH&P). Some of these include the following:

1. The fee may be determined based on the amount of direct labor. A fee that is about 50% of the direct labor cost is considered adequate protection against possible labor overruns. Using the amounts from Figure 11-2, a fee calculation would be

$$[(\$188,153 - \$64,800)](0.5) = \$61,677$$

   This fee represents about 2.7% of the subtotal prior to adding the business taxes and insurance. This is low, but it might be appropriate in a competitive market. The estimator should look at other ways to calculate a more realistic fee.

2. Another approach to fee determination is to estimate the earning power of the project superintendent and project manager. The capability of the team to organize and run a job successfully, keep costs under control, and maximize profit potential are factors that should be considered. In many cases, the superintendent and project manager will not be known at bid time, but the type of project usually dictates the capabilities required. For example, a very large job with a high labor risk will require a very experienced superintendent and project manager. Smaller projects that employ mostly subcontractors can be done successfully with a less experienced team. A highly capable superintendent and project manager should be able to earn $20,000 or more per month for a project. Those who have little experience or who cannot run high-risk work may have an earning power as low as $5,000 per month. A highly skilled superintendent and project manager for a job whose duration is 6.5 months should generate a fee of

$$(\$20,000/\text{month})(6.5 \text{ month}) = \$130,000$$

   Note that this is considerably more than the required labor protection calculated in the first method. It also represents about 5.6% of the subtotal before business taxes and insurance are added. This would be considered a reasonable fee, but it might be a little high for current market conditions. Before making a final decision, other fee determination methods should be considered. A job that is straightforward and done largely by subcontractors has a lower risk, so the work of the superintendent is primarily that of ensuring that the subcontractors perform in accordance with the contract documents. A project manager or project engineer will do much of the subcontracting and documentation work, and the superintendent can be someone who has less experience but is working to increase his or her knowledge. The estimator may decide that a fee of only $12,000 a month is warranted, which would be $78,000 for a 6.5-month project.

3. A company's backlog of work also enters into the fee consideration. The estimator and the OIC usually discuss the company's backlog and decide how important the project is. If the backlog is low, they may decide they want the job and propose to lower the fee. If the backlog is high, they might decide to use a higher fee. If they do not win the bid, at least they have responded, which usually keeps them on the owner's preferred bid list for future projects.

4. A survey of market conditions is also used to determine the fee. When the company's backlog decreases, it is usually low for an entire class of competitors. Consequently, they all will probably be bidding to get work and will use lower fees. The contractor has to be careful not to bid the job so low that there will be no profit. There is a fine balance between keeping personnel occupied on a project at almost any cost versus losing money. The final decision rests with the OIC.

5. The bid team also must assess the availability of personnel to supervise the construction activities. If all of the contractor's key personnel are committed to other projects, a higher fee may be proposed to cover the cost of hiring a new superintendent and possibly some other key field people.

The estimator should review the project with the OIC in detail. This will help the OIC assess risk in relation to determining a fee. If the project is straightforward and is the type that the contractor normally undertakes, the risk is relatively low, and a modest fee can be used. If the work is a new type for the company or there is a very large direct labor force, the risk is high, and the fee should reflect this.

At this stage, the estimator prepares the bid summary for bid day. He or she has decided to use a fee of 6% based on the following:

- The labor risk coverage calculation produces a fee that is too low.
- The work is the type that the company normally performs.
- An experienced superintendent's earning power for 7 months produces a fee of just over 6%.
- The subcontract work is significant, which lowers risk.
- Market conditions seem to indicate that projects are being bid with fees in the range of 5% to 8%.
- The company's backlog is reasonably strong but could use more work.
- The home office overhead is currently running about 2% of total work under contract.

The estimator believes that a 4% profit keeps the fee competitive and at the lower end of the market range. It also is in line with the earning power of an experienced superintendent and project manager. A figure of 6% for OH&P is therefore entered on the first run estimate.

Business Taxes and Insurance

Business taxes and insurance are a combined markup, based on the total contract amount, that covers the taxes for doing business in the state, city, and county where the project is located, and the cost of liability insurance. Most states have some sort of business tax. Many cities have their own tax for all work contracted within their city limits. Company accounting departments can usually furnish a markup rate (%) to be used for business taxes and liability insurance. If the project is in a state and city where the contractor does not normally work, the estimator must determine the cost for a business license and add it to the markup or include it in the general conditions estimate. The Training Center is being constructed in the area where Western Construction normally works, and a 1.6% markup for the business taxes and liability insurance has been established.

On certain projects, the owner will require *builder's risk insurance*, which is in addition to the insurance included in the final markups on the bid summary. The estimator must price it accordingly. Builder's risk insurance is a policy that protects the owner against financial loss due to damage to the uncompleted project. The owner may provide this insurance, or the contractor may be required to furnish it. It is important to realize that this is an additional cost to the contract and to treat it accordingly.

The estimator may want to include a contingency either in the fee or just before the final bid total. Contingencies are appropriate for negotiated projects where design information may be limited; but for lump-sum work, contingencies generally are not used. The bidder is being asked to furnish a price for the work as defined in the contract documents. It is the project team's duty prior to executing the contract to make sure that the project scope of work has not been increased. This then minimizes the need for any contingency.

An item briefly discussed earlier was what percentage of the bid amount the jobsite overhead is. Usually, a general conditions estimate that is about 5% to 8% of the total bid is considered adequate for a project. Straightforward projects, such as the Training Center, can be done with a little less field management, and 8% might be considered high. On bid day, this should be discussed with the OIC as it may affect what, if any, adjustments are made. The first-run estimate for the Training Center shows a jobsite overhead of 5%, which should be adequate for this type of job. If a project is difficult, a higher jobsite overhead will be required. On some heavy industrial projects, the general conditions can be as high as 12% due to additional management and supervision and the need for expensive specialized small tools.

Formulas are entered in the appropriate spaces in the markup section. Percentage markups are located in their own cells so that the formula will multiply the previous subtotal by the percentage entered. If the percentage needs to be changed, it can be done easily, and the markups will be recalculated automatically. The cell for the adjustment has no formula, and the amount (if any) determined by the OIC must be entered and then checked to make sure it is added correctly.

11.6 SALES TAX

Sales tax becomes an issue in an estimate in three different places: for certain items that do not become a permanent part of the project, such as concrete form material; for equipment rental; and whether or not sales tax is included in the final bid. The estimator must understand the procedures for sales tax in the state in which the project is being constructed and apply those procedures accordingly. When purchasing form material, for example, the unit prices used may need to include sales tax. If a construction company's historical information is used as the basis for pricing, it typically includes appropriate sales tax. However, if vendor pricing or estimating references are used, sales tax may not be included. Equipment rental also is subject to differing state rules regarding sales tax. At the location of the Training Center, equipment that is rented without an operator is subject to sales tax, while equipment that is rented with an operator is not subject to sales tax.

When tendering a final bid, the inclusion or exclusion of sales tax may be a matter of state law. Some states require that sales tax be added to the contract amount to calculate a bid total. Other states make it illegal to include sales tax in a bid. This becomes an important issue when a contractor is constructing a facility in a state other than his or her home location. In addition to state sales tax, the estimator needs to determine if any local sales taxes apply. Washington State, where the Training Center is being constructed, does not allow sales tax to be included in the bid.

11.7 VALIDATING THE FIRST-RUN ESTIMATE

An important function of the first-run estimate is to validate it by comparing it with the ROM estimate prepared in Chapter 6. In doing this, the estimator must take into account the level of accuracy for each type of estimate. The ROM is based on general information and square foot pricing for a structure built for a particular use. Many things can vary from one facility to the next. Remember that the model used to develop the price for the Training Center was a one-story factory with offices and a shop. The first-run estimate is based on detailed estimating of the self-performed work and OM estimates for the subcontract work. The first-run estimate should be more accurate than the ROM estimate. Neither will be as accurate as the final bid, which will have subcontractor bids.

Let's compare the first-run estimate (Figure 11-3) with the ROM estimate from Chapter 6 (Figure 6-2) and determine if the variance is within an acceptable range. The estimate totals are as follows:

ROM Estimate from Chapter 6	$2,480,000
First-Run Bid Estimate	$2,491,171
Variance	$11,171

These two estimates are within 0.5% of one another. It is fairly unusual to be this close, but the estimator should expect the variance to be less than 10%. Note that these two estimates were derived by different means, and the comparison validates that the estimate is within the expected range.

11.8 PREPARING THE ESTIMATE FOR BID DAY (*ELECTRONIC*)

As the time for tendering the bid approaches, things can get hectic in the *bid room*. This makes the process especially vulnerable to errors, however, the use of computers has greatly reduced this vulnerability, as we will discuss in Chapter 14. Much can be done ahead of time by setting up a universal bid summary template and modifying it for the particular project being bid. In most instances, modification will not be necessary, and the first-run bid estimate can be used to check all calculations.

All calculations on the bid summary are straightforward, and the formulas should be entered in the appropriate cells. All lines should sum across to the total column and columns should sum down. In addition, the sum of the labor and material column totals should equal the sum of the total column. The final setup and operation of the bid summary will be discussed in Chapter 13.

11.9 SUMMARY

An estimate is complete when a final check has been made of the work done and the figures have been entered onto the bid summary in preparation for bid day. A thorough document review is performed to ensure that all components of self-performed work have been properly quantified and priced. Estimate pages are scanned to make sure all usable totals are double underlined signifying that they have been checked, and all of these totals are circled indicating that they have been transferred to the next page in the sequence. For most modest-sized projects, the completion of the bid can be accomplished in a day.

A key point in this process is validating the results. This is done by making a first-run bid estimate and comparing the results against the ROM estimate developed at the beginning of the process. Since this is done prior to the receipt of subcontractor bids, the total of the OM estimates developed in Chapter 9 is used for subcontract work. Anticipated markup percentages are then entered, which results in the first-run total. The first-run is validated if it compares within a reasonable range to the ROM estimate. It is very important that the first-run bid estimate be prominently marked and that it is not in the bid room on bid day.

During the development of the first-run estimate, all calculations on the bid summary are checked for proper ranges and operations. Cells containing formulas are locked to avoid inadvertent entry of other numbers on bid day. A final bid summary containing the general conditions, direct work, and labor burden is then made up in preparation for use on bid day.

11.10 REVIEW QUESTIONS

1. What is an important operation that should be done first when completing the estimate?
2. Which form is used for completing the estimate?
3. The bid form is organized into five general sections. What does each section represent?
4. How are the general conditions and direct work subtotals checked?
5. What percentage range is used as a guide when comparing the total of the general conditions estimate against the total bid amount?
6. What is labor burden?
7. When would an amount be entered for a subcontractor bond?
8. What are the components of the fee?
9. What are four factors to consider in determining the fee?
10. What is a first-run estimate and how is it used?
11. What is the function of the first-run estimate on bid day?

11.11 EXERCISES

1. Make a bid summary template on a computer spreadsheet. Determine all formulas including a percentage formula next to the general conditions subtotal. Check all operations and save this template for future use.

2. Determine what the business taxes required for a general contractor are for your local area. Add 1% for liability insurance and enter it in a first-run bid summary form.

3. Modify the template created in exercise 1 to automatically calculate and include an aggregate (state and local) sales tax of 8.4% in the bid total.

4. Determine the percentages of the bid total that are attributable to the direct work and the subcontracts. Use the direct work after the addition of the labor burden. Would these percentages be useful as a guide on similar estimates?

12

UNIT PRICE ESTIMATES

12.1 INTRODUCTION

As discussed in Chapter 1, unit-price contracts or bid items are used when the exact project scope cannot be determined, but a quantity can be estimated for each element of work. The designer, either an engineer or an architect, provides an estimated quantity for each unit-price item, and the construction contractor determines the unit price. The actual contract value for each unit-price item is not determined until the project is completed. The actual quantities of work are measured during the construction of the project, and the cost is determined by multiplying the quantity used by the unit price submitted by the contractor. Many unit-price contracts have both lump-sum and unit-price bid items. Unit-price contracts are used extensively for highway projects, those involving environmental cleanup, and some sitework projects. The invitation for bids for industrial and commercial projects sometimes request that a schedule of unit prices be submitted as part of the bid. In this chapter, we will discuss the process for developing the unit prices for such contracts.

12.2 UNIT PRICE BID FORMS

There are many types of unit-price bid forms. Sometimes the majority of the work is priced as a single or lump sum with selected project components, such as sitework or foundation items, unit priced. An example of such a bid form is shown in Figure 12-1. In other instances, only bid alternates are unit priced, as illustrated in Figure 12-2. Most heavy construction and highway projects have a number of individual lump-sum and unit-price items, as illustrated in Figure 12-3.

183

The undersigned proposes to furnish all labor, materials, equipment, and services necessary to complete the work, less the drilled foundations, in strict accordance with the contract documents for the sum of

_____ Dollars ($_____)

The undersigned proposes to furnish all labor, materials, equipment, and services necessary to construct the drilled pier foundations for the following schedule of prices. Exact quantities will be determined upon completion of the work.

Item	Unit of Measure	Estimated Quantity	Unit Price	Amount
2-foot diameter drilled piers	linear feet	400		
3-foot diameter drilled piers	linear feet	350		
4-foot diameter drilled piers	linear feet	500		

Total for Unit-Priced Items:

_____ Dollars ($_____)

Total Bid Price:

_____ Dollars ($_____)

FIGURE 12–1　Bid form for lump-sum contract with unit-price bid items.

BASE BID

The undersigned proposes to furnish all labor, materials, equipment, and services necessary to complete the work in strict accordance with the contract documents for the sum of

_____ Dollars ($_____)

which sum is hereby designated as the Base Bid.

ALTERNATES

The undersigned proposes to perform the work called for in the following alternates, as described in Section 01030 and the drawings of the Contract Documents for the following schedule of prices, which are additions to the Base Bid. Exact quantities will be determined upon completion of the work.

Alternative #1: Add asphalt parking lot.

Estimated Quantity	Unit of Measure	Unit Price	Bid Amount
2,000	square yards		

Alternate #2: Add hauling of spoil material to soccer field.

Estimated Quantity	Unit of Measure	Unit Price	Bid Amount
1,000	cubic yards		

FIGURE 12–2　Bid form for lump-sum contract with unit-price alternates.

The undersigned proposes to perform the work called for in the Contract Documents for the following schedule of prices. Exact quantities will be determined upon completion of the work.

Work Items	Unit of Measure	Estimated Quantity	Unit Price	Bid Amount
1. Mobilization	lump sum	1		
2. Traffic Control	lump sum	1		
3. Erosion Control	lump sum	1		
4. Clearing and Grubbing	lump sum	1		
5. Embankment in Place	cubic yards	4,000		
6. Culvert Pipe	feet	300		
7. Aggregate Base	square yards	1,000		
8. Asphalt Pavement	square yards	6,000		

Total Bid Price:

_____ Dollars ($_____)

FIGURE 12–3   Bid form for unit-price contract.

In determining the unit price to bid for base-bid, unit-price items, the estimator needs to estimate both the direct and indirect cost associated with each item. The indirect costs include both the project indirect cost (general conditions) and company overhead and profit. Since alternate bid items may or may not be awarded by the owner, only costs directly related to the specific scope of work, company overhead, and profit should be considered when determining an appropriate unit price. This is to ensure that the contractor's general conditions costs on the project are covered by base-bid items.

12.3 DIRECT COST ESTIMATION

The first step is to estimate the quantity of work required for each unit price item. The quantity is then compared with the quantity listed on the bid form by the project designer. This is to determine if the listed quantity is reasonable. Then using either the quantity taken off the project plans or the estimated quantity on the bid form, the direct costs are estimated using procedures similar to those discussed in Chapter 7. Material costs are estimated using prices from material suppliers. Labor and equipment costs typically are determined using a crew analysis, which is described in Figure 12-4.

Let's use the embankment-in-place work item shown in Figure 12-3 as an example. The first step is to visualize the operation and the jobsite working conditions. The task is to excavate fill material from a borrow site, transport the material 1.5 miles to the jobsite, and construct a compacted earth embankment. The work is scheduled for summer months, so weather will not be a factor. The construction site will be cleared during clearing and grubbing, so it will pose no impediments to an efficient operation. The loading site is restricted, which will affect the productivity of the loading operation.

The next step is to perform a QTO for the compacted embankment. We determined the measurements from the site drawings and calculated a volume of approximately 4,000

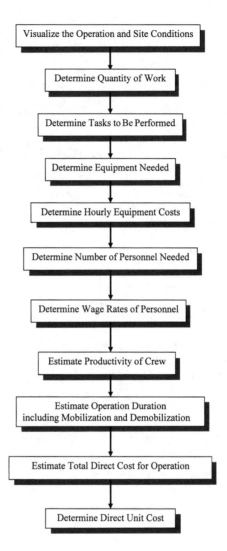

FIGURE 12–4 Crew analysis.

cubic yards, so we will use the estimated amount shown on the bid form. If the QTO had indicated a significantly lower quantity, we would have used our measured quantity to determine the unit price. Now we must select the fleet of equipment we will use. We will need a hydraulic excavator to load dump trucks at the borrow site, four dump trucks to transport and spread the fill material, a grader to shape the fill, a water truck to add moisture to help with compaction, and one compactor.

Now we need to estimate the hourly cost for each piece of equipment. This cost will include ownership, rental, or lease cost, and an operating cost. Historical records are the best source for ownership and operating costs, and vendors are the best source for rental or lease costs. The hourly ownership cost for a piece of equipment is established by deter-

Equipment	Hourly Cost
Excavator	$65 per hour
Dump Truck	$35 per hour
Grader	$40 per hour
Water Truck	$25 per hour
Compactor	$45 per hour

FIGURE 12-5 Hourly equipment costs.

mining an annual ownership cost and dividing it by the number of hours the contractor anticipates using the piece per year. The annual ownership cost is estimated using the acquisition cost, anticipated salvage value, and expected period of ownership. The hourly operating cost is estimated by adding the hourly maintenance and repair, tire, fuel, and service costs. The hourly costs for the equipment to be used are shown in Figure 12-5.

Now we need to estimate the number of personnel needed for the embankment construction. We will need one operator for each piece of equipment, a foreman, and three ground guides, for a total of twelve people. Let's assume that their average hourly wage is $40, including benefits. After analyzing the productivity of each item of equipment, we determined that the governing productivity for this operation will be that of the four dump trucks, which is estimated to be 125 cubic yards per hour. Now we can estimate the duration of the task by dividing the estimated quantity by the overall fleet productivity.

First, we must estimate the amount of fill material to be hauled. Once the soil is excavated, it expands or swells. Let's assume that the amount of swell is 25% for the type of soil that is to be excavated. Once the soil is placed in the embankment and compacted, its volume shrinks to less than it was in its natural state. Let's assume that the amount of shrinkage for the compactive effort that will be applied is 5%. Now we can estimate the amount of material to be excavated to be

$$\frac{4{,}000 \text{ compacted cubic yards}}{(1 - \text{shrinkage})} = \frac{4{,}000 \text{ compacted cubic yards}}{0.95} = 4{,}211 \text{ bank cubic yards}$$

The amount of material to be transported in the dump truck can now be estimated to be

$$(4{,}211 \text{ bank cubic yards})(1 + \text{swell}) = (4{,}211 \text{ bank cubic yards})(1.25)$$
$$= 5{,}264 \text{ loose or truck cubic yards}$$

The estimated duration for the task can now be estimated to be:

$$\frac{5{,}264 \text{ truck cubic yards}}{125 \text{ truck cubic yards per hour}} = 42 \text{ hours}$$

We should add 4 hours for mobilization and 4 hours for demobilization, for a total of 50 hours. Now we can estimate the total cost for the operation as shown in Figure 12-6.

Now we can estimate the direct unit cost by dividing the total direct cost by the estimated quantity of work, which is

($39,750) ÷ (4,000 cubic yards) = $9.94 per cubic yard or $10.00 per cubic yard

In a similar manner, we can estimate the unit prices or lump-sum amount for the remaining bid items. The results are shown in Figure 12-7.

Item	Quantity	Hourly Cost	Duration	Total
Excavator	1	$65 per hour	50 hours	$3,250
Dump Trucks	4	$35 per hour	50 hours	$7,000
Grader	1	$40 per hour	50 hours	$2,000
Water Truck	1	$25 per hour	50 hours	$1,250
Compactor	1	$45 per hour	50 hours	$2,250
Labor	12	$40 per hour	50 hours	$24,000
Total				$39,750

FIGURE 12–6 Total direct cost for embankment operation.

Work Items	Unit of Measure	Estimated Quantity	Unit Price	Bid Amount
1. Mobilization	lump sum	1	$10,000	$10,000
2. Traffic Control	lump sum	1	$2,000	$2,000
3. Erosion Control	lump sum	1	$5,000	$5,000
4. Clearing and Grubbing	lump sum	1	$8,000	$8,000
5. Embankment in Place	cubic yards	4,000	$10	$40,000
6. Culvert Pipe	feet	300	$50	$15,000
7. Aggregate Base	square yards	1,000	$9	$9,000
8. Asphalt Pavement	square yards	6,000	$36	$216,000
Total				$305,000

FIGURE 12–7 Total direct cost for bid.

The greatest risk the estimator faces in determining the direct cost for a bid item is in estimating the productivity of the crew. The condition of the equipment, experience of the operators, and weather all influence the productivity that actually will be achieved. Sometimes the estimator will reduce the estimated productivity if adverse conditions are expected while the task is scheduled to be performed. Since we are planning on constructing the embankment during the summer, we will not make any reductions to the estimated productivity.

12.4 MARKUP DETERMINATION

Now that we have determined the direct unit prices, we need to determine appropriate markups for project general conditions costs and company overhead. The process for estimating the jobsite general conditions cost was discussed in Chapter 10, and company overhead was discussed in Chapter 11. Let's assume that the estimated general conditions cost for this project is $100,000, and that this company's markup for overhead and profit is 5%. To determine an appropriate markup, divide the estimated total general conditions cost by the total estimated direct project costs, which is

$$(\$100,000) \div (\$305,000) = 0.33$$

Thus to determine the final bid, we need to mark up the direct prices by 33% to cover the jobsite general conditions, and then mark up the result by an additional 5% to cover company overhead and profit. We may choose to make some additional adjustments as contingencies for potential risks posed by the project. These risks are discussed in section 12.6.

12.5 VARIATION-IN-QUANTITY CONTRACT PROVISION

Sometimes the actual quantities of work are significantly different from the designer's estimated quantities. If the quantities are significantly less than those estimated by the designer, the contractor will not adequately cover his or her overhead costs. If the quantities are significantly greater than those estimated by the designer, the contractor will receive greater profit. To accommodate these contingencies, a variation-in-quantity provision usually is included in most unit-price contracts. This provision allows either the owner or the contractor to request a revision to the unit price for payment items that vary by more than a certain percentage, typically 15% to 20%. An example variation-in-quantity contract provision is shown in Figure 12-8. Implementation of this clause would not occur until the end of the contract when exact quantities of work are known.

Changes in the Quantity of Unit-Price Work. Where the nature of the changed Work does not differ materially from the Work that is Unit-Price Work, the change shall be measured and paid for at the established unit prices, subject to the following exceptions:

1. *Where the quantity is less than 85%.* If the quantity of an item of Unit-Price Work actually performed is less than 85% of the bid quantity for that item, the Contractor or the Owner may request a Change Order revising the unit price for the item. Such request shall be accompanied by evidence to support the requested revision. The proposed revision will be evaluated by the Owner considering such factors as the changes in actual costs to the Contractor of the item, and the share, if any, of fixed expenses properly chargeable to the change in quantity of that item. If the Owner and the Contractor agree on the change, a Change Order will be executed. If the parties cannot agree, the Owner may nevertheless issue a Change Order pursuant to the Change Order Provision of this Contract, and the Contractor will have the rights provided in the Disputes Provision of this Contract.

2. *Where the quantity is more than 115%.* If the quantity of an item of Unit-Price Work actually performed is more than 115% of the bid quantity for that item, the Contractor or the Owner may request a Change Order revising the unit price for that portion of the Work that exceeds 115% of the bid quantity. Such request shall be accompanied by evidence to support the requested revision. The proposed revision will be evaluated considering such factors as the change in actual cost to the Contractor of the portion of work exceeding 115% of the bid quantity, and share, if any, of fixed expenses properly chargeable to that portion of change in quantity that exceeds 115% of the bid quantity. If the parties cannot agree, the Owner may nevertheless issue a Change Order pursuant to the Change Order Provision of this Contract, and the Contractor will have the rights provided in the Disputes Provision of this Contract.

FIGURE 12–8 Sample variation-in-quantity contract provision.

The undersigned proposes to perform the work called for in the Contract Documents for the following schedule of prices. Exact quantities will be determined upon completion of the work.

Work Items	Unit of Measure	Estimated Quantity	Unit Price	Bid Amount
1. Mobilization	lump sum	1	$14,000	$14,000
2. Traffic Control	lump sum	1	$2,800	$2,800
3. Erosion Control	lump sum	1	$7,000	$7,000
4. Clearing and Grubbing	lump sum	1	$11,200	$11,200
5. Embankment in Place	cubic yards	4,000	$14.00	$56,000
6. Culvert Pipe	feet	300	$70.00	$21,000
7. Aggregate Base	square yards	1,000	$12.60	$12,600
8. Asphalt Pavement	square yards	6,000	$50.40	$302,400

Total Bid Price:

Four Hundred Twenty-Seven Thousand _____ Dollars ($_427,000_   )

FIGURE 12–9   Completed bid form for unit-price contract.

12.6   RISK ANALYSIS

When finalizing the bid items for individual work items, the estimator should analyze the risks to be faced and make an adjustment to add a contingency, if this is warranted based on the risk analysis. For example, if material costs or labor rates are expected to increase, an appropriate contingency in the form of an additional markup should be applied to the direct costs. Other contingencies that might be used relate to potential weather impacts on productivity or the affects of differing site conditions.

12.7   BID FINALIZATION

Based on our analysis of the risk associated with this project, we have decided to apply only the markups determined in Section 12.4. The total markup will be

$$(1.33)(1.05) = 1.40$$

Applying this markup to the direct costs shown in Figure 12-7 yields the total bid tender shown in Figure 12-9.

12.8   SUMMARY

Unit-price contracts or bid items are used when the exact scope of work cannot be determined. The designer provides an estimated quantity, and the estimator must determine an appropriate unit price considering both direct and indirect costs. Material costs are estimated using vendor quotations, and labor and equipment costs are estimated using a crew analysis. Based on an assessment of the tasks to be performed, the quantity of work, and anticipated site conditions, the number and types of equipment and the labor needed are estimated. The hourly labor and equipment costs as well as the overall crew productivity are estimated. Using the quantity of work and the crew productivity, the activity duration is estimated. Using the duration and hourly costs, the total direct costs are estimated. A general conditions estimate is prepared and used to determine a markup rate for the project. The direct costs are then marked up for both project general conditions and company overhead to produce the unit prices for tendering the bid.

12.9 REVIEW QUESTIONS

1. How does an estimator determine the direct cost for a unit-price item on a bid form?
2. How does an estimator determine an appropriate markup for a unit-price item on a bid form?
3. What markup should an estimator apply to unit-price bid alternates? What is the rationale for your answer?
4. What sources should an estimator use to determine hourly equipment costs?
5. Why are variation-in-quantity provisions used in most unit-price construction contracts?

12.10 EXERCISES

1. Develop a unit price for the culvert pipe work item shown in Figure 12-3.
2. Develop a unit price for the aggregate base work item shown in Figure 12-3.

13

PRE-BID DAY ACTIVITIES

13.1 INTRODUCTION

Now that the first-run bid estimate has been prepared, the remaining work toward tendering a bid to the owner is represented by items 9 and 10 of the lump-sum estimating process shown in Figure 6-1. Item 9 is receipt, evaluation, and totaling of the quotations or bids from subcontractors and major suppliers. Item 10 is entering the subcontractor total onto the bid summary, making any necessary adjustments, and then completing and tendering the bid form. All of this work is done on bid day. Bid day can be chaotic, especially as the time for bid submission approaches. A well-organized bid room will retain order and reduce a tendency to panic in the last minutes. Setting up the bid room a day ahead of time helps to impart order to the process so that everyone involved is able to perform his or her assigned duties efficiently.

Most owners prescribe a specific bid tendering process. Many contracts have been lost because the general contractor did not explicitly follow procedures. This may be anything from submitting the bid late to improperly filling out the proposal form to not supplying other requested documents with the bid. Some owners even define the envelope and label for submitting the bid.

Some proposals may require submission of other information after the initial bid has been tendered. Frequently the owner will ask for a list of major subcontractors and the value of their work either with the bid or within a given time after the initial bid is tendered. Public owners may require a two-envelope bid where the general contractor first submits a statement of compliance with minority subcontracting requirements and, if acceptable, then submits a bid price.

The important thing is that regardless of what an owner's requirements are, a well-organized process on bid day will assure that they are met. Setting up the bid room and organizing the activities ahead of time helps to maintain control throughout the process, so that a valid bid will be tendered on time.

13.2 SETTING UP THE BID ROOM

Most general contractors have a designated room that is used on bid day specifically for processing subcontractor bids, determining the final price, making last-minute adjustments, and forwarding information to the person who will deliver the bid to the designated location. This is commonly called the bid room. It should be organized to be functional for the work that needs to be done on bid day. The bulk of the setup is done the evening before bid day.

First, make sure that all of the proper documents are in the bid room. This includes the complete set of drawings used to create the estimate and the owner's project manual including the specifications and all addenda. Many times subcontractors or major suppliers will call with last minute questions, and someone on the bid team must provide answers immediately. Having a complete set of bid documents in the room will reduce the time needed to research an answer and respond. In addition, some subcontractor bids may list exclusions, and the bid team will need to review the documents to evaluate their impact.

A properly labeled bid package should be prepared containing a signed original bid form and all documents to be tendered. The documents are then put into an envelope, which is left unsealed. The bid form should be filled in completely with all requested information except the final price(s). Failure to do this can be a basis for disqualification. A copy of the signed bid form will be filled in with the final price on bid day, then copies of all submitted documents will be attached to it. This then becomes the contractor's file copy of the bid.

A very important item on the bid form is acknowledgement of all addenda issued during the bidding process. It is the general contractor's responsibility to know how many addenda have been issued and to make sure all information has been incorporated into the bid. On bid day, the bid takers must verify that subcontractors and major suppliers have seen all addenda or, if they have not, that they are willing to do the work for their bid prices as submitted. Failure to acknowledge all addenda can disqualify the contractor.

Other documents needed in the bid room are all the bids and bid forms from the subcontractors that have been received prior to bid day. Many subcontractors will submit a form to the general contractor listing conditions and qualifications of their bid. They will leave the amount blank and will provide it on bid day. The estimator must be familiar with each of these bid forms to ensure that they conform to the bid documents. If they do not, a choice must be made whether to disqualify the bidders or to get them to bid according to the documents.

A relatively large stack of bid proposal forms (Form F-7 in Appendix F) should be prepared for recording the subcontractor bids. Most of them will be given to the bid takers on bid day, but some will remain in the bid room for early receipt of bids. In some cases, the general contractor will be bidding two projects on the same day, and the bid takers will be receiving subcontractor pricing for both. It is a good idea to fill in the title block of the bid form with the project name and make copies on a specific color of paper, so the bid taker can easily recognize which are to be used for your project. The estimator should coordinate with his or her counterpart for the other project to make sure that different colored forms are used for each project.

Instructions should be made up for the bid takers. They should indicate the number of addenda issued and should emphasize the need for the subcontractor's bid to be correct and conform fully to the drawings and specifications. In some cases, alternate pricing or certain price breakdowns will be requested. These instructions should be brief, but complete. The estimator should keep in mind that the more complex the instructions, the more difficult it makes the bid takers' job, especially when the frequency of bidding increases as the deadline approaches. Many subcontractor bids may be received by facsimile and *electronic mail* on bid day. These bids must be managed much like those received by telephone. One or more computers may be needed to receive vendor bids by email. The estimator should assign the receipt of email bids to certain bid takers and make sure that their computers are operating properly.

It is common for the final bid summary to be completed on a computer. Two computers are recommended, so that if one crashes the other is ready to take its place. The previously prepared bid summary with all of the general conditions, self-performed work, and related information entered should be loaded onto both computers. All markup percentages should also be entered. Operations on both bid summaries should be thoroughly checked using fictitious numbers. Once it is determined that they are operating correctly, the words "FINAL RUN" should be typed at the top.

Other computers may be used for subcontractor bid evaluation. The proper forms should be loaded, and their operations checked. All forms on the computers should be properly titled. In addition to computers, one or two adding machines, preferably with tapes, and a hand calculator should be available in case they are needed for evaluation purposes. Keep in mind that the work pace will become more intense as the time for bid submission approaches. At some point, all access into and out of the room should be limited, so the bid room must be supplied with everything needed to complete the work.

Subcontractor bid evaluation worksheets should be made up for use in the bid room. All OM subcontract estimates are entered onto the worksheet and noted as "plugs." This signifies that the number is an OM estimate that should only be used if no other bids are received in a particular section. The estimate and subcontractor file should be readied for the bid room. While they will not be put in the bid room until the start of bid day, the estimator should review the files for completeness and scan all pages to ensure that all numbers have been checked and transferred properly and that they are in order for easy access on bid day. There should be an OM estimate for every section of the subcontractor or major supply item in the subcontract file. Some subcontract prices will include work that is in the direct work estimate, and the bid team must be able to evaluate quickly how to handle this situation. Once the estimate files are in the bid room, they should be considered complete for all but the subcontract bids and the final bid summary. The estimator must ensure that all previous runs of the bid total are removed from the files and that they are not in the bid room on bid day. The total from the first-run bid discussed in Chapter 11 should be on hand in note form to compare with the preliminary runs of the final bid that will be done on bid day.

13.3 BID FORMS

The bid proposal form is the heart of the bid tendering process. This is the first page that the owner sees upon reviewing the bids. In addition to the price, the owner will look for completeness and a certain amount of professionalism by the bidder. It is not necessary that the final price(s) be typed, but all information that can be filled in ahead of time should be, and the final price must be neat and readable. If a contractor has not done a good job of completing the bid proposal, the owner may wonder if this is a reflection on that company's quality of work. It is crucial that the bid form be completed in its entirety and done neatly so that it is easy to read. A typical bid form is shown in Appendix E and may contain any or all of the following:

- Project name
- Spaces for the total bid amount
- Signature line (or page)
- Spaces to acknowledge addenda
- Space for cost of a performance and payment bond
- Spaces for any desired breakdown costs of the bid
- Spaces for any desired alternate prices
- Definition of what is and is not included in the contractor's prices as far as fees and any bond costs
- Spaces or definitions of change order markups by the general contractor and subcontractors
- Treatment of sales tax
- Time of completion or duration of the project
- Definition of liquidated damages
- Type of contract to be executed (if not included in the bid documents)

The first three items are required on all bid forms, and the fourth is common on most of them. The remaining items may or may not be included depending on the type of project and the owner's desires. Some owners tend to customize their contracts, and their bid forms may require additional information.

The signature page should have all of the information typed in ready for the OIC to sign. It is a good idea to have the OIC sign the bid form a day or two before bid day. Sometimes he or she will be called out of the office on an urgent matter and may not be available to sign the document until after the bid runner has left for the tendering site.

Some owners are very specific about the envelope in which the bid is to be tendered. It must be a certain size and have a very specific label. On occasion, an owner will include the envelope label with the bid documents. Other owners are less particular and, in these cases, the general contractor must use good judgement to make sure the bid is tendered in a well-labeled, professional-looking package. All requested documents must be in the bid envelope. These might include a project summary schedule, bid bond, company financial statement, and, on occasion, a request for cost reduction suggestions.

A *bid bond* assures the owner that if the low bidder withdraws a bid after bid opening, the difference between the low bid and that of the next lowest bidder will be paid by the bonding company. The bonding company usually furnishes it at no cost. If the general contractor cannot furnish a bid bond, he or she may be required to provide other *bid security,* such as a certified or cashiers check, with the bid. It is important that either the bond certificate or check, if required, be in the bid envelope at the beginning of bid day. Bid security (bonds or checks) are required for most public projects, but are rarely required by private owners.

Some owners, in lieu of a bid proposal form, include a contract with the bid documents with instructions for the general contractor to fill in the price(s) and sign it. If accepted, the owner executes the contract and returns a copy to the bidder. This style of bidding usually limits further negotiation, and the contractor must ensure that the bid is complete and that the work can be done profitably. In many cases, these owners will interview the contractor prior to executing the contract to make sure all work has been bid and that they feel comfortable with the relationship.

13.4 THE BID DAY TEAM

An important part of the bid day organization is the make-up of the bid day team. Figure 13-1 illustrates an organization chart for Western Construction Company's team for completing the bid for the Training Center.

Each position has specific responsibilities, and when the team is well coordinated, even the most difficult bids are easier to complete. Some positions require more than one person; the number used will depend on the size and complexity of the project. Personnel requirements and duties of each position are as follows:

- Officer-in-charge—An executive officer of the company who is a financial decision-maker. He or she will make the final review of the estimate, oversee the bid day activities and make any last-minute adjustments to the final bid.
- Project manager—The person who will eventually manage the project if it is won. The project manager may or may not have been involved in the estimating process. He or she reviews the estimate and the project with the estimator and monitors the subcontractor bidding process. The project manager coordinates the time and location for tendering the bid with the bid runner.
- Chief estimator—The person who is ultimately responsible for the quality of the estimate. He or she may or may not take an active role on bid day but is always available for problem-solving and assessing special conditions.
- Estimator—The person who is responsible for preparing the estimate. He or she reviews the estimate and project with the project manager and the OIC and manages the subcontractor bid receiving and evaluation process. The estimator determines the low bidder for each subcontractor and supplier category and establishes the cutoff point for posting bids. He or she reviews the selection of low bidders with the chief estimator or project manager prior to final posting.
- Bid posters—One or more individuals who receive the subcontractor bid information from the bid takers and post it on the bid evaluation work sheets(s).
- Bid takers—Personnel who receive subcontractor or major supplier bids and record them on the bid proposal forms. They immediately forward the information to the bid room.
- Bid runner—The person who delivers the final bid. He or she takes the bid documents, in their envelope, to the location for tendering the bid; coordinates the bid room time with the owner's clock; fills in the final price; seals the bid; and delivers it. If the owner specifies a public bid opening, the bid runner usually stays and records the results.

Western Construction Company

Bid Room Organization Chart

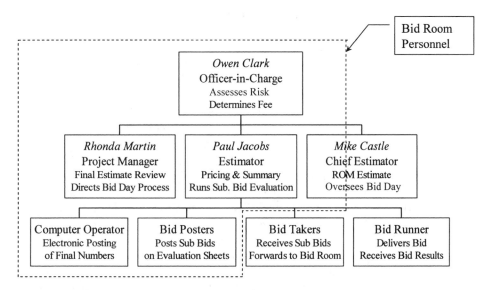

FIGURE 13–1 Bid day team organization chart.

Note that a dashed line has been drawn around certain boxes in Figure 13-1 indicating that they are bid room personnel. These are the only people who should be in the bid room as the pace of the work becomes more intense. As the time for bid submission approaches, subcontractor bids will be received at an increasing pace, and the last few minutes can be extremely hectic. The personnel within the bid room must be able to work without distraction. At a certain point, the door to the bid room is closed, and no one, including bid takers and clerical personnel, should be allowed in. Bids should be received through a slot in a door or window. This procedure allows the estimator and project manager to maintain control and avoid making a catastrophic last-minute error.

13.5 SUBCONTRACTOR BID EVALUATION PROCEDURES

Bid Evaluation Forms

The primary work of bid day is receiving and evaluating bids from subcontractors and major suppliers. Bids are posted as they are received, and the volume dictates the need for good procedures so the lowest bids and combinations can be determined quickly. As the bid time approaches, the frequency of bids increases and quick decisions must be made. Certain bid posting formats aid in carrying out the evaluation process and determining the best bids. Two methods have proven reliable for accomplishing this. One method is to use spreadsheets for positing and evaluating bids. The second method is to use an individual bid analysis sheet for each work item.

Spreadsheets made up of one or more large accounting sheets are usually used for manual operations where personnel are posting bids by hand. Boxes that represent each work specification are laid out on the sheet and are sized to include the pertinent information expected to be received. Figure 13-2 is a partial spreadsheet being used by Western Construction Company for posting and evaluating bids for the Training Center.

The boxes laid out on the spreadsheet are not of equal size because the amount of information will vary depending on the specification section. Also, more bids will be received for some work sections than for others. For example, more bids can be expected for the drywall than for skylights, and drywall contractors are more likely to submit combination bids or to bid on more than one specification section. Therefore more columns will be needed in the drywall box than for the skylights. Each box is titled with the specification division number and work description. A sequential bin number is written into the top left corner. Boxes are sized to show the name of the bidders, their price(s), and any very short but pertinent notes. No other information is necessary on the spreadsheet. It is preferable for the boxes to be laid out in the general order of the specifications starting from the upper left corner of the sheet with each succeeding work section following the previous one to the bottom of the page. This is the arrangement shown in Figure 13-2. It becomes easier to find particular work sections when placed this way rather than being placed randomly. Modest-size projects will require only one spreadsheet but more complex ones may need two or three. When multiple spreadsheets are required, it is a good idea to have a bid poster for each one.

The advantage of the spreadsheet is that it is easy to scan many categories at once. The estimator will do this often, looking at bid coverage in each section. This helps him or her determine when to make a preliminary bid total. The team can also scan key boxes that contain combination bids. Empty space or an extra spreadsheet should be available for quickly calculating the best bid combination. The bid evaluation spreadsheet is set up the day before bid day. Once prepared, all OM estimates are entered into their respective boxes, and the vendor name *plug* is used. This tells the bid team that if no bids are received in a particular category, the OM number may be used so a bid total can be calculated. Any bids that have already been received are also entered into their respective boxes.

Some bid teams prefer to use an individual sheet for each work section rather than a large spreadsheet. They are worked similarly, and bid teams can switch from one to the other quite easily. Figure 13-3 is an example of a bid evaluation sheet for a single specification section for the Training Center.

Individual bid evaluation sheets can be worked manually or electronically. The estimator needs to decide which method to use and define the procedures accordingly. It must also be decided how many bid posters are needed and how many sheets each one can manage. These sheets must be readily available for review by the estimator and others who will constantly be monitoring the process, and safeguards must be in place so that they will not be misplaced. The evaluation sheets must not be removed from the bid room during bid day.

Evaluation sheets for each specification section are made up and titled with the section number and description, and a bin number is assigned to them. Additional blank copies should be placed in the bid room to be used for combination bid evaluation. As on the spreadsheet, OM numbers are entered as plugs, and any pre-received bids are also written in. The sheets are then put into the bid room ready for bid day.

Bid Evaluation Sheet

Project Name: *The Training Center*
Bid Date & Time: June 3, 2003 @ 2:00 P.M.

#	Item	1	2	3	4	5	6	7	8	9	10	11	12
1	02200 - Demolition												
2	02.01 Earthwork												
3	02.19 Asbestos Abatement												
4	02.43 Miscellaneous Excavation												
5	02.80 Asphalt Paving												
6	02.85 Extruded Curbs & Striping												
7	02.86 CIP Curbs & Gutters												
8	02.92 Landscaping & Irrigation												
9	02.98 Buy Site Signage												
10	03.00 Concrete Subcontract												
11	03.06 Buy Reinforcing Steel												
12	0306 Place Reinforcing Steel												
13	03.60 Buy Precast Sills												
14	03.73 Sawcut Control Joints												
15	04.00 Masonry & Set Precast												
16	05.00 Buy Structural & Misc. Steel												
17	05.01												
18	05.04												
19	05.19												
20	06.49												
21	06.51												
22	06.52												

FIGURE 13-2 Bid evaluation spreadsheet.

VENDOR BID EVALUATION SHEET

Project: *The Training Center*   Estimator: *Paul Jacobs*
Location: *Kent, Washington*   Estimate: *No. TTC-1*
Architect/Engineer: *LM*   Date: *June 3, 2003*

Bin 5			
Asphalt Paving—Spec. 2510			
	Bid	Notes	

Low Bid

Notes:

FIGURE 13–3   Vendor bid evaluation sheet.

If an electronic posting process is selected, the estimator needs to ensure that the computers are properly set up and that the sheets can be accessed easily. The number of computers needed and the operators for each are determined. A short conference should be held with the operators to discuss possible combination bids and how they will be handled. The operators should check out the operation of each computer ahead of time.

Bins

The estimator makes sure that *bins* are ready for use on bid day. Bins are places where all posted subcontractor and supplier bid forms are kept during bid day. They can be anything from accordion files to built-in cubbyholes. They are numbered sequentially and correspond to the bin numbers on the evaluation sheets. After the bids are posted and reviewed by the estimator, they are put into the bins where they can be quickly accessed during the bidding process. When reviewing the bid evaluation sheets, the estimator may need more information, especially regarding combination bids or exclusions. He or she can pull the bid forms from the bins, find the ones for specific vendors and review their proposal quickly. This system helps the bid team to make informed decisions very fast. The use of bid evaluation sheets and bins will be discussed further in Chapter 14. It is important that the estimator sets these systems and procedures in place the day before bid day.

13.6 SUMMARY

A key to tendering a complete and accurate bid is organizing the bid day process. Much of this work is done on the evening before bid day. The estimator is responsible for ensuring that the proper documents are in the bid room, the computers are set up, the spreadsheets are operating properly, and other materials are ready for use. Worksheets for the subcontract bid evaluation and bid proposal forms are prepared and sufficient copies are made for bid day. Instructions for the bid takers and bid runner are written, and personnel are recruited for both jobs. The bid package is made up and readied for delivery by the bid runner. The original bid form is signed by the OIC, and copies are made for the bid package and file, and for use in the bid room. A properly labeled envelope is prepared, and all documents to be submitted are inserted with the bid form original on top. The envelope is left unsealed and is now ready to hand to the bid runner. The estimator verifies that all personnel needed to complete and tender the bid will be available on bid day. In addition, office personnel are alerted so they know how to route telephone calls and keep visitors away from the bid room. A well-organized bid day process will keep last-minute stress to a minimum and assure that a complete and accurate bid is tendered.

13.7 REVIEW QUESTIONS

1. Where is the final work usually done on a bid to prepare for bid day?
2. List five documents that should be put into the bid room in preparation for bid day?
3. What three documents will go into the bid package to be delivered to the owner?
4. How are computers prepared for bid day?
5. What are three items that will be on every owner's form of bid proposal?
6. Name five positions that are required on the bid team?
7. Will all of the positions named in question 6 be working in the bid room on bid day?
8. What is the responsibility of the officer-in-charge?
9. Who is responsible for making sure the bid runner is properly instructed?
10. Who decides when subcontractor bid posting will stop and a final price determined?

13.8 EXERCISES

1. Make up the final bid summary form and enter all of the information, including markup percentages, except the subcontract amount. Write a paragraph on the basis used for determining the fee percentage.
2. Using the bid form example shown in Appendix E, make up a bid package with two bid forms and one copy of the project summary schedule. Insert the package in an envelope with a label addressed to your instructor. Prominently display the project name and the owner on the front of the envelope. Use a large enough envelope so that the bid proposal form is not folded. Turn this package in to your instructor.

14

BID DAY ACTIVITIES

14.1 INTRODUCTION

Bid day is represented by steps 9 and 10 of the lump-sum estimating process shown in Figure 6-1, which completes the process of tendering a bid. At this point, all of the direct work estimating (Chapters 7, 8 and 12) is complete. OM estimates have been created for subcontract work (Chapter 9), and a project summary schedule and general conditions estimate has been made (Chapter 10). The first-run bid estimate has been compared and reconciled with the ROM estimate developed in Chapter 6. The estimator has prepared the bid room and assembled the owner's bid package with all required documentation and a signed copy of the bid form. The bid room is ready to receive and evaluate subcontractor bids, fill in the subcontractor bid totals on the bid summary, and complete and deliver the owner's bid form to the tendering site.

Bid day activities occur in three places. The bid takers, who are people throughout the contractor's office, will be receiving and recording subcontractor and supplier prices on bid proposal forms. The bid room team posts the bids on the evaluation sheets, determines the low prices, completes the bid summary, and forwards the total(s) to the bid runner. The bid runner, who is located near the tendering site, receives the numbers from the bid room and completes the bid form. He or she then delivers the bid package to the owner's specified location and learns the results, if it is a public bid opening.

The bid team leader, either the estimator or the project manager, must control the tempo of bid day. As the tendering deadline approaches, the atmosphere becomes stressful, and emotions can destroy the entire process and jeopardize the final bid. A smooth bid day operation minimizes emotional effects and results in the best possible bid being tendered on time.

Chapter 13 discussed organizing the bid room for bid day. At the beginning of bid day, the team captain should make sure that the organization is in place and that all people understand their duties. This will help make the work of tendering the bid go smoothly and will provide the bid team with some time for final strategizing. The team leader should verify that the OIC will be present in the bid room during the hour prior to the time the bid must be submitted.

14.2 RECEIVING SUBCONTRACTOR AND SUPPLIER BIDS

As the bidding deadline approaches, some subcontractors and suppliers will quickly give their prices and minimal information so they can proceed with calling other bidding general contractors. The information can be too incomplete for a comprehensive evaluation. When this happens, someone in the bid room will have to call the subcontractor or supplier back and get the remaining information—a time-consuming and sometimes difficult task. If the bid room activity level is high, there may not be time to do this, and a quick decision must be made whether or not to use the subcontractor or supplier's bid.

When receiving a call, the bid taker should initially indicate that he or she will ask the questions, thus pacing the call. Some subcontractors and suppliers do not like this, but this is how the general contractor can get the correct information. The bid taker must be aware that subcontractors and suppliers have other calls to make and should not waste their time by engaging in unimportant discussion. Most subcontractors and suppliers know what information general contractors need and will provide it. Conversely, some subcontractors may want to be overly detailed, which takes too much of the bid taker's time and prohibits him or her from receiving other bids.

Subcontractors and suppliers may elect to submit their bids by mail, email, or facsimile (fax). When using mail, a bid form or scope letter is received that lists the terms and conditions of the bid, including exclusions and inclusions, and has a blank(s) for prices. The estimator should review the form to ensure that it conforms to the bidding requirements and to the general contractor's subcontracting procedures. If there are discrepancies, the estimator or project manager must attempt to resolve them prior to bid day. If a subcontractor is firm on his or her conditions, a decision must be made as to whether or not to use that bid. The subcontractor or supplier then calls in prices on bid day, and the bid taker either enters the price on a copy of the submitted form or fills in a regular bid proposal form and attaches it to the subcontractor or supplier's form.

Faxed bids may be forwarded on a similar form or as a simple sheet of letterhead paper with the price on it. Some subcontractor and suppliers use the owner's bid form to submit their prices. In any case, the bid team must verify that the bids conform to the plans and specifications, and acknowledge all addenda. Bids received by email are similar to faxed bids and must meet the same criteria.

Subcontractor and supplier bids are recorded on bid proposal forms similar to the one shown in Figure 14-1. The bid team leader must stress the importance of filling out the form completely and correctly. The following is a discussion of the individual items on the form and their importance:

- Firm—The name of the firm should be filled in completely. Sometimes there are different companies with similar names, and filling in a partial name may not define adequately which company submitted the bid.

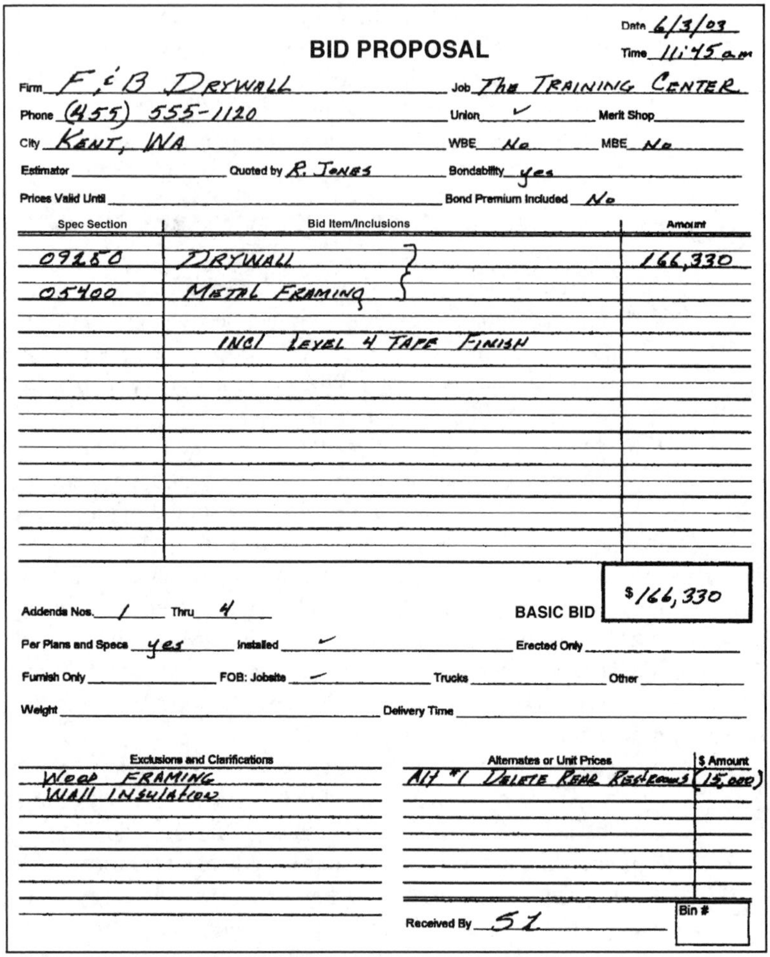

BID PROPOSAL

Date 6/3/03
Time 11:45 a.m.

Firm F & B DRYWALL
Job The TRAINING CENTER
Phone (455) 555-1120
Union ✓
Merit Shop
City KENT, WA
WBE No
MBE No
Estimator
Quoted by R. JONES
Bondability yes
Prices Valid Until
Bond Premium Included No

Spec Section	Bid Item/Inclusions	Amount
09250	DRYWALL }	166,330
05400	METAL FRAMING }	
	INCL LEVEL 4 TAPE FINISH	

Addenda Nos. 1 Thru 4
BASIC BID $166,330
Per Plans and Specs yes
Installed ✓
Erected Only
Furnish Only
FOB: Jobsite ✓
Trucks
Other
Weight
Delivery Time

Exclusions and Clarifications
WOOD FRAMING
WALL INSULATION

Alternates or Unit Prices	$ Amount
Alt #1 DELETE REAR RESTROOMS	(15,000)

Received By SL
Bin #

FIGURE 14–1 Bid proposal form.

- Job—This identifies the project for which the bid was received. This is especially important on days when more than one job is being bid.
- Vendor's telephone number and quoted by—This provides a contact if the bid team has any questions.
- Bid item/inclusions—It is very important to list all of the specification sections and inclusions. This will also be a factor in writing the subcontract or purchase order. The bid taker should also repeat the price(s) back to the bidder to verify that it has been recorded correctly.
- Addenda numbers—This verifies that the vendor has submitted a complete bid. If this is not done, it provides the vendor with an opportunity to negotiate for more money, if he or she is the low bidder.
- Per plans and specifications—A yes answer by vendors along with verification of all addenda eliminates their opportunity to try to raise their price when executing a contract.

As long as the vendors have had the opportunity to review the owner's bid package, they are responsible for all items of work affecting them, including timing and conditions of the contract between the owner and the general contractor.

- Exclusions and clarifications—These should be brief, and although many times obvious, they should always be written down.
- Alternate or unit prices—Prices that are needed to tender a complete bid. Not all bidders will be required to submit alternates or unit prices.
- Received by—The bid team may want a particular bid taker to call the vendor for clarifications; or if they call the vendor, they will want to refer to a bid given to the receiving bid taker.

All construction materials are to be quoted *FOB (free on board)* jobsite, which means that the cost includes the shipping. If the general contractor is asked to purchase owner's equipment as part of the project, the suppliers of the equipment rarely include shipping. The general contractor should accept prices only with a freight allowance added, otherwise separate shipping bids will have to be solicited, which can sometimes be difficult to obtain. The bin number box at the lower right hand corner of the proposal form is left blank at this time.

The bid taker forwards subcontractor and supplier bids to the bid room. While this sounds simple, the bid taker is usually doing more than receiving bids, and it is easy to misplace or forget about them. This could cost the contractor the chance to win the project being bid. Early on bid day when the activity level is low, bid takers can deliver the bid proposal forms at their leisure. As the deadline approaches, the frequency of calls may make it more difficult to send the bids to the bid room. It is always important for the bid takers to be available full-time to receive bids during the last two hours before the deadline, as this is when the activity is most intense. The bid team leader should monitor the bidding activity and, as it gets more intense, should have someone pick up bid proposal forms from the bid takers. This allows the bid takers to receive bids uninterrupted, and assures that all prices are delivered to the bid room.

14.3 POSTING SUBCONTRACTOR AND SUPPLIER BIDS

The bid posters receive the bids from the bid takers and post the relevant information on the bid evaluation sheet. Notes should be just a few words such as "excludes doors" or "includes sec. 09900." More detail tends to clutter the evaluation spreadsheets. If the bid team needs more information, the bid forms are in the bins and available for review. The bid poster enters the bin number on the bid form and places it in a pile for the bid captain to review and file in the designated bin.

Some subcontractors or suppliers may submit pricing for more than one specification section of work. Their price may be a single amount that includes several sections or it may list the individual sections and a cost for each. An example might be the wall insulation, drywall, and acoustical ceilings. Some bidders will supply a price for only one of these sections, but a drywall contractor may include the ceilings and drywall or all three in a single price. The team must determine whether the combination bid is lower than the sum of other individual bids. These can be easily seen, evaluated, and noted on the bid evaluation spreadsheet. Figure 14-2 illustrates how a combination bid may look.

Bid Evaluation Spreadsheet
(Partial)

29 09250 Gypsum Wallboard		Bid	Notes
PLYB		*156,200*	
Partition Contr		169,000	
Green & Gannon		172,450	
F & B		166,330	
Schneider Dry Wall		225,420	incl Paint 09900

36 09900 Painting		Bid	Notes
PLYB		*55,800*	
Portland Painters		54,948	
Schneider Drywall		See 09250	
John Smart & Sons		57,828	
Simmons Fin.Sys.		61,200	
Comm'l Painting		54,860	Excl Doors

FIGURE 14–2 Spreadsheet bid postings.

Figure 14-2 shows three prices for specification section 09250 that appear fairly close to one another. The price for Schneider Drywall is much higher, but a note indicates that it includes section 09900 Painting. The box for section 09900 located on another part of the spreadsheet shows individual prices from four firms and lists Schneider Drywall with a reference to 09250. The estimator has determined that the sum of the low prices in each box is less than the combination price tendered by Schneider. The low prices have been double underlined indicating that they should be transferred to the subcontractor list. If Schneider had been low, the price shown in the 09250 box would have been underlined, as well as the reference in the 09900 box. This process is very easy to see on the spreadsheet.

In some cases, three or more specification sections are involved. Some subcontractors or suppliers will bid on a single section, while others may bid on two or more of them. Prices may be individual or combined. When this occurs, the estimator usually evaluates them by making separate boxes for the various combinations on the spreadsheet and listing the prices in them. This is supplemental to the normal listing of the individual specification section. These combination boxes can then be referred to and used as notes regarding how the low pricing was determined.

Figure 14-3 shows how combination bids are entered onto the individual bid evaluation sheet. This sheet has been set up for two sections of the specifications because it was anticipated that at least one subcontractor would bid on both work sections. Two things to be noted are that (1) one bid (Morrison) includes foundation drainage and (2) another bid (Stefson) is for only a single work section. Morrison's bid will need to be evaluated against a combination of the other subcontractors bidding sections 02200 and 02245 and the subcontractors who are providing bids for the foundation drainage. It may be difficult to determine if Stefson's bid is low unless the other bids can be broken down into sections 02200 and 02245. If no subcontractor bids section 02245 separately, so it can be combined with Stefson's bid, the evaluation of Stefson's bid might not be possible. The bid captain needs to decide what to do about this bid. In the case of the Training Center, there was no separate bid for section 02245, so the

Subcontractor and Supplier Bid Evaluation Sheet

Project: *The Training Center*   Estimator: *Paul Jacobs*
Location: *Kent, Washington*   Estimate: *No. TTC-1*
Architect/Engineer: *LM*   Date: *June 3, 2003*

Bin 2				
Earthwork & Utilities—Spec. 2200, 2245				
	Bid	2200	2245	
Company Plug Number	$198,000	incl	incl	
G&M Excavating	211,000	incl	incl	
Earthwork Resources	184,581	incl	incl	
Morrison Excavating & Grading	225,000	incl	incl	note 1
Stefson Enterprises	189,600	incl		

Low Bid	**$184,581**	

Notes:
1. Includes 2621 Foundation Drainage System

FIGURE 14–3   Individual bid evaluation sheet.

bid captain selected the best price for the combination of sections 02200 and 02245, which was the one submitted by Earthwork Resources.

If multiple computers are being used for bid evaluation, the bid captain should consider putting the mechanical bids on one and the electrical bids on the other. Typically, during the last minutes before the deadline, many electrical and mechanical bids are received. With a few minutes to go, the bid captain may decide to select all bids except the mechanical and electrical, and have someone monitor the other incoming bids in case a significantly lower one is received. The bid team can then concentrate on evaluating the mechanical and electrical bids. These divisions can contain several combinations, and if subcontractors are lowering prices and providing alternate pricing in the last minutes, the team must be able to make quick, informed decisions.

Whichever bid evaluation method is used, the posting of bids is essentially the same. A designated team member receives bid proposals from a bid taker and forwards them to the appropriate person who then posts the subcontractor's name, price, and any pertinent notes. Notes are kept to an absolute minimum and must be brief so as not to clutter the evaluation process. Once posted, the bid poster writes the designated bin number in the box at the lower right hand corner of the bid proposal form and puts it into a pile for the estimator to review prior to filing in the appropriate bin. The use of bins makes it easy for a team member to find and review all of the bids of any specification section during the bidding process.

Spreadsheet boxes or the individual bid evaluation sheets are commonly referred to as bid tabs. They are a tabulation of vendor bids for a given work category. Bid tabs are used by the project team after a project is won to re-evaluate the bids for other combinations or situations that may result in an even lower price. Their use will be discussed in Chapter 15.

It is important for the bid team to be aware of the pace of a typical bid day. The Training Center has a bid time of 2:00 P.M. Subcontractor and supplier bid activity will be relatively low until mid-morning. A few bids are received, and the time is used to post previously received bids, to make sure the organizational work is complete, and to wait for more bids. Some members of the team may not be needed during this time. From mid-morning to about noon, the frequency of bidding will increase but will still be at a manageable level, and a single bid poster can probably handle the work. The entire bid team, including the bid takers, typically works through lunch. From noon until about 1:30 P.M., the bid frequency will increase, and more bid posters may be needed. Bids during this time typically will be from subcontractors and suppliers of all specification divisions, but usually very few will be for the mechanical and electrical work. The bidding level will become very intense during the last half hour with most of the bids being for mechanical and electrical.

14.4 EVALUATING SUBCONTRACTOR AND SUPPLIER BIDS

The bid team must be prepared to quickly determine which prices are the best and when to decide on a posting cutoff point on bid day. For most of the bidding, the subcontractors and suppliers submit prices for single categories of work, so determining the low price is straightforward. In addition to the combination bids discussed previously, the bid team needs to be aware of the specific inclusions and exclusions of each bidder. Most will bid in accordance with the plans and specifications, but some will exclude pertinent items, which may result in their having the low bid. The bid team must identify these situations and decide whether to call and ask the vendor to include the item or disqualify their bid.

Special care must be exercised if a subcontractor bids work that the general contractor typically performs. While both prices reflect the same scope of work, there are differences in how each treats variations. For example, a general contractor's cost for reinforcing steel installation has some flexibility in it, and any minor discrepancies that are encountered are just part of the job. Usually the cost to correct them can be absorbed with minimal impact to productivity. A subcontractor, on the other hand, bids the job as shown, and any discrepancy will be an extra cost. If the delivery of the material is interrupted, the general contractor can usually shift manpower to another task or even another project temporarily. The subcontractor cannot do this and will charge extra for every interruption. The estimator should discuss the inclusions and exclusions with each subcontractor.

It is important for the bid team to keep on top of subcontractor and supplier bid evaluations, so that the final minutes of the process remain under control. About 1 hour before the bid is due, the team captain should determine the state of bid coverage. The low bid in each bin is transferred to the subcontractor list. They are not double underlined or circled on the evaluation sheets at this point. Plug numbers will be put on the subcontractor list for sections for which no bids have been received. The subcontractor list is totaled and checked, and this amount is then transferred to the bid summary. Both pages are prominently marked FIRST-RUN BID. This designation differs from the FIRST-RUN estimate made in Chapter 11.

The earlier the first-run bid is generated, the more plug numbers will probably be used. As each succeeding run is made, some of the plug numbers will be replaced by low bids. The final bid run ideally should have no plug numbers in the subcontractor list or, if it does, they should be for small work categories with low risk.

The first-run bid is used as a baseline on bid day. First, it is compared with the first-run estimate total to see if the two are reasonably close. If they are not, the bid team must quickly search for a transposition error, as there is not time to do any other analysis. As the day progresses, the bid captain may make several more bid totals, numbering each one successively. They will then be compared with the previous total or the first-run bid total to see that they are still reasonably close. At this point, variations cannot be analyzed, but it can be noted where subcontractor or supplier bids differ significantly from plugs. Further analysis can be done after the bid has been tendered.

The bid captain decides how many preliminary bid totals are needed and when they are produced. If the subcontractor list and bid summary are being run on a computer, the bid captain may decide not to generate as many bids, since the numbers are constantly available for review. At least one preliminary total should be printed, so that key members of the bid team can review it for potential errors.

At a predetermined time, usually about 15 minutes before the deadline, the bid captain declares a cutoff for receiving bids for most specification sections. Low bids in each bin are double underlined and entered onto the subcontractor list. A few major categories are left open in anticipation of receiving last-minute bids. A bid team member receiving bids for closed sections compares them to the declared low bid. Only lower bids are posted at this time, and the bid captain is alerted. If a lower bid than the one already declared is received for a work section that has been closed, an adjustment is made on the subcontractor list. The bid poster determines the difference between the bid used and the new bid received. This amount is entered

Subcontractor List

Project: *The Training Center, Kent, Washington*		Estimator: *Paul Jacobs*		Estimate #: *OM-1*		
Bin	**Spec**	**Description**	**Bid**	**+ or −**	**Revised**	**Subcontractor**
	09310	*Ceramic Tile*	*34,850*	*(1,705)*	*33,145*	
	09511	*Acoustical Ceiling System*	*17,950*		*17,950*	
	09560	*Resilient Flooring*	*37,550*		*37,550*	
	09682	*Carpeting*	*incl____*		*incl____*	

FIGURE 14–4   Revised subcontractor list.

into the add/cut (+ or −) column on the proper line of the subcontractor list, and a revised to-tal is calculated. Figure 14-4 shows a portion of the subcontractor list illustrating how the cut/add column is used.

Two things should be noted in Figure 14-4. First, the revised column is a summation of the bid and + or− columns for every line item regardless of whether or not a change has been made. In this way, only the total of the revised column is used on the bid summary. Second, the resilient flooring and carpeting are a combination bid, and the price of the car-peting is included in the resilient flooring bid. A notation is made so that on the final re-view, there will be no blank lines indicating that an entry has been made for every specifi-cation section. The computer operator must ensure that any notation does not affect the column summation.

During the last few minutes of subcontractor bidding, the frequency of mechanical and electrical bids typically increases. As bids are submitted, the subcontractors may ask how their prices look. Bid takers must be instructed not to answer these questions, as that may not be in the best interests of the general construction company. A bid poster is as-signed to each of the remaining open bins, and the bid captain monitors them closely. A few minutes before the bid has to be forwarded to the bid runner, the remaining categories are closed out, the prices are entered in the subcontractor list, and a bid total is determined. The OIC then makes a decision regarding any adjustments, and the final bid total is calculated. The bid captain forwards the total to the bid runner, and a final run is printed.

14.5   PREPARING FOR DELIVERY OF THE BID

About an hour before the time for bid submission, the bid captain gives final instructions to the bid runner. The owner's bid form is reviewed so that the bid runner knows exactly what is to be filled in. Directions to the bid submission site are given, watches are checked to ensure that the bid runner has the correct time, and communications procedures are es-tablished. The bid runner carries a cellular telephone for receiving the final information that is to be entered onto the bid form.

The bid runner is sent to the bid submission site well in advance of the time when the bid must be submitted. An allowance for unusual traffic conditions should be made to assure that the runner arrives on time. Once the runner arrives at the bid submission site, he or she should contact the bid captain and inform him or her of the time required to submit the bid and the exact time on the owner's clock. The bid captain should then instruct the bid runner to call back at a designated time to receive the final bid price.

When the bid runner calls, the final bid amount is read by the bid captain and written onto the original and all copies of the bid form by the bid runner. The number should be read back to the captain for verification. The bid package will then be placed into the prepared envelope, sealed, and delivered to the owner at the designated bid submission site. The bid runner also will note the exact time the bid was turned in. If the bids are to be opened publicly, the bid runner usually remains at the bid site and records the bids that are received. The results are then reported to the bid captain.

14.6 COMPLETING AND TENDERING THE BID FOR THE TRAINING CENTER

After reviewing the subcontract bids for the Training Center, the bid captain and the OIC have noticed two very low prices from subcontractors with whom the company has no prior experience. A quick discussion ensues about the validity of these bids and the risk of lack of performance, and the bid captain and the OIC decide to add an amount to bond these subcontractors. This provides some financial protection in case one or both of them default in the performance of their work. This decision may cause them not to be the low bidder, but the bid captain and the OIC have decided to take that chance and have added $9,000 to cover the cost of the bonds. This is entered in the subcontractor section of the bid summary.

The OIC and bid captain have noted that the general conditions estimate is about 5% of the bid total. This is a little low, but after discussing personnel and duties, they decide that this project can probably be done for that amount. The chosen fee of 4.25% is approximately 53% of the direct labor cost, which is close to the desired 50% protection. The bid summary shown in Figure 14-5 indicates that only a minor adjustment was made because the fee provides sufficient labor protection and should be competitive for current market conditions. This is the type of project Western Construction likes to do, so the OIC would like to win the contract.

In the meantime, the bid runner has called in and is on the telephone waiting for the bid numbers. As soon as the OIC determines any final adjustment, the bid captain forwards the final bid amount to the bid runner, and a bid summary is printed. The bid runner verifies the final bid amount and delivers the bid, noting the exact time that it was submitted. Figure 14-6 shows the first page of Western Construction Company's bid for the Training Center.

Once the bid has been tendered, there are some wrap-up items to be completed. Bids that were received before the owner's deadline need to be posted and their prices compared against the ones used in the bid. Any bids received after the deadline should be given to the bid captain for review. If the project is won, the project manager will decide how to handle them. The bid captain then enters the name of each vendor whose price was used in the right hand column of the subcontractor list.

Bid Summary

Project: *The Training Center*   Bid Date & Time: *June 3, 2003, 2:00 P.M.*

Owner: *Carpenters Trust Fund*   Estimator: *P. Jacobs* Est. #: *TTC-2*

CODE	PAGE	DESCRIPTION	MAN HOURS	LABOR	MATERIAL	TOTAL
		Administrative		$64,000	$11,700	$75,700
		Indirect Equipment		0	30,483	30,483
		Temporary Construction		800	5,525	6,325
		General Conditions		0	13,830	13,830
		Total Job Overhead		$64,800	$61,538	$126,338
		Demolition	125	1,890	0	1,890
		Sitework	595	8,988	9,793	18,781
		Concrete	3,618	54,680	118,754	173,434
		Tilt-up Walls	2,904	43,885	72,322	116,207
		Wood & Plastics	920	13,910	9,511	23,421
		Subtotal	8,162	$188,153	$271,918	$460,071
		Labor Burden	45%		$84,669	$84,669
		Trade Travel & Subsistance				
		Labor Increase				
		Contingency				
		Subtotal		$188,153	$356,587	$544,740

Subcontracts		$1,801,028
Subcontractor Bonds		$9,000
Adjustments		
	Subtotal	$2,354,768
Fee	4.25%	$100,078
	Subtotal	$2,454,846
Business Taxes & Insurance	1.6%	$39,278
	Subtotal	$2,494,124
Adjustments		(224)
	TOTAL BID	$2,493,900

FIGURE 14–5 Final bid summary for the Training Center.

Once this work is complete, the bid proposals are removed from the bins and filed in order of the specification section and bid amounts with the lowest being on top. If individual evaluation sheets were used, they are put on top of the bids for each division and are all clipped into the subcontractor side of the bid file. If the spreadsheet was used, it is folded up and clipped onto the opposite leaf of the file folder, as are the bid proposals. Lastly, the subcontractor list is printed, attached to the bid summary printed earlier, and

```
┌─────────────────────────────────────────────────────────────────────┐
│                        FORM OF BID PROPOSAL                           │
│                                                                       │
│  Date: June 3, 2003                                                   │
│                                                                       │
│  PROJECT:                                                             │
│  THE TRAINING CENTER                                                  │
│  Kent, Washington                                                     │
│  ─────────────────────────────────────────────────────────────────   │
│                                                                       │
│                           BID  PROPOSAL                               │
│  ─────────────────────────────────────────────────────────────────   │
│                                                                       │
│  Bidder:  WESTERN CONSTRUCTION COMPANY                                │
│  To:                                                                  │
│           The undersigned bidder, having familiarized himself with    │
│           the terms of the contract, the local conditions             │
│           affecting the contract and with the Drawings and            │
│           Specifications and other Contract Documents, hereby          │
│           proposes and agrees to provide all labor, materials, and    │
│           services necessary to complete in a                         │
│           workmanlike manner all work required in connection with     │
│           the construction of                                         │
│                                                                       │
│                         THE TRAINING CENTER                           │
│                                                                       │
│  1.  All in strict accordance to Drawings, Specifications and other   │
│      Contract Documents; hereby submit a base                         │
│      bid as follows:                                                  │
│                                                                       │
│          BASE BID: $  2,493,900                                       │
│                                                                       │
│  2.  If the owner decides to purchase a 100% performance and payment  │
│      bond then the following will be in                               │
│      addition to the base bid:                                        │
│                                                                       │
│          BOND: $   6,000                                              │
│                                                                       │
│  3.  CHANGE ORDERS: All extra work not included in the Contract, if   │
│      requested, will be performed by the                              │
│      Contractor by material and labor costs plus overhead and profit. │
│      Ten percent (10%) (overhead and profit)                          │
│      will be added or deleted accordingly by the subcontractor        │
│      completing the work.  Five percent (5%)                          │
│      (overhead and profit) will be added or deleted accordingly by    │
│      the General Contractor.                                          │
│                                                                       │
│  4.  SALES TAX:  State of Washington sales tax is not included in the │
│      Base Bid.  It will be added to each                              │
│      payment request as it is submitted.                              │
│                                                                       │
│  5.  ADDENDA:  Receipt of addenda is hereby acknowledged as follows:  │
│                                                                       │
│          Addenda Nos.         Date                                    │
│               1               5/23/03                                 │
│               2               5/27/03                                 │
│               3               5/30/03                                 │
│               4               6/2/03                                  │
│                                                                       │
│  6.  GENERAL CONTRACTOR SIGNATURE                                     │
│                                                                       │
│      Western Construction Company          226 S. 4ᵗʰ. Kent WA        │
│      Bidder                                Address                     │
│      By                                    WCC 62489                  │
│           PRESIDENT                        License No.                 │
│      Title                                                            │
│                                                                       │
│                       END OF FORM OF BID PROPOSAL                     │
└─────────────────────────────────────────────────────────────────────┘
```

FIGURE 14–6 Western Construction's final bid for the Training Center.

filed in the estimate file along with a completed copy of the owner's bid form. If the bid results are known, they are filed with the estimate. This completes the lump-sum bidding process.

14.7 ADDITIONAL BID DAY ISSUES

Validity of Verbal Prices

You may question whether verbal bids taken by telephone constitute commitments by the bidders. The fact that these bids were in response to a request for quotation makes them a price for which the subcontractor is willing to sign a contract. If a subcontractor backs out after a bid has been tendered, the general contractor who won the project is still required to perform the work for the bid price. Either the low subcontractor must do the work for the price bid or the general contractor will have to find another subcontractor who will. That may be difficult to do.

It is rare that a subcontractor backs out of a bid commitment. There are cases where a major error has been made resulting in the bidder submitting an unusually low price. The bid team should contact the subcontractor and ask for verification of his or her bid, and should review all inclusions and exclusions. The subcontractor might be told that the price seems to be out of line without indicating which way or by how much. Whether to use the low price and hope it is not in error or to query the subcontractor is a decision that must be made. If a subcontractor has made an error, a corrected price may be provided, and the bid team can hope that all other general contractors also have been notified.

Ethics

General contractors may find that they are involved in a form of *bid shopping*. This happens when subcontractors determine from a bidding contractor how their prices were in relation to those of their competition. Some general contractors will divulge this information to bidders. This is a way of driving subcontractors' prices down, and thus lowering his or her own bid to the owner. This is known as bid shopping and is considered unethical. Subcontractors expect general contractors to treat their bids as confidential until the subcontracts are awarded.

The intent of the lump-sum bidding process is to have bidders submit their lowest and best price the first time for specific scopes of work. By bid shopping, general contractors are implying that subcontractors can lower their prices for the work. Some subcontractors will respond accordingly to win the work. Others will stand with their original bids. The question then arises as to whether the subcontractor who engaged in the bid shopping process really submitted the best price to start with or whether a sacrificial contingency had been included. In addition, the subcontractor may have submitted the best price initially and may not be able to complete the work for the reduced price. Finally, the subcontractor might be in financial trouble and trying to increase cash flow to avoid insolvency. Any of these situations could result in the subcontractor defaulting during the course of the work, which could cause extra costs for the general contractor.

14.8 SUMMARY

Bid day is when the final bid is completed and submitted. Early in the day, the bidding activity usually is relatively quiet. As the day progresses, the activity generally increases and can be very high just before the final bid is submitted. The bid captain must have procedures in place for controlling traffic into the bid room and making sure that each team member understands his or her duties. It is important for bid takers to understand what information is needed and to make sure that proposal forms reach the bid room in a timely manner. Bid posters are assigned to process bids for a group of specification sections. Clear and concise instructions are given to the bid runner who will deliver the bid to the location designated in the bid instructions and will remain at the site to retrieve results, if it is to be a public opening.

As the bid time approaches, the bid captain determines when a first-run bid total is to be made. Low subcontractor bids at the time are used on the subcontractor list, and items for which no bids have been received use OM plug numbers. The total is compared with the bid estimate total that was made using the OM estimates. The bid captain determines how many preliminary bid totals will be made and when they will be done. As the bid time approaches the final numbers are reviewed with the OIC, who decides if any adjustment should be made to the bid. Once this is determined, the bid summary total is forwarded to the bid runner who completes the bid form, seals the envelope, and delivers it to the owner.

There is some wrapup work to do after the bid. Prices not posted should be reviewed and filed. Bid proposals are removed from the bins and filed in order by their specification sections with the bid evaluation sheets on top. The final bid summary and electronic files are backed up. This completes the bidding process.

14.9 REVIEW QUESTIONS

1. What things need to be done in order for bid day to run smoothly?
2. On a bid day that is expected to be moderately busy, how should the estimator anticipate the activity level to change from the start of the day until time to tender the bid?
3. Who records bids coming in from the subcontractors and suppliers, and on what form?
4. What are the consequences of the bid form not being filled in completely?
5. When is the bin number filled in on the bid proposal form and by whom?
6. What are combination bids, and how are they evaluated?
7. Who evaluates the bids and determines which ones will be used in the final bid?
8. When should a preliminary bid day total be made and why?
9. What is the purpose of a preliminary bid total?

14.10 EXERCISES

1. On a bid proposal form, fill in the available information from the following call by a vendor.

   > "Hi. This is Joe at M & B, (255) 555-4430. My price for the insulation is $62,500. I have seen two addenda. Good bye."

   Four addenda have been issued. What other information is needed, and who should call him or her back? List five mistakes in this telephone proposal.
2. There are 10 minutes left before a bid is due and you are the lead estimator. The OIC is gathering information on whether or not to make a last-minute adjustment and has come to you for input. What factors do you need to address in your response? List each one and state why it should be considered. With only 10 minutes left, your answers need to be quick, clear, and concise. Each answer should be no more than two sentences long.
3. Five minutes after the owner's bidding deadline, a key subcontractor whose price was used in your bid claims error and withdraws his bid. As the estimator, what do you do now? Write a paragraph on considerations and a recommended course of action to take.

15

POST-BID DAY ACTIVITIES

15.1 INTRODUCTION

A few things remain to be done after the bid has been tendered, regardless of whether or not the contract was won. These are issues involving the bid opening, vendor queries, preparations for post-bid interviews and record keeping. In addition, whether or not the bid was won, an effort should be made to glean information from the estimate that will be useful in preparing future ones. An important issue is post-bid negotiations with private owners. Understanding the owner's position helps the contractor develop a plan for the post-bid interview.

15.2 BID OPENING

The opening of a bid by an owner may be done in one of two ways. If it is opened in the presence of the bidders and the results announced immediately, it is a public bid opening. In a private bid opening, the owner elects to open the bids without the bidders being present. Private bids are opened at the owner's convenience—on bid day or at a later time. Owners frequently state in the bid documents when they intend to enter into a contract regardless of whether or not the bid results are announced.

Public projects, such as highways or government buildings, usually are required by law to have a public bid opening. The timing of the opening is specified in the bid documents. It is also a requirement that the contract be awarded to the lowest responsive, responsible bidder. Responsive means that the bid conforms to all requirements specified in the Invitation for Bid, and responsible means that the construction company is qualified to construct the project. Bid results are published in either a government document or a recognized trade journal.

Private owners have the option of selecting a public or a private bid opening and usually will indicate which is to be used in the bid solicitation documents. They decide the timing of the opening and whether or not to make the results available to all bidders. In some cases, the bid documents state that the owner retains the right not to award to the lowest bidder. Or the owner might reject all bids because they exceed the project budget. A new round of bids may be requested after some design modifications, or the owner may select one of the bidders and contract for help in developing construction alternatives to try to reduce costs.

15.3 SUBCONTRACTOR AND SUPPLIER INQUIRIES

After a bid has been tendered, subcontractors and suppliers will begin calling and inquiring about how their bids compared with their competition. Answering them too soon after the bid has been tendered can cause problems for the winning general contractor. If a subcontractor is told that his or her price was low and the owner awards to the general contractor, the subcontractor will expect to be awarded a contract also. There are times, however, when a re-evaluation of subcontractor bids uncovers a combination that changes the results, and the subcontractor ends up not being the low bidder. If the subcontractor was told that he or she submitted the low bid, the subcontractor may have legal recourse if not awarded the subcontract from the general contractor. The estimating team must be very cautious about responding to subcontractor and supplier inquiries about their prices until final subcontractor and supplier selections have been made.

A subcontractor, who has canvassed other general contractors, especially those who were not in contention for the project, may find out that he or she was the low bidder. Not all general contractors, however, receive similar bids from the same subcontractors and they may not analyze the subcontract pricing in the same way. The winning contractor is not obligated to execute a subcontract with the specialty contractor who believes his or her bid is low but has not been told so by that general contractor.

Sometimes a bid team member will let subcontractors or suppliers know where their prices stood, if they are totally out of contention. This is done without divulging the low bidder and by indicating an approximate percentage difference from the winning bid rather than by stating the low price. Release of any subcontractor bid results should wait until the owner has issued a notice of intent to award a contract.

When conducting a subcontractor and supplier bid review, make sure that a vendor who bids more than one item is willing to contract for only one item at the price bid. Also vendors who bid a single price for a combination should be queried for a breakdown by specification section and asked the same question. Working the bids may result in a lower combination cost. The difference between this cost and the bid used is commonly known as *buyout* and is, in effect, a potential savings for the general contractor. A buyout analysis may result in a different vendor being the low bidder. Clear notes should be made regarding how the buyout was determined, and the notes should be attached to the subcontractor list in the bid files. This way if the contract is awarded, the project team has a record of all price determinations. Buyout will be discussed in more detail in Chapter 22.

15.4   POST-BID ANALYSIS

If the general contractor is not the low bidder, an analysis should be performed to determine why the bid was too high. When doing this, it is assumed that everyone had essentially the same total for the subcontractor and supplier bids, unless there is reason to believe otherwise. The self-performed work should be analyzed to see if the most efficient construction methods were used. The fee should be examined in relation to the difference between the general contractor's bid and that of the successful bidder. Many times this will be the deciding factor. Maybe a contractor wanted to establish a relationship with the owner and used a low fee. Another contractor may have determined that the project had a high potential for change orders and decided to bid a low fee with the intent of making money on them. Whatever the reason, this is a chance for the estimator and project manager to get a feel for the bidding methods of the competition (market conditions), so appropriate adjustments can be made on the next bid effort.

15.5   POST-BID ETHICS

Some general contractors, upon winning a bid, will issue subcontracts or purchase orders for an amount that is a few percent less than the price submitted by the lowest bidders. When the subcontractors complain, they are told that if they want the work they will sign the contract for the stated amount. This may work initially, but eventually this general contractor will have difficulty being low on future bids, because the subcontractors and suppliers will add a percentage to the bids anticipating the amount this general contractor will force out of them. This is similar to bid shopping, which was discussed in Chapter 14.

The bid captain and project manager should look at any subcontractor or major supplier quotations that were received after the owner's deadline. Quotations received before the deadline, but not evaluated, are legal quotations and may be used if the contract is won. Quotations received after the bidding deadline technically are late, but in some extenuating circumstances, they may be useable. For example, if no quotations were received for a category of work and an OM estimate (plug) was used in developing the bid, a late quotation may be used and the subcontractor awarded the work.

15.6   POST-BID NEGOTIATIONS

Many private owners conduct a post-bid contractor interview. The two or three lowest bidders are asked to review the project with the owner and the architect. The intent is to make sure that they have included all of the work that is required by the contract documents. The owner also may want to determine the contractor with whom he or she feels most comfortable. The owner may issue some revised bid documents that add a minor amount of work and ask the contractor to submit a revised bid price. Without saying so, the owner essentially is auctioning the project to the contending general contractors. He or she is asking them to take a second look at the project and submit a new bid. The contractor submitting the lowest price usually wins the project.

Another tactic used by some private owners is to request a best and final offer. The owner often indicates that the project is over budget and asks the contending contractors to review their bids and submit best and final offers. The contractors each must decide how badly they want the project and whether or not to lower their prices. The best and final offer approach is legal in private work and is often part of the contracting process. An owner may believe that the bidders did not submit their best bids, and this method is used to obtain the lowest possible price. During the initial bid, general contractors generally do not use inflated fees, because it may take them out of contention. Upon being asked for a new price, they usually examine the combinations of vendor bids and the self-performed work to see how much they can reasonably reduce their bid and still make a proposed profit. Fee reduction is considered last depending on the results of the other reviews.

Some owners break a project into multiple contracts. This usually occurs on larger commercial and industrial projects and is done by companies that have the staff to administer more than one contract. This will affect a contractor's fee determination and post-bid negotiations. In some cases, the contractor may bid a low fee on the first contract, anticipating that the owner may prefer to stay with the same contractor throughout the project. Changing contractors can cause a discontinuity of work, which may affect both schedule and costs. The contractor must be careful in post-bid negotiations that the owner does not commit him or her to the same fee percentage for all future work.

Some owners bid the mechanical and electrical work as separate contracts. During post-bid negotiations, they may attempt to assign these contracts to the general contractor for no additional fee. Administering these contracts can cost money by extending the job-site overhead, and the contractor deserves a profit for doing so. The risk from assigned contracts usually is lower, and a lower profit margin is warranted.

During post-bid negotiations, the contractor needs to determine which issues he or she is willing to concede and which are not negotiable, and to gain an understanding of the owner's objectives. The contractor may want the work and may yield to the owner's demands to the point of not being able to do the work profitably. An owner may try to obtain as many concessions from a contractor as possible. This is good negotiating procedure. By determining what concessions can be made and where to make a stand, the contractor can negotiate on the same level as the owner.

15.7 RECORD KEEPING

The estimator may wonder how long to keep a project estimate if the bid is not successful. If the general contractor was second or even a close third, the estimate should be retained until the owner executes a contract with the low bidder. On occasion, conditions can change, so that the low bid is rejected. The bid documents should be researched to see if there is a specified period of time that the bid is to remain valid. The estimate should be kept for at least this time period, and if the contractor was second bidder, consideration might be given to keeping it until the project is built. If the low bidder should default, the owner may want to hire the second bidder to finish it. Having the estimate available will save estimating time.

Once it is decided that a bid estimate is no longer needed, the estimator should look at it for possible historical or reference use. There may be an unusual condition that warrants retaining a portion of the estimate. For example, a project requires a pit to be constructed using sheet piling with struts and bracing. This is a type of construction not often encountered, so the estimator may elect to retain this part of the estimate in his or her reference notebook.

Perhaps the estimate was done in a very organized and neat manner and contains many common elements used for building construction. The estimator may determine that it is a valuable training tool and may want to distribute copies to less experienced estimators. If, however, there is no reason for keeping the estimate, it should be discarded once the time period that has been deemed necessary to retain it expires. If all of the bid information is on the computer, including the subcontract list, the estimator might consider making a backup onto a disk and keeping the information for a given period of time.

15.8 SUMMARY

Certain work needs to be completed after the bid has been tendered to the owner. Subcontractor queries must be handled with care, so that the contractor, if awarded the contract, is not put into a disadvantageous position. Upon notification of a post-bid interview, the contractor has to consider the owner's methods of doing business and develop an interview plan accordingly. Lastly, whether or not the contract was won, the estimate should be gleaned for its use either in training or for data that may be useful in the future. As in the actual bidding process, ethics remains an issue after the bid is submitted.

Record keeping also must be considered. Most bids have a time period for which bids are to remain valid. The estimate should be kept for at least this long and, if the bid team believes that there is a situation where the low bidder may be rejected or other negotiations will ensue, then the records should be kept until it comes to conclusion. If the project is similar to other work that the company does on a regular basis, the records may be kept for future reference.

15.9 REVIEW QUESTIONS

1. What are two common methods for the owner of a project to open bids?
2. Is the owner of a private project required to award to the low bidder?
3. Can the owner of a private project conduct a public bid opening?
4. When a subcontractor asks how his price stacked up on bid day, how should this question be answered?
5. If the subcontractor is low and inquires about his price after the bid has been tendered, how should the question be answered?
6. What is a buyout evaluation?
7. Describe a method that the owner might use to get a contractor to lower his or her bid after the time the bid was tendered.
8. How long should the bid files be kept for an unsuccessful bid?

15.10 EXERCISES

1. State your thoughts about the following ethics issues. Include the reasoning for your conclusions.
   - Bid shopping—as discussed in Chapter 14.
   - The post-bid best and final offer process.
   - Issuing subcontracts for amounts below the low bidder's price.

2. What are some of the issues you would consider when preparing for a post-bid interview with the owner?

SECTION

IV

NEGOTIATED CONTRACT ESTIMATING PROCESS

CHAPTER 16
GUARANTEED MAXIMUM PRICE ESTIMATES

CHAPTER 17
FEE DETERMINATION
FOR NEGOTIATED CONTRACTS

CHAPTER 18
GUARANTEED MAXIMUM PRICE ESTIMATE
FOR THE CASE STUDY

CHAPTER 19
COST PROPOSALS FOR NEGOTIATED CONTRACTS

16

GUARANTEED MAXIMUM PRICE ESTIMATES

16.1   INTRODUCTION

As discussed in Chapter 1, cost-plus construction contracts are often used when the exact project scope of work has not been defined. Many owners select the construction contractor early in design development to take advantage of the contractor's expertise and to foster early teaming between the design and the construction organizations. Most cost-plus contracts are awarded using the negotiated procurement process that also was introduced in Chapter 1.

In a cost-plus contract, all specified contractor's project-related costs are reimbursed by the owner, and a fee is added to cover profit and company overhead. The fee may be a fixed amount or a percentage of project costs, or it may include an incentive component. Many cost-plus contracts contain a *guaranteed maximum price (GMP)* that is negotiated between the contractor and the owner. Any costs exceeding the GMP are borne by the contractor. Some of these contracts contain a cost-sharing provision that provides for a sharing of cost savings between the owner and the contractor, if the final project cost is less than the GMP.

In this chapter, we will discuss the process for developing a GMP using semi-detailed estimating techniques. The GMP is often developed using drawings that are about 90% complete for the sitework and substructure and about 50% to 60% complete for the superstructure and finishes, as shown in Figure 1-1 in Chapter 1. The GMP includes the estimated cost of constructing the project and the fee requested by the contractor. In Chapter 17, we will discuss how to determine an appropriate fee for the GMP, and in Chapter 18, we will discuss the development of a GMP for the Training Center.

16.2   CONTRACT PROCUREMENT PROCESS

Cost-plus contracts with a GMP typically are awarded based on an agreed-upon fee and maybe a GMP, since construction costs are not known until the project is completed. The owner provides an estimated construction cost (usually a budget estimate as discussed in Chapter 3) in the solicitation documents and asks prospective contractors to submit fee proposals, maybe GMP proposals, and sometimes lump-sum or time-and-materials proposals for preconstruction services. Whether or not GMP proposals are requested will depend upon the amount of design that has been completed.

There are two approaches to awarding a cost-plus construction contract with a GMP. In one approach, the contractor and owner negotiate a fee for preconstruction services and a fee for construction services early in schematic design. Once the design is 65% to 85% complete, a GMP is negotiated. In the other approach, the owner and contractor negotiate a separate preconstruction services contract early in schematic design. Once the design is 65% to 85% complete, they negotiate a separate cost-plus construction contract with a GMP. One significant advantage of the negotiated cost-plus contract is that it allows construction to start on a fast-track basis on one portion of the project, such as excavation or foundations, before all of the other design elements are completed, such as architectural finishes.

While lump-sum bid contracts typically are awarded solely on cost, negotiated cost-plus contracts may be awarded on a combination of criteria. An owner may require that a construction schedule, quality control plan, and project management plan be submitted as well as cost proposals. Using a weighted set of evaluation criteria, the owner then evaluates each element of the contractor's proposal and awards the construction contract to the contractor whose proposal scored the highest.

16.3   DOCUMENTS

The accuracy of the GMP is directly related to the completeness of the documents upon which the estimate is based. The earlier the estimate is established, the less accurate it will be and the more reliance it will have on allowances and contingencies. Budget estimates may be developed by architects, estimating consultants, or contractors early in the design process, such as after completion of the schematic design. This may be the same time that the owner issues an RFP asking prospective general contractors to prepare preconstruction services and construction fee proposals. The GMP estimate is generally developed after the budget estimate, but before the potential for a lump-sum bid. Some design and owner teams work without the benefit of contractor input through design development and issue the RFP later, requesting GMP and fee proposals along with contractor references. The exact timing depends upon the team relationship, availability of building permits, and owner requirements. On occasion, the GMP may be competitively bid among a short list of general contractors during the later design phase, or even after the contract documents are complete.

The items of work that have the most risk for the general contractor are those that will be performed by the contractor's own workforce and those that have not been defined in the drawings and specifications at the time the GMP estimate is prepared. Appropriate contingencies should be added to the estimate as risk mitigation. Selection of appropriate contingencies was discussed in Chapter 1. The work items typically performed by a general contractor are shown on the structural and civil drawings. Often these drawings are well developed at the time the GMP estimate is prepared, while completion of other drawings may be delayed until the final design phases.

The specifications are generally assembled during the design development stage and are completed with the drawings. Outline specifications are often available during design development or at the 60% construction document stage. These may be sufficient to develop a GMP estimate. Similar to accuracy of drawings, the more developed the specifications are, the more accurate is the estimate, and allowances and contingencies can be kept to a minimum.

16.4 STRATEGIES

Owners may attempt to save design fees by negotiating a GMP with a contractor before the design is complete, and having the construction team complete the design during the Request for Information (RFI) and the submittal phases of the project. Some designers work well within these parameters, continuing during construction with limited construction administration services. In this manner, they serve more like a design-assist firm. Some owners will excuse the designer at the GMP development phase. The architect's contract may be limited to developing building permit documents, which generally are not 100% complete plans and specifications. Some contractors prefer the freedom this gives them with choices of materials. However, the contractor and owner teams are also taking on more risk with either of these two scenarios.

Some owners assume that the advantage of the negotiated GMP process is that the price is a maximum, and there will be no change orders. This is difficult for the contractor to guarantee, unless he or she is given considerable control over the design, or large contingencies were included in the GMP. If the GMP is established early, many contractors will require that they be actively involved in the completion of the design documents. The contractor should develop a detailed list of assumptions and allowances, which will accompany the GMP. Some contractors go so far as to prepare a detailed scope narrative for each specification section. If the design changes significantly and scope is added, the contractor probably has justification for an increase in the GMP. For example, if a certain curtain wall system was assumed, and the architect specifies another, the general contractor will have a justifiable reason for changing the GMP.

Some critical strategies must be established between the owner and the contractor prior to the preparation of a GMP estimate. There must be an agreement between the owner and the contractor regarding which costs will be considered reimbursable and which will be considered as non-reimbursable. Both need to be defined in the contract. The degree of involvement of the owner in the selection of subcontractors and suppliers also needs to be understood by the contractor before preparing a GMP estimate.

16.5 ESTIMATING PROCESS

A GMP estimate is more detailed than a budget estimate, and thus more accurate, but it is not as detailed or as accurate as a lump-sum estimate. Figure 16-1 shows a flow chart of the typical process used for developing a GMP estimate. The process usually is initiated with the receipt of a Request For Proposals. An example RFP is shown in Appendix D for the Training Center. Once the construction company decides to submit a proposal, an

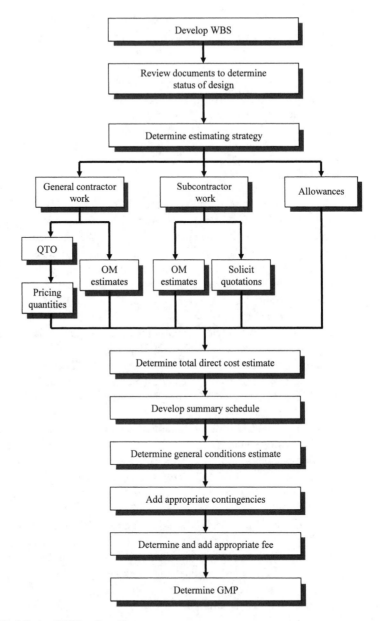

FIGURE 16–1 GMP estimating process.

estimator is assigned to prepare the GMP estimate. The process starts with the development of the WBS for the project. Next the drawings and specifications are reviewed to determine the design status of the major elements of work. Work items that are 90% or more complete can be estimated using the techniques discussed in Chapters 7, 8, and 9 for lump-sum estimating. Work items that are partially designed will be estimated using OM estimating techniques discussed in Chapters 1 and 9. Work items that have little design completed will be estimated using allowances.

The estimator next determines which elements of work will be constructed by the general contractor and which will be constructed by subcontractors. Based on this allocation of the work items and the design status for each work item, the estimator develops a strategy for preparing the estimate. Costs for contractor-performed elements of work that are reasonably well-defined are estimated by taking off the quantities of work from the drawings and pricing the resulting quantities. Costs for other contractor-performed elements of work are estimated using OM estimating techniques. OM estimates are prepared for all subcontractor elements of work that have some definition in the drawings. Subcontractors are asked to provide quotations for all elements of work that can be quantified. Allowances are established for elements of work that have little or no definition in the contract drawings. Once the total direct project costs have been estimated, the estimator prepares a summary construction schedule and estimates the general conditions costs for the project. Appropriate contingencies and the fee are added to complete the GMP estimate.

Many GMP contracts specify the use of design-build mechanical and electrical subcontractors. These firms may have been chosen prior to the general contractor's selection, or soon after. The basis for their selection may have been similar to that of the general contractor: fee and experience. Because these firms control their design, they are better able to develop a GMP early in the design process. The design fees for these firms may be included in the GMP and marked up by the general contractor, separated out and run through the architect, paid by the owner directly, or included with the preconstruction fee.

16.6   CONTINGENCIES

As discussed in Chapter 1, contingency values can range from less than 1% up to 20%, depending on the state of completion of the contract documents (drawings and specifications). The more complete the documents are, the less the contingency needed. The contingency may also be related to several project and site intangibles such as the following:

- Have the designer, owner, and contractor teams worked together before?
- Is the site a difficult one that may include unknown or hidden conditions?
- Is this a renovation project?
- What are the experiences of the different team members (owner and designer)?
- What are anticipated weather impacts during the scheduled construction?
- Will the project be constructed during a potential labor negotiation?

Hidden contingencies may be included in GMP estimates. This is sometimes done because the estimator believes that the owner will not agree with the contingency amounts. Hiding the contingencies is not usually a good idea, because they lose their identity and are more difficult to manage during the execution of the project. Some of the ways an estimator may hide contingencies in a GMP estimate are

- Using complex or ambitious work descriptions that cannot be traced to a specific measurable item of work
- Inflating material prices
- Reducing labor productivity rates

- Inflating measured work quantities
- Using higher subcontractor prices than quoted
- Inflating allowances

16.7 SUMMARY

The GMP estimate is neither a budget estimate nor a lump-sum bid, but it uses concepts from both types of estimates. The GMP process is best suited for the owner who desires a negotiated approach and has the need or sees the advantage of adding the contractor to the project delivery team early during design. The GMP process is most prevalent in private construction where the owner has the option to choose this procurement method. The contractor is usually chosen on a fee and resume basis after the schematic documents are complete. He or she completes the GMP estimate after design development is complete or approximately halfway through the construction document phase. The accuracy of the contractor's estimate is a function of the degree of completion of the design documents. If complete civil and structural drawings are available, that portion of the estimate will be taken off and priced just like a lump-sum bid. If the finishes have not been established, the contractor will use assemblies or square foot cost estimates for these areas of work. The GMP estimate may include several stated allowances. The amount of contingency is also related to the completion state of the documents. The more complete the documents are, the more accurate the GMP estimate, will be, and the less need there will be for contingencies or allowances.

16.8 REVIEW QUESTIONS

1. Which type of estimate is the most accurate and which is the least accurate: budget, GMP, or lump-sum bid?
2. What type of estimate is generally associated with negotiated contracts?
3. Will it take more estimating hours to develop a lump-sum bid or a GMP estimate?
4. Which type of estimate has the most risk for the contractor, lump-sum bid or GMP, and why?
5. Describe the major steps in developing a GMP estimate.

16.9 EXERCISES

1. Would the value of the general conditions change between a lump-sum estimate and a GMP estimate? If so, how much and why? Explain your answer.
2. Assume you were the successful estimator for a competitive lump-sum bid estimate. The client is now asking you to sign an open-book cost-plus contract with a 50%-50% savings split. Would you accept these conditions? Explain why or why not. Would you be expected to lower or raise your price? How much would you consider?
3. Assume you were the successful negotiator with a GMP estimate. The owner is now asking you to sign a closed-book lump-sum contract. Would you accept these conditions? Would you be expected to lower or raise your price? How much would you consider?

17

FEE DETERMINATION FOR NEGOTIATED CONTRACTS

17.1 INTRODUCTION

Fee determination for negotiated projects is different from the techniques used for lump-sum estimates. Most issues in negotiated contracting, including the fee and the GMP, are negotiable. One major factor in establishing the fee for a cost-plus contract will be a clear understanding of which costs are to be considered reimbursable and which are non-reimbursable. As explained in Chapter 16, the selection of a general contractor on a negotiated basis usually occurs at the completion of one of two major design phases: schematic design or design development. At the completion of schematic design, the general contractor may be selected based on qualifications and a fee proposal and enter into a preconstruction services contract with the owner. The contractor then negotiates the GMP and the terms of the contract at a later design stage. If the contractor selection process occurs later in the design process, such as at the completion of the design development documents, the RFP may emphasize the development of a competitive GMP. In either case, the fee will still need to be clearly stated.

17.2 REIMBURSABLE VERSUS NON-REIMBURSABLE COSTS

The key to establishing the fee to use in the GMP estimate will be a clear understanding of what are considered *reimbursable costs* and *non-reimbursable costs* under the terms of the contract. Any costs that are considered to be project specific costs, usually are defined as reimbursable. This would include field supervision, direct labor, material, equipment, and subcontractor costs to put the work in place. If the project manager is located at the jobsite, his or her salary usually is considered reimbursable. If the project manager is located in the home office, then the salary is considered non-reimbursable. Sometimes an agreement can be made with the owner that a portion of the project manager's salary is considered a job cost, when he or she is working specifically on project activities, regardless of their location. If this is the case, it needs to be clearly defined in the contract agreement. Typical reimbursable costs are

- Wages of construction workers
- Salaries of supervisory personnel on the jobsite
- Wages and salaries of off-site personnel who are working on the project
- Labor taxes
- Subcontract costs
- Material and equipment costs
- Costs of other materials and equipment, temporary facilities, and related items
- Miscellaneous costs including taxes, insurance, and data processing
- Other project-specific costs such as repair of damaged work

Costs that are non-reimbursable generally are those that cannot be directly related to the specific project. This includes most of the general contractor's home office overhead expenses. Any cost that exceeds the GMP that cannot be substantiated with a change order is considered non-reimbursable. For example if Western Construction Company spent $200,000 more than the final value of the GMP contract for the Training Center, it would be considered non-reimbursable. Typical non-reimbursable costs are

- Salaries of personnel working in the company's main office
- Overhead and general expenses
- Rental costs of equipment not specifically used on the project
- Costs due to rework or negligence
- Costs in excess of the GMP

Fee is overhead and profit. In this case, overhead means home office overhead. Jobsite overhead, or jobsite general conditions costs, are usually considered reimbursable project costs. Therefore, the proposed GMP fee must be sufficient to cover the estimated pro-rata share of the annual home office overhead costs plus provide a profit.

One way for owners and design teams to resolve any misunderstandings regarding reimbursable costs is to itemize them and indicate that the language is non-negotiable. Another way is to allow the contractors to provide a list of all costs that they consider reimbursable in their proposal. Any costs not listed as reimbursable, would be considered part of the fee.

Some owners may place a high emphasis on the value of a detailed general conditions estimate when selecting the construction team. They may include the proposed contractor's fee with their jobsite general conditions estimate. Some owners and designers mistakenly do not differentiate between home office overhead and jobsite general conditions costs. This may be because designers include their overhead with their fee. If contractors are required to submit detailed jobsite general conditions estimates with their early fee proposals, they may believe that selection will be based on the value of these estimated costs. They may estimate the general conditions low, assuming that they can later charge some questionable general conditions costs as project costs. This is not recommended. Experienced owners will realize the need to have a project adequately staffed and supplied and see through this shifting exercise.

17.3 HOME OFFICE OVERHEAD

Home office overhead is also referred to by different terms, including

- Indirect costs
- Fixed costs
- Home office general conditions
- Overhead
- General and Administrative costs (G&A)

These home office costs include items such as the salaries of a contractor's officers, accounting costs, home office rental, secretarial services, and home office utilities. These are considered the fixed costs of conducting business. They do not vary significantly from year to year unless there are significant workload changes.

Some additional home office expenses may be project specific and can be expensed as reimbursable, if clearly defined in the contract. This may include certain accounting or cost engineering functions that can be performed either in the field or the home office but are considered more efficient from the home office for a specific project. This can be the case in mid-sized, open-book projects that may require a substantial amount of cost reporting to the owner. On very large projects, a jobsite accountant and additional jobsite computer operations may be warranted and, therefore, they are reimbursable jobsite expenses.

Home office costs are very expensive and must be considered when a contractor is proposing a fee. Small contractors often leave this important aspect out of their estimates. The home office overhead should be known by the firm as an average annual percentage. It is computed by dividing total non-project-reimbursable annual home office costs by the firm's estimated total annual gross volume of work. Three examples are shown in Figure 17-1. The fee

Contractor A:	Home office expenses of $1,200,000
	Annual volume of $40,000,000
	Overhead percent = $1.2 mil/$40 mil (x100) = 3%
Contractor B:	Home office expenses of $5,000,000
	Annual volume of $500,000,000
	Overhead percent = $5 mil/$500 mil (x100) = 1%
Contractor C:	Home office expenses of $200,000
	Annual volume of $2,000,000
	Overhead percent = $200 k/$2 mil (x100) = 10%

FIGURE 17-1 Home office overhead percentages.

chosen by the estimator on a GMP project needs to be sufficient to cover these home office expenses and provide a profit.

17.4 RISK EVALUATION

The amount of fee chosen by the estimating team is related to anticipated risk. The GMP estimate and contract should have less risk than a lump-sum contract. If the estimator has done a proper job of qualifying his or her estimate with assumptions and exclusions and has properly analyzed the subcontractor bids, the estimate should be close. Therefore, the fee associated with a GMP estimate generally is less than that with the lump-sum estimate.

As stated in Chapter 16, the process of estimating the general contractor's direct work, such as placing foundations, is generally the same with lump-sum bidding and estimating for a GMP contract. The structural drawings generally are complete at the conclusion of the design development phase or halfway through the construction document phase, when the GMP estimate usually is produced.

The fee for a lump-sum bid generally relates to the risk of estimating the cost for those elements of work that are to be performed by the general contractor's crews. One significant difference in the risk is that the GMP is usually associated with a negotiated process. Estimators tend to use lower labor productivity rates in GMP estimates to mitigate the risk associated with incomplete documents, and they may use slightly higher material unit prices than they would on lump-sum estimates. This is because the estimator is not competing and does not need to have his or her costs estimated at the lowest level. If challenged on higher rates, the estimator usually responds by indicating that the documents are not complete and not all of the details are shown. Some of the intangibles discussed in Chapter 16 relative to team members and experiences will also not be as significant with a negotiated project as they are for a lump-sum estimate.

The second reason that the risk is not as high with the direct work portion of the GMP estimate as with a lump-sum estimate is that the estimator can have more time with the documents and should have covered all of the details. The third reason follows along the lines discussed in Chapter 6 regarding questions to the design team during the bid cycle. When contractors are competing, they do not want to divulge their estimating strategies to the other contractors by asking too many questions. When negotiating a GMP estimate, the estimator will often write many questions to the design team about details that are in conflict or not complete. These questions are early RFIs and, therefore, are tools to aid in finishing the design. A contractor who is estimating a lump-sum project very aggressively may be looking for change order opportunities and will keep any discrepancy questions until after the contract has been awarded.

The lump-sum estimating process of receiving and selecting subcontractor prices on bid day, as described in Chapter 14, is full of risks associated with incomplete subcontractor bids. The estimator in the GMP process can minimize and almost eliminate the risks associated with subcontractor pricing by

- Soliciting quotations from a select short list of prequalified subcontractors
- Allowing the owner and designer to participate in the risk by pre-approving subcontractors on the short-list

- Sending detailed RFPs to the subcontractors
- Thoroughly analyzing subcontractors' quotations when posting them to the spreadsheet and making any necessary adjustments for incomplete estimates
- Disqualifying any subcontractor who does not respond as requested to the RFP or who may have an excessively low quote that may be in error or that may appear to be set up for future change orders or claims
- Using post-bid questionnaires and interviews with subcontractors to assure complete pricing prior to forwarding the project GMP estimate to the owner
- Allowing the owner and designer to further share in the risk by proposing the subcontractor with the apparent complete low quote and asking their concurrence of selection

The estimator who is preparing a GMP estimate is not under the same tight, usually nonnegotiable estimating timeframe, as is the lump-sum estimator. If the estimator needs more time with the documents, he or she can request it. If the owner refuses to accept this request, the estimator may use or increase their "estimating contingency" percentage. The additional time with the documents and the estimate reduces the risk and associated fee with a GMP estimate.

Another way for the estimator to reduce the estimating risk is to include several stated and well-defined allowances for those portions of the work that are not fully designed. Examples would include the following:

- Allow $27 per square yard for carpet that has not been specified
- Allow $15,000 for site asphalt patching
- Allow $100,000 for dewatering
- Allow $75,000 for potential labor rate changes pending final union negotiations
- Allow $200 each for 50 pieces of undefined owner equipment that is to be installed by the contractor

Risk is not totally to be ignored when the estimator is calculating the fee on a GMP project. It is just not as significant as in the case of a lump-sum bid project.

17.5 OTHER IMPACTS ON FEE

Market Conditions

Market conditions will have an impact on the fee proposed by a contractor when negotiating a contract. The estimating team must evaluate the recent success they have had against the two or three contractors they are proposing against on this specific project. If contractor A was successful in negotiating the last project of similar size with a 4% fee, and Western Construction Company was not selected with a proposed 5% fee, then Western may have to consider lowering its fee. The construction community is a close-knit industry. In the case of a fee proposal, the owner may have shared the fees from the previous competition with all of the firms. The unsuccessful proposing contractors may even trade results among themselves. As the construction market gets busier, fees generally rise. If Western Construction Company was successful on the last project at a 5% fee in a busy market, then they may consider raising their fee to 6% on the next proposal.

Backlog

If contractors are busy and the need for additional work is lower, their fees will generally rise. A contractor may choose not to respond to a negotiated RFP or a lump-sum bid request due to a full backlog. If the owner is a repeat customer who the contractor does not want to offend, the contractor may respond honestly and indicate that he or she is too busy to properly staff the project at this time or may turn in a fee proposal with a higher than market rate fee. If the contractor gets the work at the inflated rate, he or she will need to staff the project. Problems associated with adding untested and potentially unqualified staff pose significant additional risks, which may not have warranted even the increased fee. Conversely a lower fee may be proposed if the contractor's backlog is low and the work is needed to keep key employees on the payroll.

Profit

Most contractors have a *profit* goal based on their desired return on investment. Company owners have invested their capital in the business. If they cannot return a fair profit on their investment, they would be wise to invest their money in other areas. The before-tax profit calculation will enter into fee determination. For example, if Western Construction Company has a home office overhead of 3% and proposes a fee of 3%, the anticipated profit would be zero. If they would like to return a profit to their firm of 2%, they need to propose a fee of 5%.

Opportunity Cost

Sometimes the opportunity cost of placing resources such as the project manager and superintendent on a project factor into the fee calculation. If the competition on one particular project is high and contractors can expect to barely cover their home office overhead with their fee proposals, they may choose other projects where the committed resources can generate higher fees and return greater profits to their companies.

17.6 FEE STRUCTURE

The owner has a choice in selecting the method for determining the fee for a cost-plus contract with a GMP. Any of the following contract methods may be used:

- *Cost-plus-fixed-fee.* The fee is a fixed amount irrespective of the cost of construction. The fee may be increased by change order if the scope of work is increased, but otherwise it is unchanged during the project.
- *Cost-plus-percentage-fee.* The fee is a percentage of the cost of construction.
- *Cost-plus-incentive-fee.* The fee is inversely proportional to the project cost. A target construction cost and fee are established. If the actual cost exceeds the target cost, the fee is reduced. If the actual cost is less than the target cost, the fee is increased.
- *Cost-plus-award-fee.* The fee has two components: a fixed base fee and an award fee based on periodic evaluation of the contractor's performance. The contract identifies

specific criteria to be used to evaluate the contractor's performance and states the frequency of evaluation, usually quarterly or semiannually. Criteria might include performance measures such as coordination of the work, quality of the work, safety, schedule, cleanliness of the site, and quality of project documentation.

In the RFP, the owner typically provides an estimated construction cost for the project and asks prospective contractors to provide a fee proposal. For fixed and award fee contracts, the contractor provides a percentage fee, which is multiplied by the estimated cost to determine the fixed fee or the fixed component of the fee in an award fee contract. The value of the award fee component and any incentive fee adjustments are decided by the owner and stated in the RFP. Cost-plus-percentage fee contracts are rarely used, because they provide little incentive for the contractor to reduce construction costs.

Generally the contract will state that the fee increase for change orders is the same as the contract fee. For example, let's assume that the contract fee was determined to be 5% of the estimated cost of construction. The fee increase for any changes would be 5% of the change order value. In some cases, on larger projects, it can be a *sliding scale fee*. For example a $60,000,000 project may not allow any increase in fee until the first $2,000,000 of change orders are accepted and incorporated into the contract. In this manner, the owner is trying to provide the contractor with a disincentive to generate small change orders. Some contracts will allow for a higher fee on direct work than on subcontract work, because the risk is higher with direct work as indicated earlier. Other contracts will award a larger percentage fee on smaller change orders and a smaller percentage fee on progressively higher valued change orders. Two examples are shown in Figure 17-2.

An award fee approach can be a fairly complex way to calculate a contractor's fee. The contract identifies a series of criteria that the owner will use to judge the contractor's

---

Scenario 1:

Different fee for direct versus subcontracted work:

Stated fee in the contract:	5%
Additional fee for direct labor and materials on additive change orders:	7%
Additional fee for subcontract work on additive change orders:	2%
Reduced fee for credit change orders:	0%

Scenario 2:

Different fee based upon size of change orders:

Stated fee in the contract:	7%
Additional fee for change orders valued at $10,000 or less:	10%
Additional fee for change orders valued between $10,001 and $50,000:	7%
Additional fee for change orders valued in excess of $50,001:	5%
Reduced fee for credit change orders valued at $50,000 or less:	0%
Reduced fee for credit change orders valued at $50,001 or more:	−5%

FIGURE 17–2   Sliding scale fees.

Award Fee Evaluation

Project: The Training Center
Contractor: Western Construction Company

Category	Points Possible	Points Awarded
Budget control	30	28
Communications	10	8
Safety	10	10
Quality control	15	12
City relations	5	5
Neighborhood relations	5	5
Schedule adherence	20	15
Jobsite cleanliness	5	4
Total Points:	**100**	**87**

Points as a percentage of 100:	87%
Potential additional fee:	$25,000
Additional fee awarded:	$21,750

Evaluation by: _____   _____
               Owner's Representative   LMA Project Architect

FIGURE 17–3   Award fee report card.

performance. Contractor performance reviews are conducted either at specific review periods throughout the construction of the project or at the completion of the project, and the fee is awarded based on the results of these evaluations. An example award fee evaluation form is shown in Figure 17-3. Often the contractor is first asked to evaluate his or her performance against the criteria and then submit the evaluation to the owner for review and concurrence.

17.7   CONSTRUCTION COST SAVINGS SPLIT

Many GMP contracts contain a provision that allows a split of any savings between the contractor and the owner if the actual construction costs are less than the GMP. Savings splits are usually an item the contractor is allowed to propose with the fee proposal. They can range from 50%–50% to 100% (owner) and 0% (contractor). The market range is usually in the 70%–30% to 80%–20% range. The contractor's portion of the saving split represents increased profit. For example on the Training Center, we will assume Western Construction Company had a 75%-25% savings clause and the GMP is about $2.6 million. If Western completes the project for $2.4 million or approximately $200,000 less than the contract value, then they would receive their 25% portion in the savings as an increase to their profit. This arrangement benefits both the owner and the contractor. The owner also realizes a $150,000 saving.

17.8 SUMMARY

Fee is generally defined as the sum of the home office overhead plus the desired profit the contractor is seeking. Many factors are used in determining what fee to include in a GMP estimate. The clear definition of reimbursable versus non-reimbursable costs is critical to calculating a proposed fee. The risks for the estimator associated with a guaranteed maximum price estimate should not be as high as they are for a lump sum-project for a variety of reasons, including negotiated style, less competition, select subcontractors, use of allowances, and stated contingencies. There are many ways to calculate and state a fee in a GMP contract. The fee may be a fixed amount or a percentage of construction costs, or it may have an incentive component. Savings splits are another way for the contractor to increase the fee.

17.9 REVIEW QUESTIONS

1. Which type of estimate has a higher estimated fee, lump-sum or GMP? Why?
2. What considerations should the estimator give when calculating a proposed fee?
3. Why would a contractor propose an incentive fee?
4. When would it not be advisable for a contractor to enter into an incentive-only fee contract with an owner?
5. When would a percent-only fee contract clause benefit the contractor?
6. When would a percent-only fee contract clause benefit the owner?
7. Name five non-reimbursable costs.
8. Name five reimbursable jobsite general conditions costs.
9. What risks are associated with a lump-sum bid estimate that are not as prevalent with a GMP estimate?
10. What type of contract has the potential to result in the highest end-of-construction fee, lump-sum bid or GMP?

17.10 EXERCISES

1. ACME Construction is a medium-sized general contractor who has home office general conditions that average approximately 4% of their annual volume. They are bidding on a retail tenant improvement project with an estimated cost of $1,250,000. ACME wants to receive a profit of 3%. Calculate their percentage and lump-sum fee for this bid.
2. ACME will later bid on a $5,000,000 elementary school project in a slower market. Their goal is to return a 2% profit after project completion. Calculate their percentage and lump-sum fee for this bid.
3. If Western Construction Company received most of their bids on the Training Center from unknown subcontractors because the plans were put in the plan centers, how might this affect their proposed fee?

4. Assume the Training Center project has been negotiated by Western Construction Company. They are soliciting subcontractor proposals from a narrow select list of subcontractors, rather than lump-sum competitive bids. How would this affect the fee?

5. Based upon the drawings and specifications included for the Training Center, list at least five allowances that should have been included in Western Construction Company's proposal.

6. Assume Western Construction Company's jobsite general conditions estimate developed in Chapter 10 was part of a negotiated proposal, and the selection of the contractor will be based on the lowest fee plus jobsite general conditions cost. List at least five general conditions items they may have wanted to hide in the direct cost of the work.

7. Why might an owner not want to enter a construction contract where the owner received 100% of the savings?

8. Calculate the fee Western Construction Company should propose for the Training Center based upon an estimated construction cost of $2.6 million and the following:

   • Home office overhead is 3% of annual volume
   • The desired profit is 3%

9. Calculate the total fee Western Construction Company will realize for the Training Center based upon an estimated construction cost of $2.6 million and the following:

   • Home office overhead is 4% of annual volume
   • Desired profit was 3.5%
   • The project finished $100,000 under contract value
   • The project had a stated 70% (owner) -30% (contractor) savings split
   • There was a stated ceiling for the contractor's share of shared savings as 2% of contract value

18

GUARANTEED MAXIMUM PRICE ESTIMATE FOR THE CASE STUDY

18.1 INTRODUCTION

The case study used throughout this text has been the Training Center located in Kent, Washington. In this chapter, we will discuss the development of a GMP estimate for the project. A select list of four contractors received relatively complete sets of plans and specifications. They were required to submit GMP estimates along with several other qualifying documents. The RFP for the project is shown in Appendix D. The contractors were expected to include sufficient contingency in their GMP estimates to protect the owner from design discrepancy change orders.

18.2 DESIGN STATUS

The design documents, which were forwarded to the contractors to use in preparing GMP proposals, were approximately 75% complete. The documents had been complete enough to apply for the building permit. All of the code-related life-safety systems were shown. The specification sections were all identified. An abbreviated specification manual was included in the RFP. It was more than an outline, but less than a fully detailed document. The finish schedule was prepared, but not all of the finish products or colors were identified. Allowances for items such as ceramic tile and carpet were necessary in the GMP estimate. Final finish products and pricing were to be resolved during the submittal process. A short soils report also was provided.

The following documents were issued to the competing contractors for the Training Center:

- Request for proposal, dated April 14, 2003. (Shown in Appendix D)
- Drawings issued by the Architect, LMA, all dated 4/10/00, except the civil drawings, which were dated 12/21/99, and the topographic survey drawing, which was dated 7/13/98.
- Specification manual prepared by LMA, dated April, 2000.
- Geotechnical engineering study, dated December 2, 1999.
- Addendum number one, dated April 21, 2003.
- Jobsite pre-proposal meeting agenda, dated April 21, 2003.
- Addendum number two, dated April 25, 2003.
- Blank contractor summary schedule of values, which was to be completed and turned in with the proposal.
- Addendum number three, dated April 27, 2003

18.3 ASSEMBLIES METHOD

An assemblies estimate was used for many work items for the Training Center because the design documents were not complete. The assemblies method combines labor, material, and equipment into one unit price. Databases from published estimating references, such as those by R.S. Means, can be used for this process, just as they can for detailed estimates. Either the total without markups (for direct work) or the total including markups (for subcontract work) are used in lieu of detailed unit man-hours, labor rates per hour, labor burdens, and material unit prices. Many firms prefer to rely on in-house databases. This information usually is more accurate for a specific firm in a specific geographic area performing a specific type of work, than national averages that are available in published databases.

Even if the documents are not complete enough to prepare a lump-sum bid, the more detailed the estimate and the more current the unit prices, the more accurate the GMP will be. As accuracy is increased in estimating, risk is reduced. After analyzing the documents included with the RFP, Western Construction Company decided to estimate different areas of work on the Training Center using the strategy shown in Figure 18-1.

18.4 ESTIMATING GENERAL CONTRACTOR WORK

The drawings were relatively complete for the general contractor's self-performed work for this project. The estimating techniques discussed in Chapters 6 through 8 for lump-sum estimates could be used for the direct work. Quantities are measured and taken off the drawings and posted to QTO sheets. Items of work are extended, and like items are grouped and subtotaled. These items are then posted to the pricing recapitulation sheets. Western Construction Company performed detailed estimates for the following categories of work:

- Structural excavation and backfill
- Foundations including reinforcement steel
- Slab-on-grade
- Elevated composite concrete slab on metal deck

Western Construction Company
550 South 7th Avenue
Kent, Washington 92002

Project: The Training Center
Type of Estimate: GMP
Chief Estimator: Mike Castle
Project Manager: Rhonda Martin
Proposal is due on: April 28, 2003

- Prepare a detailed estimate for normally performed Western direct work that is adequately detailed. This will include most of the cast-in-place and tilt-up concrete work.
- Take off the quantities for the balance of the direct work that is not completely detailed, increase quantities to allow for work that is yet to be designed, and use assemblies unit pricing.
- Request subcontractor quotes for the systems that have been completely designed. Prepare RFPs for select subcontractors that Western is confident can perform on the project.
- Take off the quantities for the balance of the subcontracted work. Either use assembly unit prices from Western's in-house database or request OM unit prices from subcontractors. Clearly define these areas as allowances with the proposal to the owner.
- Include stated contingencies in the GMP estimate summary sheet for <u>estimating accuracy</u> due to incomplete documents and inadequate subcontractor coverage and for the balance of <u>design completion</u>.
- Prepare a detailed general conditions estimate based upon a reasonable construction schedule for this type of facility.
- Choose a fair but competitive fee reflecting current market conditions and minimal estimating risk.
- Prepare a professional proposal responding to all issues in the RFP. Turn in the proposal on time.

FIGURE 18–1   Western Construction's estimating strategy.

- Tilt-up concrete panel form work, reinforcement steel, and concrete placing and finishing
- Door installation

There were also areas of normally self-performed work that were not designed sufficiently to perform detailed labor and material estimates. In these cases, Western Construction Company used what quantities they could measure, allowed for 5–10% additional quantity, and used assemblies estimates for each system. Some of these categories included

- Sidewalks
- Concrete tilt-up panel erection
- Structural steel erection
- Rough carpentry

Figure 18-2 is a pricing recapitulation sheet that shows this combination of detailed estimates for designed elements and OM estimates for items for which the design was not yet complete.

Project: The Training Center
Contractor: Western Construction Company
Proposal Date: April 28, 2003

CSI Division	Description	Labor	Material	Total	Type of Estimate
2	Structural excavation	$1,042	$6,442	$7,484	Detail
2	Sidewalks			$20,000	OM
3	Foundations and rebar	$13,445	$22,625	$36,070	Detail
3	Slab-on-grade	$14,445	$31,222	$45,667	Detail
3	Elevated composite slab	$6,248	$6,590	$12,838	Detail
3	Form and pour tilt-ups	$55,245	$59,967	$115,212	Detail
3	Erect tilt-up panels			$50,000	OM
5	Structural steel erection			$50,000	OM
6	Rough carpentry			$17,800	OM
8	Door installation	$2,500	$1,500	$4,000	Detail

FIGURE 18–2   Direct work estimate.

18.5   ESTIMATING SUBCONTRACTOR WORK

Western Construction Company solicited competitive subcontractor bids for the areas of work that were completely defined. The subcontractor bids were then analyzed, and the most favorable bids were selected for the estimate. The following subcontractor work items were competitively bid in this manner:

- Mass excavation and fill
- Site utilities
- Roofing
- Thermal and acoustical insulation
- Glazing
- Purchase of doors and door frames
- Drywall
- Acoustical ceiling tile
- Bridge crane
- Mechanical
- Plumbing
- Electrical

The design was not sufficiently complete to receive bids for several areas of work. Western Construction Company chose to use OM estimates based on cost per square foot for these areas. The subcontractor categories of work estimated by Western Construction Company included

- Asphalt pavement
- Curbs
- Pavement striping and markings
- Structural steel supply

- Millwork
- Door hardware
- Interior and exterior painting
- Floor coverings
- Specialties including signs, toilet partitions, and white boards
- Elevator
- Weld exhaust system

Figure 18-3 is a pricing recapitulation sheet for the subcontractor work that shows this combination of subcontractor bids for designed elements and OM estimates for items for which the design was not yet complete.

Project: The Training Center
Contractor: Western Construction Company
Proposal Date: April 28, 2003

Major Supplier and Subcontractor Categories	Quote or OM Estimate	One Quote - 1 or Competitive - C	Estimate
Earthwork and utilities	Q	C	$184,600
Asphalt	OM		$45,000
Curbs	OM		$16,000
Pavement markings	OM		$2,500
Fence	Q	C	$10,400
Landscape	Q	C	$39,000
Rebar and mesh supply	Q	C	$32,800
Rebar and mesh installation	Q	C	$17,000
Masonry	Q	C	$27,300
Structural steel supply	OM		$150,000
Millwork	OM		$26,700
Insulation	Q	1	$15,400
Roofing, flashing, skylights	Q	C	$110,000
Supply doors and frames	Q	1	$25,000
Supply door hardware	OM		$15,000
Overhead doors	Q	1	$23,000
Glazing	Q	C	$76,600
Drywall systems and acoustical ceilings	Q	1	$182,000
Painting	OM		$53,000
Floor covering	OM		$71,000
Specialties	OM		$21,000
Bridge crane	Q	1	$75,600
Elevator	OM		$30,000
Plumbing	Q	1	$66,200
HVAC	Q	1	$155,200
Fire protection	Q	C	$56,800
Electrical	Q	1	$205,600
Total subcontractors and major suppliers:			$1,732,700

FIGURE 18–3 Subcontractor estimate summary.

Western Construction Company
550 South 7th Avenue
Kent, Washington 92002

The following items have not been completely designed at the time of this proposal. Cost allowances have been included in the over-all guaranteed maximum price estimate and are identified as "allowances." The assemblies method basis for these estimated allowances is also shown for clarification. Upon completion of the design, and development and receipt of complete pricing, the allowances will be removed and rolled into the GMP as line item estimates. The contract value will be adjusted, up or down, based upon these firm values, via contract change order.

Direct Work:	Allowance:
• Sidewalks (6700 sf @ $3/sf)	$ 20,000
• Structural steel erection (100 tons @ $500/ton)	$ 50,000
• Tilt-up panel erection (25,000 sf @ $2/sf)	$ 50,000
• Rough carpentry (35,610 sff @ $0.50/sff)	$ 17,800

Subcontractors and Suppliers:	
• Asphalt (45,000 sf @ $1/sf)	$ 45,000
• Curbs (2,000 lf @ $8/lf)	$ 16,000
• Pavement striping and markings (2,500 lf @ $1/lf)	$ 2,500
• Structural steel supply (100 tons @ $1500/ton)	$150,000
• Millwork (35,610 sff @ $0.75/sff)	$ 26,700
• Door hardware (50 sets @ $300/set)	$ 15,000
• Interior and exterior painting (35,610 sff @ $1.50/sff)	$ 53,000
• Floor coverings, including tile walls (35,610 sff @ $2/sff)	$ 71,000
• Specialties (35,610 sff @ $0.60/sff)	$ 21,000
• Elevator (2 stops @ $15,000/stop)	$ 30,000

Note: All unit prices are per measured unit of item unless noted as square foot of floor (sff) in which case quantity measurements could not be made at this time.

FIGURE 18–4   Training Center GMP allowances.

A summary of all the allowances determined by the use of OM estimating techniques is shown in Figure 18-4. This summary is submitted with the final GMP estimate to justify all allowances used.

18.6 ESTIMATING CONTRACTOR GENERAL CONDITIONS

A summary construction schedule must be developed before the general conditions estimate is prepared. The contractor team can use input from the direct work estimate, early subcontractor input, and history on similar projects to develop a preliminary summary construction schedule. The owner may require that a schedule be submitted as part of the proposal. This may be in summary or more detailed format, according to the requirements of the RFP. Regardless of the level of detail, the contractor, owner, and designer teams should all realize that this is just a tool to be used to prepare the proposal. This schedule is not yet a construction tool.

Jobsite general conditions estimates are prepared in one of two ways: (1) percentage add-on to the estimated cost of the work or (2) a detailed general conditions estimate. The percentage add-on is only recommended for early budget estimates such as those discussed in Chapter 3. The preparation of a detailed general conditions estimate was discussed in Chapter 10. Any design beyond the early schematic design phase is sufficient for the construction team to prepare a detailed general conditions estimate. A lump-sum general conditions estimate for the Training Center is shown in Chapter 10 (Figure 10-2). A slightly higher general conditions value was used in the GMP estimate because additional coordination and financial documentation are expected.

18.7 MARKUPS AND ADD-ONS

The significant differences in the markups and add-ons between lump-sum estimates and GMP estimates are that fees are lower with GMP estimates, because the design is not complete, so the risks are lower and the contingencies are higher. Markups for cost of the work and add-ons such as labor taxes, liability insurance, builders risk insurance (if required), or excise taxes are the same regardless of contracting method. Because the drawings are not as complete, the estimator usually includes contingency markups. Because the drawings and specifications were only 75% complete when the GMP was requested, a 3% contingency was used in the estimate. This corresponds to an upper value as shown in Figure 1-15. Western Construction uses a company overhead rate of 3% and desires a 2% profit on the project, so a fee of 5% was used in the estimate. The final GMP estimate for the Training Center is shown in Figure 18-5.

Project: The Training Center
Contractor: Western Construction Company
Proposal Date: April 28, 2003

GMP Estimate Summary

CSI Division	Description	Labor	Material	Suppliers & Subcontractors	GMP Value
1	Jobsite general conditions	$92,900	$42,200	$0	$135,100
2	Sitework	$13,300	$26,600	$317,500	$357,400
3	Concrete	$99,800	$134,100	$49,800	$283,700
4	Masonry	$0	$0	$27,300	$27,300
5	Structural steel	$50,000	$0	$150,000	$200,000
6	Carpentry	$10,000	$7,800	$26,700	$44,500
7	Roofing and insulation	$2,500	$4,300	$125,400	$132,200
8	Doors and glazing	$2,500	$1,500	$139,600	$143,600
9	Finishes	$0	$0	$306,000	$306,000
10	Specialties	$3,500	$2,255	$21,000	$26,755
11	Bridge crane	$0	$0	$75,600	$75,600
12	Furnishings	$3,750	$2,575	$0	$6,325
13	Equipment	$0	$0	$0	$0
14	Elevators	$0	$0	$30,000	$30,000
15	Mechanical	$0	$0	$0	$0
	Plumbing	$0	$0	$66,200	$66,200
	HVAC	$0	$0	$155,200	$155,200
	Fire protection	$0	$0	$56,800	$56,800
16	Electrical	$0	$0	$205,600	$205,600
		$278,250	$221,330	$1,752,700	$2,252,280
	Labor burdens:		40% of labor	$111,300	$2,363,580
	Liability insurance		1%	$23,636	$2,387,216
	Builders risk insurance		0.20%	$4,774	$2,391,990
	State excise tax		1%	$23,920	$2,415,910
	Estimating contingency		3%	$72,477	$2,488,387
	Home office overhead and profit		5%	$124,419	$2,612,807

Total GMP Estimate: $2,612,807

FIGURE 18–5 GMP estimate summary.

18.8 SUMMARY

The contract documents provided to Western Construction from which to develop a GMP estimate were about 75% complete. A WBS was developed, and general contractor and subcontractor work items were selected. Detailed estimating techniques were used for those general contractor work items that had nearly complete design documentation. Subcontractors were asked for quotations for subcontractor work items that had nearly complete design. OM assemblies estimates were developed for general contractor and subcontractor work items with little design completed. A general conditions estimate was prepared, and markups and add-ons were selected to complete the GMP estimate.

18.9 REVIEW QUESTIONS

1. How is an OM assemblies estimate prepared?
2. How did Western Construction Company decide which general contractor work items to estimate using a QTO and unit pricing approach?
3. How did Western Construction Company decide which subcontractor work items to ask subcontractors to bid on?
4. What are two methods for estimating the general conditions for a GMP estimate?
5. How did Western Construction Company determine appropriate markups and add-ons for the GMP estimate?

18.10 EXERCISES

1. Using labor productivity and material pricing from a database, replace the assembly pricing for the structural steel package shown in Figure 18-3 with a detailed estimate.

2. Using an assemblies price, provide an alternate price to replace the tilt-up walls estimated in Figure 18-2 with structural split-face concrete block.

3. Provide an alternate price to replace the built-up roof estimated in Figure 18-2 with a single-ply EPDM product.

4. The construction drawings on the Training Center were completed after the contract with Western Construction was executed. Prepare a contract change order to replace the asphalt allowance shown in Figure 18-4 and incorporate an acceptable bid from a subcontractor for $42,500.

19

COST PROPOSALS
FOR NEGOTIATED
CONTRACTS

19.1   INTRODUCTION

The negotiated procurement process was discussed in Chapter 1 and illustrated in Figure 1-13. Prospective contractors typically are invited first to submit their qualifications to the owner for review. The best-qualified construction firms are then issued a Request For Proposals (RFP), which identifies information that is to be submitted to the owner for review and evaluation. The owner evaluates each proposal against a set of criteria and selects the firm with the highest scored proposal for contract award. The general contractor for a negotiated construction contract may be selected early in the design process based on a fee for preconstruction services, a construction fee, and qualifications. Determination of a preconstruction services fee was discussed in Chapter 5. An RFP for the Training Center is shown in Appendix D.

19.2   STRATEGIES FOR RESPONDING TO THE REQUEST FOR PROPOSAL

Just as submission of a bid concludes the lump-sum estimating process, submission of a proposal concludes the GMP estimating process. The goal of the contractor in responding to the RFP is either to be selected based upon the written response or to get an interview. It is the contractor's goal to differentiate itself from the competition. Some suggestions for responding to the written RFP include the following:

- Continue marketing while responding to the RFP. Communicating with the selection team is generally acceptable. Let the owner know you have received the RFP, have a high degree of interest in the project, and are actively working to respond.
- Only respond with the information requested. The selection team may not value excess volumes of paper, which forces them to search for information that is really important in their selection process. The owner may believe that if the contractor cannot follow directions on the RFP that he or she may not follow the plans and specifications.
- Determine the important evaluation criteria. If it is fee, then do not spend excessive time with the value engineering section.
- Know the owner. Try to find out who will be reviewing the evaluations.
- Make the response as personal and project-specific as possible. Insert the owner's name, such as Training Center, and the architect's name, such as LMA. Generic terms such as owner and architect do not win any points. It is important to tell the owner what you will do for them on this project.
- Know the competition and emphasize your strengths. Set your firm apart from the competition.
- Be professional. Make the proposal package look like it was put together with quality control in mind. The owner may believe that if the proposal package lacks quality, the construction of the building may also lack emphasis on quality.
- Respond exactly on time, if not early. If the proposal is received late, the owner may believe that the contractor cannot make a schedule.
- Provide the exact quantity of proposals requested, if not a few extra copies. If there are five people on the selection committee, but only four proposals are provided, one of the reviewers may not rate the proposal highly.

19.3 DOCUMENTS TO BE INCLUDED WITH THE WRITTEN PROPOSAL

Every RFP is different. There is no one way to respond. A contractor will have a library of the types of documents that may be requested to be included with a proposal. They all will need to be customized for any specific project. Following are some of the types of documents that may be included with a proposal:

- Cover letter thanking the owner or designer and introducing the firm
- Table of contents
- Fee proposal
- Guaranteed maximum price estimate
- Detailed general conditions estimate
- Summary or detailed schedule
- Cost-control procedures
- Quality-control plan
- Project-specific safety plan
- Insurance, financial, and bonding information

- Company history on this type of project, in this location, with this designer, with this owner, or any combination of these experiences
- References for the firm and proposed project management team
- Resumes for the proposed project management team
- Organization chart for this project
- List of reimbursable versus non-reimbursable costs
- Subcontractor selection process
- Contractor-proposed contract format, or comments on the selection team's proposed contract format
- Value engineering proposals
- Constructability analysis of the drawings and specifications
- List of documents used to prepare the guaranteed maximum price estimate
- Assumptions, clarifications, qualifications, or exclusions used when preparing the guaranteed maximum price estimate

Some of these documents may be required, and others not. It may be in the contractor's best interest to provide unrequested documents, but the contractor must exercise care when submitting extra documentation. The owner's review committee may not value voluminous proposals. The proposal should be bound to present a professional appearance.

19.4 GENERAL CONTRACTOR INTERVIEW AND SELECTION PROCESS

The contractor's goal is to get to the interview process. Experienced owners may issue a post-proposal questionnaire to the short list of contractors. The advantage of written questions is that they require written responses. The owner and design teams generally like to receive as much on the contractor's letterhead prior to selection as possible. The contractor is still selling at this stage. It is surprising how often these early responses are referred to later during the construction process. Examples of post-proposal questions for the Training Center are shown in Figure 19-1. Responses from Western Construction Company are shown in Figure 19-2.

Responses to these questions may be required prior to the interview, or they may be submitted at the time of the interview. From the owner's perspective, it is better to receive the answers prior to the interview, as these answers will often result in additional questions and issues that can be covered during the interview. If the contractor is not required to respond in writing until the interview, the contractor should bring enough copies for everyone who may be at the interview, and some extras.

An agenda should be prepared for the interview. If the owner has not given the contractor direction regarding issues that are to be covered, the contractor should ask and should be ready to respond. If the owner is not experienced in this process, the contractor may bring an agenda. An example interview agenda is shown in Figure 19-3.

The order of interview may be important for some contractors. Some prefer to be first, to set the standard. Some prefer to be last, to try to close the deal after the meeting, or to adjourn for dinner or lunch to try the informal approach. Most contractors do not want to

The Training Center
20474–72nd Avenue South
Kent, Washington 98032

May 1, 2003

Mr. Owen Clark
Western Construction Company
550 South 7th Avenue
Kent, Washington 92002

Re: Training Center Proposal—Post-Proposal Questions

Dear Mr. Clark,

Thank you for your timely and complete proposal on the Training Center. We are in the process of reviewing the four proposals we received and would like to ask you a few additional questions. It is our intent to interview one to two firms next Wednesday and make a decision at the following Trustee's meeting. Your timely, written response to these questions would be appreciated.

1. Your schedule was longer than the other firms. Please review and respond.
2. Please confirm that your estimate is based upon using prevailing wage rates.
3. There appears to be some confusion about site painting the exposed structural steel. Did you include this work? At what cost?
4. Thank you for including your proposed markups to the standard AIA A111 agreement. Unfortunately, your proposed markups are quite extensive. How flexible is your firm in negotiating these terms?
5. You did not provide any references for your superintendent. Is he new to your firm and this area? Please provide if possible.
6. Would your firm be available for an interview in the architect's office on Wednesday of next week in the early afternoon?
7. What are the major risks for your firm on this project?
8. What do you see as the major risks for the owner on this project?
9. How accurate were the documents (% = __)? How much contingency did you include in the GMP? What contingency would you recommend the owner carry for document discrepancies?

Best Regards,

William Rogers

Owner's Representative

FIGURE 19–1 Post-proposal questions.

Contractor Response to Post-Proposal Questions

Western Construction Company
550 South 7th Avenue
Kent, Washington 92002

May 2, 2003

Mr. William Rogers, Owner's Representative
The Training Center
20474–72nd Avenue South
Kent, Washington 98032

Re: Training Center Proposal—Post-Proposal Questions

Dear Mr. Rogers,

We received your post-proposal questions dated May 1, 2003. We at Western are very excited to be involved in this challenging project. I trust that our responses below address all of your questions. We look forward to sitting with you next Wednesday and introducing our team first-hand. I am confident that you will find our firm and project team are the best match for this specific project.

1. The elevator delivery is critical to our schedule duration. We may be able to save two weeks off the schedule if we can start on the foundations before the building permit is received. There are other schedule expediting possibilities we would enjoy discussing with you.

2. Our estimate is based upon prevailing wage rates.

3. We included site painting the structural steel as indicated on the finish schedule. This value is approximately $10,000 depending upon which painting firm we negotiate with. We have other value engineering items we can discuss at our interview.

4. We can discuss these teams and find mutually agreeable language.

5. References for our superintendent are attached to this letter.

6. We have blocked out the entire Wednesday afternoon to meet with you.

7. Our major risks are associated with some of the unsolicited subcontractor pricing we received on proposal day. We would like to review all of these subcontractors with you and your architect and mutually choose firms who are best qualified to build this facility.

8. We see the contractor and the owner as a team. Our risks are your risks and your risks are our risks. Unforeseen conditions, such as unstable soils and questionable subcontractor quality, are some of the issues we can discuss on Wednesday.

9. The documents are probably 75% complete. We have included a minor estimating contingency in our estimate, for those items that were not completely designed. We have not included any contingency for items such as the following:
   - Owner scope changes
   - City changes
   - Designer changes

FIGURE 19–2 Contractor response to post-proposal questions.

- Unusual weather conditions
- Unforeseen conditions
- Material and labor escalation if project award is delayed
- Document discrepancies

We would recommend the owner carry a contingency of 7–15% for all of these potential issues.

If you have any additional questions, please feel free to call me direct.

Best Regards,

Owen Clark

Officer-in-Charge
Western Construction Company

FIGURE 19–2 Continued.

Interview Agenda

May 5, 2003
Training Center
Interviewing Contractor: Western Construction Company (WCC)

AGENDA

Item	Discussion	Responsible
1.	Introductions	All
2.	Goals of the interview	William Rogers
3.	Review written responses to post-proposal questions	WCC
4.	Potential to expedite schedule	WCC
5.	Risky subcontractors	WCC
6.	Potential value engineering ideas	WCC
7.	Additional questions from the owner and design teams:	WCC
	Why is the electrical price so disproportionately high?	
	Where are the costs for site utilities?	
	Have your PM and superintendent worked together?	
	The entire project came in over budget. Why is it so expensive?	
8.	Design completion and permit schedule updates	LMA
9.	Does WCC have any exclusions other than as indicated in the proposal and the post-proposal question responses?	WCC

FIGURE 19–3 Sample interview agenda.

be the first interview after the owner's lunch break. Sometimes people lose attention immediately after eating lunch. In most cases, the contractor will not have a choice of interview times. Some suggestions for contractors during the interview include the following:

- Know the audience. Address everyone by his or her name.
- Dress appropriately.
- Bring all required personnel. This usually includes the project manager and the project superintendent. Do not bring more individuals than suggested.
- Practice the interview in front of peers.
- If the owner does not provide an agenda, offer to bring one.
- Make sure the owner's and the architect's questions and issues are covered. Do not spend 45 minutes talking about cost control, when their important issue is constructability input.
- Make sure the owner hears from the project team that is being proposed, not just the marketing department.
- If the decision process will take some time after the interview, such as a few days, contractors should follow up immediately and offer any additional answers or information that the selection team may be looking for.

If the contractor prefers to use electronic graphic presentations, some additional suggestions are as follows:

- If possible, review the interview room's layout and capabilities ahead of time.
- Bring a paper backup in case your equipment does not function.
- Ask the owner if this type of presentation is acceptable.
- Ask the owner if set-up time will be allowed in addition to the interview time.
- If only 30 to 45 minutes are allowed for the interview, the set-up time for the equipment may not warrant the electronic presentation.
- The contractor may ask the owner and designer teams to visit the contractor's office for the presentation if set-up and electronic media are that critical and are not available in the owner's office.
- Practice the presentation. Electronic presentations done well can win the project for the contractor, and those done poorly can lose the project.
- Always ensure that the electronic presentation works flawlessly.

Owners may use a variety of methods to choose the successful contractor. Some may already have decided, so the interview is just a formality. The proposing contractor can do little in this situation. Many interview processes result in a clear winner, without much debate or voting. More complicated selection processes, such as those choosing a negotiated construction manager on a public works project, may include a weighted score card. This scorecard may or may not be shared with the contractors prior to the interview. All individuals on the selection team are given a card for each contractor, and the scores are tallied and either summed or averaged. A sample of a negotiated scorecard is shown in Figure 19-4. Even after a detailed written proposal process including post-bid or post-proposal questions, an interview, and a complicated scoring system, the results may be close. The final decision may come down to a simple question: "Which contractor do we want to work with?" The answer may be subjective based upon interview chemistry, team member personalities, or past relationships.

Final Contractor Selection Scorecard

Category	Category Weight 1 (low) to 5 (high)	Training Center Western Construction Company Contractor Score 1 (low) to 5 (high)	Extended Score Weight x Score
Guaranteed maximum price	3	5	15
Fee percentage	5	4	20
Jobsite general conditions estimate	3	4	12
Project Manager	2	4	8
Superintendent	5	3	15
Approach to subcontracting	3	5	15
Professional written proposal	4	5	20
Response to RFP	4	5	20
Response to post-proposal questions	2	3	6
Interview	2	3	6
Schedule duration	1	4	4
Acceptance to contract format	4	4	16
Total score for *Western:*			**157**

Competing Contractor Comparisons:

Acme Construction Company	*120*
Northwest Constructors	*143*
Western Construction Company	**157**

Decision: Proceed with contract negotiations with Western Construction Company

FIGURE 19–4 Sample final contractor selection scorecard.

19.5 NEGOTIATED SUBCONTRACTS

The selection of negotiated subcontractors can happen any time during the design or construction phases, using a negotiated or bid procurement process. The negotiated process is similar to the selection of a negotiated general contractor. An RFP is developed. Written proposals are received. Post-proposal questionnaires, interviews, and sometimes a scorecard may conclude the selection. The same suggestion about written information applies, whether the owner, the architect, or the general contractor firms are selecting the subcontractors. The more information and commitments that can be obtained from a subcontractor in writing prior to issuing a subcontract, the better off the purchasing party will be. Following are some of the different timings and methodologies of selecting negotiated subcontractors:

- The owner or architect selects design-build mechanical and electrical subcontractors early in the design process prior to the general contractor selection. The design portion of their fee will be under the architect. The construction portion should be under the general contractor for field control and single point responsibility issues.
- The general contractor may have been selected on a fee basis early in the design process and may take the lead on selection of the design-build mechanical and electrical subcontractors.

- The general contractor may have the use of early design criteria-type documents and may solicit design-build GMP proposals from a select list of mechanical and electrical subcontractors who will finish the design and build the project.
- On occasion, complete design documents may be available in any discipline. The general contractor may then solicit lump-sum bids from a short list of subcontractors and proceed through a post-bid negotiated selection process. The 80-20 rule will apply here as well as to which subcontractors are interviewed. Some of the critical subcontractors on most projects include earthwork/utilities, structural steel supplier, drywall systems, mechanical, and electrical.

19.6   SUMMARY

Proposals for negotiated contracts are prepared by the construction team in response to an RFP. The RFP may come early in the design process, requesting a fee for construction services and a fee for preconstruction services, or later in the design process, requesting a GMP. It is important for the contractor to respond to the RFP on time and exactly as requested. Many documents can be submitted with either a fee-only or a GMP proposal. This would include items such as a detailed general conditions estimate, resumes of key personnel, and a schedule. If the contractor is invited to a post-proposal interview, he or she should address several key issues, and should provide a written response to post-proposal questions. The contractor should practice the presentation and make sure that key project personnel are available. Some owners may use a sophisticated scorecard to select the successful construction firm. Some subcontractors may be selected during early phases of the design. The RFP and the proposal and interview processes for these firms usually follow the same procedures as those for the general contractor.

19.7   REVIEW QUESTIONS

1. When would a design-build RFP not be issued to subcontractors?
2. Name five documents that the owner might request from the general contractor in a fee-only RFP.
3. List five elements needed to successfully prepare for an interview.
4. Why would an owner use a post-bid questionnaire?
5. When responding to the written RFP, what is the contractor's immediate goal?
6. List three things a general contractor might do that would cause him or her not to be selected for an interview.
7. List three criteria for a successful electronic presentation at an interview.
8. When does the contractor stop marketing?

19.8 EXERCISES

1. List five ways a general contractor can differentiate itself from its competition.
2. Assume that Western Construction Company has a post-negotiated proposal interview with the Training Center building board. The project manager who was named in the proposal does not show for the interview. What actions should the company take? How would the owner and design teams respond?
3. Assume the Training Center building board interviews Western Construction Company. You are the project manager. The questions asked from the owner and the architect teams are negative. It appears they are trying to find a way not to hire you. How do you respond?
4. Why might the owner, architect, and general construction teams decide to select subcontractors using a negotiated procedure rather than a bid procedure?
5. If you were the owner or architect on a negotiated contract, what five questions might you want the general contractor to respond to in an interview?

V

ADVANCED ESTIMATING TOPICS

CHAPTER 20
AUTOMATED ESTIMATING TECHNIQUES

CHAPTER 21
OTHER TYPES OF ESTIMATES

CHAPTER 22
PROJECT MANAGEMENT ISSUES

20

AUTOMATED ESTIMATING TECHNIQUES

20.1   INTRODUCTION

Computers have had a significant impact on the construction industry during the last ten to twenty years. They are now used in design, estimating, scheduling, project management, and communications. Estimating efficiency and speed have improved dramatically from these changes. The construction estimates produced twenty years ago were primarily developed from hand-produced design drawings. The estimating process consisted of measuring by hand with architectural and engineering scales, adding and multiplying with a ten-key adding machine, looking up unit prices in books and folders, and receiving telephone quotations from subcontractors. The estimate was manually delivered to the owner's office, often with the help of a pay telephone for last-minute bid adjustments. Cellular telephones had a significant impact on the bid submittal process ten years ago, and now electronic mail (email) and the Internet have taken bid submission to another level. The purpose of this chapter is to introduce a few of the automated techniques currently used in developing a cost estimate.

20.2   PRE-ESTIMATE AUTOMATED TECHNIQUES

Design drawings previously were prepared on mylar. Changes to the original drawings required extensive erasing and redrawing. Sticky-backs were standard details that designers had either developed themselves or could purchase. The sticky-back itself was a significant improvement from hand drawing each detail on every set of drawings.

Today drawings for many commercial projects are almost exclusively prepared electronically with CAD (computer-aided design) software. The CAD operator has replaced the draftsperson. Following are some advantages of computer-produced drawings:

- Borrowing proven details from previously prepared drawings
- Using overlays to discover and resolve conflicts between disciplines
- Creating three-dimensional views
- Making faster revisions and updates
- Easily showing alternate design schemes

CAD has allowed automated calculation of areas and quantities, such as site and building square feet. Municipalities often require this information early in the design process as part of their permit review procedures. Although the computer has made it easier to produce square foot calculations, there still is a risk in assuming that these figures are correct and not performing separate QTOs. Even if the site and building areas are printed on the cover sheet of the permit application drawing set, the estimator should make independent measurements and calculations. An estimator who relies on published figures in developing an estimate, does not perform an independent QTO, and determines later that the designer's figures were in error usually cannot recover the loss that results from underestimating the quantity of work. There generally is language in the specifications warning contractors that the figures are not for estimating purposes. In addition, the production of technical specifications is often automated. Generic specification databases are available from which the design team can select appropriate sections and make minor modifications to customize the specifications for a particular project.

20.3 AUTOMATED ESTIMATING TECHNIQUES

Subcontractor Involvement

As was discussed earlier in this text, one of the first things an estimator should do when preparing an estimate is to get subcontractors and suppliers involved. The junior estimator often is assigned the task of telephoning select subcontractors and notifying them that a project is being reviewed and that the general contractor would like their quotations on bid day. The estimator will need some knowledge of the project in order to answer preliminary questions from subcontractors, such as the type of wood doors that have been specified. Today, all subcontractors are often notified simultaneously via email. The estimator has become less reliant on personal contact. Instead of telephoning ten drywall firms, a generic notice can be sent to all ten firms at the same time.

Many contractors have also developed homepages where subcontractors can review what projects the general contractor is pursuing. These homepages usually have links to allow the subcontractor to review the projects over the Internet and even download drawings. This also saves time. Within minutes after a general contractor has a project to estimate, subcontractors can be notified and have drawings on their estimating desks.

On many projects for private owners, contractors may limit their subcontractor list to a select few firms that they believe are qualified to perform the work. In these cases, the homepage Internet link to view and access the drawings may be secured for only those select firms.

Quantity Take-Offs

Often drawings are not transmitted on paper. They can be transmitted either on a computer disc or electronically over the Internet. This saves initial reproduction cost and time in getting the drawings to contractors. Many computer-produced drawings are capable of providing the contractor (and the owner and architect) with a list of all the quantities of materials required for the project. The old system required the estimator to measure and count each item. It was discussed in Chapter 7 how estimators mark up drawings with highlighters to indicate that the work has been taken-off. With the correct combination of design and estimating software, quantities can all be downloaded ready for pricing with a few keystrokes.

Short of this completely automated take-off process, many contractors have supplemented the estimating team with electronic *digitizers*. Digitizers use a mat and an electronic wand. Drawings are taped to the mat on the estimator's desk. The wand traces over the drawings and produces a picture of the item being measured, such as a spot footing, on the computer screen. The computer is given the scale of the drawing and the quantity of that size of footing. Touching each footing with the wand can also generate the quantity of footings rather than manually counting them. The quantities of formwork, excavation, rebar, concrete, and anchor bolts are all then automatically determined. Some estimators have made errors by missing quantities, which the old highlighter system prevented. The digitizer can produce a drawing that replicates the design drawing to provide a crosscheck against these types of errors.

The digitizer, like many of the automated estimating tools, saves the estimator considerable time, not only by measuring, but also by producing the addition and multiplication math functions. Electronic spreadsheets are used as take-off sheets and pricing sheets. These spreadsheets can also quickly perform all of the math steps that the estimator used to spend hours preparing and rechecking. However, caution must be used with electronic spreadsheets. When the estimator customizes a form and cuts or inserts a row or column, the formulas may be altered. A good estimating check is to freeze these sheets and formulas and perform a math check on the totals using a calculator.

Unit Prices

Many computerized databases containing unit prices are commercially available. These databases include pricing averages for a variety of systems and materials. Estimators used to review old estimates from their estimating resource books or from other estimators to estimate labor productivity or material prices for the quantities that had been manually measured. Today, many contractors have their own databases of historical pricing developed from past projects.

An estimating software system can take the quantities produced manually, from a CAD file, or with the assistance of a digitizer, and apply a database of unit prices, calculating the pre-bid day total estimate for a project. Again, the benefit of this type of technique is speed and reduction of math errors. Many of the items that contribute to the computer estimate development are shown in Figure 20-1.

The risk for the estimator is in becoming overly reliant on the computer calculations (both quantities and pricing) and not analyzing the differences the project may have from the generic model. Some of the mental questions the estimator should consider include the following:

- What is unique about this project?
- Is the project up on a hill or down in a hole?
- What type of labor regulations does the contract for this project contain?
- Are there workday or time restrictions that may impact productivity?
- Are there site material access issues that should be analyzed?
- Does the owner need the facility turned over in phases, which could have an effect on crew size leveling?
- Is there a way it can be built faster and better?
- Would one project manager or one superintendent perform better than another on this specific project?
- Gut check questions such as "How do the labor hours feel," or "is the schedule reasonable?"

Most spreadsheets can incorporate some of these personal impact issues. If all contractors have access to the same quantities through the use of CAD or digitizers, can purchase the same electronic databases for pricing, and receive the same subcontractor bids on bid day, what differentiates the high from the low bidder? The answers lie in some of these questions, and others in the bid-day analysis discussed in Chapter 14. This construction team input to the automated estimate is also shown in Figure 20-1.

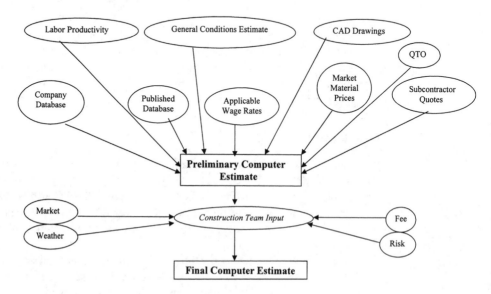

FIGURE 20-1 Computer estimate development.

Estimate Completion

Bid-day procedures have been impacted by automated estimating techniques. The computer provides for quick and effective math checks and allows for continual updates from the ROM to the final bid. The process of receiving, posting, and analyzing subcontractor quotes has changed considerably. Some contractors are using some or all of these changes for subcontractor bid analysis:

- Subcontractor estimates can be received electronically by email or fax, or over the telephone. They are then input into an electronic spreadsheet where manual selections of the most complete and economical bid can be made and automatically input into the estimate total. This process still involves the personal contact (if telephone quotes are received) and the personal review of the quotes and individual choice of the subcontractor. The computer advantage is reduction of errors in transferring the bid amounts from the manual spreadsheets to the bid posting sheet, efficient math calculations, and the ongoing total estimate update.
- Subcontractor estimates can be received electronically and input directly to the computer spreadsheet. This saves time, but misses the personal questioning of the subcontractor (for telephone quotes) and personal review of the subcontractor's inclusions and exclusions. Often a subcontractor's quote requires some minor modification to make it complete or comparable to other firms who are bidding the same specification section or groups of specification sections.
- Subcontractor estimates can be received electronically and automatically input to the computer. Software programs can then choose the least costly option and automatically recalculate the bid total, without any personal estimator input. Although this is feasible, it is extremely risky for the contractor.

The Internet and email are also changing the way some owners receive their bids. General contractors, like subcontractors, can now submit their bids to some owners via email. This allows for incorporation of very late subcontractor pricing into the general contractor's bid. This should minimize the number of times a contractor might be late submitting a bid. The pitfall of this system is the assurance that the bid is being received and opened, as was the case with a sealed envelope carried by a member of the estimating team.

Some owners are now even using a reverse auction system, where bids are posted on the Internet, for all contractors to view. The name of the firm posting the bid is usually kept confidential. Contractors may then lower their bids if they want to take the job for less money and underscore the posted low bid. This system raises many ethical questions. Contractors may become overly ambitious and lower their bid too far, taking the work for less than cost. This may result in change orders, claims, bankruptcies, and more court cases. The general contractor may in turn do the same with the subcontractors, driving their prices down below cost to make up for the shortfalls from submitting too low a bid.

Figures 20-2 and 20-4 have converted the spot footing recap and GMP estimate for the Training Center with the use of an electronic spreadsheet software system from *Win Estimator (WinEst)*. *WinEst* is driven by a number of databases that can be customized to contain company labor and equipment rates and general conditions costs. Figure 20-3 is the subcontractor list for the pre-bid-day first-run estimate previously shown as Figure 9-6.

Item Description	Takeoff Qty	Unit	Labor Prod	Labor Hours	Labor Rate	Labor Total	Mat Price	Mat Total	Grand Total
Excavate Spread Footings	125.8	cuyd	0.1780	22	28.56	640	5.05	635	1,275
Structural Fill and Compaction	76.0	cuyd	0.0120	1	27.34	25	1.46	111	136
Off-haul	93.8	cuyd	0.0120	1	28.56	32	0.70	66	98
Fine Grade	1,046.0	sqft	0.0400	42	24.71	1,034			1,034
Spot Footing Concrete Formwork	733.0	sf	0.0860	63	28.58	1,802	3.23	2,368	4,169
Formwork accessories	1.0	ls					118.00	118	118
Rebar Accessories	1.0	ls					30.00	30	30
Continuous Footing Reinforcing Steel	0.6	ton	15.2380	9	28.22	241	550.00	308	549
Spread Footings - Medium	66.5	cy	0.4000	27	26.58	707	63.00	4,190	4,897
Concrete Finishes	1,046.0	sqft	0.0100	10	26.58	278			278
Grand Total				**175**		**4,758**		**7,825**	**12,583**

Total Estimate   12,583

FIGURE 20–2   *WinEst* Spot footing recap for the Training Center.

CSI	Item Description	Takeoff Qty	Unit	Subs Total
2000	**Sitework**			
2200	Site Earthwork	1.000	LS	178,400.00
2510	Traffic Markings	1.000	LS	2,000.00
2520	Sidewalks	1.000	LS	48,920.00
2520	Concrete PIP Curbs	1.000	LS	17,300.00
2800	Chain Link Fences	1.000	LS	9,400.00
2900	Landscaping	1.000	LS	34,150.00
	Sitework Total			**290,170.00**
3000	**Concrete**			
3210	Reinforcing Steel Supply	1.000	LS	33,000.00
3210	Reinforcing Steel Installation	1.000	LS	17,650.00
	Concrete Total			**50,650.00**
5000	**Steel**			
5100	Structural Steel Supply	1.000	LS	54,150.00
5100	Structural Steel Installation	1.000	LS	50,400.00
5210	Steel Bar Joists & Deck	1.000	LS	79,000.00
5500	Metal Railings - Guard Rails	1.000	LS	4,000.00
	Steel Total			**187,550.00**
6000	**Wood & Plastics**			
6400	Architectural Woodwork	1.000	LS	12,800.00
	Wood & Plastics Total			**12,800.00**
7000	**Thermal & Moisture Protection**			
7100	Foundation Waterproofing	1.000	LS	500.00
7200	Thermal Insulation	1.000	LS	16,300.00
7250	Firestop	1.000	LS	2,000.00
7500	Built Up Roofing	1.000	LS	90,000.00
7600	Flashing and Trim	1.000	LS	17,200.00
7700	Roof Hatches	1.000	LS	500.00
7800	Skylights	1.000	LS	3,250.00
7900	Caulking and Sealants	1.000	LS	2,500.00
	Thermal & Moisture Protection Total			**132,250.00**
8000	**Doors & Windows**			

FIGURE 20–3   *WinEst* subcontractor list.

CSI	Item Description	Takeoff Qty	Unit	Subs Total
8210	Interior Doors and Frames	1.000	LS	24,890.00
8300	Overhead Doors 12x16	1.000	LS	23,000.00
8710	Door Finish Hardware Set	1.000	LS	16,500.00
8810	Windows & Glass	1.000	LS	75,000.00
	Doors & Windows Total			**139,390.00**
9000	**Finishes**			
9250	GWB Partitions to Ceiling - 1 hour	1.000	LS	156,200.00
9300	Ceramic Tile Walls	1.000	LS	32,000.00
9545	Acoustical Ceiling System	1.000	LS	18,000.00
9650	Sheet Vinyl Flooring	1.000	LS	1,750.00
9680	Carpet	1.000	LS	25,392.00
9900	Paint Walls	1.000	LS	55,000.00
	Finishes Total			**288,342.00**
10000	**Specialties**			
10100	Marker Boards	1.000	LS	3,500.00
10160	Toilet Partitions	1.000	LS	4,450.00
10400	Signage	1.000	LS	2,500.00
10500	Lockers	1.000	LS	4,000.00
10800	General Specialties	1.000	LS	1,000.00
10800	Toilet Accessories	1.000	LS	5,600.00
	Specialties Total			**21,050.00**
12000	**Furnishings**			
12500	Window Blinds	1.000	LS	4,750.00
12670	Entrance Mat Grilles	1.000	LS	1,200.00
12670	Entrance Mats	1.000	LS	1,500.00
	Furnishings Total			**7,450.00**
14000	**Conveying Systems**			
14200	Hydraulic Elevators per Stop	1.000	LS	35,000.00
	Conveying Systems Total			**35,000.00**
15000	**Mechanical**			
15300	Fire Sprinkler System	1.000	LS	55,200.00
15400	Plumbing	1.000	LS	109,695.00

CSI	Item Description	Takeoff Qty	Unit	Subs Total
15500	HVAC	1.000	LS	185,000.00
	Mechanical Total			**349,895.00**
16000	**Electrical**			
16050	Electrical	1.000	LS	253,864.00
	Electrical Total			**253,864.00**
	Grand Total			**1,768,411.00**

Total Estimate 1,768,411

FIGURE 20–3 Continued.

CSI	Division	Labor Total	Mat Total	Subs Total	Equip Total	Other Total	Grand Total
1000	General Conditions	92,900	42,200				135,100
2000	Sitework	13,300	26,600	317,500			357,400
3000	Concrete	99,800	134,100	49,800			283,700
4000	Masonry			27,300			27,300
5000	Steel	50,000		150,000			200,000
6000	Wood & Plastics	10,000	7,800	26,700			44,500
7000	Thermal & Moisture Protection	2,500	4,300	125,400			132,200
8000	Doors & Windows	2,500	1,500	139,600			143,600
9000	Finishes			306,000			306,000
10000	Specialties	3,500	2,255	21,000			26,755
11000	Equipment			75,600			75,600
12000	Furnishings	3,750	2,575				6,325
13000	Special Construction						
14000	Conveying Systems			30,000			30,000
15000	Mechanical			278,200			278,200
16000	Electrical			205,600			205,600
	Grand Total	**278,250**	**221,330**	**1,752,700**			**2,252,280**

Labor Burden	111,300
Subtotal	2,363,580
Liability Insurance	23,636
Subtotal	2,387,216
Builders Risk Insurance	4,774
Subtotal	2,391,990
State Excise Tax	23,920
Subtotal	2,415,910
Estimating and Escalation Contingen	72,477
Subtotal	2,488,387
Home Office Overhead and Profit	124,419
Total Estimate	2,612,807

FIGURE 20–4   *WinEst* GMP summary sheet for the Training Center.

20.4   PROJECT MANAGEMENT AUTOMATION TOOLS

Project management is not the subject of this text, but the automated estimating techniques discussed here provide an immediate impact to automated project management techniques. The use of labor productivity rates and man-hours in producing the estimate was discussed earlier in the book. An additional advantage of the computer in the estimating process is the ease of transforming man-hours for other project management activities. This information can be input into a scheduling program to produce a project schedule. Again, the importance of the human element with the participation of the superintendent, project scheduler, and successful subcontractors cannot be underestimated.

The computer-generated schedule provides many benefits to the project management team during the estimating process:

- An early construction schedule provides necessary duration input for field administration/jobsite overhead calculations.
- A schedule may be required for a negotiated proposal submission.
- The schedule can assist with subcontractor buyout and can be attached to the subcontract as an exhibit.
- Field work-packages can be assembled for the beginning of cost control.

Many of these project management tools and applications, which are easily initiated by the computer-generated estimate, are shown in Figure 20-5.

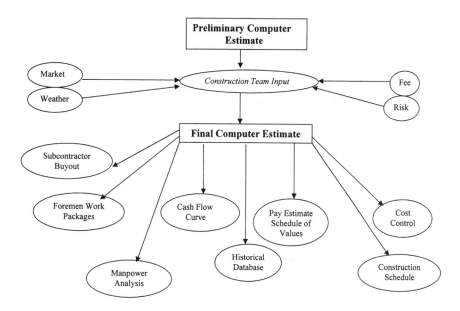

FIGURE 20–5 Project management applications.

The foreman work-packages developed from the estimate and construction schedule are used to manage the cost-control process. The work-packages can be used to record actual quantities installed and hours incurred, which can be used to calculate as-built unit prices or as-built productivity rates. This data can be provided directly to the contractor's database, which will provide the estimating team with current historical pricing to be used on the next estimate.

CAD drawings are a tool used today to minimize document discrepancies. The computer-generated design can also provide a starting point in the preparation of subcontractor submittals and shop drawings. Subcontractors are able to obtain consistent floor plans and site plans, and not redraw what others have already drawn. After completion of the drawings, subcontractors can produce computer-generated overlays, sometimes referred to as coordination drawings. These coordination drawings help identify conflicts, which would not have been apparent until field installation.

These same submittals also provide a lead for the preparation of *as-built drawings*. The major subcontractors, such as mechanical and electrical, can input their as-built information directly onto the CAD drawings, thereby producing automatic as-built drawings. The old system required subcontractors to mark up the blueprints, and then the design team was hired to incorporate those changes into the original design mylars.

20.5 SUMMARY

Computers have had an impact on the design and construction industries in several ways. CAD has reduced document discrepancies and increased the speed and ease of incorporating changes. The same CAD drawings can be used in the field to produce multiple discipline overlays, which helps to resolve field conflicts. CAD has increased the efficiency and reduced the time it takes subcontractors to produce shop drawings because the backgrounds and common floor plans do not need to be redrawn.

Automated estimating techniques have changed the way estimates are being produced and will continue to change the process as new software is developed. A contractor can receive the drawings electronically, produce the measurable quantities that require pricing, and apply a pricing database to quickly produce an estimate. Subcontractor quotes can be received electronically, and the computer can choose the low subcontractor and prepare a total bid ready to be tendered. The general contractor may be able to send the bid to the owner electronically.

The increased speed in estimate production, coupled with reduced math errors, has allowed contractors to produce more estimates in a shorter time, thereby increasing their chances of preparing a successful bid and receiving an award. But speed is not a substitute for good experienced judgment. Schedules, subcontracts, purchase orders, field workpackages, and project management plans can also be prepared by the computer as soon as the general contractor is notified of a successful bid.

There are benefits to the design and construction industries from the use of computers. There are also risks with the reduction of the human element in production of estimates. It is important for estimators to be aware of these risks when taking advantage of the new tools that are available.

20.6   REVIEW QUESTIONS

1. What is CAD?
2. How do digitizers increase estimating speed?
3. What is a risk of the digitizer and how can it be minimized?
4. Why should an estimator not rely entirely on the area calculations reported on the architectural drawing cover sheet?
5. How has the computer impacted specification production?
6. Name three ways a contractor may receive drawings from which to develop an estimate?
7. What can the computer not do in the preparation of an estimate?
8. What are three advantages of software spreadsheet systems such as *WinEst?*
9. What advantage does an in-house database have over a commercially prepared database?
10. What document is used in the field to begin the cost-control process?

21

OTHER TYPES OF ESTIMATES

21.1 INTRODUCTION

Can a house builder estimate an industrial manufacturing facility? Can an apartment developer estimate a warehouse? Does a contractor who specializes in tenant improvement projects have the tools necessary to estimate a downtown high-rise? The answer: both yes and no. Many of the procedures used to measure the concrete in a spot footing, to call a vendor for a current quote, and to apply necessary markups are consistent in whatever type of construction project is being estimated.

There are some differences, however, that require consideration. In most instances, these differences are used by a contractor to gain a competitive advantage. If general contractors do not have experience constructing oil refineries, they generally are not qualified to bid on this type of project. If contractors had an opportunity to estimate a few similar projects, they would learn that the tools required are the same, except that instead of measuring square yards of carpet, they are measuring lineal feet of pipe. This, of course, is an oversimplification. The message is that estimators should not be afraid of trying. They will often be surprised that many of the tools necessary to estimate new projects are already in their toolbox. The business decision to take on a different market, however, typically is made by a company executive, not the estimator.

It is very difficult in one textbook to describe all types of estimates. We chose a commercial case study to explain the processes. Estimating is a process, whether the estimate is a budget, a bid, a unit price, or a GMP proposal. This chapter will introduce a few different types of estimates including bid alternates, residential, industrial, change order proposals, and as-built estimates.

21.2 ESTIMATING BID ALTERNATES

Bid alternates were discussed in Chapter 12. Owners may request bid alternates to be included on the bid form. These items may be *additive alternates* or *deductive alternates* from the base bid proposal. The purpose of requesting bid alternates may be either to know the true value of an item or area of work, or to allow the owner to adjust the project scope if the bids come in under or over the allotted budget.

For example, an owner may not be sure whether he or she has sufficient funding to complete the second floor of a building. As a contingency, the owner could list finishing the second floor as an additive alternate on the bid form. If the bids are higher than anticipated, the owner may choose not to award the alternate and to leave the second floor unfinished. On the other hand, if the bids are lower than anticipated, the owner may choose to award the alternate along with the base bid.

Because the contractors do not know which, if any, of the bid alternates will be accepted, they need to estimate them correctly. Each bid alternate needs to be a stand-alone price including all direct and subcontract costs and markups. On bid day, the contractor needs to set up the bid room to allow for analysis of the bid alternates by a separate bid-day estimator. When posted to the bid spreadsheet, subcontractor quotations need to also be reviewed for the value of any alternate pricing. Failure of a general contractor to submit the requested alternate prices may result in the owner rejecting the contractor's bid as nonresponsive. Selection of acceptable bid alternates by the owner may change the order of the general contractors' bids. The initial low-bidding contractor may end up as second low after the owner has chosen the acceptable alternates.

21.3 RESIDENTIAL PROJECT ESTIMATES

There are many differences between estimating techniques used by the residential construction industry and the commercial construction industry. This text has emphasized the tools and techniques most common for the commercial industry. Many of the previous chapters describe this process. Although most of these techniques could be used on residential projects, few are. The differences can best be explained by dividing the residential contracting industry into two significant segments: the small custom builder and the large tract-home developer.

The small builder may be a one-person firm. The owner may also be the lead carpenter and the accountant. He or she may not have the expertise or the staffing to prepare detailed cost estimates. Estimating is limited to the knowledge that he or she estimated the last 2,000 square foot home at $75 per square foot, and therefore this one should be about the same. He or she may self-perform much of the work, does not cost-code time or material invoices, and does not estimate or invoice for general conditions. The small residential contractor seldom bids work. A larger fee may be charged, which is expected to cover equipment replacement and home office costs. The contractor will usually have a preferred subcontractor or supplier in each category of work. An independent builder generally does not get competitive subcontractor quotations. He or she does not have an in-house unit price database. If, at the end of the year, the contractor has made money, he or she will usually proceed in the same fashion the next year. This is one of the reasons that there is such a high failure rate among residential contractors.

A small residential contractor would benefit from the use of a simple estimate summary form as shown in Figure 21-1. This form is broken down using CSI divisions. Even

PROJECT NAME: PLAN NO. 208A
BID DATE: May 25, 2003
BID TIME: 1:00 PM
PROJECT ESTIMATOR: Terry Jones
SQUARE FOOTAGE: 1,920

MAN-HOURS	BIN	DESCRIPTION	LABOR	MATERIAL	SUBCONTRACTOR	TOTAL	$/SF
0	1.00	GENERAL CONDITIONS (markup below)	0	0	0	0	0.00
15	2.00	SITEWORK	329	1,525	0	1,854	0.97
145	3.00	CONCRETE	3,200	2,500	0	5,700	2.97
0	4.00	MASONRY	0	0	7,500	7,500	3.91
0	5.00	STRUCTURAL STEEL (with carpentry)	0	0	0	0	0.00
269	6.00	ROUGH CARPENTRY	5,920	9,436	0	15,356	8.00
106	6.00	FINISH CARPENTRY	2,340	8,746	0	11,086	5.77
264	7.00	SIDING/ROOF/INSULATION	5,800	2,000	11,000	18,800	9.79
57	8.00	DOORS AND WINDOWS	1,260	6,840	1,000	9,100	4.74
23	9.00	FINISHES	500	500	14,000	15,000	7.81
5	10.00	GAS FIREPLACE	100	100	3,300	3,500	1.82
16	11.00	APPLIANCES	360	3,000	0	3,360	1.75
8	15.00	MECHANICAL	180	555	5,050	5,785	3.01
11	15.00	PLUMBING	250	225	5,250	5,725	2.98
16	16.00	ELECTRICAL	350	175	5,500	6,025	3.14
936			20,589	35,602	52,600	108,791	56.66
MH	51.00	LABOR BURDENS	30%	6,177		6,177	3.22
		SUBTOTAL DIRECT:	20,589	41,779	52,600	$114,968	59.88
		GENERAL CONDITIONS (CSI division I)	10.00%			11,497	5.99
		FEE	10.00%			12,646	6.59
		SUBTOTAL				$139,111	72.46
		CONTINGENCY	5.00%			8,163	4.25
		INSURANCE	1.00%			1,391	0.72
		BOND	1.00%			82	0.04
		EXCISE TAX	0.80%			1,113	0.58
		CITY TAX	0.00%			0	0.00
		SUBTOTAL				$149,860	78.05
		ADJUSTMENT:				140	0.07
		ADJUSTED TOTAL:				$150,000	78

FIGURE 21–1 Residential estimate summary form.

estimating according to the assemblies method, as was introduced in Chapter 3 for budgets and Chapter 16 for the GMP proposal, would be better than just using a square-foot number based on the previous year's projects.

Larger residential contractors or developers may construct 200 tract homes per year. Such firms generally subcontract most of the work. Their direct crews often are limited to one superintendent per tract and maybe a couple of cleanup or warranty crews. They typically obtain competitive bids on all of the work. They may not have the allegiance to particular subcontractors that is common with smaller builders. These residential contractors usually perform very limited detailed quantity take-off. They generally rely on lumber suppliers to perform their own take-offs from the drawings. The large firm has a smaller percentage margin than does the smaller firm, because it can distribute the overhead costs across more projects. The larger firm's business success tends to be greater than the smaller one-person firm. The larger firm's greatest risk is in becoming overextended with too many unsold homes and being exposed to adverse economic swings. The smaller firm often can fall back on remodel projects during these situations. The tract developer usually uses many more project management tools than the smaller firm, including maintaining a historic estimating database.

The benefit that the larger residential contractor could realize from the detailed estimating techniques discussed earlier in the book would be the ability to prepare better in-house estimates prior to bidding a tract of homes. Early estimates would allow them to forecast a development's success better and to guide the designer toward designing homes that fit within a project's pro-forma. The contractor would also be better suited to analyze subcontractor change-order pricing and to prepare better estimates for owners who desire custom changes to a standard tract home.

21.4 INDUSTRIAL PROJECT ESTIMATES

The industrial market is the most difficult and the most risky to estimate as it uses the most general contractor direct labor. Often industrial project drawings are developed around machinery built overseas. The drawings might be in languages other than English and the measurements may be metric. Industrial estimating is best reserved for experienced and specialized estimators. Projects range from a small manufacturer with one or two production machines in a tilt-up warehouse to a multi-megawatt power plant costing hundreds of millions of dollars. General contractors may be firms that perform a certain amount of the work with their own forces, or they may be asked only to be the construction manager for very large projects. In either case, an estimating team will be required to develop estimated costs for the work.

Two things differentiate the industrial project from a commercial building: the types of construction and the owner's production process. Buildings will frequently require heavy concrete foundations and steel framing and may cover a very large area. It is not uncommon for several major buildings to be constructed on the same site at the same time. Automobile assembly plants are housed in one very large building and usually have several other buildings on a single site. Heavy industries such as steel production and aluminum reduction plants require very heavy foundations for the processing equipment and heavy steel to support loads of very large bridge cranes.

The general contractor may be asked to install production equipment or specialized mechanical and electrical equipment for the owner. Some contractors will do this work with their own forces while others will hire subcontractors. Millwrights and riggers usually do equipment installation work. There is, unfortunately, very little reliable estimating information published for this type of work. Contractors who are in the industrial construction business usually keep their own databases and do not make it accessible to others.

A typical characteristic of industrial projects is that they usually contain very large mechanical and electrical subcontracts. Mechanical will include service piping for all sorts of chemical processes and may have high capacity air handling systems for process exhaust. Electrical work can include installation of large service and distribution systems, high-intensity lighting, and power to large mechanical equipment.

A commercial estimator can, with a little care, develop costs for some industrial projects. Quite often the building shell may be similar in design and construction as commercial buildings and therefore use similar estimating techniques as covered earlier in this text. OM estimates for architectural and structural subcontract work can be made for construction that is common to other types of projects such as offices or warehouses. The general construction estimator, however, should be careful when preparing OM estimates for industrial mechanical and electrical work. These areas are not typical, and there are very few reliable guidelines available. The assistance from subcontractors who specialize in this area, even with early budgeting, would help minimize some of the risks of the estimator.

A team member who estimates industrial work on a regular basis should prepare equipment installation estimates. Some published references will provide general guidelines such as number of man-hours per ton of machinery, but they are too generic and are very unreliable and should be used with extreme caution and appropriate contingencies. Production equipment involves precision work and specialty tools and unless the estimator is completely familiar with the installation process he should seek qualified help for estimating this type of work. For example,

- Process machinery is installed on base plates commonly referred to as sole plates. These must be installed and leveled very accurately, otherwise it is very difficult to install the production equipment within specified tolerances. A typical sole plate may be six feet long and eighteen inches wide and will take eight man-hours per lineal foot to install and level.
- Grout is installed under the sole plates and some machine bases similar to that under steel column base plates. What is different from commercial construction is that great care is taken to get all air pockets out of the grout when it is placed so that the machine will have full bearing. This can significantly reduce the column base plate grouting productivity. The specialized grout material is also much more expensive than in commercial construction.
- Machinery must be leveled and aligned to very tight tolerances. This requires a separate millwright crew just to read and record the alignment results. They work to more precise standards than a survey crew and are on the job during the entire installation process.
- Industrial projects also include other specialized trades that most general contractors are not accustomed to working with or estimating for. This includes millwrights, surveyors, boilermakers, and pipe-fitters.

These are a few specialty items that need to be considered in an industrial estimate.

One other unique characteristic of industrial work is that owners do not use standard contract formats such as those used for commercial projects. Most large industrial owners have their own contract forms. In addition to a complex estimating process, these contracts pose additional risk for the contractors. RFQs, specifications, and general conditions are different, and there is liberal use of supplemental or special conditions. Whenever work is done on an existing process that has to be shut down for a specific period, it is common for a high liquidated damages clause to be included. A site inspection is necessary because an existing plant never looks exactly as it is represented on the drawings.

Industrial process work is challenging, high risk, and vastly different from one project to the next. The only way to develop a comprehensive estimate is to do a very detailed breakdown of the work and determine the cost on this basis. The estimator for industrial work is usually more experienced than a commercial estimator. Due to the lack of reliable historical data, a greater emphasis is made on the personal experiences of the estimator and the lead field supervisors.

21.5 CHANGE ORDER ESTIMATES

The process of estimating change orders is very similar to that explained in previous chapters for bid and negotiated estimating processes. Detailed take-offs, pricing for the general contractor work, and collection of usually one subcontract price in each area of work is similar. The general contractor gathers all input and prepares the *change order proposal (COP)*. This includes subcontractor estimates as well as estimates for anticipated direct labor and material costs. This takes a form similar to a bid summary, as shown in Figure 21-2. The contract may dictate the form and, if so, the general contractor should have evaluated it prior to submitting the original bid. The COP cover sheet can take numerous forms. Some of the important points, which should be covered on any pricing or proposal form, include the following:

- COPs are numbered sequentially.
- The COP description should be clear.
- Direct labor, hours, labor burden, and supervision costs are itemized.
- Direct material and equipment costs should be summarized.
- Subcontract costs are listed separately from direct costs.
- Markups including overhead (home office vs. field), fees, taxes, insurance, and bond are all clearly shown.
- A line for the owner or architect to sign approval is provided.

The project manager usually gets only one opportunity for additional compensation for a differing site condition, so the estimate needs to be right the first time. Owners have an understandably difficult time accepting resubmittals of the same COP because the general contractor left out one subcontractor's price from the tabulation or a math error occurred.

The estimator or project manager should do everything possible to sell the COP. Some of the attached backup to the one-page summary might include

- The originating field question or submittal
- Copies of areas of all relevant drawings and specification sections
- Subcontractor and supplier COPs and quotes
- All detailed quantity take-off and pricing recap sheets
- Any letters, memos, meeting notes, daily diaries, or phone records
- The same detailed backup from the subcontractors

CHANGE ORDER PROPOSAL

WESTERN CONSTRUCTION COMPANY
550 South 7th Avenue
Kent, WA 92002

The Training Center

CHANGE ORDER PROPOSAL NUMBER: _____ 3 _____   Date: ___ **October 27, 2003** ___

Description of work: ___ Upgrade finishes in main lobby, stair, and elevator cab ___

Referenced documents: ___ Construction Change Directive #2, Sketches 3, 4, 5, & 6 ___

ESTIMATE SUMMARY:			**Subtotal**	**Total**
1	Direct Labor	40 hours	1,200	
2	Supervision	15%	180	
3	Labor Burden	46%	635	
4	Safety	2%	40	
5	Total Labor:			2,055
6	Direct Materials and Equipment		4,500	
7	Small Tools	3%	62	
8	Consumables	3%	62	
9	Total Materials and Equipment:			4,624
10	Subtotal Direct Work Items #1:#9			6,679
11	Subcontractors (See attached subcontractor quotes)			7,500
12	5% Overhead on Direct Work Items		334	
13	5% Fee on Direct Work Items		351	
14	5% Fee on Subcontractors		375	
15	Subtotal Overhead and Fee:			1,060
16	Subtotal all costs:			15,239
17	Liability Insurance & Excise Taxes: (2.0%)			305
18	Total this COP #	3		**$15,544**

This added work has an impact on the overall project schedule, full extent to be determined. Please indicate acceptance by signing and returning one copy to our office within five days of receipt.

Approved by:

_____   _____

Training Center   Date

cc: LMA Architects, WCC Superintendent
Job No. 9821/File Code: COP #03

FIGURE 21–2   Sample change order proposal.

The ultimate goal for the contractor with respect to COPs is to have them approved. The easiest way to achieve this goal is to play it straight with respect to pricing direct and subcontract work. Overly inflated prices will only delay the process. Quantity measurements are verifiable to a large degree, and they should not be inflated. Wage rates paid to craft employees are verifiable and should not be inflated. Subcontractor quotes should be passed through as is without adjustment (unless incomplete) from the general contractor to the owner. The subcontractors and suppliers should practice the same procedures with their second- and third-tier firms.

How much is a fair markup? Markups can include a lot of items. Generally they are percentage add-ons to the direct cost of labor and material associated with change orders. Markups on change orders could include such things as

- Fee on direct work
- Fee on subcontracted work
- Field or jobsite overhead and administration costs
- Home office overhead
- Supervision and foreman costs
- Labor burden and labor taxes
- Detailing
- Builders risk and liability insurance
- State sales, business, and excise taxes
- Small tools
- Bonds
- Cartage and material handling
- Cleanup
- Dumpsters or rubbish removal
- Safety
- Cost of preparing the change order proposal estimate
- Hoisting
- Consumable materials

It is possible to see a series of markups that could double the cost of the direct work. Owners and architects are frustrated with these add-ons. They do not understand why they have to pay more than the direct costs. Many of these items are required, and sometimes it is the presentation that makes it difficult to sell. Quite often general contractors (and subcontractors) are asked to propose markups with their bid proposal. This works to minimize arguing after the first big change order is received. Some markups are listed in the bid documents. This is another reason to carefully read the general conditions of the specifications and contract prior to preparing the estimate. Some designers will try to bundle the subcontractor and general contractor markups together to prevent markups on top of markups.

Generally markups for commercial general contractors will fall in the range of 5–10%. This is usually the same percentage fee rate that was used on the original estimate. Home office overhead costs are usually included in this fee. Jobsite general conditions are not allowed unless they can be substantiated on individual change issues or can be proven to extend the project schedule.

Subcontractors receive higher fees because their volume is generally less and because their risk, which is estimated by the ratio of direct labor to contract value, is higher. Subcontractors may receive a 10% fee and an additional 10% overhead. Again, both of these fee calculations will depend on how many of the items indicated in the previous list are anticipated to be included in the base estimate, are in the fee or overhead, or are allowed in addition to the fees.

Rarely is there a project that does not require change orders. Fair play will improve the process for all principal contracting parties including the general contractor, subcontractors, suppliers, design team, and owner. This can be achieved with open book estimates with verifiable quantities and pricing systems.

21.6 CLAIM PREPARATION

Claims are the result of either unresolved change-order proposals or construction losses discovered after project completion. A subcontractor or general contractor who realizes after a project is complete that she or he lost money may submit a claim requesting the difference between the estimate and the actual costs. Claims can be very difficult to prepare and substantiate, and even more difficult to resolve.

Some costs that contractors may attempt to recover in a claim are the difference between estimated and actual costs, losses in productivity due to multiple change orders or schedule compression, or schedule delay. One of the easiest types of costs to recover, if allowed by contract, is extended jobsite general conditions. If the contractor can show that $20,000 per month was estimated for general conditions, and the job was either delayed or put on hold for weeks or months, then a math calculation would likely result in a fair reimbursement for these costs. For example

Estimated general conditions:	7 months @ $20,000 per month or $140,000
Actual project duration due to delay:	9 months
Extended general conditions:	2 months (9 less 7) @ $20,000 or $40,000

Many contractors will also attempt to cover home office overhead costs for schedule delays, asserting that they lost the opportunity for additional work during these delays. This is one of the most difficult items for the contractor to successfully negotiate. Many contracts specifically do not allow recovery of these costs.

21.7 AS-BUILT ESTIMATES

Project managers should prepare an *as-built estimate* before completely demobilizing from the project site. Dividing the actual costs spent, or hours incurred, by the actual quantities installed creates as-built unit prices. If estimators and managers do not do this throughout the course of the project or near its completion, they never will. A lot of work goes into tracking actual costs accurately. This is valuable input to the firm's ongoing ability to improve its estimating accuracy. Input of as-built unit prices to the firm's estimating database is necessary on every job if the database is to remain current.

Construction professionals are usually too busy and excited about starting the next project to develop as-built estimates. As-built estimates, like as-built drawings and as-built schedules, are important historical reporting tools. Collecting actual cost data helps to develop better future estimates, but coupling those costs with the actual quantities to develop actual unit prices is better. The units to be used are those that are likely to be used to estimate with in the future, whether they are $/sf of contact area, $/ea, $/ton, $/cy, or $/sf of floor area. Assemblies analysis would also be beneficial for future budget estimates. These figures can help with developing the firm's database as well as providing the estimator with better data to use in the future.

21.8 DATABASE UPDATES

An estimating database is a collection of unit prices and productivity rates for a variety of construction materials and systems. The price or rate given is usually an average of many prices input for that specific area. There are many different types of databases that can be used for many different purposes. Several computer-generated software systems are available that allow a contractor to prepare his or her own customized database. Ready-made databases, all filled out, are also available commercially.

The advantage of commercially available databases is that they provide unit prices for firms or individuals who do not have their own unit prices. These figures are, of course, averages and quite often not applicable for a firm to use on a specific project. It is recommended that each estimator develop a database of historical costs. The disadvantage of a company database is that it will include data from different types of projects averaged together. An estimator will need to be able to throw out the highs and the lows and sort through the data to select the values that apply to the specific project being estimated.

The best database is an in-house one that is continually maintained by the construction company's chief estimator. Historical as-built estimating data are input to the database on an ongoing basis. The ability to sort out specific types of projects makes it more usable. Many contractors will have two sets of databases, one to competitively bid work, and one for budgets, negotiated proposals, or change order estimates.

21.9 SUMMARY

Although the case study chosen for this text was a mid-sized commercial project, the processes presented for budgeting, lump-sum bidding, and proposing a GMP on negotiated projects can be applied to many other types of estimates. Estimating bid alternates requires careful organization from the bid team on bid day. The owner may choose an alternate that may alter the order of the successful bidders so that each alternate should be estimated accurately and stand alone. Residential estimators typically do not perform detailed take-offs and estimates but could benefit from many of the detailed steps followed by successful commercial estimators. Industrial estimating is one of the more complex forms of estimating and often involves a significant amount of contractor-performed work. Change orders should be estimated and detailed to allow the project manager or estimator to successfully sell the change to the owner. Project managers should take the time to develop as-built estimates, which can be input back into the company's estimating database. Databases that are too generic or include too many different types of facilities or construction peculiarities may not be accurate enough to use as a tool to prepare competitive lump-sum bids.

21.10 REVIEW QUESTIONS

1. Why should bid alternates be estimated straight?
2. How does a small residential general contractor estimate?
3. Why do larger residential developers not have select subcontractors they use on every project?
4. What are three specialized trades that work on industrial projects but may not be found on a typical commercial project?
5. What similarities might exist between commercial and industrial estimates?
6. List four types of markups that may be found on a change order.
7. Why should change orders have extensive backup attached to them?
8. What is the difference between a change order proposal and a claim?
9. What is an as-built estimate? Why is one prepared?
10. Who should prepare an as-built estimate?
11. How are as-built estimates related to databases?

21.11 EXERCISES

1. Using a cost data guide, such as *Means,* prepare an assemblies estimate for a 2000-square-foot, single-story residence with at least twenty line items. Apply all of the appropriate markups.
2. For the residential assemblies estimate prepared in exercise 1, prepare a list of at least five assumptions and allowances that were used to develop the estimate.
3. Without the benefit of drawings or specifications, would the estimate from exercise 1 be considered a budget, a guaranteed maximum price, or a lump-sum bid? If your answer was budget, what changes to the estimate and documents would be necessary to transform the estimate into a GMP? What additional changes would be necessary to transform the GMP into a lump-sum bid?
4. Prepare a change order for the Training Center for an additive scope change valued at greater than $1,000. Include all backup necessary to sell the change.
5. Assume the Training Center was put on hold for three months during the middle of construction (after tilt-up concrete and structural steel were installed, but before the interior finishes were complete). Prepare a claim requesting three-months worth of additional jobsite overhead and impact costs due to the work stoppage.
6. Revise the bid form for the Training Center included in Appendix D with the following new bid alternate: "Delete all asphalt and landscape and site lighting work. The owner may choose to do this at a later date when financing is available. Leave the site graveled and sloped to drains." Prepare a stand-alone estimate for this bid alternate.
7. Prepare a detailed industrial estimate for installation of the Training Center's bridge crane. Explain any allowances or assumptions necessary to prepare this estimate.

22

PROJECT MANAGEMENT ISSUES

22.1   INTRODUCTION

The preparation of a successful estimate may be the end of the task for some estimators. But for the construction company, the estimating step is just one of the very early phases of the construction process. The ultimate goal of most project managers is to return a clear profit to their firms for their respective projects. Estimating is one of the most important steps in obtaining work and, therefore, is an important element for generating profits for the construction firm. A project manager may not provide a profit if the estimator is not successful in the preparation of a competitive bid or proposal.

This chapter discusses the use of estimates as project management tools. The estimate document itself is an important tool for the project manager and the superintendent. It is important that they participate in developing the estimate. Their individual input regarding constructability and their personal commitment to the estimate are essential to ensure not only the success of the estimate, but also the ultimate success of the project.

22.2   THE BUYOUT PROCESS

Project buyout is the process of awarding subcontracts, procuring materials being furnished by the general contractor, and comparing the actual costs to the estimated costs. The purpose is to determine the status of the project with respect to the contractor's original estimate. A *buyout log* such as the one illustrated in Figure 22-1 can be used to buy out the project. Some project managers may choose to use an electronic spreadsheet to compare buyout costs with estimated costs.

BUYOUT LOG

WESTERN CONSTRUCTION COMPANY

Project Manager: _Ronda Martin_

Project Name: _The Training Center_

Spec Section	Description	Estimate	Buyout	Variance	Date	Sub/Supplier	Comments
02200	Mass Excavation	$184,600	$182,200	–$2,400	June 16, 2003	Dirt Construction	
05000	Supply Steel	$150,000	$145,000	–$5,000	June 16, 2003	High Iron	
07400	Roof and Flashing	$110,000	$117,500	$7,500	June 16, 2003	ACME Roofing	Low bidder dropped
09680	Carpet	$71,000	$40,000	–$31,000	June 16, 2003	Custom Floors	Carpet and tile separate
09652	Tile and Vinyl	w/carpet	$20,000	$20,000	June 16, 2003	Hard Surfacing	
15500	Fire Protection	$56,800	$59,900	$3,100	June 16, 2003	ABC Construction	Paid for weekend allowance

FIGURE 22–1 Buyout log.

283

Receiving numerous subcontractor quotations on bid day can be a hectic and error-prone event. Even with good estimating practices, it is still possible to make errors when receiving, reviewing, posting, and selecting subcontractor bids. The use of the fax machine and electronically transmitted quotes, and early bid qualifications has helped the general contractor minimize these errors.

Because of the volume of subcontractor quotations that are received at the last minute or after the bid has been forwarded to the bid runner, it is possible for the general contractor to receive subcontractor quotations that are lower than the ones used in the bid. If the general contractor is successful with its bid and receives some late quotations, the firm may improve its position during the buyout process. In addition, some subcontractors may not get their quotations out to all of the bidding contractors before the bids are due to the owner. After the successful general contractor has been declared, it may also benefit from bids that were not received at all on bid day.

Is it ethical for the contractor to use these late quotations? Most in the private industry believe that it is acceptable. What is not ethical is bid shopping, or asking subcontractors to drop their price to meet or beat another quotation. This was discussed in Chapter 15. Some project owners require the general contractor to name its subcontractors with the bid; therefore, these late bids do not provide the contractor any benefit.

Subcontractors should be selected based on the value that they contribute to the project team. Selection based solely on price often leads to problems with quality and timely execution. A subcontractor proposal analysis form, or bid tab, similar to the one illustrated in Chapter 14, can be used to assist in subcontractor selection. To ensure that the intended scope of work is included in the price quotation, the project manager uses an analysis form to compare all proposals for each scope of work. Prior to selecting the specialty contractor for each subcontract, the project manager should conduct pre-award meetings for the major or risky subcontracted areas. Following are some of the firms he or she should buy out first:

- Those with the highest values, such as mechanical and electrical
- The firms who will mobilize first, such as earthwork and utilities
- The longest lead times, such as elevators and hollow metal door-frames
- The direct materials that will be needed first, such as structural steel embeds and rein-forcement steel
- The suppliers with the longest shop drawing process, such as structural steel

The project manager's goal is to employ the firm whose bid matches the estimate and does not have obvious errors in its estimate. The project manager and the estimator should meet with one specialty firm at a time to address the following bid-related issues:

- Review the drawings and specifications to ensure the correct scope of work was considered in preparing the proposal.
- Review any exclusions listed on the proposal.
- Discuss any questions submitted with the proposal or raised by a same-discipline firm during the bid cycle.
- Review all of the addenda.
- Discuss the size of the specialty contractor's proposed work force and the anticipated schedule.

Based on the results of the pre-award meetings and annotated subcontractor proposal analysis forms, subcontractors are selected for all scopes of work that will not be performed by the general contractor's workforce. Each subcontract value is then entered in the project buyout log shown in Figure 22-1.

22.3 CORRECTING THE ESTIMATE

Is any estimate perfect? Generally the answer is no. Subcontractor posting errors were discussed previously. Even with good estimating practices, there may be errors within the direct work portion of the estimate as well. Before the estimate is input into the accounting system, and the construction team begins to monitor and control costs against it, the estimate should be corrected. It will be much easier and more fruitful to the project management team to monitor, control, and report against an estimate that has been adjusted and input as correctly as possible.

If a surplus results from the buyout and the estimate correction process, the project manager can set up a *cost code* designated as "yet-to-buy" to reflect the dollars that have not yet been assigned to an activity. Even long after the buyout process is complete, additional errors or missed activities may show up, to which some of this surplus can be applied.

Unfortunately the buyout and input process may result in the identification of an estimate shortfall. This is not good news to the construction team, but it is valuable information to have early. It is not wise to reduce the value of work activities with real estimates just to cover this shortfall. Trying to meet an estimate that cannot be met will discourage the construction team. The shortfall should be reported in the same "yet-to-buy" category, but as a negative entry. It is important that the home office management team knows that there may be a problem, and that it is not being hidden.

22.4 SCHEDULE OF VALUES

The first step in developing the pay request is establishing an agreed-upon breakdown of the contract cost, or *schedule of values (SOV)*. An example schedule of values for the Training Center is shown in Figure 22-2. Often the contract will require that a schedule of values be submitted for approval within a certain time after executing the contract; for example, two weeks. This schedule should be established and agreed upon early in the job, well before the first request for payment is submitted. Forcing the issue too early, before accurate subcontract figures have been established, may cause excessive revisions and explanations in the schedule of values. If this is done, the project manager may spend the entire job reconciling the payment requests.

Developing the schedule of values starts with the summary estimate. That estimate is first corrected for the actual buyout values, which were shown in Figure 22-1. These calculations are shown in the left three columns of Figure 22-2. The third column would be the schedule of values used on a negotiated contract because the general conditions and fee are listed separately. On a lump-sum contract, the general conditions and fee would be distributed proportionately across all payment items. The schedule of values the project manager would submit in the lump-sum case is shown in the far right column of Figure 22-2.

Schedule of Values

WESTERN CONSTRUCTION COMPANY
550 South 7th Avenue
Kent, Washington 92002
(206) 239-1422
The Training Center
4/28/2003

Columns:		1	2	3	4	5	6
CSI Division	Description	Original Bid	Buyout Adjust	GMP SOV Adjusted Estimate	% of Subtotal	Add-ons Prorated	Lump-Sum SOV Adjusted Totals
1	Jobsite general conditions	see below		0			0
2	Sitework	$357,400	−2,400	355,000	16.83%	84,725	439,725
3	Concrete	283,700	0	283,700	13.45%	67,708	351,408
4	Masonry	27,300	0	27,300	1.29%	6,515	33,815
5	Structural & misc. metals	200,000	−5,000	195,000	9.24%	46,539	241,539
6	Wood & plastic	44,500	0	44,500	2.11%	10,620	55,120
7	Thermal & moisture protection	132,200	7,500	139,700	6.62%	33,341	173,041
8	Doors, windows, glass	143,600	0	143,600	6.81%	34,272	177,872
9	Finishes	306,000	−11,000	295,000	13.99%	70,405	365,405
10	Specialties	26,755	0	26,755	1.27%	6,385	33,140
11	Equipment	75,600	0	75,600	3.58%	18,043	93,643
12	Furnishings	6,325	0	6,325	0.30%	1,510	7,835
13	Equipment	0	0	0	0.00%	0	0
14	Conveying systems (elevator)	30,000	0	30,000	1.42%	7,160	37,160
15	Mechanical Systems:	0	0	0	0.00%	0	0
	Plumbing	66,200	0	66,200	3.14%	15,799	81,999
	HVAC	155,200	0	155,200	7.36%	37,040	192,240
	Fire protection	56,800	3,100	59,900	2.84%	14,296	74,196
16	Electrical Systems	205,600	0	205,600	9.75%	49,069	254,669
	Subtotal w/o GC's and fee:	2,117,180	−7,800	2,109,380	100.00%	$503,427	$2,612,807
	General conditions	135,100	0	135,100			
	Labor burdens	111,300	0	111,300			
	Insurance and taxes	52,330	−195	52,135			
	Contingency	72,477	0	72,477			
	Fee	124,419	7,995	132,414			
	Subtotal add-ons	495,626	7,800	503,426			
	TOTAL GMP:	**$2,612,806**	**0**	**$2,612,806**			

Buyout improves fee position!

FIGURE 22–2 Schedule of values.

Some contractors try to combine items into single line items. In this way, they believe that they might be able to overbill or hide the true subcontract values from the owner. The schedule of values should be as detailed as is reasonable. The project manager should do all that is possible to assist the owner in paying completely and promptly. Nothing should be hidden. At a minimum, the 16 CSI divisions should be used as line items. Major subcontractors should be listed where possible. Separate building components, building wings, distinct site areas, separate buildings, phases, or systems should be individually shown in a detailed schedule of values.

Some project managers advocate hiding the fee and general conditions, or front loading them. This is more prevalent with bid contracting than with negotiated work. In the case of an open-book project, these items should be listed just as they would be in the project cost accounting system. The schedule of values should look like the final estimate. Trying to explain during an audit or a claim situation why the cost of the tilt-up panels was stated as $200,000 in the pay estimate but was only $100,000 in the original estimate will be difficult. Spreading, but still hiding, the fee and general conditions as a weighted average over the schedule of values may be fair, but it will be more difficult for the owner to track lien releases.

22.5 CASH FLOW CURVES

Because production of a detailed construction schedule is not part of this text, we will limit our discussion of cash flow curves to just a brief introduction. The *cash flow curve* and the cost-loaded schedule are direct by-products of a detailed estimate combined with a detailed construction schedule. There are several reasons for cost-loading the schedule and producing a cash flow curve. Often, it is one of the first things the owner will ask of the project manager, and it may be specifically required by the construction contract. The cash flow curve is a graphical estimate of when the contractor expects to have work in place and the estimated cost of that work. The curve provides a forecast to the owner and the bank of anticipated monthly pay requests to be made to the contractor for the completed work.

The cash flow curve is very easy to prepare. The estimated costs (as corrected, bought out, and input to the accounting system) are applied across the schedule activities. If the value of an activity is $100,000, and it will take five months to complete, $20,000 is spread over each of the five months. Costs such as administration, taxes, and fees should be distributed proportionately over the entire project. The cost data are summed at the bottom of the schedule for each month to develop anticipated monthly expenses. The likelihood of the general contractor being billed by each material supplier and subcontractor according to any anticipated schedule is somewhat remote.

22.6 COST CONTROL

Cost control begins with assigning cost codes to the elements of work identified in the work breakdown phase of developing the cost estimate. Work breakdown was discussed in Chapter 6. These cost codes allow the project manager to monitor project costs and compare them with the estimated costs. Cost codes usually are numerical assignments to work activities that allow accurate assignment of estimated and scheduled costs and times to which activities can be recorded. These numbers generally are consistent throughout a construction firm. The objective is not to keep the cost of each element of work under its estimated value, but to ensure that the total cost of the completed project is under the estimated cost. The cost control process involves the following series of steps:

- Cost codes are assigned to each element of work in the cost estimate.
- The cost estimated is corrected based upon buyout costs.
- Actual costs are tracked for each work item using the assigned cost codes.
- The construction process is adjusted, if necessary, to reduce cost overruns.
- Actual quantities, costs, and productivity rates are recorded and an as-built estimate is prepared.

While all costs should be monitored, the following items generally involve the greatest risk:

- Direct labor
- Equipment cost or rental
- Jobsite overhead or administration

It is possible to lose money on material purchases, but with good estimating skills, it is not probable, and the risk is not as great as with labor. The same holds true with subcontractors. They have quoted prices for specific scopes of work, so they bear the risk associated with their labor and equipment.

It is difficult to control costs if the project manager does not start with a detailed estimate. For example, let's assume there was a $1,606 cost overrun on the Training Center's 8,925 square foot second floor mezzanine structure. The assemblies cost analysis shown in Figure 22-3 does not provide sufficient detail to identify the cause. Project managers should use a more detailed cost breakdown, as shown in Figure 22-4, to determine the cause of the cost overrun.

Now it is easy to see that the problem is not with the laborers placing the slab, but the majority of the overrun is with setting screeds, edge forms, and concrete finishing. Why did this happen? Maybe the slab got rained on. Maybe there were more mechanical block-outs than were estimated. Maybe personnel changes were necessary. Maybe the estimate was too low. There could be a variety of reasons. The point is that the project manager and the superintendent can now focus on evaluating these specific issues.

To be able to control costs, they must be tracked and compared with the corrected estimate. The first step is to record the actual costs incurred and input the information into a cost control database. Cost codes are used to allow comparison of actual cost data with the estimated values. Several types of cost codes are used in the industry. The best system for most projects is the coding system selected for the project files. Such systems were discussed in Chapter 6. Many construction firms have adopted a version of the CSI Master-Format system.

Depending on the size of the construction firm, the type of work, and the type of owner and contract agreement, the project manager may perform job cost accounting in the home office or in the field. Generally, the smaller the firm and the smaller the contract

Assemblies Cost Analysis

Cost Code	Description	Quantity	Units	Estimated Unit Price	Estimated Cost	Actual Unit Price	Actual Cost	Variance
02.04.00	Elevated composite slab	8,925	sf	$0.70 /sf	$6,248	$0.88 /sf	$7,854	$1,606

FIGURE 22–3 Assemblies cost analysis.

Detailed Cost Analysis

Cost Code	Description	Quantity	Units	Estimated Unit Price	Estimated Cost	Actual Unit Price	Actual Cost	Variance
02.04.01	Set screeds	8,925	sf	$0.19 /sf	$1,696	$0.31 /sf	$2,767	$1,071
02.04.02	Edge forms at blockouts	110	lf	$1.42 /lf	$156	$7.20 /lf	$792	$636
02.04.03	Install mesh	9,800	sf	Subcontractor	Subcontractor	Subcontractor	Subcontractor	$0
02.04.04	Place concrete	83	cy	$12.10 /cy	$1,004	$8.74 /cy	$725	–$279
02.04.05	Pump concrete	83	cy	Subcontractor	Subcontractor	Subcontractor	Subcontractor	$0
02.04.06	Finish elevated slab	8,925	sf	$0.38 /sf	$3,392	$0.40 /sf	$3,570	$178
	Total System:	8,925	sf	$0.70 /sf	$6,248	$0.88 /sf	$7,854	$1,606

FIGURE 22–4 Detailed cost analysis.

value, the more likely it is that all accounting functions will be performed in the home office. Larger projects may have a jobsite accountant. The type of contract and how it addresses reimbursable costs may affect where the construction firm performs the accounting function. For example, the project is a $15 million mid-rise speculative office building with a negotiated GMP contract that allows for all on-site accounting to be reimbursed. It may be more cost-effective to perform accounting out of the home office with the assistance of the accounting department, but according to the terms of the contract, the owner will not pay for it.

Regardless of where the cost data are collected and where payment is made, most accounting functions on a project are the same. The process begins with a corrected estimate. Actual costs are then incurred in the form of direct labor, material purchase, or subcontract invoice. Cost codes (those matching the estimate) are recorded on the time sheets and invoices, and routed for approval. After the invoices are approved, the cost data are input into the cost control system.

One important aspect of this phase of cost recording is the accurate coding of actual costs. If costs are intentionally or accidentally coded incorrectly, the project team will not know how they are doing on that specific item of work. All costs should be recorded correctly to provide the project manager with an accurate accounting of all expenditures. Accurate recording will not only help with cost control, it will also provide a more realistic as-built estimate, which will be used to update the company's estimating database and help prepare better estimates in the future.

Control of direct labor and equipment rental costs is the responsibility of the superintendent. The key to getting the field supervisors involved in cost control is to get their personal commitment to the process. One successful way for the project manager to do this is to have the superintendent actively involved in developing the original estimate. If the superintendent said it would take four people working two weeks to form a particular wall, he or she will often see to it that the task is completed within that time.

Work packages are a method of breaking down the estimate into distinct packages or systems that match measurable work activities. These were previously discussed in Chapter 6. For example, footings, including forming, reinforcing steel, and concrete placement, could be a work package. The work is planned according to the number of hours in the estimate and monitored for feedback. When a system is complete, such as footings or slab on grade, the project manager and the superintendent immediately know how they are doing with respect to the overall estimate. To be able to do this, the field supervision needs to know the estimated costs, both in materials and man-hours for each work package. The advantages of estimating using unit man-hours (UMH) over unit prices for labor were discussed in Chapter 8. Field supervisors think in terms of crew size and duration. They do not think in terms of $3.50 per square foot. Estimating in this manner also makes for an easy transition into project management.

Which items should the project team track? The 80-20 rule applies here also. The project manager should evaluate the risks. The estimate should be reviewed to identify those items that have the most labor hours, or in the case of equipment rental, the most cost. Work packages should be prepared for items that the project manager and the superintendent believe are worthy of tracking and monitoring. The foreman who is responsible for accomplishing the work should develop each work package. Figure 22-5 shows an example work package cost control worksheet for the Training Center project.

Foreman's Cost Control Work-Package Worksheet

Contractor: *Western Construction Company*
Project: *The Training Center* Foreman/Superintendent: *Sam Lewis*
System/Area: *Spot Footings* Date: *7/1/2003* Page: *One*

Month/Year	June	July	July	July	July	July	July	July	July	2003
Date	30	1	2	3	4	7	8	9	10	Totals:
Estimated Crew Size	4	4	4	4	0	2	2	1	0	21
Est'd Crew Hours	32	32	32	32	0	16	16	8	0	168
Est'd Accumulated Hrs	32	64	96	128	128	144	160	168	168	168
Original Bid Estimate:										175
Actual Crew Size										0
Actual Crew Hours										0
Actual Accum'd Hrs										0

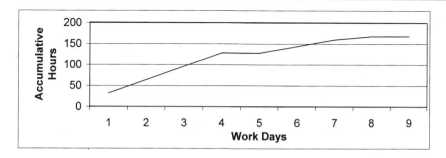

FIGURE 22–5 Foreman's work package cost control worksheet.

22.7 SUMMARY

Developing a good estimate is the most important activity for the estimating team. Without the contract, the project manager will not have a project to manage. The ultimate success of the estimating efforts, though, will be measured during the construction of the project. If the estimate was prepared properly, the project management activities such as schedule and cost control are much easier. There is no such thing as an error-free estimate or schedule. One of the first responsibilities of the project construction team is to buy out the project and to correct the estimate so that it is a workable tool during construction. The cash flow curve is developed from the estimate and the schedule, which is a tool used by the owner who may in turn need to provide such a forecast to the bank. The corrected estimate and schedule will result in a more accurate cash flow curve. It is also easier for both the owner and contractor teams to use an accurate schedule of values that has been adjusted for estimate errors and that reflects the result of the buyout process. The cost control management aspect of the construction project takes the corrected and bought out estimate and monitors it against actual costs incurred making adjustments as required. The foreman's work package is an important tool in managing field labor costs.

22.8 REVIEW QUESTIONS

1. In a private owner project, is it acceptable to use a subcontractor whose quote was received after the general contractor has telephoned his bid in to the bid runner?
2. What is the difference between bid shopping and buyout?

3. Why might a project manager want to buy fast?
4. Why is it to everyone's benefit to postpone establishing the pay request schedule of values until after buyout is complete?
5. Why might the bid estimate not be correct?
6. Why should both the project manager and the superintendent be involved with creating the original bid estimate and schedule?
7. The cost codes on a project should be the same as what other types of codes?
8. Who prepares a cost control work package?
9. Do craftspeople care if a project or an activity is completed within budget and on time?
10. How does the 80-20 rule relate to cost control?
11. What is the riskiest and most difficult part of the estimate to control?

22.9 EXERCISES

1. The GMP estimate, which was developed in Chapter 18, has the jobsite general conditions, fee, and other markups clearly stated. Assume that the Training Center is a lump-sum bid project and that the contractor wants to evenly spread these items. Prepare a revised summary estimate with this spread.
2. Assume the following buyout values for the Training Center. Beginning again with the GMP estimate developed in Chapter 18, develop a buyout log.

   - Buy reinforcement steel and mesh: $ 28,500
   - Install structural steel, deck, and joist: $ 62,750
   - Landscaping and irrigation: $ 29,000
   - Unit price for concrete: $ 72 per cubic yard
   - Plumbing and HVAC: $205,000
   - Roofing and sheet metal flashing: $100,000
   - Glazing: $ 78,800
   - Elevator: $ 31,500

3. Using the buyout values above, develop a new schedule of values for the negotiated Training Center project that was shown in Figure 22-2, third column.
4. Revise the lump-sum schedule of values for the case study (as shown in the right column of Figure 22-2) by combining items to create a 10-item schedule of values.
5. Assume that only one subcontractor bid was received for roofing on a project. After award to the general contractor, that subcontractor indicates they have a bid error. What should the general contractor do? If they re-bid that section, is that ethical? Should they just try to negotiate with one favorite subcontractor? Should the general contractor notify the owner? If they re-bid that portion of the work and the new bid price is less than the pulled quote, which firm should realize the benefit? What if the new bid is higher?
6. Revise the lump-sum schedule of values for the Training Center (as shown in the far right column of Figure 22-2) by front-end loading all of the fee and general conditions to the areas of self-performed general contractor work.
7. Using the buyout log developed in exercise 2, prepare a forecast and savings split for the project if the project were to finish with exactly those buyout costs equaling actual costs, and all other estimated costs equaling actual costs. What would the final fee for Western Construction Company be? Would the owner realize any project savings? How would those savings be reflected in the final contract amount?

A

LIST OF ABBREVIATIONS

The following abbreviations and acronyms are used in this text, are standard in the estimating and construction management industry, or may be found on the documents from which an estimator must prepare an estimate.

AGC	Associated General Contractors of America
AIA	American Institute of Architects
allow	allowance
bcf	bank cubic feet
bcy	bank cubic yards
bf	board feet
c	one hundred
CAD	computer-aided design
CD	construction documents
CE	chief estimator
C.E.A.T.	Carpenters-Employers Apprenticeship Training Trust Fund of Western Washington, the owner of the Training Center case study used in the text
cf	cubic feet
chr	crew hour
CIP	cast-in-place concrete
CJ	concrete construction joint
CO	change order
COP	change order proposal
csf	hundred square feet

csfa	contact square foot area (for formwork), see also sfca
CSI	Construction Specifications Institute
cy	cubic yards
DD	design development
Div	division
Dwg	drawing
ea	each
Est	estimate or estimator
FF&E	fixtures, furnishings, and equipment
FOB	free on board
ft	foot or feet
G&A	general and administrative cost
GC	general contractor
GCs	general conditions
GMP	guaranteed maximum price
GWB	gypsum wallboard
H	height (column on QTO form)
HM	hollow metal (door or frame)
hr	hour
HVAC	heating, ventilation, and air conditioning
IFB	invitation for bid
k	one thousand
L	length (column on QTO form)
lb	pound
L cost	labor cost
lcy	loose cubic yards
lf	lineal feet
LMA	Lance Mueller and Associates, case study project architects
loc	location
ls	lump sum
m	million
mbf	thousand board feet measure
M cost	material cost
MDO	medium density overlay
MEP	mechanical, electrical, and plumbing
mh	man hour
mil	million
mo	month
Mob	mobilization
NA	not applicable
NIC	not included or not in contract
NFPA	National Fire Protection Association
NTP	notice to proceed
OH&P	overhead and profit
OIC	officer in charge
OM	order-of-magnitude

OSB	oriented strand board
OSHA	Occupational Safety and Health Administration
PE	project engineer
PM	project manager
P.O.	purchase order
PreCon	preconstruction
psi	pounds per square inch
QTO	quantity take off
Qty	quantity
Rebar	concrete reinforcement steel
Recap	recapitulation
RFI	request for information
RFP	request for proposals
RFQ	request for qualifications
ROM	rough-order-of-magnitude
S/C	subcontract or subcontract cost
SD	schematic design
sf	square feet
sfca	square foot of contact area
sff	square foot of floor
sfw	square foot of wall
SJ	concrete sawed control joint
SOG	slab on grade
SOV	schedule of values
SQ	square or hundred square feet
Spec	specification
Sub	subcontractor or subcontract
Supt	superintendent
T & M	time and materials
tcy	truck cubic yards = bank measure × swell (expansion factor)
tn	ton
Typ	typical
UBC	Uniform Building Code
umh	unit per manhour
U.N.O.	unless noted otherwise
up	unit price
W	width (column on QTO form)
w/	with
WBS	work breakdown structure
WCC	Western Construction Company, case study hypothetical general contractor
wk	week
w/o	without
wwf	welded wire fabric
yr	year

GLOSSARY

Addenda   Additions to or changes in bid documents issued prior to bid and contract award.

Additive alternates   Alternates that add to the base bid if selected by the owner.

Agreement   A document that sets forth the provisions, responsibilities, and obligations of parties to a contract. Standard forms of agreement are available from professional organizations.

Allowance   An amount stated in the contract for inclusion in the contract sum to cover the cost of prescribed items, the full description of which is not known at the time of bidding. The actual cost of such items is determined by the contractor at the time of product selection by the architect or owner, and the total contract amount is adjusted accordingly.

Alternates   Selected items of work for which bidders are required to provide prices.

Amendments   See *addenda.*

American Institute of Architects (AIA)   A national association that promotes the practice of architecture and publishes many standard contract forms used in the construction industry.

Application for payment   See *progress payment request.*

Arbitrator   An individual who presides in an arbitration, listens to both sides of a dispute or disputes, and renders a decision regarding the issues.

As-built drawings   Contractor-corrected construction drawings depicting actual dimensions, elevations, and conditions of in-place constructed work.

As-built estimate   Assessment in which actual costs incurred are applied to the quantities installed to develop actual unit prices and productivity rates.

Assemblies analysis   Determining the number of man-hours estimated per unit of work, such as man-hours per cubic yard of concrete, and comparing the result with similar data from other projects.

Assemblies cost estimate   A semi-detailed estimate that requires quantity take-off of bulk in-place systems such as foundations, and applies a unit price for all work associated with that system, including labor, material, and subcontractor.

Associated General Contractors of America (AGC)   A national trade association made up primarily of construction firms and construction industry professionals. It publishes many standard contract forms used in the construction industry.

Bank cubic yard   A measure of the volume of soil in its natural, undisturbed condition.

Base hourly wage   That portion of a worker's gross hourly pay that does not represent deductions for fringe benefits or payroll taxes.

Best and final proposal   The final proposal submitted by a contractor in a negotiated procurement process after the owner has discussed the previous proposals received with each contractor submitting one and issued any clarifications or changes to the request for proposal.

Bid bond   A surety instrument that guarantees that the contractor, if awarded the contract, will enter into a binding contract for the price bid and provide all required bonds.

Bid documents   Drawings, specifications, and contract terms issued to general contractors to be used in developing a bid for the defined work. Bid documents are not always the same as the final construction documents.

Bid form   The form issued by a project owner on which contractors submit their bids.

Bid procurement process   Selection of a contractor based upon a lump-sum bid.

Bid room   Location where a general contractor's bid team processes subcontractor and supplier quotations and determines the final bid price.

Bid security   Money placed in escrow, a cashier's check, or bid bond offered as assurance to an owner that the bid is valid and that the bidder will enter into a contract for that price.

Bid shopping   Unethical contractor activity of sharing subcontractor or supplier bid values with competitors in order to drive down prices.

Bid summary   The estimating form onto which all previously priced work and subcontractor bid totals are entered, markups are calculated, and the final price is calculated.

Bid tab   Tabulation of vendor bids for a single category of work.

Bin   Location where posted subcontractor and supplier bids forms are stored on bid day.

Boilerplate   Standard contract language that owners include in most of their contracts.

Budget control log   Spreadsheet used to monitor changes of materials or scope throughout the design process, and the budget implications of those changes.

Budget cost estimate   Preliminary estimate based on early design documents.

Builder's risk insurance   Protects the owner in the event that the project is damaged or destroyed while under construction and protects the contractor in the event construction materials stored on the project site are damaged or destroyed.

Burden   See *labor burden.*

Buyout   The process of awarding subcontracts and issuing purchase orders for materials and equipment.

Buyout log   A project management document that is used for planning and tracking the buyout process.

Cash flow curve   A plot of the estimated value of work to be completed each month during the construction of a project.

Cash-loaded schedule   A schedule in which the value of each activity is distributed across the activity, and monthly costs are summed to produce a cash flow curve.

Change order (CO)   Modifications to contract documents made after contract award that incorporate changes in scope and adjustments in contract price and time.

Change order proposal (COP)   A request for a change order submitted to the owner by the contractor, or a proposed change sent to the contractor by the owner requesting pricing data.

Chief estimator   The head of the estimating department in a construction firm.

Claim   An unresolved request for a change order.

Close-out   The process of completing all construction and paperwork required to complete the project and close out the contract.

Conceptual cost estimate   Cost estimates developed using incomplete project documentation.

Constructability analysis   An evaluation of preferred and alternative materials and construction methods.

Construction documents   The agreement, general conditions, special conditions, drawings, and specifications.

Construction joint (CJ)   The interface or meeting surface between two successive placements of concrete.

Construction Specifications Institute (CSI)   The professional organization that developed the 16-division MasterFormat that is used to organize the technical specifications.

Contingency   Amount applied to an estimate to cover unknown issues and incomplete documents.

Contract   A legally enforceable agreement between two parties.

Control joint (SJ)   Joint cut into a concrete slab to control where cracking occurs.

Corrected estimate   Estimate that is adjusted based on buyout costs.

Cost codes   Codes established in the firm's accounting system that are used for recording specific types of costs.

Cost estimating   Process of preparing the best educated anticipated cost of a project given the parameters available.

Cost indices   Numerical values that reflect the variation in price levels at different geographic locations and/or different timeframes.

Cost-plus-award-fee contract   A kind of cost-plus contract in which the contractor's fee has two components; a fixed component and an award component based on the contractor's performance. The award component is decided at periodic intervals, for example quarterly, based on an owner-established set of criteria. Criteria might include cost control, quality of construction, safety performance, and meeting an agreed-upon schedule.

Cost-plus contract   A contract in which the contractor is reimbursed for stipulated direct and indirect costs associated with the construction of a project and is paid a fee to cover profit and company overhead.

Cost-plus contract with guaranteed maximum price (GMP)   A cost-plus contract in which the contractor agrees to bear any construction costs that exceed the guaranteed maximum price unless the project scope of work is increased.

Cost-plus-fixed-fee contract   A cost-plus contract in which the contractor is guaranteed a fixed fee irrespective of the actual construction costs.

Cost-plus-incentive-fee contract   A cost-plus contract in which the contractor's fee is based on measurable incentives, such as actual construction cost or construction time. Higher fees are paid for lower construction costs and shorter project durations.

Cost-plus-percentage-fee contract   A cost-plus contract in which the contractor's fee is a percentage of the actual construction costs.

Cost-reimbursable contract   A contract in which the contractor is reimbursed stipulated direct and indirect costs associated with the construction of a project. The contractor may or may not receive an additional fee to cover profit and company overhead.

Craftspeople   Non-managerial field labor force who construct the work, such as carpenters and electricians.

Davis-Bacon wage rates   Prevailing wage rates determined by the U. S. Department of Labor that must be met or exceeded by contractors and subcontractors on federally funded construction projects.

Deductive alternates   Alternates that subtract from the base bid if selected by the owner.

Design development documents   Plans and specifications that are about 75% to 80% complete.

Detailed cost estimate   Extensive estimate based on definitive design documents. Includes separate labor, material, equipment, and subcontractor quantities. Unit prices are applied material quantity take-offs for every item of work.

Differing site condition   Some condition of the project site that is materially more adverse than was depicted in the contract documentation, and that could not have been seen by a visit to the site. For example, encountering a buried water line where none was shown in the contract drawings.

Digitizer   Computer tool used to measure quantities from two-dimensional drawings.

Direct construction costs   Labor, material, equipment, and subcontractor costs for the contractor, exclusive of any markups.

Dispute   A contract claim between the owner and the general contractor that has not been resolved.

Eighty-twenty rule   On most projects, about 80% of the costs are included in 20% of the work items.

Electronic mail   Internet tool for sending communications and attached documents.

Escalation   Percentage added to an estimate to account for anticipated cost increases over time.

Estimate schedule   Management document used to plan and forecast the activities and durations associated with preparing the cost estimate. Not a construction schedule.

Estimating database   Collection of historical labor and material unit prices, which can be applied to quantities in future estimates.

Estimator   A person charged with preparing a cost estimate.

Extension   Calculation of quantities and pricing of line items on either the QTO or recapitulation form.

Fast track schedule   A schedule that shows construction of a project starting before the entire design is completed. Construction of the foundation would be started as soon as the foundation design is complete, even though the remainder of the building design is not finished.

Fee   Contractor's income after direct project and jobsite general conditions are subtracted. Generally includes home office overhead costs and profit.

Footprint   The ground upon which a building is situated.

Foreman   Direct supervisor of craft labor on a project.

Free on board (FOB)   An item whose quoted price includes delivery at the point specified. Any additional shipping costs are to be paid by the purchaser of the item.

Fringe benefits   The portion of the gross hourly pay that is deducted for payment of benefits such as retirement, health insurance, and life insurance.

General conditions (CGs)   A part of the construction contract that contains a set of operating procedures that the owner typically uses on all projects. They describe the relationship between the owner and the contractor, the authority of the owner's representatives or agents, and the terms of the contract. The term also is used to describe jobsite overhead costs.

General contractor (GC)   The principal party to a construction contract who agrees to construct the project in accordance with the contract documents.

General liability insurance   Protects the contractor against claims from a third party for bodily injury or property damage.

Geotechnical report   Also known as a *soils report*. A report prepared by a geotechnical engineering firm that includes the results of soil borings or test pits and recommends systems and procedures for foundations, roads, and excavation work.

Guaranteed maximum price (GMP) contract   A type of cost-plus contract in which the contractor agrees to construct the project at or below a specified cost.

Home office overhead   Contractors' operating costs that are not related to specific projects.

Incentive fee   A fee component that the owner establishes to motivate the contractor to achieve specific project objectives.

Indirect construction costs   Expenses indirectly incurred and not directly related to construction activity, such as project or home office overhead.

Indirect equipment   Construction equipment that is used for multiple purposes on a project, such as a tower crane, that cannot be charged to a single construction activity.

Invitation for Bid (IFB)   A portion of the bidding documents soliciting bids for a project.

Jobsite general conditions costs   Field indirect costs that cannot be tied to an item of work, but are project specific and, in the case of cost-reimbursable contracts, are considered part of the cost of the work.

Jobsite overhead   See *jobsite general conditions cost.*

Labor and material payment bond   A surety instrument that guarantees that the contractor (or subcontractor) will make payments to his or her craftspeople, subcontractors, and suppliers.

Labor burden   Markup of labor wage rates to account for worker benefits.

Labor taxes   See *labor burden.*

Laydown areas   Areas of the construction site that have been designated for storage of construction materials until they are used in the construction of the project.

Liquidated damages   An amount specified in the contract that is owed by the contractor to the owner as compensation for damage incurred as a result of the contractor's failure to complete the project by the date specified in the contract.

Loose cubic yards   A measure of the volume of soil after it is excavated and expands or swells.

Lump-sum contract   Also known as *fixed-price* or *stipulated-sum contract.* A contract that provides a specific price for a defined scope of work.

Major supplier   Vendor who supplies fabricated material or a large amount of material for a construction project.

Markup   Percentage added to the direct cost of the work to cover such items as overhead, fee, taxes, and insurance.

MasterFormat   A 16-division numerical system of organization developed by the Construction Specifications Institute that is used to organize contract specifications and cost estimates.

Material supplier   Vendor who provides materials but no on-site craft labor.

Mediator   An individual who presides during a mediation and attempts to facilitate a negotiated settlement between the parties participating in the mediation.

Negotiated procurement process   Selection of a contractor based on a set of criteria the owner selects.

Non-reimbursable costs   Contractor costs that are not reimbursed by the project owner under the terms of a cost-plus contract.

Notice to proceed (NTP)   Written communication issued by the owner to the contractor, authorizing the contractor to proceed with the project and establishing the date for project commencement.

Officer-in-charge (OIC)   General contractor's principal individual who supervises the project manager and is responsible for overall contract compliance.

Open shop   A nonunion firm, or one that has not signed a contract with a labor union.

Order-of-magnitude (OM) estimates   General contractor's cost estimates for subcontracted scopes of work.

Overhead   Expenses incurred that do not directly relate to a specific project; for example, rent on the contractor's home office.

Overhead burden   A percentage markup that is applied to the total estimated direct cost of a project to cover overhead or indirect costs.

Payment bond   See *labor and material payment bond.*

Payment request   See *progress payment request.*

Payroll taxes   That portion of the gross hourly pay that is used to pay federal and state employment taxes including income taxes, Social Security, and unemployment insurance.

Performance bond   A surety instrument that guarantees that the contractor will complete the project in accordance with the contract. It protects the owner from the general contractor's default and the general contractor from the subcontractor's default.

Plan center or room   Location where bid documents are available for review by both general contractors and subcontractors.

Plugs   See *order-of-magnitude estimates.*

Pre-bid conference   Meeting of bidding contractors with the project owner and architect. The purpose of the meeting is to explain the project and bid process and solicit questions regarding the design or contract requirements.

Preconstruction agreement   A short contract that describes the contractor's responsibilities and compensation for preconstruction services.

Preconstruction conference   Meeting conducted by owner or designer to introduce project participants and to discuss project issues and management procedures.

Preconstruction services   Services that a construction contractor performs for a project owner during design development and before construction starts.

Premium time   That portion of a worker's wage that represents the cost of overtime.

Pre-proposal conference   Meeting of potential contractors with the project owner and architect. The purpose of the meeting is to explain the project, the negotiating process, and the selection criteria, and to solicit questions regarding the design or contract requirements.

Prequalification of contractors   Investigating and evaluating prospective contractors based on selected criteria prior to inviting them to submit bids or proposals.

Pricing recaps   Form used by estimators to price the quantities of work determined during quantity take-off.

Profit   The contractor's net income after all expenses have been subtracted.

Pro-forma   A financial analysis of a real estate development, such as a tract of homes, to predict the anticipated costs and revenues.

Programming budget estimate   Budget estimate prepared during the programming phase to assess the financial feasibility of a project and to identify anticipated funding requirements.

Progress payment requests   Document or package of documents requesting progress payments for work performed during the period covered by the request, usually monthly.

Progress payments   Periodic (usually monthly) payments made during the course of a construction project to cover the value of work satisfactorily completed during the previous period.

Project control   The methods a project manager uses to anticipate, monitor, and adjust to risks and trends in controlling costs and schedules.

Project engineer (PE)   Project management team member who assists the project manager on larger projects. More experienced and has more responsibilities than the field engineer, but less than the project manager. Responsible for management of technical issues on the jobsite.

Project manual   A volume usually containing the instructions to bidders, the bid form, general conditions, and special conditions. It also may include a geotechnical report.

Property damage insurance   Protects the contractor against financial loss due to damage to the contractor's property.

Purchase orders (P.O.)   Written contracts for the purchase of materials and equipment from suppliers.

Quantity recaps   Form used by estimators to group like items, such as reinforcing steel or concrete, from several quantity take-off sheets.

Quantity take-off (QTO)   One of the first steps in the estimating process to measure and count items of work to which unit prices will later be applied to determine a project cost estimate.

Recapitulation (Recap)   The form upon which tabulated quantities or work are listed and priced.

Reimbursable costs   Costs incurred on a project that are reimbursed by the owner. The categories of costs that are reimbursable are specifically stated in the contract agreement.

Request for proposals (RFP)   Document containing instructions to prospective contractors regarding documentation required and the process to be used in selecting the contractor for a project.

Request for qualifications (RFQ)   A request for prospective contractors or subcontractors to submit a specific set of documents to demonstrate the firm's qualifications for a specific project.

Request for quotation   A request for a prospective subcontractor to submit a quotation for a defined scope of work.

Rough order-of-magnitude (ROM) cost estimate   A conceptual cost estimate usually based on the size of the project. It is prepared early in the estimating process to establish a preliminary budget and decide whether or not to pursue the project.

Savings split   A clause in a guaranteed maximum price contract that provides a formula for sharing the savings between the owner and the contractor, if the final cost of construction is less than the guaranteed maximum price.

Schedule of values (SOV)   An allocation of the entire project cost to each of the various work packages required to complete a project. Used to develop a cash flow curve for an owner and to support requests for progress payments.

Schematic cost estimate   A budget estimate that is prepared at the completion of schematic design.

Schematic design documents   The plans and specifications early in the design process. They typically consist of sketches and preliminary drawings.

Self-performed work   Project work performed by the general contractor's work force rather than by a subcontractor.

Semi-detailed cost estimate   An estimate that is prepared during design development that includes estimates for some components based on quantity take-off and estimates for other components based on order-of-magnitude estimates.

Short list   The list of best-qualified contractors developed after reviewing the qualifications of prospective contractors. Only those on the short list are invited to bid or submit a proposal.

Sliding scale fee   On negotiated projects, the fee typically is higher on risky items and less on items involving less risk to the contractor.

Soils report   See *geotechnical report.*

Special conditions   Also known as *supplementary conditions.* A part of the construction contract that supplements and may also modify, add to, or delete portions of the general conditions.

Specialty contractors   Construction firms that specialize in specific areas of construction work, such as painting, roofing, or mechanical. Such firms typically are involved in construction projects as subcontractors.

Statement of qualification   Documentation submitted by a contractor in response to a request for qualifications. The statements of qualification are evaluated by the owner to determine the best qualified contractors from whom to solicit proposals.

Subcontractors   Specialty contractors who contract with and are under the supervision of the general contractor.

Subcontractor call sheet   A form used to list all of the bidding firms from which the general contractor is soliciting subcontractor and vendor quotations.

Subcontracts   Written contracts between the general contractor and specialty contractors who provide craft labor and usually material for specialized areas of work.

Substantial completion   State of a project when it is sufficiently completed that the owner can use it for its intended purpose.

Substructure   The portion of a building that is constructed below ground, usually the foundation and any basements.

Summary schedule   Abbreviated version of a detailed construction schedule that may include 10 to 20 major activities.

Superintendent (Supt)   Individual from the contractor's project team who is the leader on the jobsite and who is responsible for supervision of daily field operations on the project.

Superstructure   The portion of a building that is constructed above ground.

Taxable wage rate   The base hourly wage rate plus the cost of fringe benefits upon which payroll taxes are calculated.

Technical specifications   A part of the construction contract that provides the qualitative requirements for a project in terms of materials, equipment, and workmanship.

Tilt-up concrete construction   A method of concrete construction in which members are cast horizontally and then tilted into place after the forms have been removed.

Time-and-materials contract (T & M)   A cost-plus contract in which the owner and the contractor agree to a labor rate that includes the contractor's profit and overhead. Reimbursement to the contractor is made based on the actual costs for materials and the agreed-upon labor rate times the number of hours worked.

Truck cubic yards   See *loose cubic yards*

Uniformat   A system for organizing a cost estimate that is based on building systems.

Unit-price contract   A contract that contains an estimated quantity for each element of work and a unit price. The actual cost is determined once the work is completed and the total quantity of work measured.

Value engineering   A study of the relative value of various materials and construction techniques to identify the least costly alternative without sacrificing quality or performance.

Work breakdown structure (WBS)   A list of significant work items that will have associated cost or schedule implications.

Workers' compensation insurance   Protects the contractor from a claim due to injury or death of an employee on the project site.

Work package   A defined segment of the work required to complete a project.

C ESTIMATING RESOURCES

C.1 MASTERFORMAT FOR DEVELOPING COST ESTIMATES

DIVISION 1—GENERAL REQUIREMENTS

01010	SUMMARY OF WORK
01050	FIELD ENGINEERING
01100	SPECIAL PROJECT PROCEDURES
01200	PROJECT MEETINGS
01300	SUBMITTALS
01400	QUALITY CONTROL
01500	CONSTRUCTION FACILITIES
01600	MATERIAL & EQUIPMENT
01700	CONTRACT CLOSEOUT
01800	MAINTENANCE

DIVISION 2—SITEWORK

02010	SUBSURFACE EXPLORATION
02050	DEMOLITION
02100	SITE PREPARATION
02140	DEWATERING
02150	SHORING & UNDERPINNING
02200	EARTHWORK
02500	PAVING & SURFACING
02600	UTILITY PIPING
02700	SEWERAGE & DRAINAGE
02900	LANDSCAPING

DIVISION 3—CONCRETE

03100	CONCRETE FORMWORK
03200	CONCRETE REINFORCEMENT
03250	CONCRETE ACCESSORIES
03300	CAST-IN-PLACE CONCRETE
03370	CONCRETE CURING
03400	PRECAST CONCRETE
03470	TILT-UP PRECAST CONCRETE
03600	GROUT

DIVISION 4—MASONRY

04100	MORTAR & MASONRY GROUT
04210	BRICK MASONRY
04220	CONCRETE UNIT MASONRY
04400	STONE
04550	REFRACTORIES
04700	SIMULATED MASONRY

DIVISION 5—METALS

05120	STRUCTURAL STEEL
05140	STRUCTURAL ALUMINUM
05200	METAL JOISTS
05300	METAL DECKING
05400	COLD FORMED METAL
05510	METAL STAIRS
05520	HANDRAILS & RAILINGS
05530	GRATINGS
05700	ORNAMENTAL METAL

DIVISION 6—WOOD AND PLASTICS

06100	ROUGH CARPENTRY
06200	FINISH CARPENTRY
06220	MILLWORK
06240	LAMINATES
06410	CUSTOM CASEWORK
06430	STAIRWORK
06500	STRUCTURAL PLASTIC

DIVISION 7—THERMAL AND MOISTURE PROTECTION

07100	WATERPROOFING
07200	INSULATION
07250	FIREPROOFING
07300	SHINGLES & ROOFING TILES
07400	PREFORMED ROOFING & SIDING
07500	MEMBRANE ROOFING
07600	FLASHING & SHEET METAL
07700	ROOF ACCESORIES
07800	SKYLIGHTS
07900	JOINT SEALERS

DIVISION 8—DOORS AND WINDOWS

08100	METAL DOORS & FRAMES
08200	WOOD & PLASTIC DOORS
08400	ENTRANCES & STOREFRONTS
08500	METAL WINDOWS
08600	WOOD & PLASTIC WINDOWS
08700	HARDWARE
08800	GLAZING

DIVISION 9—FINISHES

09100	METAL SUPPORTS
09200	LATH & PLASTER
09250	GYPSUM WALLBOARD
09300	TILE
09400	TERRAZZO
09500	ACOUSTICAL TREATMENT
09550	WOOD FLOORING
09650	RESILIENT FLOORING
09680	CARPETING
09800	SPECIAL COATINGS
09900	PAINTING
09950	WALL COVERING

DIVISION 10—SPECIALTIES

10100	VISUAL DISPLAY BOARDS
10150	COMPARTMENTS & CUBICLES
10200	LOUVERS & VENTS
10300	FIREPLACES & STOVES
10520	FIRE PROTECTION SPECIALTIES
10550	POSTAL SPECIALTIES
10600	PARTITIONS
10670	STORAGE SHELVING
10750	TELEPHONE SPECIALTIES
10800	TOILET & BATH SPECIALTIES

DIVISION 11—EQUIPMENT

11010	MAINTENANCE EQUIPMENT
11020	SECURITY & VAULT EQUIPMENT
11050	LIBRARY EQUIPMENT
11060	THEATER & STAGE EQUIPMENT
11120	VENDING EQUIPMENT
11130	AUDIO-VISUAL EQUIPMENT
11160	LOADING DOCK EQUIPMENT
11170	SOLID WASTE HANDLING EQUIPMENT
11400	FOOD SERVICE EQUIPMENT
11500	INDUSTRIAL & PROCESS EQUIPMENT
11680	OFFICE EQUIPMENT

DIVISION 12—FURNISHINGS

12100	ARTWORK
12300	MANUFACTURED CASEWORK
12500	WINDOW TREATMENT
12600	FURNITURE & ACCESSORIES

| 12670 | RUGS & MATS |
| 12800 | INTERIOR PLANTS & PLANTERS |

DIVISION 13—SPECIAL CONSTRUCTION

13020	INTEGRATED ASSEMBLIES
13030	SPECIAL PURPOSE ROOMS
13120	PRE-ENGINEERED STRUCTURES
13150	AQUATIC FACILITIES
13200	LIQUID & GAS STORAGE TANKS
13300	UTILITY CONTROL SYSTEMS
13400	INDUSTRIAL & PROCESS CONTROL
13600	SOLAR ENERGY SYSTEMS
13700	WIND ENERGY SYSTEMS
13750	COGENERATION SYSTEMS
13800	BUILDING AUTOMATION SYSTEMS
13900	FIRE SUPPRESSION & SUPERVISION

DIVISION 14—CONVEYING SYSTEMS

14100	DUMBWAITERS
14200	ELEVATORS
14400	LIFTS
14500	MATERIAL HANDLING SYSTEMS
14600	HOISTS & CRANES

DIVISION 15—MECHANICAL

15060	PIPE AND PIPE FITTINGS
15160	PUMPS
15250	MECHANICAL INSULATION
15300	FIRE PROTECTION
15400	PLUMBING
15500	HVAC
15550	HEAT GENERATION
15650	REFRIGERATION
15750	HEAT TRANSFER
15850	AIR HANDLING
15880	AIR DISTRIBUTION
15950	CONTROLS
15990	TESTING & BALANCING

DIVISION 16—ELECTRICAL

16200	POWER GENERATION
16300	MEDIUM VOLTAGE DISTRIBUTION
16400	SERVICE & DISTRIBUTION
16500	LIGHTING
16610	UNINTERRUPTIBLE POWER SUPPLY
16700	COMMUNICATIONS
16850	ELECTRICAL RESISTANCE HEATING
16900	CONTROLS
16950	TESTING

C.2   UNIFORMAT FOR DEVELOPING COST ESTIMATES

01—FOUNDATIONS

| 011 | STANDARD FOUNDATION SYSTEMS |
| 012 | SPECIAL FOUNDATION CONDITIONS |

02—SUBSTRUCTURE

021	SLAB ON GRADE
022	BASEMENT EXCAVATION
023	BASEMENT WALLS

03—SUPERSTRUCTURE

031	FLOOR CONSTRUCTION
032	ROOF CONSTRUCTION
033	STAIR CONSTRUCTION

04—EXTERIOR CLOSURE

| 041 | EXTERIOR WALLS |
| 042 | EXTERIOR DOORS & WINDOWS |

05—ROOFING

051   ROOFING SYSTEMS

06—INTERIOR CONSTRUCTION

061   PARTITIONS
062   INTERIOR FINISHES
063   SPECIALTIES

07—CONVEYING SYSTEMS

071   ELEVATORS

08—MECHANICAL SYSTEMS

081   PLUMBING
082   HVAC
083   FIRE PROTECTION
084   SPECIAL MECHANICAL SYSTEMS
085   MECHANICAL SERVICE & DISTRIBUTION

09—ELECTRICAL

091   ELECTRICAL SERVICE & DISTRIBUTION

092   LIGHTING & POWER
093   SPECIAL ELECTRICAL SYSTEMS

10—GENERAL CONDITIONS

101   CONTRACTOR'S OVERHEAD & PROFIT

11—EQUIPMENT

111   FIXED & MOVABLE EQUIPMENT
112   FURNISHINGS
113   SPECIAL CONSTRUCTION

12—SITEWORK

121   SITE PREPARATION
122   SITE IMPROVEMENTS
123   SITE UTILITIES
124   OFF SITE CONSTRUCTION

C.3 UNIFORMAT II FOR DEVELOPING COST ESTIMATES

A—SUBSTRUCTURE

A10   FOUNDATIONS
A20   BASEMENT CONSTRUCTION

B—SHELL

B10   SUPERSTRUCTURE
B20   EXTERIOR CLOSURE
B30   ROOFING

C—INTERIORS

C10   INTERIOR CONSTRUCTION
C20   STAIRCASES
C30   INTERIOR FINISHES

D—SERVICES

D10   CONVEYING SYSTEMS
D20   PLUMBING
D30   HVAC

D40   FIRE PROTECTION
D50   ELECTRICAL

E—EQUIPMENT & FURNISHINGS

E10   EQUIPMENT
E20   FURNISHINGS

F—SPECIAL CONSTRUCTION & DEMOLITION

F10   SPECIAL CONSTRUCTION
F20   BUILDING DEMOLITION

G—BUILDING SITEWORK

G10   SITE PREPARATION
G20   SITE IMPROVEMENTS
G30   SITE CIVIL/MECHANICAL UTILITIES
G40   SITE ELECTRICAL UTILITIES
G50   OTHER SITE CONSTRUCTION

C.4   DIMENSIONAL LUMBER BOARD FOOT CONVERSIONS

Lumber Size	Board Feet per Lineal Foot	Lumber Size	Board Feet per Lineal Foot
1 × 2	0.17	2 × 10	1.67
1 × 4	0.33	2 × 12	2.00
1 × 6	0.50	4 × 4	1.33
1 × 8	0.67	4 × 6	2.00
1 × 10	0.83	4 × 8	2.67
1 × 12	1.00	4 × 10	3.33
2 × 2	0.33	4 × 12	4.00
2 × 4	0.67	6 × 6	3.00
2 × 6	1.00	6 × 8	4.00
2 × 8	1.33	6 × 10	5.00

C.5   STANDARD CONCRETE REINFORCEMENT STEEL WEIGHT CONVERSIONS

Bar Size	Weight per Lineal Foot	Bar Size	Weight per Lineal Foot
2	0.167 lb	8	2.670 lb
3	0.376 lb	9	3.400 lb
4	0.668 lb	10	4.303 lb
5	1.043 lb	11	5.313 lb
6	1.502 lb	14	7.650 lb
7	2.044 lb	18	13.60 lb

C.6   MISCELLANEOUS WASTE AND LAP ALLOWANCES

Material	Add
Gravel	20% to convert from bank cubic yards to truck cubic yards
Earth Backfill	30–50% to convert from bank cubic yards to truck cubic yards
Concrete	3–5% for waste
Reinforcement Steel	10% for lap (or 40 times bar diameter)
Wire Mesh	10% for lap
Framing Lumber	10% for waste
Plywood	5–10% for waste
Building Paper	10% for lap
Vapor Barrier	10% for lap
Siding	20–35% for waste and lap

C.7   SAMPLE GENERAL CONTRACTOR'S COMPANY DATABASE

CSI	Work Item	Units	Labor Productivity per Hour	Material Unit Price
2	Sidewalk OM	sf sidewalk	with material	$3.00
2	Structural excavation	bcy	0.178	$5.10
2	Backfill	cy	0.012	$1.50
3	Form spot footings	sfca	0.086	$3.20
3	Footing rebar	ton	15.24	$450
3	Purchase tilt-up concrete	cy	with placement	$63
3	Place tilt-up concrete	cy	0.492	with purchase
5	Structural steel OM	ton	20	$1,500
5	Erect columns	ea	1.00	with suppliers
5	Expansion anchors	ea	0.20	$3.30
5	Rough carpentry OM	sf of floor	with material	$0.50
8	Door hardware OM	door sets	3.00	$300
9	Carpet OM with pad	sy	with material	$25.10
10	Specialties OM	sf of floor	0.25	$0.60
14	Elevators	stops	with material	$15,000
15	Plumbing OM	sf of floor	with material	$3.10
15	HVAC OM	sf of floor	with material	$5.20
15	Fire Protection OM	sf of floor	with material	$1.60
16	Electrical OM	sf of floor	with material	$7.20

C.8   INCH TO FOOT CONVERSIONS

Inches	Feet	Inches	Feet
1	0.08	7	0.58
2	0.16	8	0.67
3	0.25	9	0.75
4	0.33	10	0.83
5	0.41	11	0.91
6	0.50	12	1.00

C.9   ESTIMATING REFERENCE GUIDES

Aspen Richardson's General Construction Estimating Standards, (CD-ROM only), Cambridge, Mass.: Aspen Technology, Inc.

Assemblies Cost Data, Kingston, Mass.: R. S. Means Co. Inc., published annually.

Building Construction Cost Data, Kingston, Mass.: R. S. Means Co. Inc., published annually.

Commercial Square Foot Building Costs, Chatsworth, Calif.: Saylor Publications, Inc. published annually.

Current Construction Costs, Chatsworth, Calif.: Saylor Publications, Inc., published annually.

Electrical Cost Data, Kingston, Mass.: R. S. Means Co. Inc., published annually.

Heavy Construction Cost Data, Kingston, Mass.: R. S. Means Co. Inc., published annually.

Means Estimating Handbook, 2nd ed., Kingston, Mass.: R. S. Means Co. Inc., 2003.

Mechanical Cost Data, Kingston, Mass.: R. S. Means Co. Inc., published annually.

Plumbing Cost Data, Kingston, Mass.: R. S. Means Co. Inc., published annually.

Site Work & Landscape Cost Data, Kingston, Mass.: R. S. Means Co. Inc., published annually.

Square Foot Costs, Kingston, Mass.: R. S. Means Co. Inc., published annually.

Walker's Building Estimator's Reference Book, 26th ed., Scott Siddens, ed., Lisle, Ill.: Frank R. Walker Company, 1999.

C.10   STANDARD UNITS FOR QUANTITY TAKE-OFF AND PRICING CONVERSIONS

Work Item	Take-Off Units	Pricing Units
Asphalt	square feet	square yards
Cabinets	linear feet or each	linear feet (material) & each (labor)
Carpet	square feet	square yards
Cast-in-place concrete curbs	linear feet	linear feet or cubic yards (forms separate)
Ceramic tile	square feet	square feet
Concrete finishing	square feet	square feet
Concrete purchase/placement	cubic feet	cubic yards
Dimensional lumber	linear feet	thousand board feet
Door hardware	each or sets	each or sets
Doors	each or leaf	each or leaf
Drilled piers	each	linear feet
Drywall	square feet	square feet
Electrical	sq feet or boxes & devices	square feet or boxes & devices
Elevators	stops	stops
Excavation	cubic feet	truck cubic yards
Fire protection	square feet	square feet
Footing forms	linear feet	linear feet or square feet of contact area
Grout	cubic feet	cubic feet
HVAC	sq feet or cooling tonnage	square feet or cooling tonnage
Insulation	square feet	square feet
Landscaping & irrigation	square feet	square feet
Masonry	square feet	square feet or each
Metal bar joist	linear feet or each	linear feet (material) & each (labor)
Metal deck	square feet	square feet
Millwork & trim	linear feet	linear feet
Paint	square feet	square feet
Pavement markings	linear feet	linear feet
Plumbing	square feet or fixtures	square feet or fixtures
Plywood	square feet	sheets
Precast concrete curbs	each	each
Reinforcement steel	linear feet	tons
Roofing	square feet	square feet or squares

Work Item	Take-Off Units	Pricing Units
Rubber base	linear feet	linear feet
Sheet vinyl	square feet	square yards
Sidewalks	square feet	sq feet or cubic yards (forms separate)
Storefront	square feet	square feet
Structural steel	linear feet or each	tons (material) & each (labor)
Toilet accessories	each	each
Trees & plants	each	each
Utility piping	linear feet	linear feet
Vapor barrier	square feet	square feet
Vinyl tile	square feet	square feet
Wall covering	square feet	square feet
Wall forms	square feet	square feet
Welded wire mesh	square feet	hundred square feet
Windows	square feet or each	square feet or each
Wood floors	square feet	square feet

C.11 RECOMMENDED TABLE OF CONTENTS FOR ESTIMATOR'S NOTEBOOK

Throughout this text we have discussed the need or suggestion for the estimator to establish a notebook to use as a reference on future estimates. Some of the items that may be included in that notebook are listed below. The order of items follows the process discussed in this book for developing the estimate. This list and order are just suggestions. An experienced estimator will develop his or her own system for assembling this type of information.

1. Rough order of magnitude (ROM) estimates for types of facilities
2. Estimating forms
3. Long and short lists of potential subcontractors and suppliers to call
4. Conversion and math tables such as those in this Appendix
5. Database for labor productivity rates and current material prices
6. Current wage rates
7. Backup for labor burden or labor tax percentage markups
8. Information on tax structures and percentages for different communities and states in which the contractor may work
9. Database for subcontractor order of magnitude (OM) estimates
10. Field performance records of subcontractors and suppliers used on past projects
11. History of estimate successes for your firm and other contractors including markups
12. Copies of previous estimates
13. Building permit costing data and/or calculations
14. Insurance percentages
15. Bond costing rates

D

REQUEST FOR PROPOSAL

April 14, 2003

To: Select General Contractors

Re: The Training Center, Kent, Washington

Request For Proposal for General Construction Services

Thank you for your expressed interest in the Training Center. Your firm was one of the original 16 general construction firms who expressed a desire to propose on this exciting project. The owner and design teams have reduced that list to a select group of 4 general contractors from whom we are seeking a proposal for negotiated general construction services.

A. The project consists of sitework, shell, and phase one tenant improvements. Some of the **specifics** of the project include:
    - Tilt-up concrete shell
    - Structural steel second floor and roof structure
    - Bridge crane
    - Weld-exhaust booths
    - Elevator
    - Complete tenant improvements for phase one
    - Design-build fire protection system is the responsibility of the general contractor.
    - Mechanical, plumbing, and electrical systems will be designed by the owner's engineers.
    - All civil, landscape, on-grade parking, and site work is in the general contractor's scope.

B. The preliminary **schedule** of the project is:
- Design has been completed through the design development phase.
- Permit will be applied for at the 60% construction document stage.
- Mandatory pre-proposal site meeting will be April 21, 2003.
- RFP response is due Friday, April 28, 2003. Interviews will be scheduled the next week.
- Selection of general contractor by the end of the second week of May.
- Construction is scheduled to start June 21, 2003.
- Six-month construction duration is anticipated but we are requesting contractor input to this duration. Please provide a detailed construction schedule with your proposal.

C. The following documents are included with this RFP: architectural drawings, civil drawings, structural drawings, outline specifications, soils report, and topographic survey.

D. The following **documents** are required to be submitted with your proposal:
1. Contractor qualifications for work of similar construction, uses, and methods.
2. Experience with any of the owner and designer team members.
3. Proposed personnel, along with resumes and letters of reference.
4. A detailed guaranteed maximum price (GMP) estimate. It is understood that the design documents are not yet complete. The contractor is to include stated contingencies and allowances in order to provide the owner with a complete estimate. After the permit is received and the construction documents are finalized, any mutually agreed changes will be incorporated into the GMP.
5. A detailed jobsite general conditions estimate.
6. A proposed fee.
7. A proposed savings split.
8. A proposed ceiling on the general contractor's share of any savings.
9. Project specific safety plan.
10. A list of any assumptions, clarifications, or exclusions that were used to prepare the GMP.
11. Clear definition of cost-reimbursable versus non-reimbursable costs.
12. Construction schedule.

E. It is anticipated that the **contract** for construction will be the 1997 version AIA A111, cost of the work plus a fee with a guaranteed maximum price, along with the AIA A201 general conditions. The contractor is required to submit with its proposal any proposed changes to these standard agreements. The owner reserves the right to refuse any or all of these proposed changes.

F. The general contractor will be expected to work with the owner and designer teams through the completion of design. The scope of these **pre-construction services** during this period will include constructability reviews, schedules, pre-qualification of subcontractors, value engineering, and budget control. It is expected that a pre-construction services fee will be paid for this work and a short pre-construction services contract will be executed. The contractor is to propose and include with its proposal a standard pre-construction services contract along with a stated fee.

Thank you again for your interest in the Training Center. We look forward to meeting with you at the site on April 21, 2003 and receiving your proposal on April 28, 2003.

Best Regards,

William Rogers

William Rogers, Owner's Representative, The Training Center

Cc: John James, Project Architect, LMA Architects

E

INVITATION FOR BID

SECTION 00020

Invitation for Bid

Project Architect:
Lance Mueller and Associates
130 Lakeside, Suite 250
Seattle, Washington 98122

Project:
The Training Center
20474–72nd Avenue South
Kent, Washington 98032

1. **NOTICE TO GENERAL CONTRACTORS:** Sealed bids will be received by the owner's representative in person by 2:00 p.m. P.S.T on Tuesday, June 3, 2003. The bid form, along with any other requested documents, are required to be turned in with a sealed envelope to the Architect's office. Bids received after the time stated above will not receive consideration.

2. **DESCRIPTION OF THE WORK:** The project is to construct a shell, tenant improvements, and associated sitework as described on the enclosed drawings and specifications. The building footprint is approximately 27,000 sf plus a partial mezzanine. The building has cast-in-place concrete, tilt-up concrete, structural steel, masonry, and associated finishes.

3. **GENERAL CONTRACTOR BID LIST:** The following contractors have been selected to bid on this project:
Acme Construction
Northwest Contractors
Jones and Associates
Western Construction Company
ABBC, Incorporated
4. **BID OPENING:** Bids will be opened privately. It is the intent of the owner and architect teams to interview one to two bidders within one week of bid submission. All bidders will be notified of award within two weeks of bid submission.
5. **BIDDING DOCUMENTS:** One set of drawings and the project manual inclusive of specifications can be picked up by the contractors at the Architect's office. Additional sets can be purchased from the blue print office. The owner and Architect have not placed drawings in the plan centers.
6. **RIGHT TO REJECT BIDS:** The owner reserves the right to reject any or all bids due to pricing, irregularities, or timeliness, or for any other reason they choose.

SECTION 00100

Instructions to Bidders

Proposals to be entitled to consideration must be made in accordance with the following instructions:

1. **GENERAL:** Invitation to Bid, as included in the Specifications, shall be considered as part of these Instructions to Bidders as if repeated herein.
2. **EXAMINATION OF SITE AND DOCUMENTS:** Before submitting a proposal, the bidder shall:
    A. Carefully examine the Drawings and Specifications, Addenda, Geotechnical Report, and all other information furnished to the bidders.
    B. Visit the site of the work and fully inform itself to existing conditions and limitations.
    C. Rely upon its own judgment in preparing the proposal, and include in the bid a sum sufficient to cover all items required by the contract.
3. **INTERPRETATIONS:**
    A. Questions regarding Drawings and Specifications should be in writing and addressed to the Architect and will be answered by addenda addressed to all bidders. Neither the Owner nor the Architect will be responsible for oral interpretations.
    B. If there are discrepancies contained in the bidding documents between the drawings and the specifications, the specifications govern.
    C. The General Contractor is required to notify the Architect of all discrepancies contained in the bidding documents. In the event of an unclarified discrepancy, the contractor is required to bid the item of greater costs.
    D. Questions received less than 24 hours before the time set for bid opening cannot be answered. All addenda issued during the bidding period will be incorporated into the contract.

4. **FORM OF BID:** Submit bid in duplicate, on forms furnished by the Architect, without alterations in the form. Fill in all blank spaces in the form and sign in longhand. Failure to bid on all items listed in the bid form may cause rejection of the bid.

5. **WRITTEN, TELEGRAPHIC, OR FACSIMILE BIDS:** Only written bids will be received as indicated herein. Electronic or facsimile bids will not be accepted.

6. **SUBSTITUTIONS:** Bids shall be based on the articles and materials named in the specifications. Substitutions will only be accepted if submitted by the select list of general contractors, and approved and acknowledged via addenda. Substitutions must be submitted on the appropriate form and in accordance with the requirements of specifications.

7. **ALTERNATE BIDS:** Alternate bids other than those listed in the bid form will not be considered. The successful general contractor will be required to bid on each alternate listed on the bid form. Alternate bid amounts will be inclusive of all markups. The owner reserves the right to accept or reject any or all alternates.

8. **SUBMISSION OF BID:** Bids are required to be submitted as indicated in Section 00020.

9. **BID BOND:** A bid bond is not required at this time.

10. **WITHDRAWAL OF BIDS:** No bidder may withdraw its bid after the time announced for the opening, or before both the award and execution of the agreement, unless the award is delayed for a period in excess of thirty (30) days.

11. **EVIDENCE OF QUALIFICATION:** A bidder whose proposal is under consideration shall, upon request, promptly furnish satisfactory evidence of its financial resources, experience, organization, and references.

12. **PERFORMANCE BOND, AND LABOR AND MATERIAL PAYMENT BOND:** The contractor may be required to secure and pay for Performance Bond, and Labor and Material Payment Bonds, issued by a bonding company licensed to transact business in the locality of the project, on AIA form A311. The prices of these bonds are not to be included in the base bid amount at this time.

13. **BID PROPOSAL SUPPLEMENT:** After bids are received and prior to signing the contract, the owner or architect may request additional information:
    A. Post-bid questions and clarifications, which will require written responses.
    B. The general contractor will be required to attend a post-bid interview and bring all project personnel.
    C. Evidence of financial qualification.
    D. Performance and Payment bonds.
    E. Listing of all major successful subcontractors.
    F. Construction schedule.

14. **PROJECT SCHEDULE TIME LINE:**
    A. The project must be completed within 7 calendar months after award.
    B. The owner may, at his option, include a liquidated damages clause in the contract, wherein the contractor will forfeit $500 per day for every day the project is not completed within the contract schedule requirements.

15. **REJECTION OF BIDS:** The owner reserves the right to reject any or all bids for whatever reason.

Date: June 3, 2003

PROJECT:
THE TRAINING CENTER
Kent, Washington

BID PROPOSAL

Bidder:

The undersigned bidder, having familiarized himself with the terms of the contract, the local conditions affecting the contract, and the Drawings and Specifications and other Contract Documents, hereby proposes and agrees to provide all labor, materials, and services necessary to complete in a workmanlike manner all work required in connection with the construction of

THE TRAINING CENTER

1. All in strict accordance to Drawings, Specifications, and other Contract Documents, hereby submit a base bid as follows:

    BASE BID: $ _____

2. If the owner decides to purchase a 100% performance and payment bond then the following will be in addition to the base bid:

    BOND: $ _____

3. CHANGE ORDERS: All extra work not included in the Contract, if requested, will be performed by the Contractor by material and labor costs plus overhead and profit. Ten percent (10%) (overhead and profit) will be added or deleted accordingly by the subcontractor completing the work. Five percent (5%) (overhead and profit) will be added or deleted accordingly by the General Contractor.

4. SALES TAX: State of Washington sales tax is not included in the Base Bid. It will be added to each payment request as it is submitted.

5. ADDENDA: Receipt of addenda is hereby acknowledged as follows:

    Addenda Nos.   Date

6. GENERAL CONTRACTOR SIGNATURE

    _____   _____
    Bidder   Address

    _____   _____
    By   License No.

    _____
    Title

F

ESTIMATING FORMS

List of Forms

Form	Description
F-1	Project Item List
F-2	Call Log
F-3	Quantity Take-off Sheet (standard form)
F-4	Quantity Take-off Sheet (accounting form)
F-5	Recapitulation
F-6	General Conditions Estimating Form (4 pages)
F-7	Bid Proposal Form (for recording subcontractor bids)
F-8	Subcontractor List
F-9	Project Bid Summary
F-10	Request for Information
F-11	Composite Crew Calculation

PROJECT ITEM LIST

Project: ______________________________ Date: ________________

Estimator: ______________________________

			Provider			
			General Contractor		Subcontractor	
Line #	CSI Div	Cost Item Description	Materials	Labor	Materials	Labor

Form F-1

CALL LOG

JOB: _____ DATE: _____

FIRM	CONTACT	PHONE NUMBER	WILL BID (yes/no)

SUBCONTRACT/SUPPLY ITEM: _____

SPECIFICATION SECTION(s): _____

GENERAL SCOPE OF WORK: _____
_____

SPECIFIC INCLUSIONS: _____
_____

SPECIFIC EXCLUSIONS: _____
_____

OTHER NOTES: _____
_____

Form F-2

QUANTITY SHEET

Project: _____
Location: _____

Date: _____
Estimator: _____
Est #: _____

Div# _____

Ref	Description	Qty (ea)	L (ft)	W (ft)	H (ft)														

Form F-3

QUANTITY SHEET

Project: _____
Location: _____
Arch/Eng: _____
Classification: _____

Estimator: _____
Extensions: _____
Checked: _____

Estimate No.: _____
Sheet No.: _____
Date: _____

Code	Sec/Det	Description	No.	L	W	H/D								

Form F-4

RECAPITULATION

Project: _____
Location: _____
Arch./Engr.: _____

Date: _____
Estimator: _____
Estimate #: _____

Division													
Code	Sec/ Det	Description	Qty	Unit	UMH	Man- hours	Wage Rate	Unit L Cost	Labor Cost	Unit M Cost	Material Cost	Total Cost

Form F-5

GENERAL CONDITIONS

ADMINISTRATIVE EXPENSE

PROJECT: _____   DATE: _____   ESTIMATOR: _____

OWNER: _____   ESTIMATE #: _____

Code	Description	qty	unit	Labor up	Labor Cost	Material up	Material Cost	Total Cost
	MANAGEMENT & SUPERVISION							
	Project Manager							
	Project Superintendent							
	Assistant Superintendent							
	Assistant Superintendent							
	Field Survey/Engr							
	ENGINEERING & SAFETY							
	Project Engineer							
	Office Engineer							
	Field Engineer							
	Form Detailing							
	Plan & Schedule							
	Quality Control							
	Professional Surveying							
	Blue Printing							
	Engineering Equipment							
	Safety/Medical							
	Safety Training							
OFFICE								
	Office Manager							
	Timekeeper							
	Secretarial							
	Warehousing							
	Rent							
	Office Utilities							
	Job Telephone/Fax							
	Set Up Telephones							
	Postage							
	Office Supplies							
	Furniture & Equipment							
	Custodial Expense							
	Public Relations							
	Travel Expense							
	Supervisory Substance							

ADMINISTRATIVE EXPENSE TOTALS   _____   _____ _____

Form F-6

GENERAL CONDITIONS

EQUIPMENT

PROJECT: _____ DATE: _____ ESTIMATOR: _____

OWNER: _____   ESTIMATE #: _____

Code	Description	qty	unit	Labor up	Labor Cost	Material up	Material Cost	Total Cost
	Equipment Purchases							
	Salvage Value							
	Outside Rentals							
	Owned Equipment Rentals							
	Pickup Truck							
	Compressor							
	Welder							
	Flatbed Truck							
	Forklift							
	Scaffolding							
	Torch Set							
	Concrete Equipment							
	Equipment Transportation							
	Tower Crane Base							
	Install Tower Crane							
	Tower Crane Rent							
	Tower Crane Operator							
	Man/Mat'l Hoist Rent							
	Install Man/Mat'l Hoist							
	Hoist Operator							
	Mobile Crane Rental							
	Mobile Crane Operator							
	Saw Sharpening							
	Small Tools							
	Consummables							
	Equipment Fuel & Maint.							

EQUIPMENT TOTALS   _____   _____   _____

Form F-6

GENERAL CONDITIONS

TEMPORARY CONSTRUCTION

PROJECT: _____ DATE: _____ ESTIMATOR: _____

OWNER: _____ ESTIMATE #: _____

| Code | Description | qty | unit | Labor | | Material | | Total Cost |
				up	Cost	up	Cost	
BUILDINGS								
	Job Office							
	Owner/Arch Office							
	Dry Shacks							
	Warehouse							
	Tool Shed							
	Trailer Transportation							
	Trailer Setup							
	Saw Line							
INSTALL UTILITIES								
	Water System							
	Temp Power Hookup & Dist							
	Temporary Lighting							
	Install Heating System							
	Operate Heating System							
	Telephone/Telex Setup							
	Job Communications System							
SITE FACILITIES								
	Temporary Roads							
	Parking							
	Jobsite Bus							
	Precast/Panel Yard							
	Rubbish Chute							
	Stairs & Ladders							
	Project Sign							
	Layout & Batter Boards							
PROTECTION								
	Fences							
	Signs & Barricades							
	Covered Walks							
	Temporary Handrails							
	Fire Protection							
	Temporary Partitions							

TEMPORARY CONSTRUCTION TOTALS   _____   _____   _____

Form F-6

GENERAL CONDITIONS

GENERAL OPERATIONS

PROJECT: _____ DATE: _____ ESTIMATOR: _____

OWNER: _____ ESTIMATE #: _____

Code	Description	qty	unit	Labor up	Labor Cost	Material up	Material Cost	Total Cost
PERMITS, LICENSES, & TAXES								
	Building Permit							
	City Business Tax							
	State Excise Tax (B&O)							
	Sales Tax (exp mat'l)							
	Street Use Permit							
BOND & INSURANCE								
	Bond Premium							
	Broad Form Insurance							
	Earthquake & Flood Ins.							
	Liability Insurance (PL & PD)							
UTILITIES								
	Operate & Maintain Electrical							
	Power Bills							
	Electrical Supplies							
	Water Bills							
	Drinking Water							
	Chemical Toilet							
SECURITY & PROTECTION								
	Security							
	Flaggers							
MAINTAIN FACILITIES								
	Buildings							
	Roads							
TESTING & INSPECTION								
	Inspector							
	Testing Lab							
	Mockups							
	Samples							
	Job Photos							
CLEANUP								
	Rubbish Removal							
	Periodic Cleanup							
	Final Cleanup							
	Punchlist & Warranty							
	Clean Streets							
	Glass Cleaning							
	Damage Repair							
OTHER								
	Hauling & Freight							
	Trash Hauling							
	Environmental Mitigation							
	Hazardous Material Disposal							

GENERAL OPERATIONS TOTALS   _____   _____   _____

Form F-6

BID PROPOSAL

Date _____

Time _____

Firm _____ Job _____

Phone _____ Union _____ Merit Shop _____

City _____ WBE _____ MBE _____

Estimator _____ Quoted by _____ Bondability _____

Prices Valid Until _____ Bond Premium Included _____

Spec Section	Bid Item/Inclusions	Amount

Addenda Nos. _____ Through _____ **BASIC BID** $ _____

Per Plans and Specs _____ Installed _____ Erected Only _____

Furnish Only _____ FOB: Jobsite _____ Trucks _____ Other _____

Weight _____ Delivery Time _____

Exclusions and Clarifications	Alternates or Unit Prices	$ Amount

Received By _____ Bin _____

Form F-7

SUBCONTRACTOR LIST

Project: _____ Estimator: _____ Est. #: _____

Bin	Spec	Description	Bid	+ or −	Revised	Subcontractor

TOTAL SUBCONTRACTS   _____   _____   _____

Form F-8

BID SUMMARY

Project: _____ Bid Date & Time: _____

Owner: _____ Estimator: _____ Est. #: _____

Code	Page	Description	MH	Labor	Material	Total
		Administrative				
		Indirect Equipment				
		Temporary Construction				
		General Conditions				
		Total Job Overhead				
		Subtotal				
		Labor Burden _____%				
		Trade Travel & Subsistence				
		Labor Increase				
		Contingency				
		Subtotal				
			Subcontracts		
			Subcontractor Bonds		
			Adjustments		
			Subtotal		
			Fee _____%		
			Subtotal		
			Bus. Taxes & Ins. ___%		
			Subtotal		
			Adjustments		
			TOTAL BID		

Form F-9

REQUEST FOR INFORMATION

Project: _____   Date: _____

Area/System: _____   RFI Number: _____

To: _____

Address: _____   Related RFI   _____
          _____   Number(s):   _____
          _____   _____

Attn: _____

Return Submittal by: _____

Subcontractor/Supplier providing RFI: _____   Originator's Number: _____

Subject: _____

Detailed Description/Request: _____
_____
_____
_____
_____
_____
_____
_____

Attached/Referenced/Supporting Documentation: _____
_____
_____

Please Reply to: _____

Space below for Architect/Engineer

Reply: _____
_____
_____
_____
_____
_____
_____
_____

Signed: _____ Dated: _____

Contractor's Job No./File code: _____

Form F-10

Project: _____
Location: _____

Date: _____
Est #: _____

Trade/Rank	Base Wage	No.	Cost	No.	Cost	No.	Cost	No.	Cost	No.	Cost	No.	Cost

Total No. in Crew

Composite Wage

Notes:
1. Base wage is the base hourly rate without fringes and payroll taxes.
2. Field supervision that supervises more than one crew is to show the fractional amount to be applied to a single crew.

Form F-11

G

SELECTED PROJECT SPECIFICATIONS FOR THE TRAINING CENTER

List of Specifications

1. Temporary Facilities and Controls
2. Precast Concrete
3. Ceramic Tile

SECTION 01500
TEMPORARY FACILITIES AND CONTROLS

PART 1. GENERAL

1.1 SUMMARY

  A. Section includes:
    1. Temporary Utilities: Electricity, lighting, heat, ventilation, telephone service, water, and sanitary facilities.
    2. Temporary controls: Barriers, enclosures and fencing, protection of the work, and water control.
    3. Construction facilities: All-weather access roads, parking, progress cleaning, temporary buildings, and staging areas.

1.2 TEMPORARY ELECTRICITY

  A. Connect to existing power service. Contractor will pay cost of electricity used. Exercise measures to conserve energy.

  B. Provide adequate distribution equipment, wiring, and outlets to provide single-phase branch circuits for power and lighting. Provide temporary feeders to limit voltage loss to 5% overall from local utility power lines to provide electric requirements for project during construction.

  C. Provide main service disconnect and over-current protection at convenient location. Provide necessary transformers, meters, cables, protective devises, switches, etc. as required.

1.3 TEMPORARY LIGHTING

  A. Provide and maintain lighting for construction operations.

  B. Permanent building lighting may be utilized during construction.

1.4 TEMPORARY HEAT AND VENTILATION

  A. Provide and pay for heat devices and heat as required to maintain specified conditions for construction operations.

  B. Prior to operation of permanent equipment for temporary heating purposes, verify that installation is approved for operation, equipment is lubricated, and filters are in place. Provide and pay for operation, maintenance, and regular replacement of filters and worn components.

  C. Maintain minimum ambient temperature of 50 degrees F in areas where interior construction is in progress, unless indicated in the specifications.

  D. Ventilate enclosed areas to assist cure of materials, to dissipate humidity and to prevent accumulation of dust, fumes, vapors, or gases.

1.5 TELEPHONE SERVICE

  A. Provide, maintain, and pay for telephone services to field offices at time of project mobilization.

1.6 TEMPORARY WATER SERVICE

  A. Provide, maintain, and pay for suitable quality water service required for construction operations.

  B. Extend branch piping with outlets located so water is available by hoses with threaded connections. Provide temporary pipe insulation to prevent freezing.

1.7 TEMPORARY SANITARY FACILITIES

  A. Provide and maintain required chemical toilet facilities.

  B. Locate as required. Maintain facilities clean and serviced as necessary and in compliance with local health code requirements.

1.8 BARRIERS AND FENCING

A. Protect non-owned vehicular traffic, stored materials, site, and structures from damage.

B. Provide barriers to prevent unauthorized entry to construction areas to allow for Owner's use of site and to protect existing facilities and adjacent properties from damage due to construction operations.

C. Provide barricades and covered walkways required by governing authorities for public rights-of-way, to allow for owner's use of site, and for public access to existing building.
    1. Erect barricades using 1/2 inch plywood on 2×4 frame. Supports shall be as required to support barricade.
    2. Construct 8 foot high unless otherwise directed by the owner.

D. Construction: Commercial grade chain link fence, 6 feet high.
    1. Provide fence around area of expansion and staging areas.
    2. Coordinate installation and relocation with all trades.
    3. Equip with vehicular and pedestrian gates with locks.

1.9 FIELD OFFICES AND SHEDS

A. Contractor's office:
    1. Size as required for contractor's use and to provide space for project meetings.
    2. Adequate electrical power, lighting, heating, and cooling to maintain human comfort.
    3. Office space with desk and chair, layout table, plan rack, and facilities for storage of project record documents.
    4. Furnishings in meeting area:
        a. Conference table and chairs for at least eight persons.
        b. Racks and files for project record documents in, or adjacent to, the meeting area.
        c. Other furnishings: Contractor's option.
    5. Contractor's office and sheds not to be used as living accommodations.

B. Storage Sheds: Structurally sound, weather tight, on proper foundations, with floors raised above the ground.

C. Locate office and sheds a minimum of 30 feet from existing structures.

1.10 ACCESS ROADS AND PARKING

A. Construct and maintain temporary all weather roads accessing public thoroughfares to serve building pad and construction staging areas.

B. Extend and relocate as work progress requires.

C. Provide and maintain access to fire hydrants, free of obstructions.

D. Provide temporary parking areas to accommodate construction personnel.

E. When site space is not adequate, provide additional off-site parking.

END OF SECTION

SECTION 03400
PRECAST CONCRETE

PART 1. GENERAL

1.1 DESCRIPTION

    A. Related work specified elsewhere:
    Coordinate/requirements in other sections including:

      1. Testing Laboratory Services   01410
      2. Inspection Services   01420
      3. Project Meetings   01200
      4. Concrete Formwork   03100
      5. Steel Reinforcement   03200
      6. Metal Fabrication   05500
      7. Welding   05060
      8. Painting   09900
      9. Joint Sealants   07900

    B. Description of the work:
      1. Provide detailed drawings of all precast elements.
      2. Provide all precast concrete work as indicated on the drawing and specified herein.

    C. Coordination:
      1. Coordinate work and scheduling with other trades.

1.2 QUALITY ASSURANCE

    A. Requirements of Regulatory Agencies:
      1. Building Code:
      Conform to the requirements of referenced Uniform Building Code/00810 and Standard ACI 318 Building Code.
      2. Standard:
      Conform to Referenced Standard ACI 301 except as otherwise indicated.

    B. Reference Standards:

ACI 301-72	American Concrete Institute's Specifications for Structural Concrete Buildings.
ACI 318-71	American Concrete Institute Building Code.
ASTM C31-69 (1975)	Making and Curing Concrete Test Specimens in the Field.
ASTM C39-72	Test for Compressive Strength of Cylindrical Concrete Specimens.
ASTM C94-74a	Specifications for Ready-Mixed Concrete.
ASTM C143-74	Test for Slump of Portland Cement Concrete.
ASTM C150-76a	Specification for Portland Cement.
ASTM C260-74	Specification for Air-Entraining Admixtures for Concrete.
ASTM C494-71	Specification for Chemical Admixtures for Concrete.

    C. Erector:
    Use only erectors who are "specialists" in this type of work.

    D. Welding:
    Conform to Section 05060.

    E. Inspections:
      1. Provide Field Inspection to show conformance to the Referenced Standards.
      2. Provide Laboratory Inspection per City of Kent requirements.

F. Measurements:
Verify all dimensions shown on drawings with field measurements. Proper fit and attachment to adjacent work is required.

G. Allowable tolerances:
1. Casting tolerances:
Maintain casting, bowing, warping, and dimension tolerances within the following maximums:
a. Overall dimension for height and width of units shall be plus zero of unit dimension to minus 3/32" for 10'-0" and over.
b. Thickness of units shall be plus or minus 1/8" maximum.
c. Bowing or warping shall not exceed 1/360 of the span.
d. Insert locations shall be within plus or minus 1/4" in each direction.
e. Opening dimensions to figured dimensions shall be within a tolerance of plus 1/8" to minus zero.

1.3 SUBMITTALS

A. Submit any design mixes to architect and engineer:
1. Do not proceed until authorized by architect.
2. Use of design mix required batch plant inspection.

B. Drawings:
1. Submit steel reinforcing shop drawing for each element. Use element numbers indicated on architect's drawing.
2. Submit layout drawings for element drawings to indicate location of all openings and dimensions of all elements.
a. Drawing to indicate type and location of all items to be embedded in concrete.
b. Reference embedded items to detail number on architect's drawings.
c. Use element numbers given on architect's drawings.

PART 2. MATERIALS

2.1 PRODUCTS

A. Material:
See drawings.

B. Reinforcing:
See drawings.

C. Sealants:
Conform to Section 07900.

2.2 CONCRETE TESTING

A. Conform to City of Kent requirements.

PART 3. EXECUTION

3.1 FABRICATION

A. General:
Fabricate the work of this section to sizes and shapes indicated, and of texture matching approved Samples:
1. Finished units shall be straight, true to size and shape, and within specified casting tolerances.
2. Exposed edges shall be sharp, straight, and square and all flat surfaces in a true plane.

    3. Warped, cracked, broken, spalled, stained, and otherwise defective units will not be acceptable.

    4. Place and secure in forms all anchors, clips, inserts, reglets, lifting devices, stud bolts, shear ties, and other devices required for handling and installing precast units, and for attachment of subsequent items as indicated or specified.

3.2 SURFACE FINISH

A. Exterior—Smooth.

B. Interior unpainted—Industry Standard.

3.3 HANDLING AND STORAGE

A. Handle all precast concrete by such methods as will guard against soiling, mutilation, or chipping. Protect from damage to arises, and from accumulation of dirt, dust, grease, or other staining or disfiguring elements. Any chipping, cracking, staining, or other damage due to mishandling is responsibility of contractor. Correct any such damage at no cost to owner.

3.4 ERECTION

A. Erect no precast units until design strength is achieved. Use equipment of capacity adequate to handle size and weight of units fabricated. Use only experienced erection crews; provide all necessary safeguards to existing work. Align edges of individual panels carefully; secure to supporting members as shown. Provide temporary bracing, if required.

B. Install the work of this section in strict accordance with approved shop drawings, the original design and all pertinent codes and regulations.

C. Shims:
Install steel bearing shims where indicated on approved drawings. Set shims on level and uniform bearing surface; maintain in correct position until recast units are in place.

D. Erect plumb, square, and true to line and level allowable tolerances specified previously. Installation shall be performed by a specialist in erection of panels. Units have been designed for stresses resulting from the final-in-place position only. Additional stresses incurred during lifting processes and proper allowance for same shall be contractor's responsibility. Engage such persons as are necessary for any redesign required to safely raise the units into their final position without damage and bear the cost of same. Method of lift, type, and location of embedded anchors, if required, etc., shall be the contractor's sole responsibility.

E. Secure in final position with connections and anchorage features as indicated on drawings.

F. Perform any welding required to complete unit attachments with certified welders.

G. Power-actuated fasteners:
Do not use power-actuated fasteners for surface attachment of accessory items except where specifically approved by architect and specifically accepted by precast unit manufacturer.

H. Grouting:
    1. After precast units have been placed and secured, grout open spaces between footing and foundation.
    2. Use only grout system or systems recommended by manufacturer of precast units and approved by architect.
    3. Pack spaces with stiff grout material, tamping voids completely full.

3.5 CAULKING

A. Conform to Section 07900 Joint Sealants.

3.6   PROTECTION

A. Protection after erection:
Where concrete work, roofing, or other activities may damage precast elements already in place, cover with non-staining rosin-sized paper applied with a non-staining waterproof adhesive allowing easy removal.

3.7   REPAIR AND CLEANING

A. After erection, repair any damaged surfaced, if requested by architect.

B. After all setting, grouting, and caulking is complete, thoroughly clean with fibre brushes, soap, and water; then rinse with clear water preferably from a hose.

3.8   CLEAN UP

A. Per GENERAL CONDITIONS.

END OF SECTION

SECTION 09310
CERAMIC TILE

PART 1. GENERAL

1.1 DESCRIPTION

A. Related work specified elsewhere:

(Note: Add Sections 9320, 0330 as required)

    1. Gypsum wallboard   09250
    2. Rough carpentry   06100

B. Description of System:
    1. Ceramic tile installations over substrates.
        a. Work includes floors, walls, integral coved base, counters, metal divider strips, and accessories.
            1) Floors:
                a) Toilet rooms:
                    Floor tile and coved base installed/latex
                    Portland Cement thinset mortar.
                b) Entrances:
                    Where membrane is required for wet areas or as detailed on drawings, tile to be installed over liquid-applied elastomeric adhesive membrane.

1.2 QUALITY ASSURANCE

A. Requirement of regulatory agencies:
    1. Conform to Standard Specifications as Architect judges applicable, and as modified this Section:
        a. General:
            1) Tile Council of America. "Handbook for Ceramic Tile Installation," edition current as of specification date.
        b. Materials:
            1) Tile/Tile Council of America A137.1-1988, Recommended Standard Specifications for Ceramic Tile.
            2) American National Standards Institute (ANSI).
        c. Installation:
            American National Standards Institute (ANSI):
            ANSI-A 108.4-1985   Ceramic Tile Installed with Water-Resistant Organic Adhesives.
            ANSI-A 108.5-1985   Ceramic Tile Installed with Latex Portland Cement Mortar.
            ANSI-A 108.6-1985   Installation of Ceramic Tile with Chemical Resistant, Water Cleanable Tile Setting, and Grouting Epoxy.

B. Grade in Accordance With:
    1. Recommended Standard Specifications for Ceramic Tile, TCA A137.1-1988.
        a. All "Standard Grade."

1.3 SUBMITTALS

A. Submit/01340:
    1. Samples:
        a. Submit duplicate tile manufacturer's standard colors and patterns for selection by architect.
            1) Samples to show color variation extremes.
        b. Cured grout color selected.

2. Manufacturers' literature.
3. Submit definitive brochures.
   a. Include grout manufacturer's color chart.
B. Submit test reports and certificates:
   1. Before setting tile, furnish evidence satisfactory to architect that tile is type and grade specified.

1.4   PRODUCT DELIVERY, STORAGE, AND HANDLING

A. In accordance with 01600 and following:
   1. Protect at all times from damage.
      a. Environmental requirements:
         In accordance with referenced quality assurances.

PART 2. PRODUCTS

2.1   MATERIALS

A. Expansion Joints in accordance with referenced standards:
   1. Include sealant-filled joint at perimeters and abutments with rigid surfaces.
   2. Expansion joints in field in accordance with referenced standard. Sealant color to match grout color.

B. Unglazed pavers at entrances:
   1. Penetrating sealer for entrance pavers:
      a. Sealer as recommended by tile manufacturer to their specifications.

C. Ceramic mosaic walls, floors, and counters:
   1. Unless otherwise indicated, size 2″ × 2″ × 1/4″ thick modular size. Porcelain ceramic mosaic. As manufactured by Dallas Ceramic Co., or approved.

D. Tile base:
   Coved-segments matching floor or wall tile.

E. Special tile shapes:
   Provide as shown on drawings or required for complete finished installations. Include bullnose and all other trim units.

F. Grout:
   1. Commercially prepared grout (Bostik's "Hydroment" grout, or equal), modified with "Hydroment" acrylic latex additive #425 for toilet room floor, base, and any other installations except entrances and counters.
   2. 100% solids epoxy grout Kerapoxy or Latapoxy 210, or approved for counters and entrances.

G. Metal edge strip:
   1/4″ wide "heavy top" one piece terrazzo strip, half-hard brass or zinc as noted. Provide for juncture and joining of tile flooring with other materials.

H. Adhesive/Walls:
   In accordance with referenced ANSI A136.1 - 1985. Mastic Type I, A0/1700, or approved. Type I adhesive for dry area walls with latex modified grout equal to Laticrete 3701.
   Alternate: Latamastic #11 Latacrete, or equal.

I. Latex Portland cement mortar:
   In accordance with ANSI A118.4–1985.

J. Entrance membrane:
   Latocrete 9235, or approved, liquid applied, reinforced. Set tile with latex modified thinset for heavy traffic over slabs, use Laticete 301335.

K. Special conditions as detailed:
   1. Bostik's "Hydroment" flexible mortar/grout system. Install per manufacturer's recommendations.

L. All other materials:
   Conform to standard specifications. Submit for architect's approval.

PART 3. EXECUTION

3.1 INSPECTION AND PREPARATION

A. Laying of work of this section constitutes acceptance of backing conditions.

3.2 INSTALLATION/APPLICATION/PERFORMANCE

A. Follow specified quality assurances and manufacturer's recommendations.

B. Control temperature and ventilation for best results.

C. Pointing:
   1. Tool to dense, smooth surface. Joints completely filled flush.

D. Threshold/metal edge strip:
   1. Set securely straight and true.
   2. Position in center of doors, and as directed.
   3. Brace to prevent distortion during installation. Coordinate with other trades.
   4. Set high, then grind to close tolerance with adjacent floorings.

E. Trim:
   1. Provide screed per detail at all doors where a change in floor materials occur.
   2. Corners:
      Provide preformed inside and outside corners.
   3. Base:
      Provide cove base at all walls.

F. Wall tile tops:
   At top of all wall tiles, provide bull edge piece.

3.3 CLEANING

A. Leave surfaces clean, free from plaster materials and stains.

B. Protect from damage until owner's acceptance of project.

3.4 CURING

A. Damp cure for 3 days in accordance with referenced standards.

3.5 SEALER AT ENTRANCES

A. Seal in accordance to material manufacturer's recommendations.

B. Install one coat prior to grouting.

C. Install one finish coat after grouting.

3.6 SCHEDULE

A. Install where indicated:
   1. Where vertical surface indicated, provide around any columns, projections, and entire perimeter of room or space except as otherwise shown.

END OF SECTION

H

SELECTED PROJECT DRAWINGS FOR THE TRAINING CENTER

List of Drawings

Note: The drawings are foldout inserts located at the end of the book.

INDEX

A

Accessory items, 131
Accordion file, 200
Accounting, 290
Accuracy of estimate. *See* estimate accuracy.
Addenda, 18, 67–69, 84, 94, 121, 170, 193, 194, 203, 204, 284
Additive alternate, 272
Add-ons, 245
Administrative expense, 160–164
Adverse weather, 20
Agreement, 67
Allowance, 21, 32, 224, 225, 227, 228, 233, 237, 244
Alternate bid item, 16, 17, 46, 183, 205, 272
American Institute of Architects (AIA), 67
American Society for Testing and Materials (ASTM), 11
Application for payment, 65, 66
Arbitrator, 5
Architect, 40, 43, 44, 47, 48, 65, 93, 94, 109, 121, 142, 183, 218, 224, 225, 227, 254, 255, 263, 276
Architectural wood, 117, 149
As-built drawing, 269, 279
As-built estimate, 5, 269, 279, 280
As-built schedule, 279
Assemblies analysis, 89, 133, 136, 280, 288
Assemblies check, 133, 138
Assemblies Cost Data, 7

Assemblies cost estimate, 6–9, 33, 36–38, 42, 44, 240, 241, 274
Assemblies pricing, 147
Assembly pricing recap sheet, 86
Assigned contract, 219
Assumptions, 38, 47, 225, 232
Automated estimating techniques. *See* estimating software.
Average wage method, 140

B

Backlog, 178, 179, 234
Bank cubic yard (bcy), 100, 101, 187
Bankruptcy, 20
Base bid, 26, 185, 272
Base hourly wage, 129, 131
Best and final proposal, 18, 218
Better Business Bureau, 66
Bid, 5, 16, 142–145, 166, 171, 177, 180, 181, 211–214, 216–219
Bid alternatives, 48, 57, 272
Bid bond, 195
Bid captain, 209, 218
Bid date, 68
Bid day, 64, 70, 123, 131, 155, 170, 177, 182, 192–194, 196, 200, 202, 203, 205, 214, 216, 232, 265, 272, 284
Bid decision, 64, 65, 71